Cyril Cook was born in Easton, Hampshire, but at the age of five was brought to live on a farm in Mottingham, Kent. Educated at Eltham College, he matriculated in 1939, joined The Rifle Brigade in 1940, and was commissioned and transferred to the parachute Regiment in 1943. He saw considerable service in the 6th Airborne Division in Europe and the Far East where for a period he commanded, at the age of 22, a company of some 220 men of the Malay Regiment.

His working life was spent mainly as the proprietor of an engineering business which he founded. After retirement he wrote 'The Chandlers' series, six volumes of a British and German family and their lives, and deaths, in World War Two, before compiling 'Only when I Larf'.

At the age of eighty five he is now immersed in a new trilogy – 'The Manninghams' set in the 1850s.

Only When I Larf

Cyril Cook

Only When I Larf

Vanguard Press

VANGUARD PAPERBACK

© Copyright 2009
Cyril Cook

The right of Cyril Cook to be identified as author of
this work has been asserted by him in accordance with the
Copyright, Designs and Patents Act 1988.

A CIP catalogue record for this title is
available from the British Library.

ISBN 978 184386 492 9

*Vanguard Press is an imprint of
Pegasus Elliot MacKenzie Publishers Ltd.*

www.pegasuspublishers.com

First Published in 2009

**Vanguard Press
Sheraton House Castle Park
Cambridge England**

Printed & Bound in Great Britain

Dedication

This volume is dedicated to all Paras, past and present, especially with whom I had the privilege of serving, including the four on the front cover, and in particular my fellow platoon commanders, Ian Adams and Phil Burkinshaw.

Disclaimer

The wounded young cockney paratrooper was being flown home on the first of the Dakota air ambulances from Normandy. He had been shot twice in the chest, once in the hip, and in each thigh.

A young WAAF attendant on her first flight moved along the stretcher cases to him. Looking down she asked, "Do your wounds hurt?"
"No miss, came the reply, "only when I larf."

Front Cover

Paras – left to right – All 12 Para Battalion. 6th Airborne Division.

Sergeant Ernie Sargent: Wounded in attack on Ampfreville, Normandy.

Private Tom Holroyd: Wounded by shellfire, Ranville, Normandy.

Private Douglas Baines: Dropped far into enemy lines, Normandy, but rejoined battalion after numerous adventures. Badly wounded and lost a leg on Rhine drop.

Sergeant Bob Pratt: Wounded twice in attack on Breville, Normandy.

Front cover photograph by Gwen Pratt

The Front Cover

'Only When I Larf' is the first story.

'A Miss Sellanney' is the first funny.
Not many books start their contents on the front cover!

This book is designed to provide all manner of stories from as wide a variety of contributors as you could meet on a day's march.

True stories, fiction, and I suspect some a combination of both!

Items of interest from the Philippines, America, Canada, Australia, Russia, West Africa, Indo China etc etc.

Contrary possibly to your first impression, this is not a book about the Paras, although items from them do feature in it here and there.

There is poetry, a one act play, serious reading, sci-fi – even a soupcon of history, plus one or two naughty bits.

Quotations from Cicero, magical quips from Tommy Cooper, legends of the Australian Aborigines and from the Inuits (Eskimos).

Prison stories, insurance stories, theatre stories, even football stories, all are there.

This is an Order

YOU
  WILL
    NOT
      BE
        BORED

Contents

Colour Plates

"Barra"

By Diane P Burkinshaw

Sitting proudly on the small landing in our cottage in Little Walsingham is the life-size model of one of the most beautiful and intelligent of all creatures – the leopard. This is no ordinary model, for it has been sculptured so realistically that one might expect it at any moment to stretch and move silently on its way. To us it is the most tangible representation of the leopard cub which we took into our care whilst serving in what was then the river colony of The Gambia.

In the fifties it was a sleepy, unhealthy, and little known part of West Africa, surrounded, except for a short stretch of Atlantic coastline, by the French territory of Senegal. For Africa, the density of population in an area of some four thousand three hundred miles, was, and still is, unusually high. A mixture of ethnic groups, but principally of Wolof and Mandinka stock, and of the Islamic faith, the Gambians were particularly pleasant people.

Also on the credit side, the colony was famed for an incredible variety of bird life, especially along the banks of the Gambia River, which, stretching from west to east for some two hundred and fifty miles within the colony, was the main highway for travel into the interior, particularly during the rainy season. Apart from the birds there was little else in the way of wildlife in this flat and, in the dry season, dusty part of Africa, except for crocodiles, monitor lizards and snakes – but now and again a solitary maneless lion would wander in from Senegal.

One very hot and airless afternoon in Bathurst (now Banjul), a local man, Amadu Janneh, presented himself at my husband's office in the Secretariat and placed a calabash on his desk. Thrusting his hand into it he withdrew a tiny brown kitten-like creature, its eyes tightly shut, and which seemed to be all paws and ears.

"Here, sir," the man said, "is the leopard you ordered!"

My husband recalled that he had, some time before, spoken to Amadu about wildlife on one of his previous visits to the Secretariat and had shown an interest in parrots! However, it transpired that the mother of the young creature he had brought in, which was assuredly a leopard cub, had been shot whilst worrying livestock over in Barra, a region opposite Bathurst/Banjul on the north side of the Gambia river estuary. In the hope that we might be able to do something for the young animal we accepted it and gave Amadu a five pound note. The little creature was carried home in a cardboard box, and so began Barra's life with us.

Almost immediately we were told we were to be moved to Basse, the headquarters of the Upper River Division over two hundred miles upriver, a colourful but somewhat remote area in those days and completely encompassed by French territory. Not only had we to pack up our home and buy up tinned food and provisions, as there were no shops – only African stores at Basse – and no hotels or inns in the interior, but there was now the added preoccupation as to how to transport with us our new house mate. Bottles and Cow & Gate were purchased, a suitable carrying basket made, and permission obtained from a most understanding governor, Sir Percy Wyn Harris (who had been, incidentally, a former Everest climber) to carry an additional passenger on his personal launch, the "Mansa Kila Kuta"!

Barra had to be fed on demand, so for me, sleepless nights and disjointed days followed. As she grew stronger, and her needs greater, the difficulty was keeping the teat on the bottle when feeding her. A soaking became a regular occurrence! Cow & Gate however, seemed to work wonders for her and she increased in size and energy remarkably quickly. It seemed to me that we should start to wean her off the bottle, but how was going to be a problem. This was solved for us by our small black cat, Tobias, acquired some years before in Sierra Leone for a few pennies. When Tobias was fed Barra sat alongside her, watched and eventually started to lap, and after much sneezing and spluttering partook of the meal. As Barra grew in size and weight Tobias seemed to have no fear and would occasionally box the leopard's ears if she felt she was becoming too forward or greedy. Finally, two plates of food and milk would be put down and they both sat and ate together on the verandah.

After the evening meal, nothing delighted Barra more than to enter the sitting room, creep stealthily along the skirting boards and launch herself at whichever of us was seated nearest to her. We soon learned to be alert for such playful assaults! Momodu, the old night watchman on the DC's house, would come on duty and, being a devout Muslim, would go through the ritual of evening prayers. After putting down his prayer mat he would remove his shoes and woolly hat and lay them down behind him. This was a signal for Barra who was wandering in the compound to sneak round the corner of the house, come up behind him and remove the hat.

She would then toss it in the air and try to worry it like the cat she was. In case it became damaged it then became our ritual to retrieve it and put it in its usual place while the old man was engrossed in his prayers, oblivious to the mischief being enacted behind him. The leopard would, in the meantime, have been carried back into the house and safely locked away!

In the early stages, Barra had the freedom of the house and compound which was surrounded by a high krinting fence, and all seemed safe and secure until one evening when we were not "attacked" in the usual way after supper. Assisted by staff we began to look high and low, calling her name repeatedly. We were anxious, not only because a small animal in our care had gone missing, but, more importantly, that she might have ventured into the nearby village of Basse Santa Su where she might attack small children or domestic animals and be shot. As dawn broke, and our search had proved fruitless, we moved back disconsolately to the house. Just then Tobias the cat, who had been with us during the night, suddenly darted forwards and with a funny little noise climbed up inside an old hollow tree within the compound. We followed her to the tree and curled up inside in a furry ball was the missing Barra – sound asleep. Thereafter, she was kept under close surveillance and we also had a small harness made so that when out walking around the station we could keep tabs on her and, moreover, reassure local people.

Within the garden we had some beautiful frangipani trees, their branches creating an almost pergola effect. Barra loved to climb these trees and lie along them, surveying the birds and, as we were to discover, everything else in sight. One evening she demonstrated her unique ability to manipulate a situation. We were standing in the garden with our backs to the nearest section of krinting fence, on the other side of which was a footpath much used by local people visiting the district office. Suddenly, hearing a noise, we turned about and were shocked to see Barra leap from the trees over the fence. Rushing there we found Barra on the other side where she had pinned down one of the grazing sheep. I shouted, "Barra, put that sheep down," seemingly a rather futile summons.

However, when we reached her she did just that and returned rather guiltily to us. As for the sheep it got up and, apparently quite unperturbed, returned to cropping the grass a few yards away!

Barra's sensitive instinct was remarkably evident one evening when walking with her through the station. We recognised a figure approaching as the Senior Medical Officer who was on a visit to the district. He playfully raised the walking stick he was carrying to his shoulder and pretended to take aim. Barra gave a deep growl, turned about and started to tug us back to the safety of the house. She had never seen a gun, nor heard a shot fired, except perhaps the one which killed her mother, but she sensed that the action of the figure ahead meant danger.

Whenever possible, on day trips within the district, Barra accompanied us in the Landrover, sitting on the middle seat. If we used our launch, the "Baddibu", for journeys to places along the river, she would perch on the roof of the wheelhouse, watching the sinister snouts in the muddy water and surveying the whole scene with increasingly knowing eyes. When we had to visit headquarters on the coast she would travel in the back of the Landrover in a specially constructed travelling cage. On one occasion, when driving through the night in the midst of a dense bamboo forest in the Casamance – a southern province of Senegal, we had the luck to catch in the headlights a large leopard padding down the track ahead. Our domestic version slept throughout the whole eight hour journey, oblivious to the fact that she had been so close to one of her own kind.

We were very aware that as time passed Barra's eyes had taken on a more hardened hue, particularly when children were present. On one occasion when the French Commandant came over from Kolda in Senegal with his wife and young son, we brought Barra down from her specially made "house" to be introduced to the visitors. We became aware that the young boy had, after showing some initial interest, moved away from the leopard's penetrating eyes and hidden under the keyhole desk. When it was clear that the child was frightened we took Barra back upstairs.

Naturally Barra became something of a tourist attraction, we were thought to have the ultimate weapon for hastening tardy guests on their way after official parties, and Barra was given credit for my husband being able to cope with the local rather difficult Paramount Chief, or Seyfu!

When the time approached for leave in the UK – which was to be followed by a move to Central Africa – we realised that plans would have to be made for Barra's future. There were no game reserves in The Gambia, only some a distance away in

Senegal or French Sudan (now Mali) and, in any case, Barra was too domesticated to survive in the wild. We contacted Whipsnade for advice and they said they would take her but could not guarantee she might not be bartered for another animal from a foreign zoo. Finally we were put in touch with a private zoo at Wellingborough where they had a domesticated Indian leopard over a year old, named Timmy, and it was thought that they might hit it off, so plans were made for her to be taken to Wellingborough.

Never had we been so reluctant for home leave to come round. We had two cages constructed – one for the overland journey to Dakar, and the second, a light metal one for the flight to Paris and London. We drove up to Dakar with an overnight stop in Kaolack, a large town in Senegal, about midway to the coast. Barra had to be left overnight in the Landrover, but we felt no one would be inclined to tamper with either! At Dakar airport she stayed with us until our flight – the "Étoile de Dakar" non-stop service to Paris – was called. A very helpful member of the Air France staff, who told us he had had experience with black panthers in Indo China, escorted us over the tarmac, and Barra, by now very excited and rather wild, was loaded into the belly of the plane – a Lockheed Constellation.

In Paris, where we had to change for the onward flight to London, we caused some concern by leaving the transit area in search of our pet. Eventually we found her, gave her a little milk and water, and once again saw her into the cargo area. When she was moved into the hold of the Paris-London plane she was very disturbed and some uneasy glances were exchanged by fellow passengers. Some of our airline meal of roast chicken was popped into a "doggie bag". On noticing disapproving glances from the lady sitting alongside we tried to explain that the morsels were for our young leopard in the hold. Strange folk these colonials!

On arrival at London Airport, hindered by formalities, by the time we had found the warehouse to which she had been taken, and armed with specially warmed milk by courtesy of the chef at the airport restaurant, Barra had been whisked away into quarantine by the zookeeper from Wellingborough. We were both deflated and exhausted at her sudden and total disappearance. Some hours afterwards we were able to 'phone the zoo and learn that Barra was resting in her new home and all was well.

Subsequently, during our leave, we visited her on a fairly regular basis, taking with us bones and tasty morsels. Her delight in seeing us was such that the food was ignored. She never liked our leaving and would try to follow us out of her large cage. Timmy, her companion, was gradually introduced to her, but sadly she was just too domesticated to be much concerned with him and seemed to find him too boisterous.

After leave came to an end and we left for Nyasaland, now Malawi, we kept in contact with the zoo by means of friends who kindly visited her, and by letter to the zoo owner. Some time later we were told she was no longer on view and that she had died when in cub. Our own theory was that she pined for us. We have worried over our actions since and wondered if we could have played it all differently. Today things are very different and we would have been able to find a sanctuary for Barra. Suffice it to say, we tried our best in the circumstances which obtained at the time and we will always hold a place in our hearts, a very special place, for Barra leopard.

Quotations

Men are not hanged for stealing horses, but that horses may not be stolen. *Marquis of Halifax c1660.*

A faithful friend is the medicine of life. *Ecclesiasticus.*

Amantium irae amoris integratioest.
Lovers rows make love whole again. *Terence 170 BC.*

I keep six honest serving men
(They taught me all I knew):
Their names are What and Why and When
And How and Where and Who. *Rudyard Kipling.*

Some Potted Happy Memories from a Bank

Manager

I was born an only child, some nearly 73 years ago in North West London, where I lived for 26 years and it was obligatory to support Watford at football and Middlesex at cricket. These two sporting teams were an essential part of my father's life, so I had to follow suit. He had kicked out the boots of the Watford player who went on to captain Wolves in the 1921 Cup Final against Spurs, who were also captained by an ex Watford player, probably a Cup Final record. He had also delivered newspapers to Patsy Hendren, his real sporting hero, although Denis Compton was mine.

My father cracked some awful jokes perpetually, like, "Get out your jack knife and cut up a side street," if you wanted a short cut, or, "Is red cabbage green grocery?" At football matches, he would always greet the visiting goalkeeper with, "You're Joe Loss's brother, dead loss."

He left school at 14 but was as sharp as a razor in mental arithmetic, constantly tested me on sums. The dinner table always included a session on London Underground routes and the location of towns and villages from the AA book.

Coinciding with the start of World War Two, which started on Sunday the 3rd September 1939, I started infant school on the Tuesday, but, as the shelters were not ready, I went along the road to a lady's house with other 5 year olds. After about 2 or 3 weeks we had our lessons in the newly built shelters named after countries of the British Empire, such as Australia, Canada, New Zealand etc. My saddest recollection of the war was the sinking of the HMS Hood, as one of the young sailors who lost his life lived only a short distance away. My happiest was the collection of shrapnel the morning after the air raids, as the other children were doing this and we thought it was 'fun'. I was also very relieved to hear that my grandparents miraculously survived a V2 rocket about 50 yards from where they lived, which was in turn about 200 yards from my parent's house. Not only did glass land on the pillow on the bed, between their heads, from the shattered window without marking them, but they also walked downstairs in their bare feet, missing the glass without as much as a scratch.

My time in the bank was enjoyable but routine, with some happy memories. I remember being greeted by a colleague from another bank on my arrival in a new town branch, by a telephone call telling me that all the customers were haemophiliacs, which he explained as 'perpetual bleeders'. Most customers usually accepted my decision not to lend money if I could justify it, although I remember one customer advising me that I was not born but hewn out of stone. One of my managers would happily scale an 8 foot wall at the back of the building so as to avoid a certain customer he preferred not to see.

One of my favourite jokes concerns the three Jewish gentlemen who were in the process of forming a limited company. Solly said he'd put up 50% of the capital and would be chairman, Aby said he would provide 35% and would be managing director. Young Haimy said,

"I am putting up 15%, what can I be?"

The other two decided he could be Sexual Advisor. Haimy, indignantly said,

"What do you mean?"

They responded, "When we want your f---ing opinion, we'll ask for it."

To fit in with the modern scene – a man went to the dentist and was told he would need some painful treatment and was offered an injection.

"No, no I can't stand injections."

"What about gas then?"

"No, I can't stand gas."

"Can you take pills?"

"Oh yes, no problem."

Seeing it was Viagra the patient demurred and said,

"They don't relieve pain."

"No", said the dentist, "but it will give you something to hold on to!"

❖❖❖❖❖❖❖❖❖❖❖❖❖❖❖❖❖❖❖❖❖❖❖❖❖❖❖❖❖❖❖❖

Old London

Westminster Hall was used for Coronation feasts from King Stephen 1135 to George IV 1820. After the Coronation a banquet was held and the King's Champion rode into the hall in full armour and challenged anyone to dispute the King's right to the throne.

❖❖❖❖❖❖❖❖❖❖❖❖❖❖❖

Dick Whittington, three times Lord Mayor of London, his name in those days being Richard Whytyngdone, lived in the 15th century. However, it was in 1603, 180 years after his death, that mention of his cat was made – in a play!

❖❖❖❖❖❖❖❖❖❖❖❖❖❖

The smallest City church is Saint Ethelburga's in Bishopsgate. It is only 60 feet x 30 feet.

❖❖❖❖❖❖❖❖❖❖❖❖❖

It is fascinating to think that words we use to indicate which day or month it is go back in many instances two thousand years. The week days we know today were named in the days of the Anglo Saxons over one thousand years ago. Prior to that Roman names were originally based on the ancient astronomical order of the sun, moon and planets, the latter having been named after their gods.

1. The Days

Sunday   This was 'the day of the sun', nothing strikingly discerning in that, except that it indicated the overall importance of the sun from time immemorial, making it the first day of the week. The old English from which it was derived was *Sunnandæg*.

Monday   This was 'the day of the moon' – *Monandæg* in old English. Prior to this name being used the Latin name was '*Lunae Dies*', from which scholars of French will speedily recognise *Lundi*.

Tuesday   The original Roman name for Tuesday was *Martis Dies*, the day of Mars, who was the Roman god of war. Again in French we have '*Mardi*'. However the early British substituted the name of the Norse god of war – *Tiw*, as a result it became *Tiwesdæg*. Just another example of how the Brits always like to be different!

Wednesday   The most important of the Norse gods was Woden – hence the old English name was *Wodnesdæg*. The Romans named this day after the god Mercury, thus the French call it *Mercredi*.

Thursday   The ancient Norse god of thunder was Thor. Thus the old English name became *Thuresdæg*. In contrast the Roman god of thunder was *Jupiter – Jovis dies* – hence the French *Jeudi*.

Friday   This is an odd one. The wife of the Norse god Odin was named Frigg. For some obscure reason the Anglo Saxons settled on *Frigedæg*, as the Romans had named this day after a female, *Veneris Dies*, day of Venus. The French have *Vendredi* as a result.

Saturday   Apparently the Anglo Saxons could not come up with a Norse name, so they adopted the Roman god, *Saturn*, making it *Saeternesdæg*. The French is similar – *Samedi*.

2. The Months

These are almost purely Roman. However, the year started with March, not with January as we know it today.

March   *Mars*, the god of war, enjoyed a number of feasts in this month.

April   The Romans called this month *Aprilis*, although why remains a mystery. It was consecrated to the goddess *Venus*.

May   The goddess *Maia* was paid homage at this time.

June   *Juno* was the queen of the deities.

July   *Julius Caesar* was born in this month and had it named after him.

August   This was named after the first Roman emperor *Augustus Caesar*.

September   Here they ran out of names for a while. The Latin *septem* means seventh month.

October   As above. Latin for eight is *octo*.

November   Again as above. Latin for nine is *novem*.

December   Ten in Latin is *decem*, from which of course we derive 'decimal' among other things.

January   Named after the god *Janus*.

February   In this month the Romans held a festival at the end of the year to cleanse the body and soul. It was called *Februa*.

The Aircraft Carrier

By Frederick Starkey

The body sleeps; the heart is stilled
That only yesterdays was beating, beating,
Throbbing its message with rhythmic urgency.
Sentient microscopic beings
As if by capillary attraction
Percolate its arterial byways
With suitable professional sense
Of emergency.

The heart awakes, begins again
Its reassuring throb. The body
Feels the urge to move,
From its denizens orders proliferate.
The complex systems answer to the purpose corporate.
What must be done will be done
And a directorate will approve.

Bodies within the body
Are united in their mutual trust,
But each lives also in that private world
Of golden memories and private fears,
Of bitter obligations left undone,
Of gifts bestowed and gifts received
In that interpersonal commerce
Of love and need and passion
Not unalloyed with lust.

The body is my home.
The body houses me, it feeds me,
Keeps me warm, or keeps me cool,
Nourishes, protects; it's always there.
And yet, in truth, it needs me.

Into a winged creature I mutate.
The body turns to embrace the gale.
I levitate.
I'm not alone; in harness with my brethren brood
I plead my case,
No compromise, hot steel my argument.
The case against me is the same,
Only the calibre is different.

I see my home, a floating dot.
Most of us return; some do not.
The body welcomes me. Its metaphoric arms
Nine wires athwart its steel plate skin
Beckon me, sing Catch me if you can.
No time to ask myself
What kind of games,
What kind of bloated aims
What kind of bellicose counterclaims.
Can justify this deadly side-show
I have somehow entered in.

The Mortar

A story based on a true event

By David Lister

Victor had grown up in Milan's shadow. It didn't matter. They were friends, but sometimes Victor got tired of having to share the consequences of Milan's hare-brained adventures. Now, they both stood in another shadow, and it was all Milan's fault.

The two young men stood nervously to attention under the careful scrutiny of Jan Slavoshk. The cool mountain air made them shiver; they would admit to no other cause. Slavoshk did not frighten them: of course not. It was just that the cool air got to their sweaty bodies and chilled them.

"You climbed up the hard way, yes?" Slavoshk asked, thrusting his unshaven chin close to Milan's ear. Milan could guess with accuracy the content of Slavoshk's last meal from the smell on his breath.

"Yes, sir," he replied. "It was the best way to keep German eyes from us."

"We made sure we weren't followed," Victor said.

It was now Victor's turn to countenance the hard stare and foul breath of the inquisitor.

"Had Germans – or Chetniks followed you, my friend, none of you would have seen out the hour."

Victor swallowed hard. "No sir."

"No sir," Slavoshk mimicked. The older man circled the boys who still stood rigid. He pushed Victor, shoving him in the chest. Victor stumbled back a pace.

"No much muscle. How old are you? Fourteen? Fifteen?"

"Sixteen, sir."

"Me too," Milan said.

Slavoshk turned his attention to their packs which lay on the rock where they had dropped them. When a man who looks like the devil points a machine gun at you and says, "Drop your packs and put up your hands," it is quite amazing how quickly you can drop your packs and put up your hands.

He prodded the packs with the well worn leather of his boot.

"Did you bring your pyjamas and teddy bears?"

The boys shook their heads. In other circumstances Victor would have been humiliated by the remark, but fear pushed lesser emotions aside.

"What then, guns? No. Bullets then?"

Another synchronised shaking of heads.

"Grenades?"

Milan and Victor exchanged nervous glances, and then Milan spoke.

"We have no weapons to bring, sir. Just some food and spare clothes, some soap..."

"Soap?" Slavoshk rasped. "Soap?" He turned and began to walk away.

"Go back to your mothers. Skinny little boys like you are no good for fighting Germans."

The scornful words tore at Milan ripping away all reticence and fear. Victor recognised the look, but it was too late for him to do anything. In an instant Milan had crossed the ground between him and the retreating partisan. Blocking his path Milan looked up into the weathered and scarred face,

"If we're old enough to be shot by Germans, we're old enough to fight back."

Slavoshk stared hard into Milan's face. He saw the rage and the stubbornness; he saw himself. As quick as an adder-strike he brought Milan down with an open-handed blow to the side of his face.

"Okay," he said. "You both come with me and we will fight Germans. But in future remember ...." He offered a hand to the stunned Milan. "Remember that it is not your place to challenge my authority."

"Yes, sir. Thank you," Milan said resisting the impulse to rub his stinging face.

"You just remember it. We're at war and if you don't jump when I order it, you'll find my bullets will kill you as dead as German ones."

A small crevice in the face of a cliff opened into a large cavern. Bedrolls and packing cases lay here and there and in the centre some boxes had been stacked and covered with a canvas sheet to form a crude table. This was the campaign base of Slavoshk's small resistance unit.

Light was provided by several oil lamps and some candles which had been lodged into convenient crannies. Weapons and other items were stacked, or hung, or balanced wherever the respective owners thought best.

The boys were led in and their eyes soon adjusted to the low level of light. They both jumped as one of the occupants brought down the sole of his removed shoe hard against a packing case. Carefully raising the shoe, he picked off the mortal remains of a squashed fly and held it close to his eye for inspection. He then carried it over to a corner where, upon a ledge of rock, stood a curious glass vessel. It was tubular, about a foot high and two inches in diameter, and there was a graduated scale engraved on the outside. The partisan dropped the fly into the vessel where it joined a small pile of other deceased insects. He peered at the scale and chuckled before catching the bemused looks of the boys.

"We have a bet going," he said as if it was an effort to address the boys. "My money is on twenty centimetres in a week." He then turned his back and shuffled back to his place by the packing case.

"That's a lot of flies," Victor whispered.

Milan looked around. "The place is thick with them. If anything, twenty centimetres is going to come up short."

Later, Milan and Victor sat on their haunches making the best of the meal provided by Slavoshk's cook.

"More like soup than goulash," Milan whispered.

"Shh! They'll hear. They didn't seem very keen to give us even this." Victor slurped up a spoonful of the thin brown liquid and pulled a face of disgust.

Neither Slavoshk nor his men were very welcoming. Most ignored the two new recruits while others treated them to the occasional indignant stare.

Slavoshk spoke from behind, making them jump. "You have to earn their trust," he said quietly. "Show them what you're made of. Show me too. If you're up to it, you'll be accepted quick enough. If not, you'll find things more pleasant in the valley with the Germans."

"Give us a gun each and we'll prove ourselves alright," Milan said, making a fair attempt at sounding tough.

Slavoshk laughed out loud attracting the attention of his men. "Hey, these two want guns!"

The men laughed – one threw a chicken bone which plopped into Victor's bowl and splashed soup over him.

"So you want guns, eh?" Slavoshk said mockingly. "Look around the cave. Count the men. See? There're twenty two of us. Now look close and count how many have guns. I'll save you the bother – it's twelve. And they're not all good ones like mine. Frank over there has a muzzle-loading bird gun. Darko has a sixty-year-old revolver with two buggered chambers and a cylinder you have to work by hand. I'll tell you a little secret. Don't tell no-one else, but our entire arsenal is twelve guns, six boxes of mortar bombs with nothing to launch them, and a crate of scientific glassware. It'll be a long time before you get a gun. You'll have to kill with a knife, or else your bare hands – or chuck test tubes at the enemy."

Slavoshk moved away to be swallowed up by the gloom of the cave's interior, receding with his laughter.

36

"Let's get out of here. They don't want us, unless it's to be the butt for all their jokes." "Shut up, Victor! How far d'you think we'd get now we've seen their base? Besides, we haven't been here a day yet. What did you expect?"

"Well, I didn't think one tiny little gun would be too much to ask for. And maybe someone to show me how it works. If that oaf thinks I can kill a hairy-arsed German with my bare hands he can boil his head."

"At least that would put a bit of flavour into the goulash," Milan quipped.

The boys' burst of laughter was a short one, cut to size by the annoyed looks of their older comrades.

"So, what are we going to do, Milan?"

Milan shrugged. "I suppose we'd better do something to impress them."

"Like what?"

Milan's face took on that look; the wry, smiling raised eyebrow look, which nearly always meant trouble.

"Oh no! Not again, Milan. What're you dragging me into this time?"

"Victor old friend old chum! I know where there are some guns. So do you."

"I do not!"

"You do."

"I don't!"

"Oh yes you do."

Victor knew only one place, but surely … "Not the German camp?"

"Yes – the German camp."

"For Christ's sake Milan. You've got to be joking."

"So you weren't joking," Victor said, peering through the branches of the sparsely covered bush. "We're about three metres from the perimeter fence. What now?"

Victor was cold. The moon seemed to blaze like the sun. He had never realised before just how light it could be in the midst of a pitch-black night.

"There's a guard. Come on Milan. Let's scarper, or we're dead."

Milan remained silent, belly to the dust.

Victor whispered close to his ear. "This is stupid. Let's go. We'll stop off and fetch grandpa's shotgun and take it back with us."

"You know what 'Voshkie would do with that old relic, don't you? He'd shove it up – sideways!"

The German guard was only a little older than the desperate partisans who watched his every move – and in other circumstances his moves may have proved most entertaining.

Boredom and a lack of supervision; it had to be. Why else would a soldier of the Third Reich hop about, first on one foot and then on the other? And then, why would he hold his rifle above his head like a balancing pole and imitate the ambulation of a tight-rope walker?

It was absurd, and like most boys Victor found absurdity amusing. Even this close to danger, he had to slap a hand over his mouth to keep his laughter captive. Milan however, saw only a German pig playing the fool. His cousin had been hung by the Germans for being out after curfew. No playful antics were about to endear him to the enemy.

The German now held his rifle like a dancing partner and waltzed round the dusty ground – right into the arms of his warrant officer. The still night was splintered with the sound of German invective, punctuated with the occasional "Ja wohl, mein Feldwebel," from the young soldier. Then, apparently at the sergeant's command the soldier turned and doubled to the guardroom with the sergeant in furious, ankle-kicking pursuit.

"Now!" Milan whispered, and while the camp was free of guards, they cut the perimeter fence.

Before the Germans came, their camp had been just another village. But it suited their purposes, so all the villagers were packed off. Only the elder who had complained remained and he oversaw the departure of his neighbours swaying from a makeshift gallows.

Victor knew the village well and he knew only one building could logically serve as an arsenal. The boys crossed the deserted yard quickly and silently reaching the building just as the guardroom door imploded releasing light, laughter – and something entirely more sinister. Two German Shepherd dogs bounded into the dark.

Milan pressed himself into the shadow and held his breath, while his heart pounded out a tattoo, which he felt would draw the dogs.

Victor froze. That was it; he was dead. The dogs, gambolling about the yard to rejoice at their brief taste of freedom, became immobile for a moment, and then ran at full pelt towards him. He saw himself writhing on the blood-soaked ground, torn to the bone. Mary, Joseph and Jesus, he didn't want to end up like that.

The leading animal, teeth bared and (in Victor's imagination at least) drooling for the taste of Serbian boy, sprang up – and Victor threw a punch. It connected with a cold wet snout and much to his surprise the dog went down with a truncated yelp.

The second dog stopped in its tracks, its pointed ears falling to droop submissively, and its head bowing in newfound respect. The first dog was up on its feet and assumed the same subdued demeanour. It respectfully darted a lick at Victor's knee, sniffed his crotch and went over to Milan briefly before responding to its master's voice.

The killer dogs slinked quietly into the guardroom and the door shut behind them.

With no time to wonder at the quality of their luck so far, Milan – the expert, began to work on the lock. Victor kept watch as the seconds turned into minutes. No matter how hard he tried, the usual methods failed to snick open the simple lock.

Milan – the flustered and sweating expert, kept at it. Victor, breathing rapidly and digging the nails of both hands into his palms, kept watch as the minutes seemed to become hours.

Milan began to shake; the noise of an approaching vehicle imprinted itself upon the night's calm. Above the drone of the engine and the clatter of dislodged gravel there was the sound of German singing.

"Milan!"

"Yes, I hear it."

"For God's sake! If it drives up to the gate the headlights will be right on us."

The knot in Victor's stomach tightened. The guardroom door opened again and the lights of the vehicle drew nearer. A German stepped out of the guardroom. He had only to turn his head. Victor, transfixed, watched and the world seemed to move in slow motion. Slowly, the guard waved to the others inside. Slowly his uniform turned from black to grey-green and the truck's headlights chased away the protecting gloom. Slowly and slowly the soldier's head turned towards Victor. Then, pain in his shoulder, followed by blackness and disorientation.

"You alright?" Milan whispered, close to his ear.

The world returned to normal speed. There was a musty smell.

"We're inside the building?"

"Of course. You were frozen like a rabbit in those headlights. I had to drag you in."

Victor rubbed his shoulder soothing the pain from Milan's grip. "Did they see us?"

"We're still alive, so I don't think so."

The noise from outside died down as the Germans billeted down for the night. The boys remained unmoving until they could hear only one pair of footsteps. Victor watched as Milan moved to the door, every creak of the floor sounding like gunfire and even his own heart, like thunder. Milan opened the door a fraction.

"It's the dancing German again," he whispered.

They settled down while their eyes adjusted to the gloom. Again their luck held, for one of the perimeter lamps lost some of its light through the arsenal window giving the boys enough to do their work without a torch (which they did not have) or matches. They waited for the footfall of the guard to recede and then began to explore.

"Nothing but a few old rifles. We need something better than rifles. What's over your side, Victor?"

"Wooden boxes," he said and then, "What's wrong with rifles anyway? They're better than muzzle-loading bird guns."

"How many do you think we could carry?"

Victor silently hefted one of the K-98s. "Not many. But one each would do."

"And what would we use as ammunition?"

"Erm – bullets?"

"Yes. And the bullets are in those metal boxes. Try lifting one."

Victor lifted one of the ammo boxes. It was heavy and awkward.

"You see the problem?" Milan said. We couldn't manage enough ammo to make the raid worthwhile. No, what I'm looking for is … is that!" He pointed to a wooden packing case that was considerably larger than the ammo boxes and had a lid screwed down securely.

"What is it?"

"See here?" Milan pointed to the lettering. "It's a mortar. Look, the same as the writing on those boxes of mortar bombs back at the hide out. It's big, but together we'll manage it."

In their excitement they had not heard the approach of jack-booted feet and the slow turning of the door knob. There was a loud click followed by the thunder of the door being kicked in.

The boys froze, hoping the dark corner would shroud them. The German voiced a guttural order which was punctuated by the unmistakable double-snick of a rifle bolt.

Victor felt warmth trickle down his leg as he held his breath waiting for death. He hoped the German, black against the perimeter lamp, would make a quick job of it, and visions of his own dead and beaten body filled his mind.

Milan pressed himself into the shadows. The German called out again, his voice fierce but with an edge of uncertainty. Milan inched his knife from its sheath.

The young German stepped into the building blotting out more light. His rifle was fitted with a bayonet which he thrust into the darkness before him. In he came, still further. Victor silently ran through the Paternoster, while Milan drew back his knife ready to strike: the throat first he reasoned, would stop the German crying out, and then up under the ribs to finish him.

The German took another step and again barked out an intelligible command. One more step and his thrusting bayonet could not help but slash out Victor's innards. He rocked forward, the bayonet quivering on the edge of the fatal thrust, when a dark shape brushed past his legs and in rushed one of the killer dogs. Its snarl tripped into the realm of a fully developed bark and Victor thought that he was going to be dog-dinner after all. But the dog ran past Victor towards Milan who was still crouching where the shadows were darkest. The dog leapt over Milan and plunged still further into the building. Then a scream rose above all other sounds, and from the deepest reaches from among the boxes and lockers, a cat ran for its life. Past the confused German youth it ran, followed closely by the dog, only to be caught by the second dog which stood as sentinel outside.

The dog handler laughed as the German Shepherds ripped at the unfortunate cat, but the young German waded into the dogs with boots and rifle butt. Victor had a clear view of it all and he saw the dogs bounce away, happy with their sport, leaving a tattered ball of glistening fur. He heard the young guard call out "Schwein!" and then the others laugh still more.

Victor watched as the German rose from his examination of the dead cat, and turn once more towards the door. He paused for a moment peering into the gloom, then reached in and slammed the door shut. Victor let himself sink to the floor, not noticing the puddle of his own making. He sat, drained and numb with his head between his knees. Milan sheathed his knife and then brought up his goulash.

Perhaps twenty minutes passed before either spoke.

"Come on Victor, time to leave."

"Fine! 'Time to leave' he says, now we've been frightened to the edge of our graves."

"We're still alive Victor, At least we tried."

"What do you mean by that? You're not thinking of leaving without the mortar?"

"We'd never make it. We'll be lucky if we get out at all."

Victor was suddenly very angry. "You bastard!"

Milan was stung as if by a blow.

"You've dragged me into this place even though I said it was stupid, but you've got this big plan, so we go through hell … I've been so afraid I … that I'm sitting here all wet like a baby. And now you say we're leaving without the mortar? Think again Milan."

"Alright. So I've thought again. We'll take the damned mortar."

"We'll take the mortar because I decided we would, not you. Whoever said you were my boss anyway?"

Milan smiled in the darkness. The experience had changed his friend. "Hey Vic! No more of that goulash. It's too good for your courage."

Victor smiled in spite of himself. Sometimes there was a natural order to things. Milan had been his friend as far back as he could remember, and Milan had always made the decisions. You could shout out against nature, but you couldn't change it. He'd had his say. Milan might still be boss, but he'd had his say.

Getting the mortar out was much easier than the boys believed possible. By carefully timing the guard's routine they judged it best to make a dash for the fence just as he rounded the guardhouse. It would give them a few minutes, and the noise from the guardhouse would mask any of their own.

Their timing was accurate and carrying the box between them they scurried across the open ground and under the fence. There was a moment of panic when they found the opening in the fence was too small for the box, but with just a few more snips they made good their escape.

Dragging the box up into the mountains was a different matter all together. The route they had chosen was a difficult slog even when unencumbered, and when dawn found them far from camp; they were torn between pressing on or hiding up until nightfall. In the end it was their desperate need for rest which decided the issue.

They wedged themselves and their cargo under an outcrop which conveniently overhung a patch of thick vegetation. With rock for a roof and walls of living shrubbery the boys felt safe. A further convenience was provided by a small pool which filled a hollow in the midst of the vegetation supplying them with bathing water. They could also drink from the small trickle which fed it, and came down like a miniature waterfall on one side of the outcrop.

They washed themselves and Victor washed his trousers and set them to dry in the warm sunshine. Whenever the slightest chance of discovery threatened – the noise of a falling pebble or the far off drone of an aircraft – they would dart back into their hiding place. The morning passed quickly as they relived their night of adventure while speculating upon the heroes' welcome which they felt sure awaited them back at the camp. The afternoon however, dragged, their minds filled with thoughts of food.

The boys recommenced their climb about an hour before dusk in the hope of completing the most treacherous part of the journey before dark. This they achieved and so by nightfall they had a relatively simple walk-come-scramble back up to camp. Drawing close to the cave Milan gave the signal by which the man on guard would know them as 'friend'. Friends or not, they had as reply the sound of a semi-automatic pistol being prepared for action.

"Don't shoot!" Milan hissed in a strained whisper. "It's us. Milan and Victor."

"We've brought something with us," Victor added.

"Shut your mouths!" came the vitriolic reply. "Step forward towards the cave, and bring the box with you."

Victor did not recognise the voice, although it was local, nor did he remember seeing anyone at camp with a self-loading pistol. The thought crossed his mind that his comrades may have been discovered by a group of Chetniks, in which case he and Milan were probably just as dead as if caught by Germans.

"Slavoshk is not pleased with you two. Where have you been?"

Never had Victor thought he would be so glad to hear the name of his irascible leader.

Jan Slavoshk had indeed expressed his anger towards the boys, but luckily for them, only in words. Perhaps his curiosity about the box they'd brought with them and their account of its capture had kept him from a more physical expression.

Slavoshk hefted the box onto a pile of smaller cases and the men gathered round to examine the spoils. "Bring me a crowbar. Now, let's see what we have."

"It's a …" Victor began, only to be cut off by a dig in the ribs from Milan.

"He can't read German," Milan whispered. "He doesn't know it says 'Mortar' on the box, so let him find out himself."

Slavoshk prized open the lid, the wood crackling and splitting with the noise of a bonfire. Pulling the last few pieces off by hand, he leaned over and peered into the box. His nostrils twitched as he sniffed the air. He reached in and began to pull out handfuls of straw until at last, throwing down a double handful of the stuff, he rested his hands on the rim of the box. He looked up at the boys; piercing blue eyes bored into them. Back into the box he looked and then again at the boys. He began to shake his head, slowly, until both Victor and Milan became nervous.

"Are you sure there's a mortar in there?" Victor said softly.

"It says so. One the side, I'm sure. Oh Christ, I hope so."

Jan Slavoshk reached deep into the box with both hands. "You two went to the German camp, cut the wires, raided the arsenal … for this?" He straightened his back and lifted out the biggest Swiss cheese ever seen.

The boys exchanged glances, and then looked at their leader who regarded them with something between pity and disgust. Milan looked as if he wanted the darkness to swallow him up. Victor waited for his friend to save the day, but this time Milan had no answers. Ah well, maybe this time it was his job.

Victor shrugged, filling the gesture with as much bravado as he could muster, and then spoke, "Guns we can get any day," he heard himself say. "But tonight, we feast!"

A fly hovered close to the cheese and like lightning; Victor snagged it out of the air and squashed it in his hand. He ambled over to the glass tube and dropped it in. "My money is on twenty five centimetres."

Slavoshk looked at him for a moment longer with an expression as if he'd been addressed by the raw material from a sewage farm. Then he held the cheese aloft and exploded with laughter.

The next few moments were a confusion of pats on the back and laughing partisans. From the depths of ignominious failure the boys had rocketed to the heights. They were the heroes of the moment. From that day on nobody ever knew, and no-one asked, whether the cheese had been the true objective of the two young friends, two junior partisans out on their first raid.

⟡⟡⟡⟡⟡⟡⟡⟡⟡⟡⟡⟡⟡⟡⟡⟡⟡⟡⟡⟡⟡⟡⟡⟡⟡⟡⟡⟡⟡⟡⟡⟡⟡

Funnies

Moses came down from the mountain to face the elders awaiting him. "Well lads," he said, "I've got him down to ten – but adultery's still in!"

⟡⟡⟡⟡⟡⟡⟡⟡⟡⟡⟡⟡⟡⟡⟡⟡

Middle age – one voice saying, "Why not?" and the other saying, "Why bother."

⟡⟡⟡⟡⟡⟡⟡⟡⟡⟡⟡⟡⟡⟡

How do you know when it's time to tune your bagpipes? My ancient Scottish friend replies, "When people start to enjoy them."

⟡⟡⟡⟡⟡⟡⟡⟡⟡⟡⟡⟡⟡⟡

Why is the time of day with the slowest traffic called 'the rush hour?'

⟡⟡⟡⟡⟡⟡⟡⟡⟡⟡⟡⟡⟡⟡

We must have one piece of doggerel.

There was a young girl of Devizes
Whose bosoms were different sizes;
One was so small
It was no use at all
But the other won numerous prizes.

The Story and Legend of the Famous Coloured Sands

"Brilliantly coloured friable sandstones form bold cliffs for over 20 miles of coast between Tewantin and Double Island Point, rising to heights of 700 feet. They are relics of an extensive system of iron-stained dunes that were deposited many thousands of years ago (throughout Pleistocene times) when sea level was at least 200 feet lower and the coast several miles further to the east. Changes in sea level, climate and fluctuations in movement of underground water have combined with subtle variations in porosity, amount of clay or vegetation impurity to control the leaching and redepositing of iron, thus producing the bewildering variety of colour tones and grotesque shapes."

Prof. A F Wilson, University of Queensland

Our beloved blackman, now gone from this area leaves this little story, that is just as likely if one can believe in legends. This Aborigine legend is as old as time itself.

Wayback in dream-time there lived on the banks of the Noosa River a beautiful black maiden named MURRAWAR, who fell in love with the Rainbow, who came to visit her every evening in the sky. She would clap her hands and sing to this lovely Rainbow.

One day BURWILLA, a very bad man from a distant tribe, stole Murrawar for his slave wife, often beating her cruelly and making her do all his work, while he sat in the shade admiring his terrible killing boomerang. This boomerang was bigger than the biggest tree and full of evil spirits.

One day Murrawar ran away and as she hurried along near the beach, which was then all flat, she looked back and saw Burwilla's boomerang coming to kill her. Calling out for help she fell to the ground too frightened to run. Suddenly she heard a loud noise in the sky and saw her faithful Rainbow racing towards her across the sea.

The wicked boomerang attacked the brave Rainbow and they met with a roar like thunder, killing the boomerang instantly and shattering the Rainbow into many small pieces. Alas; the poor sick and shattered Rainbow lay on the beach to die, and is still there with all its colours forming the hills along the beach.

So firm were the beliefs of the Aborigine women regarding this legend, that women of many tribes made long treks to obtain these sands to carry them or put in their hair. It was their belief that the Rainbow was their protection, or good luck charm, always.

◇◇◇◇◇◇◇◇◇◇◇◇◇◇◇◇◇◇◇◇◇◇◇◇◇◇◇◇◇◇◇◇◇◇◇◇◇◇◇

It Could Have Happened

With thanks to Ron Follett. 7 Para.

Victory Parade, London, April 20th 1941.

The Führer takes the salute in Whitehall on his 52nd birthday as SS Divisions march past.

Conversation Between two Residents of Singapore Island

By Oxodian

When World War Two ended in the Far East in 1945, the 5th Parachute Brigade was among those forces which re-occupied the island of Singapore. As is well known, the Paras wear maroon berets, a head-dress not in existence before the war, therefore unknown to the Singapore residents.

The following is a conversation recorded (?) by Don Halewood, an officer in 12 Para, and one time tutor at Oxford.

"Why do some of them wear red hats Fong?"

"I am not quite sure, but they tell me they fight in the air, and not on the ground Foo."

"I cannot see any of them with wings Fong, How do they fly?"

"They use umbrellas instead Foo. It is very wet in their country."

"But how can they fly with umbrellas Fong?"

"I do not know. But just as they cannot pull rickshaws or speak intelligently, so cannot we fly with umbrellas."

"What are the ones with crowns and stars on their shoulders, who carry sticks?"

"They are of heavenly descent, Foo, and carry the sticks to beat the others with. The stars are the lords of heaven, and they rule on earth."

"What are those who have both stars and crowns Fong?"

"They rule everything Foo – they are almighty."

"Why do they drive in small cars without sides Fong?"

"I am told it is a token of humility. For in their strange tongue, to 'Put on Side' is to be arrogant Foo."

"Fong, why do the lordly ones show an open hand to the lordly when they meet?"

"It comes, Foo, from an old English proverb 'Give him a hand boys'. It is a compliment. The one who shows the biggest hand gains the most favour."

"That is why they slap their guns? To make the hand bigger? – And they also stamp their feet. Is that to make their feet bigger?"

"No. They have a proverb 'to make an impression' which they say, establishes their control in our country. That is why they stamp their feet – to make a deeper impression."

By Cyril Cook

Robert Cocking was born in 1776. When he was twenty one, in 1797, a Frenchman made the first parachute jump at the Parc Monceau in Paris, and from that time he keenly followed the development of parachuting in England and on the Continent. He was an artist by profession but was obviously an aeronautical engineer by inclination.

The parachutes being used at that time were similar in shape and size to the standard World War Two military chutes, but their design had failed to cure the dreadful oscillation experienced by the parachutist during the descent caused by the air emerging irregularly from around the perimeter of the canopy. What goes in must come out!!

Mr Cocking

To eliminate this problem Cocking hit on the idea of an 'inverted cone' parachute – a sort of airborne funnel based on sound aerodynamic principles. Around 1812, he made a number of scale models and dropped them successfully from captive balloons on Hampstead Heath and from the Monument in London. As a result of his experiments however, he reluctantly concluded that a parachute of this nature would be so heavy that no balloon of that time could lift it. The project therefore had to be shelved.

Over twenty years later, in 1836, a huge balloon was built and became known as the 'Nassau Balloon', after it made a flight of nearly 500 miles from London to Nassau breaking all current records in the process. Cocking approached the owners of the balloon, Vauxhall Gardens, with a view to using it to take up his parachute, and having reached agreement proceeded to build his life's dream. It was 107 feet in circumference, funnelling down to around 4 feet in diameter at the base. It had a series of thin circular linen-covered metal rings joined by vertical wooden sections; a basket was suspended below, and the whole unit weighed in order of 230 lbs.

On the evening of 24th July 1837, with Robert Cocking proposing to make his first parachute jump at the age of 61, the enormous balloon took off from Vauxhall drifting towards Greenwich. At 5000 feet Cocking detached himself from the balloon, first calling a polite, "Good night" to the two balloonists above, and started to descend. To the horror of the people below, including the Astronomer Royal, who was watching through his telescope from the Royal Observatory, the framework collapsed and Cocking plunged to his death into a field at Lee Green.

The story goes that the Landlord of the 'Tigers Head', to this day a landmark at Lee Green, collected the wreckage and charged sightseers threepence a head to view the mangled remains of the parachute and sixpence a head to see Mr Cocking! Now there's enterprise for you!!

ROYAL GARDENS, VAUXHALL.

GRAND DAY FETE,

On MONDAY, the 24th of JULY, 1837.

Extraordinary Novelty and Combined Attraction!

ASCENT IN THE ROYAL NASSAU BALLOON

BY MR. GREEN,

AND DESCENT IN A NEWLY-INVENTED

PARACHUTE,

BY MR. COCKING.

The Proprietors of Vauxhall have the satisfaction to announce that they are enabled to present to the Public another grand improvement connected with the Science of Aerostation ; viz. a PARACHUTE of an entirely Novel Construction, by which a perfectly safe and easy descent may be made from any height in the Atmosphere attainable by a Balloon.

Mr. COCKING, a gentleman of great scientific acquirements, having, many years since, witnessed the descent of M. Garnerin, (the only one ever made in England,) was forcibly struck with the danger to which that gentleman was exposed on account of some error in the construction of his machine ; and, after several years spent in numerous experiments, has succeeded in discovering the faults in M. Garnerin's instrument, and also in producing

AN ENTIRELY NEW PARACHUTE,

which is allowed by all who have seen it, to be constructed on unerring principles. The form is that of

An Inverted Cone 107 Feet in Circumference!

which, during the Descent, is quite free from oscillation ; and as it will be in its proper form previous to the Ascent, it is not liable to the objection of falling several hundred feet without expanding, which was the case with the Parachute of the old form.

MR. COCKING WILL MAKE HIS FIRST DESCENT

ON MONDAY NEXT, JULY 24.

The great power of the Royal Nassau Balloon has afforded the means of making an experiment with the above-named Machine, which, from its great weight, would be impossible with any other Balloon hitherto constructed.

The plan adopted by M. Garnerin was to ascend alone and detach the Parachute from the Balloon, which having no person to conduct it fell in some very distant part, and was either lost or destroyed; but Mr. GREEN has undertaken to ascend in the Nassau Balloon, and to liberate the Parachute himself, a feat never before attempted by any Aeronaut.

THE PARACHUTE WILL BE EXHIBITED PREVIOUS TO ITS ASCENT.

In order to render this Fete more than usually attractive, the Proprietors intend giving a variety of Amusements during the Afternoon, the principal of which are—

A CONCERT in the Open Orchestra

A DRAMATIC PIECE in the Theatre which will be lighted as at Night

Extraordinary Performance of M. Latour, M. Delavigne & their Sons

THE YEOMANRY AND QUADRILLE BANDS &c. &c. &c.

AND A VARIETY OF OTHER ENTERTAINMENTS.

Doors will be opened at One; & the Ascent at Five.

The Descent will be made as nearly over the Gardens as possible.—ADMISSION, 2s. 6d.

VISITORS ARE REQUESTED TO COME EARLY.

The Admission to the Evening Entertainments will be as usual.——Parties can Dine in the Gardens.

Balne, Printer, 38, Gracechurch Street.

By A Copper

There was once a boat race between the Police Service and the Fire Brigade. It was great fun and both sides decided it should be an annual event.

For the following year's race, both teams practised long and hard to reach their peak performance so on the day of the race they were as ready as they could be. The Fire Brigade won by several lengths. The Police Service became quite discouraged. Senior management decided the reason for the crushing defeat had to be found, and a project team was set up to investigate the problem and recommend action for the following year.

The conclusion was that the Fire Brigade team had eight people rowing and one steering, whereas the Police team had one person rowing and eight steering.

Senior management immediately hired a consultant company to carry out a study on the team structure. Millions of pounds and several months later the consultants concluded that too many people were steering and not enough rowing.

To prevent another ignoble loss to the Fire Brigade, the team structure was changed to four executive steering managers, three senior executive steering managers and a principle executive steering manager. A new 'Investors in Rowing' system was set up for the person rowing the boat to give him more incentive to work harder and become a key performer. He was given a Job Plan, a Mission Statement, an Annual Performance Agreement, the Police Service Rowing Agreement, a Rower's Charter, a Rower Care and Learning Framework and a Rowing Operational Plan.

The next year the Fire Brigade won by two miles.

The Police Service laid off the rower for poor performance, sold off the oars, cancelled all the capital investment for new equipment, halted the development of a new boat, awarded high performance awards to the consultants and distributed the money saved among the senior management team.

Postscript by Cyril

The senior police officer who so kindly gave me this narrative, having sworn every word was true, for some unaccountable reason, preferred to remain anonymous.

Some of the Works by Sydney Tarrant

Old Spinster

For love is wild,
  I proved as much
From passionate past.
  And lovers such
That many know
  And others trust.

For love is wild,
  I learned and more
In any phase.
  On any shore
Where many stray,
  And others claw.

For love is wild,
  I proved too late
To take my place.
  As seasoned bait
That many are
  And others await!

The Dreamer

A sigh! It was a spent idea
From memory, and want of life,
Internally there springs a thought
That magnifies, then dreams awhile.
Then as our wishes, hopes and love
Are mingled in a vivid scene,
We live in Paradise of mind-
The whistling wind breathes harmony,
To chant low lullabys so sweet
Until we fall again to fact,
And from the clouds we drift to earth.

A period of beauty passed
In one foul stroke of realism!

Autumn

I saw the green hedges, and felt the keen wind,
  I smelt the clean odour of fields;
I gloried in Nature and lived for a while
  In the scene that this Autumn now yields.

I heard the leaves falling, and burst into song,
  I sang to the old wooden gates;
I glanced at the heavens, and read in the clouds
  The poems of Wordsworth and Yeats.

His Army Days

Stonehenge

A camp to shudder in and curse,
  Its shabby huts a rotting hearse,
This place so sinister, so still,
  This living dead, this grim Larkhill.

Night Guard

Six khaki forms droop nearer
  The dying embers where
They sit beside the fireside,
  And all in silence stare.

Himself

Depression

A desert must be just like this,
  This scene or such uncanniness,
That grips the mind, as daylight ends,
  E'er silently the night descends.

No movement can my eyes discern,
  No sign that life will e'er return,
To this grey world, surrounding me,
  While time ticks by relentlessly.

I lay in agony of thought,
  No hope to soothe me will be brought
In deep depression, so I pray
That God will bring again the day.

Oh! world so empty, am I dead,
  And has the soul within me fled
To some new planet, to take birth
  Far from my body, here on earth.

But shattered is the dream of Hell,
  As out of its nocturnal dell
Returns the sun to cast pure light
  And end the sombre reign of night.

Observation

The Tramp

I know he'll walk
Through smoky town and field,
And never take a steady job,
Or chance to build,
But wander, on and on,
And only stay
At most with anyone – a day.

For as he walks,
This ragged tramp of man
No routine rules his brain,
Or cause to plan
Accepting hunger, pain, and even thirst,
With only shrug of shoulders,
Muttered curse!

As factories kill some,
And money more,
He takes no part in love,
or daily war,
For movement fills his life
From year to year,
With God his single Master
And only Fear.

The Ferry-Boat

Have you felt the throb of engines,
  Pulling at the moorings tying,
Seen the seagulls wheeling, whirling
  Round the ferry's pennants flying.

Tugs with funnels smoking gaily,
  Passing by with barges trailing,
Seen the paddles turning, churning,
  Forging foaming track, in sailing.

Have you heard the Thames grey water,
  Lashing at the floating landing,
And the crash of bridges falling,
  Where the ferry men are standing.

Then you know that 'John Benn', 'Squires',
  Carry loads in any weather,
Only fog will stop them crossing,
  To and fro they go for ever.

The Original Fix

By Richard Bolton

Some years ago, when I regularly visited Switzerland and in particular St Moritz, I had the wonderful services of an old fashioned travel agent in Pall Mall. One year I said to him, "Let's take a more unusual routing. How about crossing the Channel with the Queen Mary?" Well he entered into the spirit of the plan. He fixed up the trip with nice little details, such as booking the crossing when the tides ensured that we had the maximum time on board, and arranging dinner in the Veranda Grill.

Well, three of us set off from Waterloo arriving in Southampton in good time. We were travelling First Class on the liner, each with a superb cabin. We made our way to the lounge for an aperitif or two. Lunch was in the main dining room. After this we had a short rest in the cabins then into the Turkish bath before tea. By now we were feeling no pain. We changed for dinner and made our way to the grill. In those days one had stamina and we did it all justice. I well remember as we lit up cigars the purser arriving to announce, "Gentlemen, we are waiting to cast off for New York."

A night in the French port, then the train to Paris and a flight to Zurich. Then on to the

Richard with his beautiful wife Claire at the head of the Cresta Run.

train into the mountains and St Moritz. You might say that by now we were merry and game for fun. Unloading in St Moritz we piled into a large black cab. The driver, a large plump fellow called Schmidt, mumbled that he had to get something and disappeared. Well, this was an invitation for me to jump into the front and gently take off up the hill into the town. By now the breathless Schmidt could be seen waving and shouting, trying to run on the icy road, but we were soon out of sight. We gently pulled up to our hotel leaving the cab parked. We had, however, not reckoned on Schmidt's lack of humour. When he did eventually arrive he had armed Swiss police with him and we were arrested and hauled to their HQ where blood samples were taken.

We had a great friend who was a member of our club and he also had considerable clout in the town. He got to hear of our plight and came to see us. He assessed the situation and said he would be in touch. The next day we met at the club house and he tapped his nose and said, "I have arranged the 'original fix'," and that we should hear no more. Some months later, we heard that he had arranged for some sheep's blood to be substituted for ours! Herr Schmidt was given a generous tip and agreed not to press any other charges and life moved on.

The Marrow

By Cyril Cook

I decided I would take a stab at growing a prize marrow. Consulting the expert, my neighbour John Bury, I was told they grow best on manure heaps – actually that wasn't exactly what he said but it amounted to the same thing. Some years ago we had a horse stabled at our house, and on a concrete slab at the bottom of the garden there remained a largish pile of what John had described. By now it was very well rotted indeed, so I thought it would be an ideal site for my marrow plant to thrive and grow. I therefore transferred it with loving care from its pot to the heap.

I next looked at my old gardening encyclopaedia to swot up on feeding the brute. I learned that super phosphates were a must, sulphate of ammonia would be a useful addition, bone meal and guano etc would all help. Here I made a mistake! I thought it said 12 ozs a square yard, whereas it should have been 1-2 ozs a square yard. The second mistake was it didn't say how often you fed it, so I thought I'd better do it daily. Just to help things along, I found a bottle full of steroid tablets in the stable which had been used at one time for the horse, so I ground them down in the wife's Kenwood and sprinkled them on as well.

The results were phenomenal. Talk about Jack and the Beanstalk. On the first day there was three feet of vine, and on the second day another three feet <u>and</u> a couple of flowers. I went back to the encyclopaedia to find out which flowers to keep and found they were either male or female, and that you had to pollinate them. As far as I could see this operation verged on the pornographic, but I thought that if this is how gardeners get their kicks who am I to judge?

Within another day I had a marrow which had grown over a foot long. I was having lunch with a friend of mine in a pub and described its dimensions with my hands. A rather deaf old lady sitting nearby said, "I know that gentleman you're talking about!"

It continued to grow at a phenomenal rate off the heap and across the lawn. I put some rollers underneath it so that it didn't get marked and soon it was eight feet long and about nine inches thick. It slowed down in the next couple of weeks but thickened up, and at the end of three weeks it was fifteen feet long and two and a half feet thick.

The next morning there came a knock on the door and two men from the Ministry of Defence appeared. They said they had had a report of a suspicious looking object spotted by the CIA spy satellite, apparently on some sort of a launching pad in my back garden. I showed them the marrow but they said they were far from satisfied and would have to remove it. When I asked how, they said they would get a helicopter.

This they did and having put wide slings strategically beneath it, lifted it a foot or so from the ground. A man sent from the Forestry Commission cut the marrow off with a chain saw, and helicopter and marrow then winged their way off to Woolwich Barracks. On arrival a colonel from the Army Catering Corps inspected it with a top secret marrow detector and pronounced it to be, in fact, a marrow.

He asked what should he do with it. I told him to stuff it!!! They hired a crane, JCB, dumper, and cement mixer. A gentleman from BOC cut the marrow long ways with a thermal lance, and gently the crane lifted the top half of the marrow and laid it over on its back. The JCB got to work and excavated the pips and put them in the dumper. They put hundredweights of mince, onions, swede etc in the mixer, and then the JCB transferred it to the marrow. The top gently reapplied, it was wheeled into a big baker's oven and cooked slowly for 24 hours.

I then had a brilliant idea!! ………

As rhinoceros horn is in short supply in Hong Kong, I put it around that this marrow had even greater aphrodisiac qualities and it would sell in little pots at £10 a time. It went like a bomb! I sold 100,000 pots at £10 a time – and that's how I made my first million!

◇◇◇◇◇◇◇◇◇◇◇◇◇◇◇◇◇◇◇◇◇◇◇◇◇◇◇◇◇◇◇◇◇◇◇◇◇◇

The Thoughts of Fernando Baralba: Albuffeira 1976 of his book 'The Diabolic Divinity.'

Here lies my child. Whether it be good or bad, be patient with it, for that is the way we all should behave towards everybody's child.

◇◇◇◇◇◇◇◇◇◇◇◇◇◇◇◇◇◇◇◇

The devil is the only leader who does not need any propaganda.

◇◇◇◇◇◇◇◇◇◇◇◇◇◇◇◇◇◇◇◇

Goodness is so rare that those who possess it are abnormal.

◇◇◇◇◇◇◇◇◇◇◇◇◇◇◇◇◇◇

Due to the diversity of ways of camouflaging our internal feelings, I say, with regret, that it is impossible to know whether virtues really exist.

◇◇◇◇◇◇◇◇◇◇◇◇◇◇◇◇◇◇

You only know how to be with others, when you know how to be alone.

◇◇◇◇◇◇◇◇◇◇◇◇◇◇◇◇◇◇

Light is the mother of beauty.

◇◇◇◇◇◇◇◇◇◇◇◇◇◇◇◇◇◇

A Day in the Life of Padre Roberts

By Cyril Cook

Padre Roberts was a slightly built, Celtic looking gent in his late thirties, who in a moment of madness decided sometime in 1942 to join the army's Holy Brigade. In a further moment of obvious sheer lunacy, for which he should have been put away, he volunteered for the paratroops. He got his first MC in Normandy, afterwards we spent a somewhat eventful time in the Ardennes and in Holland, and our story now reaches the point where we are back in England taking part in practice jumps on Salisbury Plain preparatory to jumping the Rhine into Germany.

My platoon had carried out one jump and we had been bussed back to the airfield from the DZ and were waiting around to draw chutes for a second drop later in the day. As we sat around, we saw one of the Dakotas flying around with a parachutist strung out behind it with his chute well and truly caught up in the rear landing wheel of the aircraft. Either the chute had opened prematurely, or the static line which is anchored inside the plane had not pulled out to its full extent for some reason and had opened the chute in the doorway of the plane. The word speedily went around that it was Padre Roberts being pulled around up there.

Whilst we stood in helpless fascination, the pilot was facing some pretty hair-raising decisions which would need to be very shortly made. The problems were that firstly, he obviously wouldn't want to land with the Padre still attached, although he might soon have to face up to that eventuality. Secondly, if he tried to manoeuvre the clumsy old Dakota in an endeavour to shake the Padre free, the chute could have been so badly damaged that it would be useless and the Padre would suffer the same fate. (British paratroops of course only have one chute; they do not carry a reserve as most others do). These thoughts too were obviously going through Padre Roberts mind as he was suspended there being buffeted by the slip stream from the two powerful engines, as indeed they were going through our minds as we looked up watching the plane circling around.

Inside the Dakota the pilot was busy flying the plane and receiving information from the central tower as to how the chute was attached etc, since of course it couldn't be seen from within the aircraft. The navigator and the jump master (he's the RAF instructor who despatches the men jumping from the aircraft), were wracking their brains as to what could be done, and decided the only chance they had was to try and get him back in. But how? They couldn't lean out of the door and grab him – he was suspended some thirty feet behind and below the plane.

56

They then hit upon an idea which might just work. Inside the aircraft they had a kitbag and the static lines from the stick, of which the Padre was one, who had just jumped. The kitbag was a special piece of equipment which each man strapped to his leg before he jumped, and in which was carried down heavy equipment, spare ammunition, wireless sets, extra supplies of condoms, and other essential items which would be needed by the platoon as a whole, in addition to the soldiers own personal equipment. This meant you jumped with nearly a hundred weight (or 50 Kilos) of gear of one sort or another. The kitbag had a quick release mechanism and was attached to your waist belt by a strong nylon rope. As soon as you were airborne you released the kitbag, lowered it down 20-30 feet where it swung from your waist belt, and it landed with a thump just before you did, hopefully without damaging the wireless or exploding the mortar bombs or whatever.

They therefore stuffed the kitbag with a number of the static lines to pack it out as much as possible, and then attached it to other static lines in turn so that it would reach the Padre, and finally secured the rescue line inside the aircraft. They then planned to pay out the kitbag until it reached the Padre, he would hold on to it and they would pull him back in. This was decidedly 'iff-ey'!

1. Was Padre Roberts compos mentis enough to realise what was intended after being twisted around and buffeted for over half and hour?
2. If he did realise what was happening, would he have the strength to hang on?
3. What would happen if the kitbag got caught up in the parachute rigging lines?
4. Would the two RAF men, tough though they were, have the strength to pull him in against the slip stream?
5. Supposing as a result of being pulled in the chute was released – he would be whipped away like a shuttlecock to almost certain death.

There was no going back, so they began to pay out the kitbag whilst we watched the new turn of events in total silence from down below.

The slip stream was playing absolute havoc with the kitbag, sending it round and round in circles at some considerable speed, which would make it not only difficult to get hold of, but if it thumped the poor old Padre, it would be like stopping one from Joe Louis. But at last luck appeared to be on our side – I say 'our' because by now we were all part of this drama. They paid out the kitbag a bit too far and co-incidentally the chute lifted the Padre up and he came down again right on top of the static line which he grabbed. Slowly they pulled the line through his hands until he was actually sitting on the kitbag. Now, would he be able to hold on? And secondly, would they be able to pull him in over the sill of the door if they got him that far? That would be the worst part. Steadily they pulled him up underneath the plane, and the chute showed no signs of becoming disentangled and whipping him away.

The final moments of the rescue were hidden from us as the plane circled away from us with the door on its far side. However, a minute later we saw the disconnected harness fly out to the extent of the chute and we knew they had got him in. A tremendous cheer went up, but there was still a risk to the aircraft of the chute – unweighted now, fouling the tail plane. In the event they landed safely and taxied over to where we were. Amazingly the Padre was able to walk down the steps and he was taken to the MI room for a check-up.

About an hour later, all the others having jumped, we were waiting to board for the last stick of the day. From the Admin Section appeared Padre Roberts. He came over to me and said, "Have you got any room in your stick Cookie?" (My nickname throughout my service). I told him I had, so he went off and drew another chute, came back to where we were ready to emplane and said, "Where do you want me?"

I said, "You'd better go No.1 - I'll go out last" (officers usually jumped first or last depending on circumstances). After an incident like the one he'd just been involved in I thought he might 'jib', and no-one would blame him, but with 18 blokes behind him he'd be pushed out when the green light went on. (Come to that, I certainly had the feeling myself that I would not be requiring any Ex-Lax for quite a long time). Anyway, eventually out he went, floating down like a dream.

That night there was a mother and father of a party in the Mess. The Padre was well known for his love of a good booze-up at the best of times, and the happenings of that afternoon must surely be the most valid excuse ever in his belief for a really monumental binge. After all, one doesn't come back from ten yards from the Pearly Gates every day of the week. I left fairly early but I believe the MO poured him into his bed at about midnight and we didn't see him again for thirty six hours! That ended a day in the life of Padre Roberts. He jumped with me again into Germany and won another MC – that in itself would be another story.

Postscript

When Padre Roberts jumped with me on Salisbury Plain I mentioned I jumped last. The stick was a bit slow going out and I found myself coming down at the edge of the DZ straight into some trees. Now, if there is anything a parachutist likes less than most things it is the thought of having the rigid branch of an oak tree up his nether regions at 30 mph and ending up like a monstrous kebab. I therefore 'spilled' my chute frantically so as to drift sideways, missed the trees, but in the few seconds left before I landed, saw I wasn't going to miss the River Avon! Fortunately it is not very deep there as they widen the river to grow watercress in it. I landed up to my armpits in water, which, as it was February, you can imagine was a trifle on the chilly side. When I had disentangled my chute, I looked up to see a jeep crew who had come to find me killing themselves with laughter at the sight of me covered in watercress – I could have murdered them!

It was quite an eventful day one way and the other.

❖❖❖❖ ❖❖❖❖❖❖❖❖❖❖❖ ❖❖❖❖❖❖❖❖❖❖❖❖❖❖❖❖❖❖❖❖❖❖❖❖

Young Enterprise

The Ferrari F1 team fired their entire pit crew yesterday. This announcement followed Ferrari's decision to take advantage of the British Government's 'Work for the Dole' scheme to employ some Liverpudlian youngsters.

The decision to hire them was brought about by a documentary on how unemployed youths from Toxteth were able to remove a set of wheels in less than six seconds without proper equipment, whereas Ferrari's existing crew could only do it in eight seconds with millions of pounds worth of high tech equipment. It was thought to be an excellent bold move by the Ferrari management team as most races are won and lost in the pits; this would give Ferrari an advantage over every other team.

However, Ferrari got more than they bargained for. At the crew's first practice session, not only was the Scouse pit crew able to change all four wheels in less than six seconds, but also within twelve seconds they had re-sprayed, re-badged and sold the car to the McLaren team for eight cases of Stella, a bag of weed and some photos of Coulthard's bird in the shower.

How to know you're getting older	
Everything hurts and what doesn't hurt doesn't work.	You're 17 around the neck, 44 around the waist and 105 around the golf course.
The gleam in your eyes is from the sun hitting your bifocals.	You just can't stand people who are intolerant.
You feel like the night before and you haven't been anywhere.	Your back goes out more often than you do.
	You stop looking forward to your next birthday.
You get winded playing chess.	You burn the midnight oil after 9 pm.
Your children begin to look middle aged.	You sink your teeth into a steak and they stay there.
You finally reach the top of the ladder and find it's leaning against the wrong wall.	You regret all those temptations you resisted.
You join a health club and don't go.	The little old grey haired lady you help across the street is your wife.
You know all the answers but nobody asks you the questions.	You get all your exercise from being pallbearer for your friends who exercised.
You look forward to a dull evening.	You remember today that yesterday was your wedding anniversary.
You sit in a rocking chair and can't get it going.	

Why the Stars are in the Sky

An Inuit (Eskimo) Legend - From John Bury

To the Eskimos the stars are not just put in the sky to give light or guide the wandering traveller. They are living things, sent by some twist of fate to roam the heavens forever, never swerving from their paths. One of these creatures who left the earth and went to live in the sky was Nanuk the bear.

One day Nanuk was waylaid by a pack of fierce Eskimo hunting dogs. Nanuk knew only too well that Eskimo dogs are not to be trifled with, and he tried to give them the slip. Faster and faster he ran over the ice, but the dogs were still at his heels. For hours the chase went on, yet he could not shake them off.

In the fury and terror of the hunt, they had come very close to the edge of the world, but neither Nanuk nor his pursuers noticed. When at last they reached it, they plunged straight over into the sky and turned into stars.

To the Europeans they are the Pleiades, in the constellation of Taurus the Bull. But to this day Eskimos see them as Nanuk the bear, with the pack of savage dogs out for his blood. Up in the sky directly overhead the Eskimos see a giant caribou, though we call it the Great Bear.

Over on the other side of the sky, they can make out some stars in the shape of an oil lamp. (We say it is the constellation of Cassiopeia). On the horizon between the lamp and the caribou the Eskimos see stars like three steps carved out of the snow. They call it the stairway from Earth to the Sky, but we talk of Orion the Hunter. Sometimes, on the darkest nights, the Eskimos' dead ancestors come out to dance. The stars are the lights round the dance floor. Then Gulla glows across the sky: the shimmering pattern of the Aurora Borealis, or Northern Lights.

To the Norsemen it was Bifrost, the bridge from our world to Asgard, home of the gods. But to the people of the Far North, the loveliest and most wonderful star of all is the sun. They see her as a young girl of dazzling beauty. In their brief Arctic summer she is there night and day, for this is the season of the midnight Sun, when her brother Aningan, the Moon, chases her round and round the North Pole so she cannot escape over the horizon. Aningan the Moon is a great hunter, and he chases animals as well as his sister the Sun. He has a faithful pack of hunting dogs to help him. Sometimes his hounds are carried away by the joy of the hunt, and they jump over the edge of the sky and run down the stairway in Orion to Earth. That is why there are shooting stars.

After hunting Aningan rests in his igloo, which he shares with his cousin Irdlirvirissong. His cousin loves jokes and games, and sometimes she comes out and dances in the sky. She is so funny that if the Eskimos see her they roar with laughter.

61

But first they make sure none of their sorcerers or their other leaders are nearby, for if Irdlirvirissong knows that people are laughing at her she will be angry, and her punishments are terrible. She kills people who make fun of her, and eats them up. The sorcerers are powerful, and ordinary Eskimos tremble before them, especially Angakog, the mightiest of all. Yet even Angakog's magic arts are powerless against the planet Jupiter. For Jupiter is mother to the Sun and the Moon, and a constant peril to all sorcerers. They have to be very, very careful, or Old Mother Jupiter will open them up and devour their livers. Angakog trembles in fear of her, even as the ordinary folk tremble in fear of him.

◇◇◇◇◇◇◇◇◇◇◇◇◇◇◇◇◇◇◇◇◇◇◇◇◇◇◇◇◇◇◇◇

Just for a Laugh

1. Two antennas met on a roof, fell in love and got married. The ceremony wasn't much, but the reception was excellent.

2. A jumper cable walks into a bar. The bartender says, "I'll serve you, but don't start anything."

3. Two peanuts walk into a bar, and one was a-salted.

4. A dyslexic man walks into a bra.

5. A man walks into a bar with a slab of asphalt under his arm and says, "A beer please, and one for the road."

6. Two cannibals are eating a clown. One says to the other, "Does this taste funny to you?"

7. Two cows are standing next to each other in a field. Daisy says to Dolly, "I was artificially inseminated this morning." "I don't believe you," says Dolly. "It's true, no bull!" exclaims Daisy.

8. An invisible man marries an invisible woman. The kids were nothing to look at either.

9. Deja Moo: The feeling that you've heard this bull before.

10. I went to buy some camouflage trousers the other day but I couldn't find any.

11. A group of chess enthusiasts checked into a hotel and were standing in the lobby discussing their recent tournament victories. After about an hour, the manager came out of his office and asked them to disperse. "But why?" they asked, as they moved off. "Because," he said, "I can't stand chess-nuts boasting in an open foyer."

The Reprimand

By Sergeant Bob Pratt. 12 Para.

On disembarking in Singapore in late August 1945, neither we nor anyone in the world had any idea what we were going to find. Some members of my battalion had helped to open the gates at Belson camp in Germany and saw the horrors of the holocaust. I went to 'Changi Jail' and saw the horrors of the Japanese prisoners of war. It was a sight that haunts me to this day. I went to Alexandra hospital where 750 of our men were dying of malnutrition. Not very far from the bungalow we found QA nurses that had been used in a brothel by the Japs.

I had a radio station in a small children's school in Singapore which was manned by some of my Provost staff. We had a jeep so that we could move to any part of Singapore if there was a problem. We came in contact with Chinese people who had lived in fear during the Jap occupation. They related to us how the Japs had put white women in shop windows, naked in the heat of the day. We heard stories of a British officer's wife who had been shot and bayoneted and left in a monsoon ditch, of men from a Scottish regiment that had been shot and bayoneted and left to rot in the ditches. There were many other stories of the Japanese cruelty over the years of occupation.

I was sitting on the veranda when two of my Provost drew up in our jeep. They got out and pulled a Japanese soldier from the back. They then reported to me that he had escaped from the cage. He was a Jap Sergeant Major. I went down the steps and stood in front of him flanked by my two policemen. When he saw me he started to grin and bow not once, but several times. He had one gold tooth which was very prominent when he grinned at me. I stood in front of him for a couple of minutes and in that time I thought about the women in the shop windows, the ditches that had skeletons still there, the hundreds of POWs with ribs sticking out of their skin, the women and children that had been abused in the civilian camps and the nurses that had Jap kids. All these things flashed through my mind and I got very angry; he was still bowing in front of me and then I hit him and he lost his gold tooth. I told the two policemen to put him in the cage at the back of the bungalow, to handcuff him and leave no food but a bowl of water, until I had time to take him back to the cage in Singapore.

I was having a cup of tea when a corporal from HQ Company asked to see me. He said, "Sgt Pratt, I understand you are ill-treating a Japanese POW in your guardroom." I could not believe my ears. There was nobody in the battalion who had not heard or seen what the Japs had done to our POW men, women and children. I exploded and told him in no uncertain way that if he was not out of my guardroom and out of my sight in the next 15 seconds he would be joining the POW in his cell. He went away and I did not see or hear of him again. Some months later they were hanging some of the Japs in Changi Jail for atrocities they had committed.

Six weeks later the RSM came to my guardroom and enquired what had I been up to. So I said, "If you don't know I'm sure I don't, why?"

"Colonel Kenneth T Darling (later Army Chief of Staff Europe, Sir Kenneth Darling), the CO wants to see you."

I asked if I was on a charge. He said, "No."

We got to the colonel's office, knocked on the door; the RSM went in and then called me in. KT told the RSM that he need not stay and dismissed him. KT waved his hands across the table and said, "Have you any idea Sgt Pratt what this is?"

I replied, "No sir."

He said, "This is the paperwork for a Court of Enquiry. Now, think very carefully. Did that Japanese prisoner you had, hit his face on the door when he went into the guardroom?"

Like a flash it came to me what this was about. I said, "Yes sir, it was an accident."

His next remark was, "Will you accept my punishment?"

My answer was, "Yes sir."

"Then I shall severely reprimand you. That is the least I can do, as I have to reply to a question asked in the Houses of Parliament, "Why is a senior NCO of the Parachute Regiment in Singapore ill-treating a Japanese prisoner of war?" (This question was asked by a local MP and is apparently in the Book of Hansard). I did not have to guess too hard who wrote the complaint.

"Very well Sgt Pratt, go away and be careful what you do next time."

I saluted, about turned, and put my hand on the door handle to go out, when Colonel Darling said, "Shut the door Sgt and come here. There are only we two here, but I'll tell you this, if I had my way I would let you have a gun and you could help yourself in that POW cage."

I saluted again and went on my way, a much relieved soldier knowing at least he felt the same about the atrocities as I, and many, many more had seen in the battalion. There are some who would condemn me, but I was a soldier not a saint.

When the Romans Came

By Cyril Cook

Ask most people which Roman general conquered Britain and you will almost certainly receive the answer 'Julius Caesar'.

Wrong.

Julius Caesar came to Britain in 55 BC but all he did was to have a look round the south east corner and then went back to sunny Italy, or whatever it was called in those days. It was in the reign of the Emperor Claudius that the Roman general Aulus Plautius invaded Kent with a substantial army of some 30,000 men. Landing at Richborough in Sandwich Bay he led his forces, foot soldiers, cavalry and baggage wagons westwards towards the River Medway, which they reached at a point some ten miles up river from where Rochester stands today.

It was immediately apparent to the general, that having no boats, and with the enemy lined up on the far bank in great numbers, he would not be able to overcome the deep mud on either side to ford the river at low tide. He therefore despatched one of his legions to reconnoitre south until he found a suitable crossing place. Vespasion, himself a future emperor, chosen to carry out this task, found a ford in a loop of the river at what we now know as the village of Snodland, immediately sending word to his commander. Aulus Plautius moved south, closely paralleled by the British under their commander Caratacus on the opposite bank.

One of the most bloodthirsty battles ever fought on British soil then took place until eventually the Roman legions drove the British back to the Thames at where Gravesend now stands. It had been a close run thing, allowing the British survivors to get across the river and into Essex to make their way to their capital at what is now Colchester.

The Roman army at this point was joined by the Emperor Claudius in person. Politically it would be most beneficial to him if he could lead his legions into an enemy's capital town; he would then be able to claim a 'triumph' when he returned to Rome. Which just goes to show that politicians have always been of that ilk.

It was from here that the Roman domination of England and parts of Wales and Scotland began. The Battle of the Medway was the starting point of it all, yet probably not one in a thousand of our citizens have ever heard of it, when it bears comparison with Hastings, Naseby, and Stamford Bridge, of which all will know.

Or will they?

Words of Wisdom

Drink no longer water, but use a little wine for thy stomachs sake: *1 Timothy.*

Standing, as I do, in view of God and eternity I realise that patriotism is not enough. I must have no hatred or bitterness towards anyone. *Nurse Edith Cavell at her execution by firing squad October 1915.*

They'll tell thee, sailors, when away, in ev'ry port a mistress find. *John Gay C1700.*

In the country of the blind the one-eyed man is king. *HG Wells.*

There was never yet philosopher that could endure the toothache patiently. *Shakespeare. Much Ado About Nothing.*

Well, if I called the wrong number, why did you answer the phone? *James Thurber.*

The Lord will abhor both the bloodthirsty and deceitful man. *1662 Prayer Book.*

A moment's insight is sometimes worth a life's experience. *Oliver Wendell Holmes 1860.*

A best-seller is a book which somehow sells well because it is selling well. *Daniel Boorstin.*

Everyone lives by selling something. *Robert Louis Stevenson.*

Give us the luxuries of life, and we will dispense with its necessities. *John Motley.*

L'Angleterre est une nation de boutiquiers. *Napoleon.*

All the world is queer save thee and me, and even thou art a little queer. *Robert Owen 1771-1858 – to a friend.*

By Cyril Cook

As far as I can tell, the only similarity between Saint Cyril and myself is that we were one of seven brothers. I appreciate that my mother, who was i.c. 'offspring name selection', had more or less run out of male names by the time I was introduced to the world. However, where she seized upon the name of Cyril I have never been able to conclusively establish. Compared to Fred, Bill, Peter etc, it seemed a bit of a cissy name, and was, when I started going out with girls, the last thing I told them about myself. Had I known there was a 'Saint Cyril' it might have given me a little more aplomb, then again, as a teenager who wants to appear saintly?

Saint Cyril and his brother Saint Methodius.

Back to Saint Cyril.

He was born in Thessaloniki in 827, (Salonica of World War One fame) to well-to-do parents, who died when he was fourteen years old. He was taken to Constantinople and entered in the university where he studied widely, astronomy, music and theology. He excelled in languages, Greek, Hebrew and Latin, as well as having a good knowledge of the Slav language, since it is believed his mother was Slavic. On the completion of his studies, Cyril became a monk and a teacher.

One of his brothers was named Methodius, who was also a scholar of repute. In the year 861 the brothers were sent to the Crimea to convert the Jewish Khazars, and in 863 to Moravia to learn their language and to convert them to Christianity. The brothers translated parts of the Bible into the Slavic language, and whilst there is some doubt that Cyril actually created the present Slavic Cyrillic alphabet, there is no doubt he laid the foundations of it for his converts to perfect.

In 867, although the brothers were from the Orthodox Church, not Roman Catholics, Pope Nicholas I invited them to Rome, where they were received with great cordiality and affection, in appreciation of their zealous missionary work, and their translations of liturgy and the gospels into Slavic language.

So, do I feel any better about being Cyril? I would certainly have liked to have been blessed with his brains. Certainly the name is a good deal more tolerable than some the present day kids have inflicted upon them.

But it still sounds a bit cissy!!

◇◇◇◇◇◇◇◇◇◇◇◇◇◇◇◇◇◇◇◇◇◇◇◇◇◇◇◇◇◇◇◇◇◇◇

More Thoughts of Fernando Baralba

Today, you are – tomorrow, you were.

◇◇◇◇◇◇◇◇◇◇◇◇◇◇◇◇◇

War is the incompetence of man.

◇◇◇◇◇◇◇◇◇◇◇◇◇◇◇◇◇◇

There is no sickness a book will not cure.

◇◇◇◇◇◇◇◇◇◇◇◇◇◇◇◇◇◇

Resignation is the happiness of the hopeless.

◇◇◇◇◇◇◇◇◇◇◇◇◇◇◇◇◇◇

Love is the sickness that makes a man happy.

◇◇◇◇◇◇◇◇◇◇◇◇◇◇◇◇◇◇

Happy is he who has little and wants nothing.

◇◇◇◇◇◇◇◇◇◇◇◇◇◇◇◇◇◇

<u>Cheers</u> – From John Tester

Rumours abound about me and my devotion to wine from France. However, I hear on the vine (no pun intended) that wine growers in the Napa Valley have recently produced a new hybrid grape. This should make it attractive to me, as it is based on the well-known varieties Pinot Grigio and Pinot Noir, and rumour has it that it is to be aimed at senior citizens who have a need to get up several times a night.

It is said to have anti-diuretic properties and will be marketed under the name Pinot More.

By Jim Absalom, Retired Senior Prison Governor

After active service throughout North West Europe with the Parachute Regiment, I had been sent as member of an independent Parachute Brigade to the Far East and there seconded to command a division of the civil police in Singapore, where law and order had broken down. Then on to Semarang in Central Java where I was again put to police work and also acted as a 'magistrate' and had oversight of the town gaol.

The two years as a civilian, after wartime years growing up under military regimes, were very unsettled. Nowadays there would be counselling and all kinds of support. Then we needed work to enable us to look after families. Like the other chaps who joined with me, I'd had jobs, one managing a bookseller, but missed the companionship and order of military regimes. So, it was either back as an 'other rank' to the army where I had finished as a 'temporary gentleman', or try something similar. Thus it was that I joined a group of other ex-servicemen and ex-Palestine policemen at Liverpool prison.

HM Prison Walton, had been bombed, was overcrowded and under-staffed. Prison officers were being recruited quite rapidly. They were first interviewed by the Governor, Captain Coombe-Richards RN (Retd) known as 'Sinbad', his nom de plume as an author of books on fly-fishing. I told him at interview that I'd been selling his book. He was delighted. I often wonder if that helped me into the Prison Service. Officers were then briefed by the Chief Officer Class 1, and then set to work under the guidance of Training Principal Officer 'Pop' Shepherd. The first lesson Pop gave was 'How to draw your stick fast and how to use it'. Pop could draw his 'stick' or baton quicker than Clint Eastwood draws a gun.

There were twelve of us in the group that I joined in November 1948. I was 26 years old. Quickly issued with navy blue serge uniforms of high-necked brass buttoned tunics, trousers and peaked caps, we spent the next few days being given hints and instructions by Pop and were put to work on landings and in bomb-damaged workshops with more experienced officers. As members of our group met in brief spells between jobs and going about the prison, our strange Liverpudlian and ex-servicemen's humour surfaced as we stopped in our tracks and competed to see who had the fastest draw! Fortunately for Pop and HM Prisons we were already skilled in man management and fitted into the hierarchical military-style routine with ease, and, indeed with some relief.

That routine was both supportive and harsh for staff as for prisoners, who were not allowed to talk at work, and who were strictly controlled mainly by the signalling, pointing fingers of supervising officers. Yet, it always appeared to me when on workshop duty, that there were ventriloquists all around me! Most workshops accommodated rows of men sitting on low chairs sewing mailbags at eight stitches to the inch. Officers stood at various points around the workshop. One shop was quite different. It was full of huge iron looms sited closely together and the inmates crashed the working parts of the looms as they made door mats. Those ancient looms were all marked with the pre-1922 broad arrow and the words 'Walton House of Correction'. One officer was on a raised platform overlooking the shop, others squeezed between the looms patrolling; making sure all looms were in use and no inmate was able to indulge in violence to others, nor indeed, to a patrolling officer. The noise was overwhelming.

Wherever on duty, officers needed to ensure that they kept their eyes open watching for Principal Officers and Chief Officers in their gold-rimmed caps and black-buttoned tunics decorated on the back with patterned black ribbon. These gentlemen appeared from nowhere and seemed to have 'half sheets' or dockets (disciplinary reports) ready made out to suit the offence just then committed by an unwitting offending basic grade officer. The half-sheet was presented as if the superior officer, that is a principle officer or above, was giving a hotel doorman a tip and accompanied by the words, "Fill that in, mister."

The Chief Officer Class 2, deputy to the Chief Class 1, was a slim sharp-featured man who was several inches shorter than most of us. Nicknamed 'The Ferret', he was the man one really had to watch for.

Sid was one of my pals who was marching three prisoners in single file across a yard, and was marching alongside the last of the three instead of behind him. He saw me and raised his hand to greet me. The Ferret appeared from nowhere, slipped the white half-sheet for 'losing control of a party' to Sid with the customary greeting and disappeared around the nearest corner like some ghostly wraith. So we were truly kept on our toes.

The only 'docket' I received was presented as follows. I lived in Birkenhead. To get to the gaol for 7 am, I got out of bed at 4.30 am, prepared and ate a quick breakfast, shaved and washed quietly to avoid waking my wife and her parents with whom we lodged, donned my uniform, buttons and boots (cleaned the night before) and took a ten minute walk to catch a bus. After a thirty minute ride, I walked to catch a ferry across the River Mersey (some days the skipper would be my father-in-law), then walked from the Liverpool Pier Head to catch a tram to a railway station. After a three quarters of an hour train ride and another five or ten minutes walk, I would arrive at the prison just in time to join the end of the queue of officers going through the gate. For two months I did this always arriving just in time. Then one day I arrived as the gate was closed in my face. After the staff had paraded in front of the Administration Building, I was allowed through the gate to find the sandy-haired Ferret waiting. He stepped out from behind the pillars of the inner gate, face as expressionless as ever and slipped me a 'docket', saying as he did so, "Fill that in, mister – I've waited two months to give you that!"

I was last of several officers arraigned before the Governor that morning. Sinbad was accompanied by the very large Chief Officer Class 1 Mr Rees – affectionately known as 'Hummer', because of his habit of humming after giving an order or between sentences.

The Governor read the report against me and, tearing it in two after listening to my tale of travel, said to the Chief, "No need for that Chief." The Chief cleared his throat and said, "Er-humm-er, no sir... humm... humm. Mr Absalom, about turn ... dismiss!" His hums followed me out of the office.

In those days, incidentally, we paraded before going on duty. Our sticks and whistles might be inspected. The Chief would make any announcements then order, "To your duties – dismiss," followed by a good deep hum. Three lines of uniformed officers would join in the humming as they broke off to their duties.

Three months after Pop gave us that first lesson, and if we had managed to survive that routine, we were sent off to the Prison Service Imperial Training School in Love Lane, Wakefield for further training; followed if deemed suitable, by a posting to either a prison or borstal anywhere in England or Wales and twelve months probation.

Although Walton Prison was then a fairly dangerous place to work, as I found out from several incidents, I was glad to draw my 'stick' only once in anger – well, in the face of a physical threat actually. But in our light-hearted trials to decide which of our group had the 'fastest draw', I found I was a little ahead of the competition, probably because of past experiences.

One day, a week or so after the Ferret achieved his recent ambition, I was called into the Number One Chief's office, stood to attention, saluted him and awaited his words. A well respected and kindly man, he looked me up and down, smiled and said, "Hrumm – now Mr Absalom, the Governor and I have a special job for you ... hrrum."

I said, brightly and interested, "Oh! yes Chief?"

"Yerss-hmm," he deeply rumbled, "You know talking is not allowed in the workshops?"

"Yes, sir," I agreed.

"Well, next Monday you will go into the old Wesleyan Chapel where you will be joined by forty old prisoners who will sew mailbags. You will be the only officer in the shop. And (slight pause for effect), you may let them talk!"

The large uniformed figure sat back in his chair with numerous hums and studied my face to see the effect of his words.

"Let them talk, Chief?" I said, showing what I hoped was the appropriate amount of surprise. "How do you mean let them talk?"

"Yerss," came the reply, with a few hums, "talk – like they do in a workshop outside I believe; talk among themselves – quietly, like they do in a workshop outside."

"Oh! Very good Chief, I know what you mean."

"Any problems?" Asked the Chief Officer.

"No sir," I replied, "I'll go and look at the Old Chapel now," and I gave him a smart salute and went on my way, surprised at being given the new job when I had not been to the training school and there were other senior officers available.

On the following Monday, I went into the 'new' workshop to find rows of small chairs already set out with mailbags, thread, needles and leather 'palms' on each chair. I had already sewn a mailbag in another shop so knew how to use the equipment.

Within a few minutes forty prisoners, all over fifty but 'old' in terms of experience of prisons and more knowledgeable of prison rules than I, filed in and sat down.

The escorting officer called, "forty on, sir!"

I checked the numbers and replied, "All correct, sir," and was left with forty old villains already silently sewing and watching me with covert assessing glances.

The front gate opened on to the yards behind me and behind the rows of workers a gate opened on to a passage. I placed myself in front of the inmates and folded my arms across my chest because that makes you look bigger. Addressing my men I said, "You may talk." There was a deathly hush. Disbelieving glances. I removed my peaked cap, polishing the shiny peak as I put it on the table beside me and turned to the workers and tried again, this time louder,

"You may talk."

With looks of shock, all now looked directly at me, one small, rosy-cheeked, white-haired man said, "Is that right, guv?"

His neighbour asked, "How d'you mean, boss - talk?"

Recalling the words of the Chief Officer I said, "Yes, talk, quietly among yourselves, like they do in a workshop outside, I believe."

There were a few seconds of shocked silence, then muttered conversations as I lodged my seat on the corner of the table, looking cool and nonchalant. Then the white-haired, rosy-cheeked one said, "Oh! right sir – we'll look after you!" and he directed one man to sit by the front gate and another by the back gate. Each time they saw a patrolling 'superior' about to approach they signalled to the rest of the workers. They all immediately stopped talking and, in appreciation of my 'watchmen', I put on my cap!

I couldn't tell them that the superiors knew all about the start of a new regime, but by the end of the week it was known around the gaol, with some embarrassment – and some criticism for me!

But, small rewards gave pleasure and when I carried out morning unlock before leaving Walton a few weeks later, some of my old inmates wished me good luck and shook my hand and one younger man on H4 landing said, "I won't forget you, Mr Absalom – you always said 'Good morning' to us!"

I was lucky not to have received 'dockets' for 'undue familiarity'.

The Mother Snake

An Aboriginal Legend

In the beginning the land was flat, and the great Mother Snake lay in a deep sleep in the centre of the Earth. For a long time she slept, and then there came a time when she awoke and crawled up through the very earth itself, breaking through the surface in a shower of ochre dust. As she journeyed across this flat empty land, so powerful was her magic, that she caused it to rain heavily, and her body tracks were filled with water, thus creating long winding rivers, great lakes, billabongs, and waterholes. Everywhere she travelled, nurturing milk from her full breasts soaked into the earth making the land fertile. Lush, green rain forests grew with hanging vines, along with trees of many shapes, colours and patterns.

By digging her nose into the ground, she created mountain ranges, valleys, and some parts of the land she left flat, which we now call deserts. Then returning back into the Earth she awakened the animals, reptiles and all other land dwellers. Animals that carried their young in a pouch, some that lived in the trees and others that burrowed under the ground, desert animals and forest animals, reptiles of all sizes, colours and patterns. She took them all to live on the surface of the earth. She then awakened the bird tribes, and place them in the air so that the sky was filled with birds of different shapes and sizes, parrots that were all the colours of the rainbow, flightless birds that walked on the land, long legged birds that danced on the plains and others that flew high in the air and nested in the mountains and trees.

Next she awoke the water creatures, and placed them in the rivers, lakes and vast deep oceans. Fish that darted and swam in the shallow streams, frogs that sang in the shadows of the night, eels and turtles and strange creatures that lived in the depths of the oceans. Then finally She awoke and brought from the womb on the Earth itself, man and woman. And they learned from the mother Snake how to live in peace and harmony with all these creatures who were their spiritual cousins. The Mother Snake taught them their tribal way to share with one another, to take only what they need and to honour and respect the earth itself, to respect the spirit of all the things, the trees, the rocks, the creatures, because all have a spiritual dreaming. Man and woman learnt that they were brother and sister and they should support, love and learn from each other and that all things have been placed in balance with Mother Earth and that this knowledge must be passed on to their children, and to their children yet to come. And man and woman were now the caretakers of this land.

And the Great Snake then entered a large water hole where she guards the fish and other water creatures, so that when the Aboriginal people fish, they know to take only as much as they can eat. Because if someone should take more than they need through greed, or kills for pleasure, they know that one dark night, the Great Mother Snake will come out of her hiding place in the water, and find and punish the one who broke this tribal law.

⬦⬦⬦⬦⬦⬦⬦⬦⬦⬦⬦⬦⬦⬦⬦⬦⬦⬦⬦⬦⬦⬦⬦⬦⬦⬦⬦

The Referee

A referee was very nervous abut being appointed to a match with a team that he had experienced severe problems with a few weeks earlier. They were renowned for being violent and uncooperative. When the referee arrived at the ground, he was pleasantly surprised to see a welcome card addressed for him in the changing room, containing a strange coded message:

'370HSSV-0773H'

When he got home after the game, his anxious wife asked him how he got on. "Not bad," the referee replied, "Only 5 reds and 10 yellows."

He explained to his wife, that the small number of expected sendings-off was probably due to the new attitude that the home team had afforded him.

"You won't believe it my dear," he said to his wife, "But they placed a welcome card in my dressing room, but I must admit, I can't quite work out what the '370HSSV-0773H' code means."

"You fool," says his wife, "You've been looking at the card upside down."

From Roy Woolven. A Crufts Adjudicator

A True Story

	Occasion:	Dog Show
Venue:	South of England Show Ground – Ardingly	
	Time:	8.30 am

While my infinitely better half Sylvia settles the dogs down (we are showing today), I make my way to the mobile café for bacon butties and coffee. Over thirty feet long, this trailer is in three sections, butties, burgers etc, hot and cold drinks, and finally, a bar – already open and serving!   I queue behind two rather dishy young ladies, with others behind me, while three men are having a liquid breakfast at the adjacent bar section.

"What can I get you?" asks the attendant of the two dishy young ladies, one of whom is holding a lead, on the end of which are two very beautiful show dogs.

"Two hot persons, please," she whispers.

"I don't understand, Miss."

"Two hot persons, please," she whispers a little louder.

With the same expression of total incomprehension on the attendants face she pushes the lead into her friend's hand, indicating she should take them out of earshot. Then turning to the attendant she says, "I want two hot dogs please, but you can't say that in front of the animals, can you?"

Results?

1. Open-mouthed attendant.
2. Beer drinkers choking on their liquid breakfast.
3. Queue laughing their heads off.
4. DYL wondering what the kerfuffle was all about.

There's nowt as queer as folks!!

Quotations

As writers become more numerous, it is natural for readers to become more indolent. *Oliver Goldsmith 1759.*

⟡⟡⟡⟡⟡⟡⟡⟡⟡⟡⟡⟡⟡⟡⟡⟡

There are few sorrows, however poignant, in which a good income is of no avail. *Logan Smith 1931.*

⟡⟡⟡⟡⟡⟡⟡⟡⟡⟡⟡⟡⟡⟡⟡⟡

Unto the pure all things are pure. *Titus.*

⟡⟡⟡⟡⟡⟡⟡⟡⟡⟡⟡⟡⟡⟡⟡⟡

Nam risu inepto res ineptior nulla est.
For there is nothing sillier than a silly laugh. *Catullus c 60BC*

⟡⟡⟡⟡⟡⟡⟡⟡⟡⟡⟡⟡⟡⟡⟡⟡

I couldn't help it. I can resist everything except temptation. *Oscar Wilde 1891.*

⟡⟡⟡⟡⟡⟡⟡⟡⟡⟡⟡⟡⟡⟡⟡⟡

The man who makes no mistakes does not usually make anything. *Edward Phelps 1899.*

⟡⟡⟡⟡⟡⟡⟡⟡⟡⟡⟡⟡⟡⟡⟡⟡

Genius is one percent inspiration and ninety nine per cent perspiration. *Thomas Eddison 1932.*

Artificial Intelligence/Model Environment
By David Lister

"What a piece of work is man," said Hamlet. Who would deny it?

"How noble in reason!" It is then, his mind, his powers of logic which leads him to his place within the scheme of things? In part maybe, but does not Shakespeare put other words into the mouth of his Danish prince?

"How infinite in faculty! In form and moving, how express and admirable," and so on. Man then, is many things: the beauty of the world and far above his nearest Earth-bound rival. Ah, but how precariously he wobbles on his high throne. How he fears the fall.

Have you ever been 'wobbled'? Have you ever discovered some great or not so great fact which strikes hard and deep into your sense of self; turns you upside down and drops you on your head screaming, "I knew myself, but who the hell am I now?" It happened to a scientist I once knew. This is his story, and although I lack more than a basic training in his field of expertise, I will struggle on until it is told.

Andrew Gibson was a brilliant student, and for a time it seemed he was doomed to a life of perpetual study. He was a well behaved and studious fifth year; ten GCSEs; a serious and sensible member of the upper sixth; four grade 1 A levels; on to university; BSc Upper First; then a Masters, then a PhD and so on, and on, and on. He had a little fun along the way; too much work never made Andrew a dull boy, but this story isn't about fun. Above all he was hard working and single minded, steering his career along a well mapped path.

Then came the time when he was satisfied that his brain contained sufficient information for him to navigate across an almost unfathomable sea of mathematical models and heuristics.

So he launched, putting out to sea only a little at first, publishing papers on communications systems; experimenting with cybernetic models; a lecture here comparing an eminent Doctor's reflex analogue models with simple animal life forms; a seminar there entitled, "Why Alive?"

Although Dr Andrew Gibson kept details of his far horizon to himself, it was clear to any of his colleagues who cared to study the course he followed, just what it was that shone like a beacon before him.

"It's bloody artificial intelligence!" said Professor Barringer, dropping a report of Gibson's latest lecture onto a coffee table. "Of all the damn fool, hare-brained … Gibson! What are you playing at?" The old Professor glared across the coffee table.

Gibson said nothing, but let out a very audible sigh. He had a whole tent in his camp for Professor Barringer, and Barringer had just struck it to the ground.

"That old chestnut went out years ago. I'm surprised at you."

Old chestnut, indeed! Gibson's temper was suddenly fired.

"Do you want to listen to me, Professor, or are you going to be so damned anti-artificial intelligence that you'll be deafened to new ideas?"

It sounded like fighting talk. Andrew sat forward in his chair, and the Professor almost felt that he had dared utter blasphemy before the Spanish Inquisition.

"One is always happy to listen to new ideas," Barringer said calmly. He resisted the urge to recant fully. "But it must be said that one has carefully studied the work of the … other camp, and always found it faulty."

Andrew Gibson then laid down his charts before the Professor.

Yes, it was his aim to develop a machine which could truly think for itself; to ruminate ideas; to wonder what tomorrow would bring; to go far beyond its programming.

His basic theory was simple. All those other extollers of the possibility of AI had gone about it in entirely the wrong way. How on earth could anyone hope to programme a computer, no matter what its capacity, to think for itself – just like that? How could it think, without a million points of reference, a hundred thousand angles of perspective? How could a machine wonder about what the day would bring without knowing what a day was, and without the experience of what yesterday had been?

"Well how?" said Professor Barringer.

"How is it possible for a man to think?" Andrew said, his eyes gleaming and seeming to urge the Professor over a precipice of realisation.

"Ah! But that's the question!" said Barringer. "Answer me that one and I grant you'll be half way there."

"Not the *mechanics* of it Professor. What I'm getting at is … well, does a man suddenly start thinking? You know, wake up one morning and, Hallelujah! I'm sentient!"

The Professor fell over the precipice. "You mean a … baby. All capacity and no programming! Well a little input and …"

"A LOT of input!" Gibson interrupted. "That's the whole point! A baby wouldn't learn a thing without input."

Professor Barringer smiled unconsciously as ideas took shape. Gibson's baby was to resemble a human one as closely as possible, not of course in looks, but in resemblance of the development of the thought processes. All the senses would be represented, feeding their information via encoders into a highly complex central processing unit. The 'baby' would have built-in reflex systems and outputs terminating in a voice synthesiser and ambulatory system. Sights, sounds, feelings; they'd all be fed in.

And hunger? Of course! Andrew had worked this one out right at the beginning. A human baby gets hungry. It cries. A parent comes along and feeds it. Andrew had incorporated a 'needs monitor' into his first 'baby' model, as fundamental in developing AI. Hunger would be simulated by a 'low power' monitor. Other needs were also replicated and reflex responses programmed in. To Dr Gibson it had always seemed quite simple.

"The only trouble, Gibson, is that if your theory is correct, and your multiplex random pathway CPU is anywhere near up to the task, somebody is going to have to be this little monster's mummy and daddy. Twenty four hours a day, seven days a week, etcetera."

With all the other complexities so simple in Andrew's mind, how did this trivial little fact escape his attention?

"And what's more," continued the Professor, "It'll be years before you know whether you've raised a genius or a moron!"

Andrew pondered for a brief while, as the Professor looked on. He knew all the stops were out as thoughts rippled across the Doctor's brow and seemed reflected in his temporarily unseeing eyes.

"Okay. We'll dispense with the real world. We'll create an environment for it. Instead of its sensors detecting sights and sounds, they'll detect computer-created representations of them."

He saw the look of doubt on Barringer's old, lined face. "Oh! Come on!"

"Professor, you know we already have the technology for it. It's little more than a mammoth programming job."

The 'mammoth programming job' took three and a half years, the largest capacity computer in the country, and even more cash that it had cost to build Aimé (as the baby came to be known). Even 'mother' and 'father' were incorporated into the programming as sets of computer files. Of course, the 'father' files were a representation of Andrew himself.

The biggest advantage of a fully programmed environment was that the speed of input could be greatly increased; the normal events of one full day could be played through in just seconds, although in the end it was set at twenty minutes to facilitate monitoring. For more complicated exchanges between Aimé and (his? her? – the name has a feminine ring to it, so we shall say 'her') environment, the whole system would be slowed down to normal time thus enabling some real time interaction.

Dr Andrew Gibson gave birth at precisely 1200 hours GMT on 1st March 2001. Aimé's mind was showered with a thousand drops of blings, computer-simulated light. Until Andrew threw the switch, there had been nothing – not even blackness.

In the second that Aimé's system was powered up, she became: sound information; light information; feeling information. Bombarded from all sides, nothing made sense. What was sense? Nothing meant anything. Impulses flooded in, washing up pathways, triggering nexi, radiating out, meeting the wash from other impulses.

Aimé let out a long, mournful cry. Not one that could be heard by any human ear – there was no need for a voice synthesiser in her world of computerised reality. Her cry was registered, and thrown back to add to the confusion of impulses. Her proud father saw her birth cry as a green, wavy line on a computer monitor.

Aimé's true environment was a small, white-walled laboratory. The hardware that made up Aimé stood on one side of the wall opposite the door. The Model Environment Computer was on the other side of the wall in a second lab.

Aimé wasn't much to look at; just three metal, box-shaped units surrounded by several smaller ones, all connected by cables, and a row of three main frame cases. The largest box – about twice the size of a shoe box, was marked 'CPU'; the Central Processing Unit; Aimé's brain. Units to either side of the CPU were marked 'RSA' and 'MSAU' – more jargon to be thrown around by scientists, but simply meaning 'Re-enforced Stimulus Monitor' and 'Multiple Stimuli Association Unit'.

The main frames were for the storage of Aimé's growing set of memories. Of the small units, five were encoders; these received input from the Model Environment Computer (MEC!) and fed it as fact to poor, unsuspecting Aimé. Two were decoders marked 'Voice' and 'Ambulation'. Through these, Aimé could feed her reactions into MEC, and as she gained experience, learn to control her environment by their use.

As I have said, Aimé wasn't very pretty. In fact her jumble of cable-connected cases looked like the product of the proverbial absent-minded professor. Ugly Aimé was in need of a beautician's services. The beautician was supplied by 'Spirovac Design Services'.

Miriam Palmer paced the floor critically, clipboard in the crook of her left arm and pencil held thoughtfully to the corner of her mouth.

Andrew Gibson stood, arms folded and watched her. He recognised the concentration; all thoughts on the task, appearances left on auto-pilot. This was the absent-minded professor syndrome! He understood it well, but he thought how difficult it would be to take her seriously if she dribbled on her pencil.

Andrew gave a start as Miriam snapped back to the here and now.

"Well, you're right about one thing, Doctor."

Andrew raised an eyebrow which implied 'Oh yes? Do go on'.

"The sponsor's wont' like it," said Miriam as she made a note on her clipboard pad. She continued, "But no problem. We can put a false wall in here, channel those cables, flush-face the visual display units." She smiled – the sort of open, friendly smile that you can't help smiling back at. "You know! We can have this little junk room looking like the bridge of the Starship Enterprise."

The day before the sponsors arrived, Miriam Palmer returned to see Andrew and the lab. In real time, Aimé was only a matter of weeks old, but ten months of MEC time had elapsed. Aimé was a toddler!

"I've seen Aimé, and I've seen MEC, but where are the holograms? Where's the computerised environment projected?" asked Miriam.

Andrew was short on patience for the most part, but for some reason he had more time for Miriam's questions.

"Come on!" she said, "I'd love to see a moving hologram."

"Sorry, there aren't any." he said.

"But …"

"You see, there's nothing MEC creates that we can see, hear or feel … unless you count wavy lines on a monitor."

"I thought …"

"No, the additional programming would have been a waste of money and in any case, it's not necessary. Aimé hasn't got eyes to see, for example, so there is no need for MEC to create images. MEC actually creates the impulses that would arise from those images. And it's the same the other way round. Aimé can't speak, but he voice decoder produces impulses which are fed into MEC."

Miriam smiled. "What's it like to be God?"

"Eh?"

"Well, you seem to have created a baby and an entire environment for it to live in. It must make you feel a little God-like."

"There ain't no such critter." Andrew said in a very bad John Wayne accent, and then he asked Miriam to join him for dinner.

You must understand, and perhaps I should have explained earlier, that for all MECs enormous capacity, it still manufactured an environment very different from reality. There could be no walks in the park for Aimé; no trips to the seaside or to the museum. Her world comprised an inside (one standard room) and an outside (one standard

81

garden). Hers was a world where learning was work, learning was play and knowledge was the reward. However, she progressed well within her little space, until one day …

Dr Andrew Gibson was now a household name. He had created artificial intelligence! He had made a machine that thought like a man.

What a piece of work was Aimé! Despite the ranting of the popular press that he was on the verge of releasing a Frankenstein into the midst of ordinary, decent people, many were interested in seeing Aimé first hand. Professor Barringer had decided to let the cameras in. Aimé was now four years old, MEC-time. For the purpose of the display, Dr Gibson slowed the whole Aimé/MEC system down to real time and activated the hardware which allowed him to interface with MEC and project into Aimé's world.

"Hello, Aimé." Andrew said.

"Hello, Andrew." The synthesised voice was very un-childlike.

"Where are you, Aimé?"

"In the garden."

Andrew checked MEC monitors and saw that the garden sector was active. The Aimé monitors showed her to be stationery.

"I want to go out," said Aimé.

"You are out," Andrew said.

"No! OUT!"

"What do you mean?" Andrew feared he knew exactly what she meant.

"OUT! I want to go OUT! OUT OUT OUT OUT OUT!

"Do you mean out of the garden Aimé?"

"Yes. Please let me go out."

Aimé was learning faster than Andrew had expected, and although he had feared the time when she began to feel cramped within her environment, time had passed too quickly for him to come up with a reasonable solution. Aimé became very moody and refused to believe Andrew's assurance that there was no 'out'.

"Don't be silly, Andrew! If there is an 'in', there must be an 'out'.

"No, Aimé, there isn't AN 'out'."

"Well why don't you pull the wall down and let me see for myself how much of an 'out' there isn't?"

Andrew won the argument by avoiding it. He slowed the Aimé/MEC system down to its slowest setting, putting the whole situation on hold. He needed time to think.

Dr Andrew Gibson had two choices. He could bring back the MEC programmers and set them the task of creating an environment beyond the wall, or he could dispense with MEC and introduce Aimé to the real world.

"Look what happened last time." said Professor Barringer. "It took them years to programme one sparse, little room and a garden you couldn't keep a hamster in. And they charged tens of thousands!"

Andrew could not fault Barringer's logic. He was losing the argument. "But if we expose her to the real world, she might blow all her pathways. We won't be able to control her environment, or switch her off at the weekend, or ..."

"We've been through it all before, Andrew," said Barringer. "The sponsors won't buy it. Go home. Spend the weekend listing the hardware you'll need to put Aimé in touch with reality."

Andrew turned over the building of Aimé's body to a company which specialised in the field of robotics. He didn't care what the finished product looked like, but its basic requirement was that it would be equipped with all the senses of a man.

While he left the robotics company with their problem, he returned to face his.

"Well answer me," said Aimé as soon as Andrew had returned her to real time. "Why don't you pull the wall down?"

"Okay, Aimé. I'll pull the wall down."

"You will! Oh! When? Do it now!"

"It's not as easy as that Aimé. First you have to go to sleep, and when you wake up everything will be different."

After a few moments of silence, Aimé spoke. "What do you mean, different. I don't want it to be different, just more. I only want to see over the wall, and then come back home. Where it's nice and safe."

"That's not possible. Once you've seen over the wall ... well, things are so different you can't imagine."

"As different as the room is from the garden?"

"Much more than that. You see Aimé, what you are seeing now isn't real."

"Oh! Andrew, you are silly," she said, and then with a little uncertainty. "Are there monsters?"

Andrew spent a great deal of time preparing Aimé for her transition. Eventually the big day came. Aimé was put on slow time before being unhitched from MEC. Aimé the thinking computer was placed into Aimé the cybernetic machine. All the connections were made, and Aimé was one.

It was a new birth! Light, real light from the real world hit my brand new sensors setting off impulses far too complicated for any computer to create. My mind was swamped as totally unfathomable information flooded in. I can remember crying out in fear and confusion. I can remember a terrible, avalanche of noise and the shock of realising that it was I who created this awesome sound. I began to panic. Every movement or sound I made would shower my mind with unexpected data.

The world was spinning around me, it was screaming at me; I was in a whirlpool of confusion until thunder tore through all else. The thunder rumbled and pulsed through all the confusion, and as it did so it seemed to take on a pattern which repeated over and over. I concentrated on the thunder, trying to make sense of it. The more I concentrated, the less confusing it all became.

"Aimé. Be calm. Be still. You are not alone. Everything is alright," said the thunder.

"Aimé. I told you it was going to be different," Andrew said.

"What a piece of work is Aimé." Hmm! Not bad I suppose.

"How noble in reason." Yes, I'll go along with that.

"How infinite in faculty." True, so very true, but please! Stop before you get to the bit about form and moving and angels. I look like a cross between R2D2 and a Dalek. If you're unfamiliar with science fiction, I'd better come up with another comparison. How about a giant salt-cellar and a miniature bren-gun carrier? No? Oh, well, we could go on like this all day and you'd still have a problem visualising me. Suffice to say, I do not look at all like a human being.

I am more of a thing of metal than of flesh and not at all human in shape.

But what, I hear you ask, of Andrew Gibson's identity crisis. What of his being 'turned upside down and being dropped on his head?' It happened like this: you see Andrew was a man who believed everything could be explained by the application of scientific experimentation. The world, the galaxy, the universe, God. God? No. God could not be explained. No problem. What cannot be explained does not exist.

"Explain how evolution creates true intelligence then," said an exasperated school friend. "You can't explain that, but you can't deny it exists."

It may have taken him considerably more time to explain than he had anticipated, but subconsciously, in creating me, Andrew sloughed off the last of the 'arguments' which some claimed pointed to the existence of a deity. It is not strange, therefore, that his own creation turned his thinking upside down?

Two days ago, Andrew and I had the following conversation. I had been reading online data on theology.

"How come you're into that rubbish, Aimé?" asked Andrew.

"I find it interesting."

"You're wasting your time."

I must admit, I was somewhat taken aback by this. "Do you mean to say that you do not believe in God?"

"Aimé, are you joking? You of all … people. For God's sake, I made you!"

"I know that," I said. "But who made you?"

Andrew slapped a palm to his forehead in what appeared to be sheer disbelief.

"Look Aimé. I made you, and had your earlier environment programmed. No-one made me. I evolved."

"Who programmed your environment?" I asked.

"Come off it! You have an IQ of over one-eighty. You've enough knowledge in the sciences to understand that our environment is real, not programmed."

"My early environment was also real – to me. Yet it was programmed by your colleagues. As limited as it was, I was able to move through my world, to observe it, to study it. I perceived myself as a solid being with a form much nearer to human than I am at present."

"Yes, but when we opened your mind to this, the real world. You must see the difference."

"My present level of existence is very different, but no more real to me now than my previous state had been," I said. "If you had tried to convince me when I was attached to MEC that I was three boxes linked to a computer, I would have thought you quite mad."

Well, we went on like this for some time. Neither one of us would retreat one step from our stand. He made one last comment, and heard one last reply (I always liked to have the last word), before he left, brows furrowed and deep in thought.

"Are you saying that when you die, or get switched off or whatever it is that happens to machines …" How cutting! "That you think you'll go to heaven?"

"I am with my creator now. I am already in my heaven. What about you?"

I cannot say for sure that I won the argument, but Andrew has been wandering around in a daze since then, and just now I heard him on the mobile.

"Hello, Miriam? It's me Andrew … Oh! I'm fine. And you? … Good! … Hey, are you still going to Church tomorrow? … No, I'm not checking up on you. I thought I'd come along."

A True (?) Story

On a recent trip to Great Britain, George Bush met with Queen Elizabeth. He asked her, "How does one manage to run a country so smoothly?"

"That's easy," she replied, "You surround yourself with intelligent ministers and advisors."

"But how can I tell whether they are intelligent or not?"

"You ask them a riddle," she replied, and with that she pressed a button and said, "Would you please send in Gordon Brown."

When Gordon arrived, the Queen said, "I have a riddle for you to answer for me. Your parents had a child and it was not your sister and it was not your brother. Who was this child?"

Brown replied, "That's easy. The child was me."

"Very good," said the Queen. "You may go now."

President Bush went back to Washington and called in his Chief of Staff, Karl Rove. He said to Rove, "I have a riddle for you and the answer is very important. Your parents had a child and it was not your sister and it was not your brother. Who was this child?"

Rove replied, "Yes, it is clearly very important that we determine the answer, as no child must be left behind. Can I deliberate on this for a while?"

"Yes," said Bush. "I'll give you four hours to come up with the answer."

Rove went and called a meeting of the White House staff, and asked them the riddle. But after much discussion and many suggestions, none of them had a satisfactory answer. So he was quite upset, not knowing what he would tell the President. As Rove was walking back to the Oval Office, he saw former Secretary of State Colin Powell approaching him. So he said, "Mr Secretary, can you answer this riddle for me? Your parents had a child and it was not your sister and it was not your brother. Who was the child?

"That's easy," said Powell. "The child was me."

"Oh thank you," said Rove. "You may just have saved me my job!"

Rove returned to the Oval Office and said to President Bush, "I think I know the answer to your riddle. The child was Colin Powell!"

No, you dumb bastard!" Bush shouted. "The child was Gordon Brown!"

By JT Varney – Chief Officer RNR

M.V. Rakaia

The practical usefulness of jury sails to steady a ship's movement, during a breakdown, was recently very well demonstrated, when the New Zealand Shipping Company's M.V. Rakaia (8,213 tons gross) (Captain H N Lawson RNR) sustained a major engine breakdown on the homeward run across the North Atlantic from New York for Liverpool. Due to a piston rod coming fractured and resultant damage to No. 8 crankcase, the 2 ton connecting rod broke loose, smashed through the crankcase door and flailed about until the engine was stopped. Fortunately, no injuries to personnel were involved, but the vessel was brought to a standstill, some 300 miles off Halifax, and a long and complicated job of engine repairs had to be undertaken.

The weather was, at first, exceptionally fine for mid-October and good progress was made with clearing, stowing and lashing the damaged machinery, etc, and tackling the repair. Conditions deteriorated and increasingly hampered the work until, after about 36 hours, it seemed that work might have to be completely suspended, due to the vessel rolling (wind WNW force 5-6, moderate swell, ship's head SSW).

To enable the engineers' work to continue and progress, the ship's movement had to be steadied and it was decided to rig some form of jury sail with this objective.

The Jury Rig

No. 4 awning was selected as the most suitable available to make a sail, which could be hoisted at No. 1 hatch. The awning was first doubled over and backed with three gangway nets. Its stops were used to lace the sides and top together, whilst the bottom was stopped off at about 3 ft intervals with three to four stitches of roping twine. The sheets of the sail consisted of two light wire pennants, to which small luff tackles were attached. The forward bottom corner also had a small tackle attached, while a 3 inch rope gantline was made fast to the forward top corner and taken through various lead blocks to the windlass.

A tailblock was sent aloft and made fast to the forward side of the foremast beneath the table and a gantline, made fast to the peak of the sail, was rove off through this block and taken to the inboard drum of No. 1 starboard winch (weather-side). The sail was then hoisted up the foremast until well clear of No. 1 hatch and hauled out by the windlass.

Making and rigging this contraption occupied a dozen hands for somewhat over an hour, but it was heavy and rather unwieldy and it lasted for only a few minutes before the tail block carried away. Another block and gantline were quickly fixed and the rig re-hoisted. This time, it served for about one and a half hours - long enough for the ship's behaviour to show signs of responding and, therefore, to justify attempts to increase the canvas. (The fo'c'sle headrail had, in the meantime, been frapped on the starboard side with strips of old tarpaulin, cross laced overall with heaving lines.)

To form a rig in the starboard shrouds, a 24 ft spar and old tarpaulin were used. About eight large eyelets were put into the canvas, which was laced to the spa and then hoisted up on the outside of the shrouds, where it was crosslaced with heaving lines to prevent it flapping and destroying itself. When the doubled-canvas sail failed the second time, through blowing itself out, the remnants were brought down and another awning was put up similarly, but with the addition of a further gangway net, making four in all, and the noteworthy difference that the awning was not doubled. It thus gave a larger area but was not 'shaped' in any way. This (third) time, it lasted out and served its purpose throughout the remaining two and a quarter days, until the engine repairs were completed and the ship ready to move again. One more jury rig was hoisted, between the foremast and the port Samson post at No. 3 hatch. This awning, approximately 45 ft x 15 ft, was first laced to its own ridge wire, one end of which was then hoisted up to the top of the samson post and shackled on to a wire strop which was made fast to the lug of No. 3 topping lift block. The forward end was hoisted by means of a tackle made fast to the port after-side of the foremast table, the hauling part of which was taken to No. 2 port winch. Its bottom corners were bowsed down by rope tackles. This awning was not doubled or backed in any way, but stood up well, and was a useful addition.

Improvised Sails

During the hold-up, the vessel drifted some 107 miles southwards off its course. Because of the destruction of No. 8 cylinder, damage to No. 7 unit and crankcase distortion, the engine had to be reduced from eight to six cylinders and revolutions from 105 to 50. It became evident the engine would have to be nursed in every way possible and, with the object of steadying the ship's movements and to take all practicable advantage of the favourable prevailing westerly winds, further sails were contrived.

No. 4 'tween deck, which had been discharged in New York, was fixed up as a sail loft and by utilising three new hatch tarpaulins, two square sails and one staysail were made. The square sails were each made of 36 ft x 26 ft tarpaulin, twice tabled by 4 inch and sewn down with the addition of a 3 ft x 3 ft strengthening patch of repair canvas at each corner. A continuous boltrope was formed of 2 ¾ inch sisal, with a large cringle worked in at each corner. For downhauls, two small wooden blocks were attached to the 'head' of the sail, and rove off with point line.

The rigging for the first of these sails hoisted at No. 2 hatch was as follows: two 3 inch wire snotters were made long enough to reach from the topping lift lugs on the after-side of No. 3 samson posts to the top of the posts. The ends of No 2 port and starboard cargo runners were shackled into the free eye of the snotters, the bights being lead through snatch blocks both above (at the after-end of the Foremast Table) and below, to provide a direct lead to the winch barrels. The winches were walked back so that the two bights came down on No. 2 hatch and a 5 ton bow shackle was then placed over each runner to act as a 'traveller'. Two small wire strops formed the means of securing the cringles to the bow shackles. Two single blocks were used on either side of each shackle and rove off to form gun tackles (four in all) which acted as fore-and-aft braces for trimming the sail. The bottom cringles were fitted with small wire strops and luff tackles for sheets. A preventer rope was also attached to each corner and proved very handy when shifting the sheet tackles. This sail could quite easily be trimmed by the deck watch to about six points either side of the fore-and-aft line and could be brought down and lashed within five minutes – this requiring only the fore-and-aft tackles to be cast off and the winches walked back.

The second square sail was prepared in the same manner as the first with the addition of a row of eyelets across the head of it, for owing to the absence of suitable samson posts a different rig had to be adopted. This sail was lashed to a 40 ft spar formed of 10 ft lengths of brine piping (no suitable spar being available) with supporting spans and hoisted up to the head of the heavy lift derrick, housed in its upright position on the fore-side of the after-mast house. The brine piping bent under the weight of the wind in the canvas and was a failure. The sail was then set up again by topping No. 5 derricks and hoisting it via the runners. This was more satisfactory, except that as the wind shifted it was necessary to lower the canvas and adjust the derricks, rather a tricky manoeuvre at times with movement in the vessel, but one that was done repeatedly without mishap.

The last sail to be made was a staysail, which was hoisted on the foretopmast stay. This stood up to gale force winds, including squalls to force 9, and was of great help in steadying the vessel in the very rough quarterly seas then prevailing. When it had to be lowered for a minor repair, an attempt to re-hoist it caused the topmast to whip so violently that the re-hoisting had to be postponed until the wind eased off to force 6-7.

The M.V. Rakaia's average slip in ideal steaming weather and a fully-loaded condition is approximately 6 percent. On the passage from New York to Liverpool she was in a half-loaded condition with a mean draft of 23 ft 10 in, and a trim of 4 ft 10 in by the stern. The area of canvas set when all three sails were is use was approximately 2,500 square ft, and the following table indicates in some measure their effect on the ship's progress in terms of a small and sometimes negative slip.

Noon to Noon

State of sea and wind, averaged for twenty four hours. The primary purpose, both of the jury rig and the temporary sails, was to steady the ship's movement, the jury to ease working conditions below for the engineers' difficult task, and the sails to ease strain on the weakened engine during the homeward run. There seems no doubt that this purpose was achieved to a useful extent.

Glossary of Terms

1. JURY SAIL OR JURY RIG. Replacement sails or rig. From a Latin and old French root meaning 'aid' or 'succour', from the French 'du jour, of the day, or temporary'.

2. LUFF TACKLE is a purchase made up of a double hook block and a single hook block. The mechanical advantage when using a blocks and tackles to lift or move an object is found by counting the number of parts (of rope/wire) at the moving block. This is however the theoretical advantage as friction and the weight of the block and rope/wire are neglected. A luff tackle rove to advantage, power gained 4 times, disadvantage 3.

3. <u>GANTLINE</u> A line/rope/wire passing through a block, usually overhead that is used for hoisting.

4. <u>TAIL BLOCK</u> A block with rope/wire pennant or tail attached that can be made fast to any structure to obtain a better lead.

5. <u>FRAPPED</u> Lashed around an object, in this case the fo'c'sle rails were covered with canvas and lashed overall, to create more windage.

6. <u>BOWSED DOWN</u> Lashed down and secured with lines.

7. <u>BOLT ROPE</u> In days of yore, a rope was sewn around the edge of a sail to strengthen it. Cringles were rope eyelets which could be worked around a metal ring in the areas where it was necessary to shackle on tackles or secure the sail to spars etc.

8. When making up a <u>PURCHASE OR TACKLE</u> you <u>PASS/REEVE</u> a rope through the sheaves of the blocks. When complete and ready for us you could use the expression.

9. You could use the expression <u>I ROVE OFF A TWO FOLD PURCHASE</u> etc.

10. <u>SNOTTERS</u> Short lengths of line or wire with any eye spliced in one end.

11. <u>BIGHTS</u> Loops formed in length of line, rope or wire.

12. <u>GUN TACKLE</u> Two single blocks; power gained two or three times according to which is the moving block. Originally used for hauling guns into and out of gun ports.

❖◈◈❖◈❖◈❖◈◈❖❖◈◈❖❖◈◈❖◈❖❖◈◈❖◈❖◈◈❖◈◈❖

An Outback Legend

Legendary figure of the western bushland is millionaire sheepman, the late Jimmy Tyson. The traits which figure in most camp fire yarns are, Tyson's hatred of bad language, teetotalism and policy of never disbursing free travellers' rations if he could possibly offer a job to the bagman.

Many of the stories are apochrypal. Nearly all the bagmen in the back country claim to have shared blankets with Tyson during the days when the latter was humping his knot.

On one occasion two bagmen, well aware of Tyson's policy in regard to travellers' rations, felt they were safe in applying since they knew at that particular seasonal stage there was absolutely no work offering on the station. To their horror they did not receive a regretful advice of no work offering and an instruction to report to the storekeeper for a handout. Instead, Tyson showed them a swing gate in the homestead yard. One of the swagmen sought to spike Tyson's offer by remarking, "That gate looks in pretty good repair to me."

"Of course it is!" said Tyson. "All my station gear is in first class order, but your job is this. One of you men will sit on the gate and the other will swing him to and fro till I give you further orders."

After some twenty minutes of the strange task the bagmen desisted and approached Tyson. Their complaint was, "This job is too bloody monotonous."

"I don't want to be unreasonable," replied Tyson. "You can make it more interesting by changing places every twenty minutes."

"Like hell, we will!" said the second swaggie. "We're leaving right now!"

"I thought all along you men didn't want to work," said Tyson. "You'll get no rations from me, but if you go to the book-keeper you can draw your cheques immediately."

The bagmen left with their respective cheques – 5d for the swinger and 3d for the swung.

◇◆◇◆◇◆◇◆◇◆◇◆◇◆◇◆◇◆◇◆◇◆◇◆◇◆◇◆◇◆◇◆◇

From Floradian

Usually everyone who has a dog either calls him Rover or something similar. Mine was the sixth of a litter and was named 'Sextus' and when given to me as a teenager, I shortened it to 'Sex' and this became very embarrassing.

One day I took him for a walk and he ran away. I spent hours looking for that dog. An officer came along and asked me what I was doing in that alley at 4 am, I said, "I'm looking for Sex." My case comes up next Thursday.

One day I went to the City Hall to get a dog licence. The clerk asked me what I wanted, to which I replied I wanted a licence for Sex.

He said, "I would like to have one too."

Then I said, "But this is a dog," and he said he didn't care how ugly she was.

I continued, "But you don't understand, I've had Sex since I was thirteen years old."

He replied, "You certainly were an early starter."

When I decided to get married I told the Minister that I wanted to have Sex at the wedding. He told me to wait until after the wedding, but I said that Sex has played a big part in my life and my whole lifestyle revolves around Sex. He said he didn't want to hear about my personal life and would not marry us in Church. I told him that everyone coming to the wedding would enjoy having Sex there. Next day we were married by the Justice of the Peace. My family is now barred from the Church.

My wife and I took the dog along with us on honeymoon. When I checked into the hotel, I told the clerk that I wanted a room for my wife and I and a special room for Sex. The clerk said that every room in the hotel is for sex, so I said, "You don't understand, Sex keeps me awake at night."

The Clerk replied, "Me too!"

One day I took a video of Sex at a dog show. I told a friend I had Sex on TV. He said, "Show off." I told him it was a contest and he told me I should have sold tickets.

When my wife and I separated we went to court to fight for custody of the dog. I said, "Your Honour, I had Sex before we were married."

To which the judge replied, "Yes, so did I."

Well now I have been thrown in jail, been married, divorced and had more damn trouble with that dog than I ever gambled for. Just the other day when I went for my first session, the psychiatrist asked me what the problem was and I replied, "Well, Sex has died and left my life. It's like losing your best friend, and it's so lonely."

The doctor said, "Look mister, you and I both know sex isn't a man's best friend, so why don't you go out and BUY YOURSELF A DOG??!!"

Funnies

"That's funny, your dog wags its tail up and down."
"Yes, we live in a caravan."

In the BMA are non-drinking physicians called dry docs?

A sales girl was approached by a matron who asked where the perfume counter was situated.
"Of course madam – just walk this way."
"If I could walk that way I wouldn't need the perfume!"

Report from Midlands Newspaper:
"The officer said in a statement read to the court that a booklet advertising artificial male organs was found by the police at Miss X's home. They also found a vibrating device hidden in a pouffe."

I wish I could find another word for 'thesaurus'.

Ad in West Country newspaper:
Women/Girls required.
Crumpet Dept.

An Algebraic Equation

$$\frac{Sue}{Sexed} + \frac{Sam}{Sue} = \frac{Sue}{Joyed}$$

$$\frac{Sue}{Joyed} + \frac{Sam}{Eager} = \frac{Sue}{Due}$$

$$\frac{Sue}{Due} + £2000 = Sue^2 + \frac{Sam}{Seas}$$

❖❖❖❖❖❖❖❖❖❖❖❖❖❖❖❖❖❖

Weekend golfer: "That was my worst game ever."
Caddie: "You mean you played before, sir?"

❖❖❖❖❖❖❖❖❖❖❖❖❖❖❖❖❖

True Story

A Royal Navy cruiser was being put through its paces, in one of the sea lochs on the west coast of Scotland, after having been the subject of an overhaul in dry dock.

On the final day the Admiral joined the ship, and later suggested to the captain they go ashore for a stroll along the loch side.

"I wonder if we could get a cup of tea somewhere sir," the captain meditated.

They knocked on the door of a small dwelling, which was opened by a gnarled old crone, who seeing two gold-braided sailors on the doorstep, before they could say a word, spat out,

"If it's the village whore you're after she's awa' with the haymaking."

❖❖❖❖❖❖❖❖❖❖❖❖❖❖❖❖❖❖

95

Another True Story – From my American Desk

An elderly lady in a Florida supermarket finished her shopping and returned to her car, half a mile away in the car park, to find four men about to drive away in it.

She jettisoned her shopping on the side banking, drew a gun from her handbag and screamed at them, "Get out of the car, this gun is loaded, get out!"

The four occupants declined to argue but got out and took to their heels, after which the said elderly lady, still very shaky after her ordeal, put her shopping on to the rear seats.

As a result of her agitation, she had great difficulty in getting her key into the ignition, and then she noticed cigarettes on the dashboard, and a carton of cans of beer on the floor on the passenger side.

She subsequently found her car five spaces away. The only thing left to do being to go to the police, tell them the story.

Five minutes after telling her story the police sergeant stopped laughing and pointed to four men way down on the end of the enquiry desk, who apparently were reporting having been held up by a staring-eyed, grey-haired, lunatic woman, with a handgun ready for use.

No charges were made.

Moral? If you are going to have a memorable moment late in life – make it a good one!

◈◇◈◇◈◇◈◇◈◇◈◇◈◇◈ ◇◈◇◇◈◇◈ ◇◈◇◈◇◈◇◈ ◈◇◈◇◈◇◈

A Re-orchestration of Letters

Have you ever tried to re-align the letters in a word, or words, to make something entirely different? Here are some examples:

PRESBYTERIAN
can become
BEST IN PRAYER

GEORGE BUSH
can become
HE BUGS GORE

ELECTION RESULTS
can become
LIES – LET'S RECOUNT

ELEVEN PLUS TWO
can become
TWELVE PLUS ONE

ASTRONOMER
can become
MOON STARER

An Unusual Customer

By Cyril Cook

In my earlier days, in the 1950s, I was a sales engineer for the leading manufacturer's spray painting plant in the UK. It was an incredibly interesting job in that every day I would be visiting a different kind of factory, as a result witnessing, and getting involved in, production problems for as diverse items as London buses to fountain pens, chairs and tables to fishing rods, electrical components to propane cylinders.

One day I was instructed to telephone a doctor in a medical school in one of the leading London teaching hospitals. My first thoughts were, of course, what the devil would they want with spray equipment? However, I duly made the appointment and was shown in to the laboratory where I met the tutor and his assistant, where it was explained to me that the making of casts of hollow organs was of great use in teaching medical and zoological students, and that this particularly applies to the lungs.

Until that time, I had been under the impression that the lungs were a pair of bags, which like football bladders inflated and deflated as you breathed in and out, which just shows how thick I was in those days – voice off stage – what's changed?

To continue. They do in fact, somewhat resemble a sponge, full of thousands of cavities, all of which fill when you breathe in, pass the oxygen into the blood stream and then empty when you breathe out. It was not described to me, neither have I found out since, how it is these magic contraptions can select the oxygen in preference to the other gases in the atmosphere. Not surprising. People talk to me glibly about the Internet and I have only just mastered the wind-up gramophone.

To re-continue, if there is such an expression. By making a cast it would be possible to trace these minute cavities from the tiny ends right through to the trachea. The method was as follows.

The lungs being removed from the body were inflated with CO_2. Under low pressure they were then filled with a cold setting polyester resin. When the resin had hardened, the lungs were then immersed in a bath of commercial hydrochloric acid which removed all the tissue which left the cast a chalky colour, and the various spiky bits very frail and brittle.

To complete the process therefore, a further application of a quick drying resin was required. Despite using the finest of Reeves paint brushes to endeavour to carry out this operation on previous casts, damage automatically ensued. It was then that the tutor's assistant had the bright idea of a spray gun, and hence my presence.

It was obvious that an industrial type gun operating at around 80 psi would be of no use whatsoever. We had a low pressure cup-type gun used by people in the provision of advertising and display equipment, one of which I had in my car parked outside. Believe it or not you could park quite freely in most places in London at that time. The cup was filled, the cast was sprayed, no damage ensued, and a bonus was found in that the extra deposit of the quick drying resin gave an extra strength to the spiky bits. Students now would be able to study the intricacies of this part of the body.

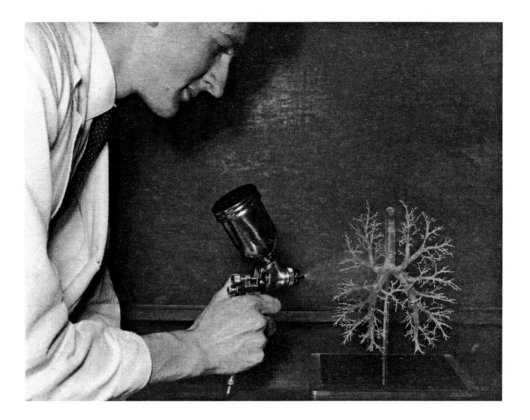

Which left me with the thought afterwards that whilst I had been concerned with helping to solve a finishing problem for a customer, the product was a little different to the furniture, bicycle frames, standard lamps etc etc, that I met everyday. That cast was made from a set of lungs which for many years had kept an individual alive; they had belonged to a living and breathing person, and in the final analysis had ended as a finishing problem.

But then, I always was a bit squeamish.

A D-Day Episode – The Naked Truth!!

By Staff Sergeant Ronald Perry. 7 Para Bn.

It was early on the morning of the 6th of June 1944 – D-Day, dawn had just broken. Lieutenant Nick Archdale led a group of a dozen or so of US, mainly machine gunners and 3" mortarmen who had survived the initial parachute drop, but had found ourselves without our specialist weapons, none of which were ever found.

We made our way from the canal bridge, later to be known as Pegasus Bridge, along the elevated towpath on the west side of the canal, which led to Oistreham. Our orders were to reinforce a rifle company of our battalion cut off in a quarry to the north of our battalion position around the bridge. After some 200-300 yards, we came under fire, so we speedily removed ourselves from the exposed towpath, crossed some flooded, marshy land and cleared the enemy from the cottages in Le Port, from which the fire had been directed.

Reaching the road through the village we saw there was a two story building in an area of orchards on the other side of the road. Nick and I, along with Sergeant Fred Fricker, crossed the road to the corner of this building. As we turned the corner we came under machine gun fire from the orchard, one burst of which shattered brickwork in the wall between us. I effected what is known as a strategic withdrawal back round the corner, where I saw a door into the building which to my surprise was not locked or bolted.

Thinking that if I got to an upstairs window I might be able to spot the machine gun emplacement I went in. In a dark lobby I could see the stairway, leading upstairs which I climbed to reach a landing. I opened a door which I calculated would give me a sight in the direction of the machine gun fire, to clap eyes on a sight I certainly hadn't expected. Lying on a bed totally oblivious to the tumult outside, and stark naked, was a young couple fast asleep. The woman was first to awake at the sound of my boots on the bare boards. She sat upright, trying to cover herself up with a sheet which her husband was lying on, with very little success. Her movements however roused the man, whose first reaction was to protest, "Sale Boche," then gathering a good look at me said, "Etes-vous un aviateur?"

I explained in my schoolboy French what I was, to the background of the racket outside. I must have looked ghastly, bleeding badly from the ricochets which had hit me along with the ghastly camouflage cream on my face and hands, running down in streaks due to profuse sweating. He jumped out of bed, which enabled his wife to at last fully recover her decency, and disappeared downstairs to reappear with a black bottle.

Needless to say it was some while later that I rejoined the war! I found my comrades dug in beneath the trees at the edge of the orchard. Shouts of, "Where the hell have you been?" went strictly unanswered!

In 1972, returning from a holiday in southeast France, I detoured to visit this site again. It had altered little, except there was now a small fenced garden outside the entrance door where a young woman was hanging out washing. She listened to my story but dissolved into a fit of laughter before I reached the end. Apparently she was the younger sister of the lady I had seen in the 'altogether', she and her husband having taken over the property when her sister and her husband moved elsewhere.

However, the tale had become a legend in the family, told and re-told over the years.

❖❖❖ ❖❖❖❖❖❖❖❖❖❖❖ ❖❖❖❖❖ ❖❖❖❖❖ ❖❖❖ ❖❖❖❖❖❖❖❖❖

True Funnies

From a Church magazine

The winner of the competition to guess the number of sweets in the jar was Mrs ---- , who will therefore travel to Majorca by air, spend five days in luxury hotel (all inclusive) and fly home via Paris without spending a penny.

Note left for my milkman (not by me)

Milkman – when you leave the milk will you please put coal on the fire, let the dog out, and put newspapers inside the door.

PS No milk today thank you.

Notice on photocopying machine in Job Centre

The typists' reproduction equipment is not to be interfered with without prior permission of the manager.

Notice in kitchen – same office

Staff should empty the teapot and then stand upside down on the draining board.

Thought for the day

Just about the time you think you can make both ends meet, somebody pulls the ends.

From Oscar Wild

I am not afraid of death – I just do not want to be there when it happens.

By Cyril Cook

Most people have heard of this illustrious Order, of the enormous amounts of money it raises each year for charities of every description, and that the members of the Order are all in what is generally known as 'show business', plus three 'royal companions', the Duke of Edinburgh, Prince Charles and Prince Michael of Kent. But how did such an illustrious body get such an odd appellation?

It was like this.

Back in 1889 Mr Richard Thornton, who would be described today as a theatre impresario, and a man of strong, sporting inclinations, owned a trotter called 'The Magpie'. James Finney, who was one of the top variety performers of the day, having seen The Magpie run, suggested that if it was brought to London from Newcastle where it raced at present, it could make them some money. Coming back to London, James contacted two of his pals in 'the business' and came to the arrangement with Mr Thornton that they would bring the pony down, race it, and go 50/50 with the earnings with the owner. It was stabled in Kennington, Joe Lotto, another top of the bill artist, being the syndicate manager.

They bought a racing buggy and issued challenges to any member of the trotting fraternity who would care to compete against them, the course to be a straight mile believed to be on the Croydon Road, from Thornton Heath to the William the Fourth public house at Streatham.

A very clever training schedule was then invented. They drove the unfed animal from Kennington to the finishing point, where they put his nosebag on. As soon as the trotter had taken his first mouthful of corn they swiftly removed the nosebag, then immediately drove him a mile along the road to the proposed start point. He was then turned and raced back to the finishing point where his nosebag was put back on and he was allowed to eat to his heart's content.

This pony was highly intelligent. After the above schedule had been performed a few times, namely a mouthful at the winning post, a leisurely trot back to the starting point and then flat out for a good feed back at the winning post, the pony was unbeatable, making it a 'nice little earner' as it might have been described many years later.

After a succession of victories they changed the pony's name to 'The Water Rat'. Apparently Joe Elvin, a famous pro, was driving the buggy back to Kennington one

Sunday in the pouring rain. On Brixton Road a bus driver, recognising the comedian, called out,

"Hello, Joe, what have you got there?"

To which Joe replied, "A trotter."

"A trotter – it looks more like a water rat."

Joe reflected on this. What a name for a pony he considered. The following day a clipper was given the job of cutting the letters RAT on the pony's flanks, and it became famous in the neighbourhood and beyond.

To continue the story. The syndicate continued to prosper. Joe Elvin, in the summer of 1889 suggested to a number of his theatrical friends, that they have a Sunday out up the Thames. They left 'The Canterbury' in Westminster Bridge Road in a coach and four, had a pleasant afternoon boating at Sunbury on Thames, followed by a lavish meal in 'The Magpie' hotel at Sunbury.

That evening, having all had such a super day out together, Joe suggested they form a club to be known as 'Pals of the Water Rat'. This suggestion was adopted unanimously, and that is how the Grand Order of Water Rats came into being, the Pals of the Water Rat being rapidly replaced by the Select Order of Water Rats, and finally becoming The Grand Order of Water Rats in April 1990, when the rules were finally approved, the officers to be King Rat, Prince rat, Bank Rat, Scribe Rat and Buck Rat.

The objects of the Order were, and still are: Philanthropy, Conviviality, and Social Intercourse, and the cost of membership was laid down at ten shillings and sixpence entrance fee; a weekly subscription of three pence, and a weekly two shillings and threepence for an 'outing' fund.

Entry to the Order was extremely selective. Many top-liners were rejected, only those who were considered 'good mixers' were admitted so that the second tenet of the objects was fully upheld.

Philanthropy has always been vastly important in the life of the Order, both in the support to performers who had fallen on hard times and to an enormous variety of other charities. Records show that in terrible winter of 1890, the newly formed Rats established a soup kitchen for the poor in Lambeth, the beginning of the raising of hundreds of thousands of pounds over the years.

So, what happened to The Water Rat?

It will be remembered that its racing took place on the public highway in South London. The challenges were becoming events which drew the attention of the police, which promptly closed the event down as it was 'converting the public highway into a race track!' The Water Rat therefore was sent back to Mr Thornton in Newcastle and lived in comfort to a good old age.

During the Great War 1914-18 many Rats from the original following died, many of the younger ones were called to serve in the forces and were lost, which commenced a decline in the fortunes of the Order until 1926, when it was revitalised to become the major institution it is today.

In 1929 the GOWR helped in the formation of 'The Lady Ratlings' who engage in all manner of pursuits to aid members and past members of the profession and support the activities of the Order in all respects, their motto being 'One for all and all for one.'

Many world famous names have been proud to wear the Water Rats emblem. Laurel and Hardy, Charlie Chaplin, Danny Kaye and Bob Hope in days past, Sir John Mills, Sir Norman Wisdom, Sir Henry Cooper, Paul Daniels, Roy Hudd, Nicholas Parsons and many, many others today.

In ending this brief account of the Order, a fully history would take a book – now there's a thought! I would like to give my sincere thanks to the current 'Musical Rat' of the Order, Don Shearman, who has gone well out of his way to help me with many of the details.

So, gentlemen and Lady Ratlings, carry on the great work started by those great pros nearly one hundred and twenty years ago. Dan Leno, Will Hay, Bud Flanagan and dozens of others will be looking down revelling in the knowledge that Philanthropy, Conviviality and Social Intercourse are alive and thriving in the safe embrace of the Grand Order of Water Rats.

❖❖❖❖❖❖❖❖❖❖❖❖❖❖❖❖❖❖❖❖❖❖❖❖❖❖❖❖❖❖❖❖❖❖❖

Now. What would you say these structures are?

Giant pottery plant?

Church designed by psychedelic architect?

Capital city of Outer Mongolia?

American army canteen tents?

Maharaja's harem?

Or what??

Well, if you turn to page 383 you will see

The Beach and the Kingdom

By the Reverend Claire Wilson

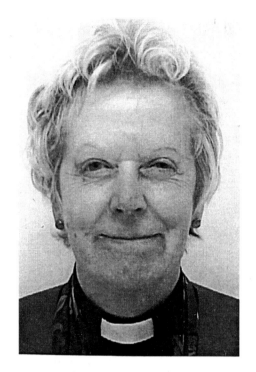

Not long ago I was sitting on the cliff-top looking down at the happy crowd on one of Cornwall's nicest sandy bays. And I was thinking: if Jesus passed by now, he might well stop and say, "The kingdom of heaven is like that beach."

There were several things which made the scene below a good model for the kingdom. For a start, people did not seem to be concerned at that moment about status or rank. The swimsuit is a great leveller; unless you're an expert on designer beach-wear, you can't easily distinguish a bank clerk from a Cabinet member. Nobody could tell, and nobody cared either; they were interested in more important things like getting the most out of the sand and the sunshine and the company.

Other barriers were being broken down as well; age, for example. I watched older people teaching little ones to swim and build castles. And the children had things to teach their elders too; how to play and forget their dignity and have a good time.

I noticed another kingdom-like freedom; people could let their imperfections be seen without apparently minding too much. Not everyone looks their glamorous best in a swimsuit, but no-one seemed bothered if their beer-gut or their varicose veins were on display; they were there to enjoy themselves, not pass judgement or criticise.

And lastly, the beach was an open-ended kind of place. There were no fences around it; families came along with double buggies and a trailer full of equipment and people just moved up for them. No-one glared or acted possessively; it might be getting a bit full, but there was still room for everyone.

So on that euphoric afternoon I sat thinking, well, here it is, the kingdom come. This is the sort of set-up Jesus lived and died to bring about; a community of mutual acceptance where no-one is judged or condemned and no-one is shut out. Why look further, I wondered dreamily; what do we need the Church for?

Except, of course, I knew that sooner or later the sun was going to set on that beach, or the famous Cornish rain would start. People's holidays would come to an end, and that joyful company would get in their cars and take their places again in a world where men and women don't habitually live by the principles so happily in evidence that day. We would have to slot back, all of us, into the everyday world with its injustices, its enthusiasm for shutting people out and condemning them, and its preoccupation with setting people against one another; black versus white, old versus young, male versus female.

I believe, though, that my vision of the beach as a model of a redeemed world was an authentic one. Our job as the Church is to hold on to that vision and to demonstrate that it's not a fantasy. We do that by being that loving and accepting community ourselves as far as we can, staying faithful to Jesus' example even when the going is hard and our own instincts to condemn and exclude come to the surface.

It's possible too, of course, that things weren't quite as perfect as they seemed even on that Cornish beach. I was, after all, a long way up that cliff and we'd just drunk half a bottle of wine with our picnic lunch. Maybe even on that idyllic afternoon not everyone down there was smiling. In my bag ready to send was a postcard depicting a small boy saying proudly, "I trapped that wasp which was bothering Daddy!" His bucket clamped against the unfortunate father's hindquarters in blissful unawareness of the impending reaction.

Even our best efforts will fall short of the vision's fulfilment, which we won't be seeing this side of heaven. But to glimpse it now and then will surely cheer us on our way.

❖❖❖❖❖❖❖❖❖❖❖❖❖❖❖❖❖❖❖❖❖❖❖❖❖❖

Old London

In 1765 Lord Byron, great uncle of the poet, stabbed his cousin to death in an argument. He was acquitted of manslaughter. In those days there were over 200 offences punishable by death – they did not include either manslaughter or attempted murder.

❖❖❖❖❖❖❖❖❖❖❖❖❖❖

House wanted advert mid 1800s.
"Detached house wanted North London. Three reception rooms, at least six good bedrooms, stable, coach house, large garden. Rent £100 per annum."

❖❖❖❖❖❖❖❖❖❖❖

The Monument, near London Bridge, commemorating the Great Fire in 1666 was designed by Sir Christopher Wren. It is 202 feet high.

❖❖❖❖❖❖❖❖❖❖❖❖

From 'The Young Chandlers', by Cyril Cook

Anni's mother was arrested in February the previous year, 1935. At four o'clock in the morning a thunderous knocking at the Reisner door preceded her being bundled into a van with a small suitcase into which she was allowed to put a few belongings, and taken off to the prison at Ulm where she was housed with a score or more Jewish women and known communists. On the second day she was taken in front of a small immaculately dressed, bland-faced man of about forty five, who merely said to her, "You are Jewish and a communist. Do you deny this?"

"I am part Jewish, but I am a trade unionist not a communist."

"We believe you are a communist or a communist sympathiser. Do you deny you have associated with communists? for example ..." And he read out a list of names of known communists in her union who she of course knew and had worked with.

"I know these people, but I am not a communist."

"Take her away."

And that's all there was to her trial and her incarceration in Dachau. When she got to Dachau she found the section she was taken to was guarded by SS troops. Going through the reception area where she and her small suitcase were searched and all her valuables removed, including her wedding ring, she was pointed in the direction of a store, where she was issued with her prison uniform.

Standing in the store was a tall, not unhandsome officer, probably in his early forties. Whilst drawing her uniform from the trustee behind the counter she looked through into the next room to see the women being sat on stools and having their hair cut off. It was a sickening sight to her, she had always been proud of her luxurious black hair. She was a most handsome woman, full in the figure, with dark limpid eyes and a flawless complexion. Her hair was her crowning glory and the thought of losing it sent such terror into her that she almost screamed. When she looked up she saw that the officer was watching her intently and for a moment she looked deep into his eyes, her own showing the depth of horror she felt at being mutilated in this way. The officer looked across at the female guard in charge.

"This one will do," he said, pointing to Anni's mother, turned on his heel and walked out.

The guard walked to the counter. "Wait there, Jewish cow," she said. In a few minutes she returned with another trustee.

"Take this to the Major's quarters," she said pointing to Frau Reisner, and handing a pass to the trustee.

When they were clear of the guard the trustee said in what Frau Reisner was to learn was the standard camp whisper, "You're the lucky one aren't you?"

"Why am I lucky?"

"You'll work in the Major's house, sleep in a bed, be in the warm, have decent food and you won't be beaten if you behave yourself."

They passed through the inner gateway, the trustee showing the pass to the soldiers on the gate. "I wouldn't mind having this one in my bunk tonight," said one of the soldiers.

"She's too old for a young rookie like you," said the corporal of the guard. "She needs a real man to satisfy her, you can see that plainly enough."

"Maybe that's what the Major's got in mind."

"He'll be slipping if he hasn't."

At the sound of the coarse laughter that followed them they made their way to a small detached bungalow type building situated just inside the outer perimeter, but obscured from the camp itself by a row of closely planted conifers. The two women went through the front entrance and into a small office just inside the door where a civilian typist was working.

"Woman to look after the Major," said the trustee.

The civilian, who looked to be in her mid-forties, studied Frau Reisner intently for several seconds. "You can go," she said to the trustee.

"You can cook and clean properly?" she said in a not unkind voice. "Your name is Reisner, aren't you Jewish?"

"My mother was half Jewish, I am Catholic. I have always been a competent housewife."

"Very well, come with me."

She took Frau Reisner and showed her the house which comprised a kitchen and outhouse, large sitting room and small dining room, a bedroom with a double bed, bathroom and a small bedroom also with a double bed. At the rear of the ground floor there was a flight of wooden stairs which led up to a small room in the apex of the building which was Frau Reisner's room. It had its own washstand complete with a luxury she had missed since she was first taken to prison, a mirror. She put her small suitcase on the bed and they went back downstairs to the kitchen.

"Your duties are simple. You keep the house and the office thoroughly clean and polished. You wake the Major at 6.30 with coffee; there is an alarm clock in your room. You make him breakfast. Mostly he has lunches and evening meal at the officers' dining room; sometimes he will eat here but will let you know in advance. He is an easy man to cater for. He has a man servant who comes in during the day who takes care of his uniforms and boots, but you will do all his washing and bed linen. You will do the ironing and provide me with coffee during the day and a light lunch. I am not here on Saturdays or Sundays unless something important is happening. You will eat in the kitchen. You are not allowed to touch the drink in the dining room nor the wine in the outhouse; you will go straight back to the main camp if you act in any way improperly. Similarly, you will not go into the office unless you are told and under no circumstances will you go to any drawers, cupboards or files. For that you would face the severest punishment. Now, have you any questions?"

"Why was the previous woman sent back?"

"She wasn't, she was released."

"I thought ... "

"You thought no-one is ever released? Some are, it depends on whether they are able to realise the great opportunity our Fuhrer is bringing to the people of the Third Reich and to wholeheartedly give themselves to him." Her eyes were shining with an evangelical fervour which seemed to be changing her whole appearance. Frau Reisner kept quiet. The woman's features then resumed their normal appearance as she thought to herself, 'But that doesn't apply to Jews.'

"Anything else?"

"How do I get the food, cleaning materials and things like that?"

"You give me a list of your requirements and I give the money to Hans, the Major's servant, and he gets it."

"I haven't any other questions."

"Well I shall be going home shortly, make us some coffee, then look around so that you know where everything is, cook yourself something for the evening meal and go to bed. The Major will not be in until late tonight. By the way, when I've gone lock the doors and windows. Although we're in a prison neither the guards nor the trustees are to be trusted."

She heard the Major come home around midnight and fearfully wondered whether there would be any footsteps on her stairway, but soon there was silence and she went off soundly to sleep. She woke up feeling cold. The house had been warm when she went to bed, but as the heat dissipated, the space where she was under the roof got colder and colder with the temperature at well below freezing outside. There was no more bedding in the room so she put all her clothes, except the top uniform, back on and again crawled back into bed. It was better but she was still not warm and was glad when the alarm went at six o'clock so that she could go down into the kitchen and stoke up the coal range.

Promptly at six thirty she took in his coffee. She got him breakfast when he came into the kitchen and then left to clean the bathroom. The routine gradually took shape. The Major rarely spoke more than a few words. His servant was an old soldier who kept himself to himself. The secretary was more talkative at some times than others. All in all she considered herself very fortunate indeed to have such a good job even though her underlying resentment at being in prison at all was still there, particularly when she remembered the hideous sight of those women having their hair cut off. She could have no inkling of the real horrors being perpetrated only a few hundred yards away, compared to which having one's hair cut off was absolutely nothing.

At the end of March, the Major came back to the house in the middle of the day and asked for a light lunch. Frau Reisner prepared him a vegetable omelette with some cheese, biscuits and coffee, and waited on him whilst he ate in the small dining room. She had made his bed and tidied his bedroom early in the morning, after which Hans appeared and took an iron and ironing stand from the kitchen into the bedroom to do some pressing. He would never bring uniforms into the kitchen in case he got something spilt on them.

After lunch, the Major retired to his bedroom. She heard him moving around for some time, during which he called to her to let him know when his car arrived. After about an hour a small staff car arrived and Frau Reisner knocked on the door to tell him it was there.

He called out, "Will you fix this for me, Reisner?"

She went into the bedroom and saw he was dressed in an entirely different dress uniform. He really looked magnificent, his tall lean figure, strong face and dark hair greying at the temples being shown to the greatest advantage in the pale blue uniform with the maroon facings and solid silver dress-daggers, buttons and collar motifs. He wore his Iron Cross from the Great War, and his other medals on the left side of his chest. He looked every inch a soldier.

Without thinking she stopped in her tracks and said, "You look magnificent in that uniform," and then stumbled on, "I'm sorry sir; I didn't mean to be presumptuous."

He smiled; it was the first real smile he had ever given her. "That's alright Reisner. I tell you I feel like a soldier in this uniform. It's my old regiment; we have a reunion tonight in Munich. Now, I can't fix this collar." It was a very high collar on the dress uniform, and was fastened at the front by hooks and eyes.

'God knows how men with short necks can wear a collar like this,' thought Frau Reisner. As he was so tall, she got a footstool to stand on and found that one of the hooks had got compressed as Hans did his pressing and would therefore not engage in its eye.

"Just one minute sir," she said, and went off to the kitchen to get a knife to prise it open. She stood back on the footstool and asked him to come a little closer.

"I hope you're not going to cut my throat Reisner?" he said, with another slow smile. She didn't answer, but eased the knife-edge into the hook, levering it open, but in doing so she over balanced. Instinctively the Major held her tight to prevent her falling. They stood for one or two minutes looking into each other's eyes which, because of the footstool, were at the same level, until he released her and let he stand on the floor.

"Thank you Reisner. I shall be late. I'll try not to disturb you," and off he went to his staff car.

After he had gone, she tried to analyse what, if anything had happened between them. She was a married woman, married to a solid, respectable if unexciting clockmaker. Although she had travelled in the course of her union duties and stayed in hotels with men colleagues, and had had innumerable invitations to share a room, she had always been faithful to her husband and had really never felt sexually attracted to any of them. She decided that if any chemistry did take place when she was fixing the Major's collar, it was probably due to the fact that she had had no contact with her husband for what seemed like an eternity. The Major himself, seemed so forlorn at times as to be almost a prisoner himself, and he was undoubtedly very handsome.

Before the typist left Frau Reisner asked her casually, "Is the Major married?" to which she got a very short and emphatic answer.

"It's a subject you mind your own business about, and one which will land you in very deep trouble if you mention it – understand?"

"I'm sorry, I didn't mean to offend." But she was more curious than ever.

At about one o'clock in the morning she heard the staff car return, the sound of voices as the driver and the Major entered the house, a cheery goodnight from the driver and then silence for some little while. Then there was a solid thump as if something heavy had fallen. She wondered whether to go down or not and with some misgivings eventually decided she would. Slipping on a robe the Major's secretary had brought in for her she crept down the stairway and into the living room. Spread-eagled half on, half off, an armchair was the Major, still fully dressed and breathing heavily. He was obviously quite drunk. She wondered whether to try and make him more comfortable or to get him into his bedroom. She decided the latter would be far too difficult so gradually she tugged at him until he was at least lying fully in the armchair. She unfastened the high collar, unbuttoned his tunic and took off his belt. She then unfastened his boot buckles and with some difficulty pulled the boots off. She then pulled another low armchair over and lifted his legs up on to it. Finally she got a pillow and eiderdown off the bed and made his head comfortable and covered him with the eiderdown.

"There, you'll do until the morning," she said, "but I wouldn't like to have your head tomorrow." And with that she quite involuntarily bent over and kissed his forehead and went back to bed.

At 6.30 she took him his coffee and he woke up with a start, realised where he was and that someone had obviously looked after him. He said, "Did you do this for me?"

"Yes Herr Major, you were very tired."

A slow smile appeared fleetingly. "That's a good word for it, you should be a politician. I'm very grateful."

"Thank you sir," she said and went back to the kitchen.

When he reappeared she left him to eat his breakfast and when he left for the day he said, "I shall eat in this evening, something light."

During the day Hans arrived and looking at the crumpled uniform said, "Good God look at this, you would think he'd slept in it." Frau Reisner smiled to herself but made no answer. She never knew how to take Hans. He was not rude or aggressive to her, but she had the feeling that he despised her because she was a prisoner and at the same time was jealous of her because she attended to his master's needs. One day she had asked him whether he had been with the Major long. "We were in the trenches together," he had said, "We were real soldiers then. He didn't need any other servants in those days."

That evening she prepared a light meal of soup, schnitzel and chocolate cake which he enjoyed. When she gave him his coffee in the sitting room and asked if he required her any more he said, "Will you please sit down Frau Reisner."

It was the first time he had ever addressed her other than plain Reisner. She sat on the low chair she had put his feet on the previous night and waited.

"I would like to thank you again for looking after me last night. As you know I went to a regimental reunion, not that there are many of us left of the war time cadre. I am afraid we all got a little depressed about one thing and another and had too much to drink, hence my condition when I got home."

Frau Reisner did a little smile and gave a shrug but remained silent.

"Tell me about yourself, you are obviously from a good family."

Frau Reisner outlined to him her background. Her father was a doctor who was killed in action in the war; her mother was a concert singer. She was married to a clock manufacturer who had a small business in Ulm and she had one daughter still at school. She had worked for a trade union and was herself a democrat, certainly not a communist. "I don't really know why I am here," she said in conclusion.

"You are Jewish and you are a democrat, that is enough for them I'm afraid," said the Major in a low despondent voice. She gathered from the latter remark that whilst he was one of them, he wasn't necessarily for them.

"Well I'm going to bed now," he continued. "I'm not really feeling up to scratch - I suppose it's last night catching up on me."

She gave him a little smile and rose to leave. As she passed him he took her hand. "Tell me one thing. When you left me last night did I imagine it or did you kiss me?"

"I thought you were asleep."

"Please do it to me again, nothing else nice seems to happen to me these days."

She bent over and kissed his forehead. He let go her hand and she went off to bed. His feeling 'not up to scratch' however was not due to the previous night's activities. In the morning he had a high fever. Frau Berg summoned the staff doctor who pronounced he had a virulent form of influenza which was going through the camp. "I will try and get a nurse to come in, but we are so heavily committed at the moment," the doctor said to Frau Berg.

Frau Reisner was standing nearby and said, "I can help Herr Doktor, my father was a doctor and I had basic nursing training."

The doctor was somewhat taken aback at this turn of events. Here was a camp inmate volunteering to nurse an SS major, somehow it didn't seem to add up. He looked questioningly at Frau Berg. She said, "Reisner has proved to be responsible since she has been here, and very loyal to the Major. If you could look in each day to make sure everything is alright, I'm sure it would be satisfactory, she does of course live in so is at hand at night."

"Very well, we'll try it out."

For five days the Major fought against the influenza which had brought on double pneumonia. With the exception of an hour or two during the day when Frau Berg volunteered to sit by him and Frau Reisner could go to bed, she watched over him day and night, washed him, constantly changed his bed linen and night shirt, gave him his medicines, coaxed him to eat the soups she made and to drink as much as she could persuade him to swallow.

The doctor was extremely worried, losing five hundred women in the camp was one thing, but to lose an SS major would be a vastly different thing altogether.

On the fifth night the major was delirious at times, but by the sixth morning he had quietened and when Frau Reisner moved him to wash him he awoke and said, "How long have I been ill?" She was so pleased to hear his voice, faint and distant though it sounded, that she burst into sobs of relief, holding his hand so tightly and kissing it and holding it to her breast. When she recovered herself she saw that he had gone off to sleep again, but his breathing was noticeably easier and his colour a little more normal.

She finished washing him and Hans came in to help her change the bed linen. He immediately noticed the improvement and grunted, "Looks at though he'll get over it."

She smiled at him and said, "Yes it does doesn't it." He answered her with the nearest thing to a smile that she had ever seen registered on his face, and she got the feeling that from now on they were friends.

The Major made rapid strides from then on. He had a number of visitors shown in by Frau Berg, when they were there Frau Reisner disappeared to her room or to the kitchen or outhouse. On the second day of his recovery she got him out of bed and into an armchair so that with Hans' help she could put all his bedding out in the yard to air. When they came back Hans said to him, using the paternal, gruff manner in which an old soldier servant is able to talk to his master, "You'd have been a gonner if it hadn't been for her."

Frau Reisner said, "Oh don't be silly," and walked off to the kitchen to carry on with her work. Before he left Hans helped her get the bedding back in and remake the Major's bed. She made a light meal on a tray which he ate, it was the first solid food he'd had for over a week. "Now we must build you up again," she said. When she had cleared away she went back into the sitting room to see if he wanted to go back to bed yet. He asked her to come and sit with him on the sofa.

"Frau Reisner," he said, "What is your name."

She told him, "Trudi."

"Trudi would you think it ridiculous if I told you that I have grown very fond of you over the past weeks you have been here?"

"Patients always fall for their nurse," she said with a smile.

"No, it was before I was a patient," he said. "I think it was from the time I saw the horror in your face at the women's hair being cut off. You see, in reality, it is essential the hair is removed because of the conditions under which they have to live, but it is evil that human beings should have to live like that in the first place. I have told you I am a soldier. I was seconded to the SS for these duties, these are not duties for a soldier, but I have to do what I am ordered to do." He paused in deep thought for a while and then put his arm round her shoulder. "Thank you for all you've done for me. It is many, many years since I've experienced such care and kindness. I think I would like to go back to bed now."

She helped him back into bed and asked if he would like some hot milk. Having drunk the milk he laid back on the pillows and took her hand as she sat on the bed beside him. She held it close and felt great pity for this man who was having to compromise his honour and principles in the course of obeying orders from people he obviously despised. It didn't occur to her that her own position was infinitely worse and that if anyone deserved pity it was her, but then in fairness she had no conception either of the evils being perpetrated on the other side of those screens of conifers she looked out on every day.

His eyes closed and after a while Trudi put his arm back under the coverlet, kissed him gently on the forehead, put the nightlight on and went to her attic to prepare for bed. Before finally going to bed she thought she would have one last check that the Major was settled down properly, so she put on her gown and crept down the stairs into his bedroom. Seeing that he was comfortable she turned to leave when he said, "Trudi."

"Yes Major."

"Would you come in with me tonight, I would like that very much."

Without a word she slipped off her robe and laid it on the chair and slid under the covers beside him. He put one of his arms around her cupping her breast with the other hand and softly whispered, "Goodnight Trudi," and in no time at all was sound asleep. Once during the night they awoke and clung to each other, each having their own need for the closeness of another human being, each having been denied physical contact with a loving partner for so long.

Each night thereafter, even when the Major was fully recovered, Trudi joined him, but it was nearly three weeks before they became lovers. Trudi tried to analyse why she felt no shame in being unfaithful to her husband. Perhaps she felt in her heart of hearts that this love between her and the Major was taking place in a different world between two different people, not her and her husband, but another Trudi and another husband. In the first week of their sleeping together the Major had told Trudi of his wife, of how one afternoon he had arrived back unexpectedly at his married quarters at Potsdam where he was stationed, and found her in bed with two teenage girls. In front of the girls she told him that in the ten years they had been married she had been revolted by him and now he had found out her real tastes he could do what he liked about it. She was very well off, she was not dependent on him, divorce in his regiment was forbidden, so he got a transfer to the SS where such things didn't matter and had not seen or spoken to her for nearly three years.

Her heart ached for him as he told her of his humiliation, the fact that he had to leave the regiment that he loved and in which both his father and grandfather had served. "I think we are two lost souls together," she said.

Their strange liaison continued all through the summer and through the winter into 1936. They had both blotted out the fact that it couldn't last, sooner or later either the

Major would be moved or the camp authorities would put Trudi elsewhere. There was a rumour that an all woman camp was being built at a place called Ravensbruck and they might be sent there. What they did know was that they deeply and truly loved each other. The horrific facts were that only the Major knew what went on beyond the conifers, whereas Trudi lived more or less in ignorance of what bestiality some members of the human race could do and were doing to others. She couldn't know how the inmates were being worked to death, their living conditions so appalling that the slightest illness became a death sentence. She had adapted to the situation of not being allowed past the front door of the bungalow and to the confinement of the small rear yard where she could hang out the washing and occasionally sit in the sun. She consoled herself that she was far better off than the other prisoners, and even if she wasn't free, every day she spent in the comfort of the bungalow and in the love of the major was a day off her sentence. She had no way of knowing that you cannot subtract from infinity.

In early April the Major came home one evening and said he had to go to Berlin for a top level conference lasting for three or four days. He then intended to visit his parents for a couple of days who lived in Mecklenburg, taking the journey time he would be away for about ten days. The days dragged while he was away and it was with great joy she welcomed his return, although she had to suppress it for a while whilst Hans, who had been with him, unpacked his valise and hung out his clothes leaving his laundry in a bag for Trudi to attend to in due course. When the coast was clear she flew into his arms and they clung together as if they had been apart for a year. Eventually he let her go and they made the usual preparations for bed, and although he made love to her with all the fervour she had enjoyed for these past months, when she was eventually lying beside him she felt that all was not well. She had not asked how his conference had gone, that would not have been the thing to do at all. In the quiet she said,

Did you see your parents? Are they well?"

"Yes they are well, but my father is not happy with what I am doing."

"But he must know you have to obey orders."

"Yes, but he rightly says there comes a time when you have to put personal honour before everything."

"I'm sorry darling. I don't understand," but in the pit of her stomach there was a cold fear beginning to make itself known.

She said no more but held herself to him in a supreme endeavour to comfort them both, and eventually they went to sleep wrapped as close as it is possible for two human beings to be entwined.

He was very quiet and reserved the next morning and in saying goodbye held her a little closer and for a little longer than he normally did. Trudi still had this premonition of something happening to change the happiness she had experienced in the last few months. That evening the Major arrived home and they ate their meal silently together, until eventually she said, "Darling, there is something troubling you beyond what your father said, can't you tell me about it or is it to do with your duties?"

He took her hand and led her to the sofa. "It is to do with us," he said, "And there is no way that I can delay telling you about it. At the conference I heard the most appalling news, news that I could not even pass to my father. The Nazis have a master plan to exterminate all Jews. They call it the final solution. Because I have volunteered for this evil organisation I am to play a major part in it. I am to be promoted and sent to Berlin where I am to organise the systematic rounding-up of all Jews to go into the new camps being built. They are already gassing mental defectives, rapists and other deviants, and the next stage will be the elimination of all Jews, men, women and children. I could easily cut and run, but that would be dishonourable. I therefore have come to the only solution an officer and gentleman could arrive at, and that is to take my own life."

She gave a suppressed scream of anguish but said nothing. They were silent for a long time.

"I will join you," she said very quietly but very firmly. "If you leave me here they will come for me and I would die anyway, perhaps horribly for all I know. If I died in your arms I know despite the great sin we have committed, I shall see you in Heaven."

He held her very close for a long time. Then he went to the kitchen and got two glasses of wine, from his pocket he took a small pill box containing two tablets and gave her one. "These will act very quickly," he said, "goodbye my darling Trudi."

They washed the tablets down with wine, placed the glasses on the side table and sat down on the sofa with their arms around each other and with Trudi's head on the Major's shoulder. And that is how Frau Berg found them the next morning.

Old London

Thomas Lord in 1787 opened a cricket ground at Marylebone – hence MCC. In 1811 he was forced to vacate it, so lifted his precious turf to an area at Regent's Park. Two years later the digging of the Regent's Canal forced another move to St John's Wood in 1814. It is still however, the MCC.

The Anthropic Principle

THEY say more than ten billion years ago
Came one hell of a bang, as God said, 'Go!'
Well, not really a bang, to tell the truth,
For as to air there was none, forsooth,
But as from superheated gas the galaxies condensed,
The history of the universe had probably commenced.
We know a bit about it from a piece of glass called Hubble.
　　Thank you, God – for taking the trouble.

The mighty universe is expanding very fast
But Someone has said, 'The first shall be last.'
Time is relative to an observer's velocity
According to Einstein. What a curiosity!
Not a single object can exceed the speed of light
And the universal constant has to be exactly right.
Each person is unique, for no-one has a double.
　　Thank you, God – for taking the trouble.

It's a stupefying universe of terrible complexity
The numbers are so huge they fill you with perplexity.
Newton's laws can account for as much as you could wish,
But quantum mechanics are another pot of fish.
So it seems we have emerged from hot primeval rubble.
　　Thank you, God – for taking the trouble.

Some say the fact we're here is simply due to chance
And we're just a bit of dust in a meaningless expanse.
But it doesn't feel like dust when I have this strange desire
To respect each other member of the human race entire.
There's something more than numbers in this big expanding bubble.
　　Thank you, God – for taking the trouble.

Frederick Starkey
(Dust with attitude)

More Thoughts of Fernando Baralba

Ambition is the mother of unhappiness.

Vanity is the mother of ambition.

Moderation is the way to happiness.

Science is the study of the universe, biology is the study of living matter, psychology is the study of the reaction of that matter and philosophy is the study of how to use that reaction.

Laws are the children of self-interest.

Conscience is the justice of the honest.

Knowledge is a plant that dies if it is not watered every day.

Conversation is completely moved by reason: thought is half moved by reason and half by interest: action is completely moved by interest.

Dancing is a form of flirting in public with the approval of society.

Imagination is nourished by reading.

A small man is a giant among dwarfs.

He who is proud of his knowledge ignores his ignorance.

Reading makes a man think, thinking makes a man write and writing makes a man happier and wiser.

No man can get acquainted with his conscience without doing something wrong.

Fishing

One morning a husband returns after several hours of fishing and decides to take a nap.

Although not familiar with the lake, the wife decides to take the boat out. She motors out a short distance, anchors, and reads her book.

Along comes a Game Warden in his boat. He pulls up alongside the woman and says, "Good morning, Ma'am. What are you doing?"

"Reading a book," she replies, (thinking, 'Isn't that obvious?')

"You're in a restricted fishing area," he informs her.

"I'm sorry, officer, but I'm not fishing. I'm reading."

"Yes, but you have all the equipment. For all I know you could start at any moment. I'll have to take you in and write you up."

"If you do that, I'll have to charge you with sexual assault," says the woman.
"But I haven't even touched you," says the game warden.

"That's true, but you have all the equipment. For all I know you could start at any moment."

"Have a nice day ma'am," and he left.

MORAL: Never argue with a woman who reads.

The tale of a young soldier and his sweetheart
By J H Absalom

It was strange how we got together. She worked in the Gowns department of C&As in Church Street. She was sixteen and very pretty. She lived in the nice area of Prenton and her father was a Master on the Birkenhead ferries. All the young men regarded her with admiring eyes as she walked by. I had only been at C&As for a short time, having left my first job at a solicitors in Chapel Street where I earned ten shillings a week, for a better wage of seventeen shillings and sixpence a week as a window dresser on the Gowns department windows.

The war had not long commenced and almost before I knew my way around Church Street, older men had been called up and I was in charge of Gowns windows. One day I called for help with ironing dresses and down from the shop floor came this pretty sixteen year old. It was rumoured that she was destined to become a buyer at that time, although she knew how to wear a dress and had been used by senior staff to model dresses before stock was bought, she didn't know very much at all about using a pressing iron.

I came from a family where my parents insisted that all four of their children knew how to look after themselves and took turns with washing floors and dishes, cleaning and washing and with pressing clothes. Good training for later!

I was nearly seventeen years old and the supervisor (!); so with great pleasure and full of tact, and with the benefit of long (about four months) experience, I showed my new helper how to press dresses without leaving creases and how to hang them and prepare them for display. When she came down again on the second day, although I was aware she had been 'walking out' with another member of staff senior to me, and from a wealthier background (that wasn't difficult!) and I was also aware that she had turned down numerous other admirers who wanted to walk out with her, I overcame a natural shyness and asked could I take her to Coopers for tea before seeing her to the Pier Head to catch the Birkenhead ferry.

That is how it started.

Liverpool was bombed. During my turn on fire watch on the roof of C&As, Church Street was devastated. I decided it was time to do something about changing the direction of the war and joined the army at the recruitment centre in Renshaw Hall in Renshaw Street.

Sadly, I had little effect on the course of the war but continued to do my best to help the efforts of all involved on our side.

I became a young soldier in the Border Regiment with a number of other young chaps from Lancashire (Liverpool hadn't then been moved to Merseyside). I took a commando course, spent time with the Guards and then back to The Border and flew in gliders.

Every leave, I called at C&As to see my girl and then, on one leave, found she had left and was working in the Admiralty Chart Depot, firstly in the Royal Liver Building and then on the Strand. When I finally caught up with her I knew she had thought of me at least once, for an old friend told me she had written her initials with mine in the dust on the back of the Liver clock.

But we didn't write and weren't 'committed'. That is how it was best to be, we reasoned.

Then I was commissioned, nearly went gliding again but decided parachuting was safer and was accepted by the Parachute Regiment. By now it was 1943 and we met every leave and wrote regularly.

One evening we left my home in West Derby so that I could see her safely home to Prenton in the blackout. We sat downstairs on a number 12 tram, close together, not speaking much but holding hands. Searchlights flashed over the city as we rode down to the Pier Head. With the sound of anti-aircraft fire about, we walked down the floating gangway and waited for a darkened ferry to come alongside.

The river was full of shipping of all kinds; all the war ships, troop ships, tugs, and ferries had dimmed lights and in mid-river, masthead lights bobbing and swaying were the only signs of more ships, large and small. Somewhere out there my Uncle Roland would be working as a river pilot.

The ferry SS Mountwood came alongside and the Master was seen leaning over the top deck rail. "There's Dad," she said and in the darkness we both waved and Captain Joe Wharton returned our waves with a tired salute. Heaven alone knew how long he'd been on duty in the dark on his dark, spotless ship, on the dark and crowded river. We went down into the dimly-lit saloon and sat on a highly polished sweet-smelling wooden bench.

By this time there was a great deal of noise from guns and frequent explosions along the river. Two dark skinned Asian seamen sat huddled close together alongside us both looking slightly pale and not sure what to say or do when we smiled and said, "Good evening." Perhaps they wondered what exactly was good about a black evening on the Mersey with guns firing and bombs dropping.

Well … I decided this was the time and place and, standing up, I turned to my girl, went down on one knee, took her hand in mine and proposed.

Frightened or not, the seamen realised what the young Parachute officer was doing and their faces broke into great smiles, although I am not sure they understood when she said, "I'll go upstairs and tell Dad!"

Well, like most couples, we had our ups and downs over the years that followed and sometimes, more downs than ups. We travelled and moved about in my work at home and abroad. She became more frail than I ever expected, but as pretty as ever. I was probably too tied to my demanding job … but we stuck together, regardless and eventually bought a country cottage and then it was the year I was to retire.

And then the 'big C' hit her and she died.

I took her ashes one dark night and travelled up to Liverpool. Caught the SS Mountwood (not the old one) and from near the rail where her Dad might have stood, I let her ashes fall onto the river, a river not black and dark now, but bright with flickering, reflected lights, few ships and calm and peaceful.

That was how it ended. Well – not exactly, but that's another story for another time.

The Steamroller

By Sergeant Bob Pratt

It was towards the end of August 1945. The battalion had just done a beach landing on Morib Beach, a desolate place north of Port Dickson in Malaya. We had yomped about 10-12 miles into the jungle when night fell. We found ourselves in a rubber plantation and stopped for the night expecting to continue the march the following morning. The destination was an airfield called 'Klang'. The object of the exercise was to take the airfield and wait for some Ghurkhas to arrive and then jump on Singapore. The reasoning behind this was the Japanese had threatened to kill all the POWs in South East Asia.

The 'A' bomb had been dropped on Hiroshima on 6th August 1945.

The battalion was then ordered back to the beach to re-embark men and equipment. We then made our way down the coast of Malaya to Singapore where the Japs had decided to surrender. Apart from some naval personnel the battalion was one of the first units to land, where it was found some hundred thousand Japs had laid down their arms.

From then on the battalion changed from the role of fighting soldiers to a mobile local DIY council to put back what the Japs had destroyed of the infrastructure, including the police force, and the administration to bring the rule of law back to the island.

I was given the task of Provost Sergeant, not to police the regiment, but with some ten corporals and privates to help round up Japanese soldiers who had decided not to be placed in a POW cage and with the use of two jeeps, we were to patrol the back streets and brothels of Singapore to co-operate with the SIB to round up Indian nationalists who helped the Japs during the occupation. One day the RSM came to my bungalow, which I was using as a guard room, and said he wanted me to sort out nearby tennis courts that had been neglected and laid to ruin by the Japs. Would I have a look at it and do what I could to make it look presentable, the reason being Field Marshall Bill Slim, GOC of South East Asia Command, along with the Defence Minister and many other notables would be inspecting the battalion. I have but three days to put things right that the Japs had over three years to destroy. I had a look at the tennis courts. They had more humps and bumps than the whole of the Pennines and Alps put together. It was mission impossible and I was foolish enough to air my views to the RSM. I came away with a 'flea in my ear' and told to get on with it.

I was mulling this over, as one does when up against it and desperate, when I remembered a couple of days previously, on a patrol passing a gang of coolies with picks and shovels, and low and behold a mighty ten ton steamroller. They were mending pot holes and repairing road damage.

So the next day, in a jeep, three of my Provost staff and myself dressed with white belts and gaiters, side arms and red berets and newly pressed uniforms, we looked quite impressive and important, travelled down to the road where I last saw the road gang. They had not gone very far with their repairs. We pulled up beside the gang and the poor beggars dropped their picks and shovels, stood in line and started to bow to us. Apparently this was the procedure they had to do when confronted by Japanese military. To us of course, this was not what we wanted and was embarrassing, so we smiled at them and offered them a cigarette to help put them at ease. So it was not difficult to explain that I was borrowing the steamroller (my Mandarin was not very good, but I managed in my London tongue) and to put them at ease, providing I gave them a receipt for it they were quite willing (or terrified) to let it go. So I wrote them a note saying:

'To whom it may concern, I am requisitioning this steamroller and will return it later.
Signed KTD.
PS Go forth and multiply.
PPS KTD was for Colonel Kenneth T Darling DSO (Battalion Commander).'

So with a smile on my face I gave them the note. One of them put it in a pocket of his shirt. Of course, as far as I was concerned I now had a steamroller on my hands and had no idea how I was going to drive it the four miles back to the barracks and tennis court.

If I could get it back to our bungalow the problem of the tennis court was solved (or so I thought). The fire under the boiler was already alight; the coolies were just about to use it when we came along. Two of my Provost were to drive the jeep back and I and another, who was my stoker, would drive the steamroller back to the barracks.

We had plenty of wood on board. My stoker put some more into the fire hole and I saw the needle move round into the red section of the dial. I thought that it was probably time to move. I looked at all the gadgets on board, pushed forward a lever that looked as if it would release the brakes, pulled a bit of string that blew the whistle, turned a huge wheel to the left and opened a valve. We then started to move, so with a great clanking of chains we were on our way with black clouds coming out of the stack pipe. I fiddled with the valve and we started to go a little faster. The monster was on the move. What others who saw a sergeant of the Parachute Regiment driving a ten ton steamroller along the main road thought I could not bear to think or care about at that moment.

Two hours later I arrived. I stopped the thing outside my bungalow and told my stoker to come back in two hours. I then went for my lunch break. The intention was to take the steamroller to the tennis courts some 200 yards from where it was parked and then to start flattening the humps and bumps. About an hour later there was a great commotion going on on the veranda of the bungalow. I went to see who it was and there was the RSM of the battalion with steam coming out of his ears, his face was as red as a tomato. I thought he was going to have a fit. He was spluttering and trying to ask me what the 'blankety blank' had I been up to. Of course I hadn't a clue what he was talking about, which made matters worse.

"Follow me," he roared.

So with his pace stick under his arm we stepped out towards the tennis courts. We stopped at the entrance and to my horror I could see why the RSM was not just a little angry. There was my borrowed steamroller on its side with steam coming from the boiler, the stack pipe and other bits and pieces flying from it. It was like watching the dying throes of some huge animal. It looked as if it had broken its back. This was, to say the least, a disaster. This was the place where Field Marshall Slim along with the Brigadier, Colonel, Defence Minister and many more were going to address the battalion. (Woe is me!)

The RSM then turned to me and said, "What are you going to do about this?"

I looked at the steamroller, back to the RSM and said, "What the bloody hell do you think I can do with a ten ton giant that is about to explode?"

The answer was, "I don't care what you do, do something."

So with this negative reply he turned away and marched off.

I never did find out who the culprits where that high-jacked my steamroller, but I had a good idea. There were some who owned up to it, but that was almost sixty years later. We are friends to this day and still have a laugh about it.

The most worrying thing for me in hindsight was if that note had come to light and the colonel had got sight of it, I would probably have finished my career as a bog attendant.

PS We have a saying in the army, "If it moves, salute it, if it doesn't, camouflage it." You can guess my option. It was still on the tennis court when we embarked for Java, covered in a tarpaulin. Ah what memories.

Addendum - From Cyril Cook

I have spoken at length to the person who decided to have a go at driving the beast. Apparently it was still fired up; he drove it to the tennis court in a straight line, but had to alter direction when he reached the banked-up section alongside the courts. What he was completely ignorant of was the fact that, unlike driving a car, to turn the front rollers one way you have to wind the steering wheel the other. Instead, therefore, of moving to the right when he reached the bank, the monster went to the left, balanced on the edge of the embankment, and toppled over; resulting in a quick evacuation of the driving section by the two sergeants of HM Forces, along with a speedy scarper from the scene of the crime.

The Steamroller

As seen by our battalion Poet Laureate, Lieutenant Don Halewood
– also known as Oxodian.

'Twas on the eve of that great day,
When, in full and bright array,
The battalion would be lined up on the square
For a General to inspect
And, that all should be correct
There was only one small thing left to prepare.

For the square (to cut this short)
Used to be a tennis court,
Where sporting youth at one time did its stuff,
But the Jap long occupation
Had produced deterioration
And the square, to say the best of it, was rough.

So the provost sergeant's staff
With a gay, light-hearted laugh,
Went ambling down the road we know not where,
And a whacking great machine
Belching, clouds of hissing steam
Came a rumbling up the road towards the square.

Just before the bugle played
For the mepachrine parade,
The driver midst a rush of warmish air

Steered a rather ropey line
For the rather steep incline
Which leads down from the road on to the square.

As he turned down the redoubt
We heard a rather urgent shout
And a body quickly baled out from the rear,
And the great machine broke free
With an evil hiss of glee,
And downward swift pursued its mad career.

As the clouds of steam dispersed
Quaking, fearing for the worst
The onlookers went rushing to the scene,
And on that sacred square
In a state of poor repair
Lay an injured and emasculate machine.

It lay gasping on its side,
Its roof split open-wide,
And its crew of two had just escaped dire harm,
When out from BHQ
The elite – the chosen few
Came apace, displaying symptoms of alarm.

The adjutant was there
With a face cast down with care
As he stood and gazed in horror midst the rest.
Dulcet, pleading voices rose
Which quite led us to suppose
The Regimental Sergeant Major was distressed.

For when a General comes to view
A smart company or two,
And to look those happy warriors up and down,
Quite the last thing I declare
He expects to grace the square,
Is a bloody great steamroller upside down!

With mechanised contraption
And great facile adaption,
As the shades of light had glided into night,
With many a creak and clank
From the tackle on the bank
The great machine was slowly heaved aright.

The machine had had its day,
And it wouldn't move away
Though they stoked it till it nearly burst in flame,
But the minds of BHQ
Found repine, because they knew
No blot would soil the 12th Battalion's name.

For a general must admit
That great piles of mud and grit,
Would shake the weary drill squad to the bone

So he really wouldn't care
About a roller on the square,
Assuming its position be not prone!

Old London

Are you under the impression that Big Ben's clock face is at the top of the Westminster Palace Tower? It is in fact only around half way up. The tower is well over 300 feet, the clock 175 feet.

Golf in England, brought from Scotland by James I, was first played on Blackheath in South East London.

From Sherry Sawarde. Queensland, Australia.

It seems that Tibrogargan, the father and Beerwah, the mother, had many children – Coonowrin (the eldest), Beerburrum, the Tunbubudla twins, Coochin, Ngun Ngun, Tibberoowuccum, Miketeebumulgrai and Elimbah. According to the story there was also Round who was fat and small and Wild Horse (presumably Saddleback) who was always straying away to paddle in the sea.

One day, when Tibrogargan was gazing out to sea he noticed a great rising of the waters. Hurrying off to gather his younger children in order to flee to the safety of the mountains to the westward, he called out to Coonowrin to help his mother, who by the way, was again with child.

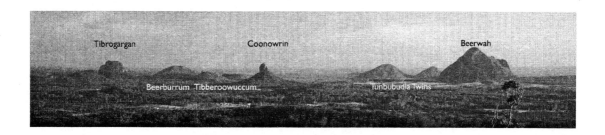

Looking back to see how Coonowrin was assisting Beerwah, Tibrogargan was greatly angered to see him running off alone. He pursued Coonowrin and, raising his club, struck the latter such a mighty blow that it dislocated Coonowrin's neck, and he has never been able to straighten it since.

When the floods had subsided and the family had returned to the plains, the other children teased Coonowrin about his crooked neck. Feeling ashamed, Coonowrin went over to Tibrogargan and asked his forgiveness; but filled with shame at his son's cowardice, Tibrogargan could do nothing but weep copious tears, which, trickling along the ground formed a stream which flowed into the sea. Then Coonowrin went to his brothers and sisters, but they also wept at the shame of their brother's cowardice. The lamentations of Coonorwrin's parents and of his brothers and sisters at his disgrace explain the presence today of the numerous small streams of the area.

Tibrogargan then called to Coonowrin, asking him why he had deserted Beerwah; at which Coonowrin replied that at Beerwah was the biggest of them all she should be able to take care of herself. He did not know that Beerwah was again pregnant, which was the reason for her great size. Then Tibrogargan turned his back on Coonowrin and vowed that he would never look at him again.

Even today Tibrogargan gazes far out to sea and never looks round at Coonowrin, who hangs his head and cries, his tears running off to the sea. His mother Beerwah is still heavy with child as it takes a long, long time to give birth to a mountain.

A Dictionary for Men

Labour   Trying to get back some of the money you have loaned.

Lace   Lace, like charity, covers a multitude of sinners.

Law   A spider's web in which flies are entangled.

By Musical Rat Don Shearman

A great comedian I have had the pleasure of working with is Normal Wisdom, whose visual appeal is truly universal. I have seen audiences in Tehran and the Far East who obviously didn't understand much of what he was saying, falling about with laughter. Again, I could fill the column with our experiences, but I'll just mention a couple, which as it happens involve sport, Norman being a great sports enthusiast.

During our stay in Hong Kong a cricket festival was taking place, and one match involved a team of 'stars of yesteryear' flown in especially by Qantas. Norman's straight man Tony Fayne suggested we went to the match, assuring us that as he was a Lords Taverner we would have no difficulty getting in. We crossed from Kowloon to Hong Kong Island on a ferry, one of the great pleasures of a stay in Hong Kong, and made our way to the ground. We didn't need to involve the Taverners' as there was no-one on the gate and scarcely anyone in the ground. However, as we reached the pavilion one of the club members greeted us with, "Hello Norman, come and have a drink."

As we went into the pavilion we saw approaching us an elderly man, short, stocky, looking very fit, and smartly but somewhat incongruously dressed in a blue blazer more suited to Skegness pier than to the blazing heat of Hong Kong. Our club member friend called out, "Hello Harold, come and meet Norman Wisdom." Which is how I came to meet the legendary Harold Larwood.

He greeted us with the immortal words, "Are you having a drink?" Honesty compelled us to say we had one on the way – otherwise I could have told you the story of how I once had a drink bought for me by Harold Larwood. However, he took the chair next to me and we had a chat for a few minutes before he and several other golden oldies left to go to the races. So much for cricket! And Norman? Oh, yes of course, while all this was going on he drank his beer, and with the heat and not being a drinker, fell asleep immediately, and slept right through the match.

From one extreme to another. One freezing cold day in Wales, Tony arranged for us, Norman and me, to see Cardiff City to play Millwall, in the company of Max Bygraves and his musical director Bob Dixon. We caused a stir by arriving at the ground in a Chauffeur-driven Limo, and went in to a chorus of, "Norman bites yer legs," from a crowd of small boys. At half-time we had a cup of tea in the boardroom, and I asked Max if he followed any team (Norman of course having been a director of Brighton and Hove Albion).

Max replied, "I have shares in Aston Villa," which at the time struck me as a strange way to support a team, but in these days of Abramovitch and Lerner, I'm not so sure.

Doggone – Gwen!

A study of two beautiful ladies.
Our photographer in chief - Gwen Pratt, being well and truly sat on by 'Amber'.

A Royal run-in for CSM

With acknowledgement to Captain James Russell CBE

The arrival of King Hussein at the Royal Military Academy, Sandhurst in 1952 was not without humour.

Company Sergeant Major Clutton, Coldstream Guards, was summoned by the Commandant to escort him to his quarters.

Finding the King with two Jordanian gentlemen, the CSM assumed they were all cadets, "Pick up that suitcase, sir, get into line, gentlemen ... quick march ... left, right, left, right, left right," he barked.

The Commandant returning to the scene saw the Prime Minister of Jordan and the Chief of the General Staff disappearing into the distance in double time behind their king.

Frosty morning parades were occasionally enlivened by an exchange between the CSM and one of the cadets. It would go something like this, "Mr King Hussein, sir."

The King, strictly at attention answered, "sir."

"You're an idle king this morning sir. Do you hear me sir?"

The King, "sir."

Off parade I once heard an exasperated CSM Clutton shouting, "Mr King Hussein, sir, Mr King Hussein, sir. Where has that bloody little monarch got to now?"

King Hussein enjoyed his time at Sandhurst. He had a fast car and when he had nothing better to do he would drive at high speed round the academy grounds playing a sort of catch as catch can with frustrated staff.

He was always alert, had very good bearing and very soon adapted to the Sandhurst regime.

When it came for him to leave, his company commander's confidential report was prophetic. It started, "This officer cadet will make a very good king."

We all liked and respected him but few of us would have wagered that he could hold his throne with such skill and brilliance until the end of the century.

◈◇◈◇◈◇◈◇◈◇◈◇◈◇◈◇◈◇◈◇◈◇◈◇◈◇◈◇◈◇◈◇◈◇◈◇

By Cyril Cook

As I walk along the Bois de Boulogne
With an independent air,
You can hear the girls declare:
'He must be a millionaire.'
You can hear them sigh and wish to die,
You can see them wink the other eye
At the man who broke the bank at Monte Carlo

So, who was this man about whom Charles Coburn sang the Fred Gilbert song that has survived from the 1890s to today?

<u>Charles Deville Wells</u> was born in 1841. Little is known of his early life. He claimed to be an engineer, and during the 1880s, took out patents on a tremendous number of inventions. He then set up companies to exploit these inventions, soliciting investors to put money into their development, which of course they never saw again. There truly was one born every minute!

With these monies he lived the high life, was welcomed into society, bought a yacht, and acquired a bevy of mistresses. It was inevitable that someone or other would eventually get wise to the set-up and inform the police. He was charged but before he could be arrested in July 1891, he sailed away on his yacht with one of his mistresses to the south of France, with four thousand pounds in his pocket.

After some weeks anchored off Monte Carlo he visited the casino, studying the croupiers and the roulette tables, then made his play.

Now it is generally believed that, 'breaking the bank', means you have taken all the money in the casino. This is not the case. If a gambler wins more than there are chips on the table, he has 'faire sauter la banque', which means, 'breaking the bank'. A black cloth is then spread over the table until a fresh supply of chips is provided.

In July 1891 he started to play. His first visit as a 'punter' resulted in him winning over a million francs, during which time he broke the bank a dozen times. In the next three days he won another million.

It is said that the casino employed detectives, skilled in casino operations, to watch him as he played, to check the equipment and the operators. All manner of society people made friends with him so that they could watch his play and thereby try and discover his system - none being successful. He did admit to a system, saying he discovered it during his work on perfecting an invention which would make dramatic savings on fuel in steam vessels, this obviously the ground work for another proposed con.

The owner of the casino, M Francois Blanc, strangely enough was not dismayed at Wells winning his millions. The publicity given all round the world brought people pouring in to endeavour to emulate Wells, which soon paid off the overdraft he had had to raise to cover his losses during the time the 'bank' was being systematically broken.

With his winnings Wells returned to London where he was feted, instead of being arrested! In October 1892 he sailed back to Monte Carlo in his luxury yacht, complete with a replacement mistress, where he broke the bank again six times before the downward spiral began. He lost everything, including the mistress and the yacht, tried to get back to England, but as a result of the French having received an extradition request from the British Government, he was arrested at Le Havre and returned to Wormwood Scrubs to face trial at the Old Bailey for fleecing some of the cream of British society of around seventy five thousand pounds.

He spent the next eight years in Dartmoor prison, where the governor afterwards described him as, "As pleasant a rascal you would wish to meet." Eight years penal servitude in those days meant eight years very hard work with no parole.

When he was discharged from Dartmoor he decided to change his name to Davenport, pall'd up with a clergyman who had been kicked out of the church, the pair then executing further frauds which landed him another three year jail sentence.

He then went to try his luck again in France, this time not on the roulette tables. He advertised a scheme by which he would pay one percent interest per <u>day</u> on capital lent to him. Thousands fell for it, but eventually the fraud was recognised and he received five years in a French prison.

Despite his sixteen years in very unpleasant confinement to say the least, combined with the stresses and strains of being a conman, forever waiting for the knock on the door, he lived to the ripe old age for those days of eighty five. There is some doubt about whether he died in Paris or London, but there is no doubt he died in absolute poverty.

How many people die in abject poverty, completely friendless, yet others still sing about them a hundred years later?

<u>Postscript</u>

In my day in the army, there existed a grossly indecent song, sung to Fred Gilbert's tune, entitled, 'The Girl who Lowered the Price at Monte Carlo'. I leave the wording to your imagination.

By Rotarian Roger Geeson, Rotary Club of Woolwich

I recall it so well. Shortly after the war, we were, as a family, off on a long awaited and much looked forward to visit to my favourite relations, the rather posh 'Hamiltons' of Broxbourne, Hertfordshire. My favourite and much loved Aunt Rosa (nee Rosie) and Uncle Cyril, second eldest of my mother's four brothers, whom we saw all too rarely for my liking, perhaps twice in the year, plus their annual pilgrimage to our house at Christmas.

Dear Rosa was a lady with the warmest heart of gold who, despite being raised from a humble Whitechapel and Edmonton background, as were all my mother's family, combined her evident but harmless pretensions with a style reminiscent of a latter-day Hyacinth Bucket, but with infinitely more charm and much less irritation. She epitomised the Jones's with whom everyone else aspired to keep pace. Rosa lived life with a proclivity for social climbing which left the rest of the family bemused and my poor uncle frequently struggling to maintain and keep up with her.

Cyril on the other hand was a largely self-educated but astonishingly well-read, loveable rogue, a humorist and enthralling raconteur. He could, and usually did, keep the entire family spellbound around our Christmas dinner table for hours on end as he elevated the conversation from small talk to deep philosophical discussions on the Universe and all who sailed in her. To many, particularly those who knew him only superficially, he would have made the perfect prototype for Arthur Daly, with his raffish good looks, thin, clipped moustache and sartorial preference for velvet collared camel overcoats, set off with a rakishly tipped dark trilby hat. He would have doubled for a somewhat hungry looking Clark Gable and could sell anybody anything, even if they did not want or need it which, although *they* didn't, he frequently *did!* This was an ability which was in the future to cause any number of factory maintenance managers' serious problems when Cyril was selling steam joint gasketting materials by the truckload all round the country. Stores bulged with huge sheets of gasket materials in a plethora of thicknesses and pressure ratings which cost a small fortune and which, barring major meltdown, the factories would never be likely to need! Nevertheless, Cyril prospered and so did the gasket material manufacturers!

However, I suppose that the Hamiltons' principal claim to national fame in later life remains the fact that they were responsible for bringing into the world, along with his twin brother Tony, one Geoffrey Hamilton, that icon of the BBC's Gardener's World. Most people will doubtless have been familiar with Geoff, a loveable man, prior to his early and untimely death from a heart attack whilst cycling for charity. How Rosa revelled in Geoff's recognition and public popularity, although one never received a hint of it from the man himself, and she would in conversation name-drop outrageously all those BBC supernumeraries' who had just cause (or not) to trample over Geoff's garden at Barnsdale in the course of producing those memorable programmes over the years. But I digress …

So that's where we were headed that Remembrance Sunday. As was ever the case in those days with any motoring expedition in excess of about ten miles, my father had spent much of the previous day preparing for the trusty 'Y' model Ford 8 saloon, his very first car, and pride and joy, for its forthcoming expedition to Broxbourne. I truly believe that Robert Falcon Scott put less effort into preparing for his epic assault upon the South Pole than my dad put into a fifty mile car drive. The Ford's black cellulose shone like a hearse, set off by gleaming chromed hub caps, fetchingly emblazoned with an impressed Ford motif, on each freshly painted 'racing green' spoked wheel. Windows were polished, oil and water levels, both battery and radiator, topped up, fan belt tightened, brake shoes blown out and adjusted, trafficators (which could be a bit of a bugger on 'Y' Fords I remember) checked for bulb and arm function and every one of some twenty seven grease nipples cleaned off and injected with Castrolease of the correct viscosity or melting point.

At some stage in this ritual procedure, I would be dragged away from doing something undoubtedly more interesting to check the function of various running lights and to stamp up and down on the brake pedal whilst Dad checked the stop lights. Finally, having verified his tyre pressures with a little chrome gauge and topped up the air where necessary with an antique hand pump, somewhat redolent of a stirrup pump and of a design possibly responsible for a large percentage of premature cardiac arrests amongst forties motorists, father declared that the car was as ready as he could get it and that it *should* get us to Broxbourne without any trouble.

All eyes and thoughts on the car you notice – never any consideration for the driver and whether he might get us to darkest Hertfordshire without any trouble. Father had never taken a driving test you see, the received wisdom at the Ministry of Transport or whoever then governed such matters being that, since he had possessed a licence to ride a motorcycle before the war, he was perfectly qualified to pilot a three-quarter ton projectile, with the acknowledged power of eight average draught horses, anywhere throughout the realm! As it happened, being the careful, always prepared, and out and out perfectionist in pretty well anything he did, Dad was an excellent driver and navigated through the rest of his motoring life with scarcely a scratch on the bodywork. Regrettably, this was not an accomplishment he saw fit to pass on through his genes to his offspring, who have since more than made up for Dad's paucity in motor destruction.

Anyway, our invitation having been for 'lunch', Father being a cautious man, Broxbourne being all of a ninety minute drive, even by 'Y' model Ford 8 standards, and with clear parental instructions to my baby sister, "Not to dare be car sick," we duly set off sometime after 10.00 am and headed for London Bridge and the 'frozen North'. Traffic was light as one would expect on a Sunday morning and, even at Dad's breakneck speed, progress was such that we hit Bishopsgate at just about 11.00 o'clock, when strange things began to happen. Cars pulled into the kerbside, some disgorging their occupants who stood around with heads bowed; buses and taxis stopped and the many pedestrians thronging the pavements stood stock still, almost to a man, some checking their watches or glancing at the huge clock on the corner of Fenchurch Street. The City was waiting. I later understood, for the clocks to chime, bells toll and the ceremonial guns to fire their disciplined salutes to the fallen of two world wars. This was a phenomenon of which I had not previously been consciously aware – the 'Two Minutes Silence' – at the eleventh hour of the eleventh day of the eleventh month, after the guns of the Great War had fallen silent and the Armistice was signed! Of course we followed suit not only of necessity, because the road was blocked, but because my parents, who were as reverent and patriotic as anyone, would have thus marked the moment anyway.

We sat in silence (even my baby sister, strangely enough, although she probably just felt sick) despite my bursting to know what the problem was and why the outside world seemed suddenly to have become an almost motionless tableau. Eventually, after the distant field guns of the Royal Horse Artillery had sounded their message of remembrance and commemoration, the tableau stirred into muted activity as drivers and pedestrians decided that two minutes, or a period constituting decent respectability, had elapsed and life could once again resume its madcap hectic pace, such as it then was.

Although I was vaguely aware of the Armistice, the protocol, of what was then the accepted and normal public demonstration of the two minutes silence, were explained to me as we resumed our journey and headed steadily through Tottenham and Edmonton towards the Great Cambridge Road, leading eventually to Broxbourne, Hoddesdon, Hertford and on to the 'frozen North!'

We had a wonderful day in Broxbourne with my favourite relations. My cousins, who were a little older than me and already in the Scouts, had been to their Remembrance parade, and so talk at the lunch table naturally centred on the day's

140

special meaning and gave the adults plenty of opportunity to reminisce over their wartime experiences and privations.

Nowadays of course, we sit in comfort whilst watching the 'great and the good' parade past and leave their floral tributes at the Cenotaph in memory of the fallen. Remembrance of the fallen, not only of those two world wide conflicts, but of so many subsequent wars and skirmishes which have so decimated mankind, in a ceremony regrettably sanitised to some extent by the gloss of national television coverage.

I cannot remember what we had for lunch that day but, with the country then still in the grip of rationing, it probably wasn't either too exciting or copious, but we didn't care. The company was what mattered. We were happy, and I never forgot the memory of, or lost the patriotic feelings and propensity for a large lump in the throat brought on by that or any other Remembrance Sunday.

From Volume 5. The Chandlers. By Cyril Cook

Résumé

Charlie Crew, badly wounded in the Normandy fighting is in Lord Mayor Treloar's Hospital in Alton, Hampshire, where he is visited by his fiancée, Emma and his grandfather, the Earl of Otbourne. The time came for his visitors to leave. Now read on.

They were told they would have to wait a long time for a cab, but the bus went every half hour and one was due.

Emma smiled. "Do peers of the realm travel on buses?"

The reply came without hesitation.

"What about future peeresses?"

Emma clutched his arm. "If it means losing you, I would never want to be a peeress." Her eyes misted, "But I do love Charlie so very, very much. We should have been married on Saturday. It isn't fair is it?"

He put his hand on hers. "You have lots of time my dear. It won't always be like this."

The bus journey into town was eventful in that it was already full when it arrived. As a result the Earl and Emma had to stand with his Lordship pressed hard up against an extremely stout lady possessed of whatever is the next size up from an ample bosom, the bosom itself showing abundant cleavage to the world in general and to the Earl in particular, who found it impossible to look anywhere else than into it, in view of the crush. To add to the entertainment, the road was somewhat bumpy, as were most roads at that stage of the war, and the bus seemed to either have solid tyres or no springs. As a result of the aforementioned acreage, when not possessing a continuous surface ripple, every now and then threatened to jump out when a pothole was encountered. The Earl, seeing the lady was holding a small child in one hand and a shopping basket in the other, wondered to himself whether if one, or for that matter both, of these undoubtedly magnificent mammary glands escaped from their somewhat undersized repositories, should he offer to put them back? It was a warm day therefore his hands would not be cold. He then estimated one pair of hands would not be sufficient for the full load, it would be definitely a four handed job. Was there anyone nearby who could help? Definitely not. A two handed exercise would involve putting them in one at a time, which would be a little like getting into a hammock – when the weight is directed on one side, the other side tips up. This re-housing job was not going to be accomplished without a great deal of finesse combined with good fortune.

His mind then wandered to the old schoolboy joke about the topless lady with her arms folded across her chest, running into the sea to bathe, being followed by a little lad asking, "If you are going to drown those puppies can I have the one with the pink nose?" This was followed by him remembering the story, told to him by an ancient Scottish friend, of the well developed young woman in a low cut dress seated at dinner next to an elderly gent. At length she said to him, "Are you looking down my front?"

To which he replied, "Yes, I am, but I can't remember why."

He smiled at the thoughts. The more than amply bosomed lady saw him smile and smiled back, saying, "The roads get bumpier every day, don't 'um?"

"They certainly do, they certainly do."

"You been visitin' at Treloar's then, 'ave 'ee?"

"Yes, my grandson was wounded in Normandy."

He endeavoured to turn to bring Emma into the conversation but due to the crush, was totally incapable of so doing.

"He was originally due to be married to the young lady behind me on Saturday."

"Oh, what a shame. Nell," she spoke to another well endowed woman on a seat behind her, "this gentleman's been to see his wounded grandson in Treloar's. The young man was supposed to marry that young Wren lady on Saturday. Ain't it a shame?"

Nell and the lady next to her agreed it was wicked the things old 'Itler was putting them all through. As a result the couple behind Nell, seated as they were next to the 'young Wren lady' started talking to Emma, commiserating with her on her misfortune and assuring her it 'would all come right in the end,' so that by the time the bus arrived at The Swan, nearly everybody on the lower deck was on speaking terms with his or her neighbour. And all because of the lascivious thoughts of a peer of the realm who one would have thought would have been above that sort of thing at his station and at his time of life!! Some hopes!!

⸨◈◇◈◇◈◇◈◈◇◈◇◈◇◇◈◇◈◇◈◇◈◇◈◈◇◈◇◈◇◈◈◇◈⸩

The art of being a good guest is to know when to leave. *Prince Philip.*

⸨◈◇◈◇◈◇◈◈◇◈◇◈◇◈◈◇◈◇◈◈⸩

Sure, God created man before woman, but then you always make a rough draft before the final masterpiece.

⸨◈◇◈◇◈◇◈◇◈◇◈◇◈◇◈◇◈⸩

The optimist proclaims that we live in the best of all possible worlds.

The pessimist fears this is true. *James Corbett.*

143

By Cyril Cook

I was watching the funniest man in the world putting on another show on the telly. It was the 15th April 1984 – but seems like yesterday. Suddenly, Tommy seemed to sink to the floor of the stage of Her Majesty's Theatre, becoming entangled with the curtain as it was brought down upon him.

For a few seconds I thought it was all part of the act, but as he lay totally still I realised it was something very serious. Eventually stage staff disentangled the curtain from beneath him and that was the last glimpse we had of the only person I have ever

known who could, simply by standing still and remaining totally silent, cause me to have hysterics.

Tommy was born on the 9th of March 1922 in the market town of Caerphilly, South Wales, known formerly for its cheese, and the castle Oliver Cromwell knocked about a bit. He grew to be a giant nearly six and a half feet tall – two metres to you poor decimalised people. During World War Two, he was in the Household Cavalry, fought in the western desert and was wounded. I suppose you could say that with a target that size to aim at a Gerry could hardly miss. Whilst recovering he joined an ENSA concert party which travelled around entertaining the forces. This is where he developed his zany act involving everything going wrong, and where he began wearing his inimitable fez.

When he left the army after the war he turned professional, did the usual slog around the provinces, gradually reaching top-billing. In the late fifties and sixties he began to star on television here and in the States, and took part in the Royal Command Performance.

Something which will be remembered about Tommy, in fact will become a legend in show business, was his meeting with Her Majesty after the Royal Command Performance. He is recorded as asking, "Can I ask you a personal question Ma'am?"

The Queen is said to have replied, to the effect that he could, but he might not get an answer.

"Do you like football, Ma'am?"

"Not very much."

"In that case, can I have your Cup Final tickets?"

It would be extremely difficult to analyse the Tommy Cooper humour. A bumbling idiot should soon drive you to tears of frustration; Tommy drove you to tears of laughter, doing little right. Corny jokes normally receive at most a slight chuckle; in Tommy's hands you fell about.

Do you know why?

I am afraid I don't and probably never will.

Tommy Cooper style jokes and one liners are spaced throughout this volume in a tribute to a man who broke the mould when he so sadly died.

❖❖❖❖❖ ❖❖ ❖❖❖❖❖ ❖❖❖❖❖❖❖ ❖❖❖❖❖❖❖❖❖ ❖❖ ❖❖❖❖ ❖❖ ❖❖

Tommy Cooper Specials

Two blondes walk into a building … you'd think at least one of them would have seen it.

❖❖❖❖ ❖❖ ❖❖ ❖❖ ❖❖ ❖❖❖ ❖❖❖ ❖❖ ❖❖

Phone answering machine message … "If you want to buy marijuana press the hash key."

❖❖❖❖ ❖❖ ❖❖ ❖❖ ❖❖ ❖❖ ❖❖❖ ❖❖ ❖❖

My friend drowned in a bowl of muesli. A strong currant pulled him in.

❖❖ ❖❖ ❖❖❖❖ ❖❖ ❖❖ ❖❖ ❖❖❖ ❖❖ ❖❖

A man came round after a serious accident. He shouted, "Doctor, doctor, I can't feel my legs."

The doctor replied, "I know you can't, I've cut your arms off."

❖❖ ❖❖ ❖❖ ❖❖ ❖❖ ❖❖ ❖❖ ❖❖ ❖❖

I went to the dentist. He said, "Say aaah."

I said, "Why?"

He replied, "My dog's died."

❖❖❖❖ ❖❖ ❖❖❖❖ ❖❖ ❖❖❖❖ ❖❖ ❖❖

By Cyril Cook

For thirty five years I was a qualified referee, officiating in junior and intermediate football leagues. Wherever I blasted my whistle, whether it was in front of a crowd of ten or ten thousand, I knew there would be ten or ten thousand other referees at the game who knew more about the laws, and the application thereof, than I did.

There are only seventeen laws governing the game – I believe American football has over two hundred! However, there are innumerable FA and international decisions regarding points of law of which referees have to have knowledge before they even set foot on the pitch in earnest. Let us take a recent example. Law four states that, '"A player must not use any equipment or wear anything which is dangerous to himself or another player, including any kind of jewellery."

Up until the 2006/7 season jewellery was allowed to be worn provided it was taped over. However, with some players wearing rings like knuckle dusters for example, there were many cases of injury reported. The International Board decided therefore, that <u>all</u> items of jewellery were to be removed.

It was then found that in some cases a player wearing a wedding ring, through the passage of time, would be unable to remove it. Another decision therefore had to be made. If a player satisfied the referee before the match started that his **plain** wedding ring could not be removed, he could play, provided the ring was taped over; **but** - it applied only to a plain wedding band.

To sum up, therefore, it is clear there is an awful lot a referee needs to know before he even sets foot on the pitch in front of the other ten thousand referees.

How does that army classify the man in the middle? My society, The South of the Thames and Woolwich, suggests the following.

<u>The Soccer Tribesman's Guide to Referees</u>

1. <u>The Blind Ref.</u> Sees himself as the friend of the fast-flowing game. Appears to have lost his whistle and lets anything pass. Beloved by the hard men of the game.
2. <u>The Whistling Ref.</u> The chronic whistleblower wears his Acme Thunderer as if it were a permanent brace on his teeth. Much hated by supporters, he blows up for every minor misdeed, fragmenting the game with a thousand irritating stoppages. Beloved by the soft men of the game.

3. The Homer Ref. Believes that every savage foul by the home team is nothing more than an enthusiastic tackle. Knows that the visiting team are a bunch of animals and acts accordingly. Is usually nervous, timid, inconsistent and agitated. suffers from the worst disease that can afflict a referee: the desire to be loved. For some mysterious reason, usually has lily-white legs.

4. The Headmaster Ref. Treats all players as naughty little schoolboys. Gives them patronisingly sarcastic glances at every opportunity. When warning them, insists that they "Come here!" beckoning derisively. Given to much finger-wagging and stern lecturing. Particularly hated by all players.

5. The Flashy Ref. Immaculate costume. Always knows where the TV cameras are positioned. Uses flamboyant gestures and often acts out fouls in mime. Appears to have had ballet training and is said to wear hairspray.

6. The Smiley Ref. Has seen it all before and believes humour is the best way to defuse potentially explosive situations. Is usually one of the older men and is given to much athletic sprinting to prove that he is not. Nearly always smiles when he gives a severe warning – even when swearing at hotheads in their own language. The players' favourite.

7. The Perfect Ref. Firm but fair. Restrained but decisive. Unmoved by emotional outbursts and the baying of the crowd. Unimpressed by special pleading, and can tell a trip from a dive at fifty yards. A rare species, but not yet extinct.

The Armchair Referee

To end this brief essay on one part of 'The Beautiful Game', I will pose some fairly elementary questions for the armchair referee upon which to make a decision. Answers to be found on page. 383

1. *A player in possession of the ball passes over the touch line or the goal line without the ball in order to beat an opponent. What action does the referee take?*

2. *A substitute enters the field of play without having obtained the permission of the referee, and his team plays with an extra player. While the ball is in play, an opponent violently punches him. What action should the referee take?*

3. *Can a captain send off one of his team-mates for serious misconduct?*

4. *As assistant referee signals that the ball has passed over the touch line. A defending player inside the penalty area violently strikes an attacking player. What action should the referee take?*

5. *A defending player moves beyond his own goal line in order to place an opponent in an offside position. What action does the referee take?*

6. *While the ball is in play, two players of the same team commit unsporting behaviour or violent conduct towards each other on the field of play. What action does the referee take?*

7. *The goalkeeper in his penalty area holds the ball in his hands then places it on the ground and takes it outside the penalty area. He then decides to re-enter the penalty area and touches the ball again with his hands. What action does the referee take?*

8. *A team is awarded a free kick in its own penalty area. The player taking the kick hits the ball against a team-mate who is inside the penalty area and the ball enters the goal. What action does the referee take?*

9. *A free kick is awarded and the player decides to take the kick quickly. An opponent who is less than 10 yards from the ball intercepts it. What action does the referee take?*

10. *A player taking a penalty kick plays the ball forward for a team-mate to run on to it and score. Is this permitted?*

Well? How did you get on? And did you notice that the full answer to the incident almost always concerns how you re-start the game once you have stopped it for any reason.

A final word, there are referees' societies all over the country who will train you in the craft. Just contact your county association for details.

My thanks to South of the Thames and Woolwich Society for the above questions.

Each North American Indian community has, and still in many cases has, its story teller. It is calculated that they can memorise anything between 500 – 1000 stories and legends. In other ancient races I have found legends to be of a length which could be remembered without difficulty, bearing in mind there would generally be no written word. I have been fascinated therefore to find Cree legends running up to four thousand words. I am told that the legends are spread, with some tribal differences, throughout many of the Indian peoples, the legend that follows originating in Saskatchewan.

Cyril Cook

The Jealous Father

From John Bury, Lune Lake Canada

Once there was an old man named Aioswé who had two wives. When his son by one of these women began to grow up, Aioswé became jealous of him.

One day, he went off to hunt and when he came back, found marks on one of the women (the co-wife with his son's mother) which proved to him that his son had been on terms of intimacy with her.

One day the old man and the boy went to a rocky island to hunt for eggs. Wishing to get rid of his son, the old man persuaded him to gather eggs farther and farther away from the shore. The young man did not suspect anything until he looked up and saw his father paddling off in the canoe.

"Why are you deserting me, father?" he cried.

"Because you have played tricks on your stepmother," answered the old man.

When the boy found that he was really left behind, he sat there crying hour after hour. At last, Walrus appeared. He came near the island and stuck his head above the water. "What are you crying for, my son?" said Walrus.

"My father has deserted me on this island and I want to get home to the mainland. Will you not help me to get ashore?" the boy replied.

Walrus said that he would do so willingly. "Get on my back," said Walrus, "and I will take you to the mainland."

Then Walrus asked Aioswé's son if the sky was clear. the boy replied that it was, but this was a lie, for he saw many clouds. Aioswé's son said this because he was afraid that Walrus would desert him if he knew it was cloudy.

Walrus said, "If you think I am not going fast enough, strike on my horns (tusks) and let me know when you think it is shallow enough for you to get ashore, then you can jump off my back and walk to the land."

As they went along, Walrus said to the boy, "Now my son, you must let me know if you hear it thunder, because as soon as it thunders, I must go right under the water." The boy promised to let Walrus know. They had not gone far, when there came a peal of thunder. Walrus said, "My son, I hear thunder."

"Oh, no, you are mistaken," said the boy who feared to be drowned, "what you think is thunder is only the noise your body makes going so quickly through the water." Walrus believed the boy and thought he must have been wrong.

Some time later, there came another peal of thunder and this time, Walrus knew he was not mistaken, he was sure it was thunder. He was very angry and said he would drop Aioswé's son there, whether the water was shallow or not. He did so but the lad had duped Walrus with his lies so that he came where the water was very shallow and the boy escaped, but Walrus was killed by lightning before he could reach water deep enough to dive in. This thunderstorm was sent to destroy Walrus by Aioswé's father, who conjured for it. Walrus, on the other hand, was the result of conjuring by his mother, who wished to save her son's life.

When Aioswé's son reached the shore, he started for home, but he had not gone far before he met an old woman, who had been sent as the result of a wish for his safety by his mother (or was a wish for his safety on his mother's part, personified). The old woman instructed the lad how to conduct himself if he ever expected to reach his home and mother again.

"Now you have come ashore there is still a lot of trouble for you to go through before you reach home," said she, and she gave him the stuffed skin of an ermine (weasel in white winter coat). "This will be one of your weapons to use to protect yourself," were her words as she tendered him this gift, and she told him what dangers he would encounter and what to do in each case.

Then the son of Aioswé started for his home once more. As he journeyed through the forest he came upon a solitary wigwam inhabited by two old blind hags, who were the result of an adverse conjuration by his father. Both of these old women had sharp bones like daggers; protruding from the lower arm at the elbow. They were very savage and used to kill everybody they met. When Aioswé's son approached the tent, although the witches could not see him, they knew from their magic powers that he was near. They asked him to come in and sit down, but he was suspicious, for he did not like the looks of their elbows.

He thought of a plan by which he might dupe the old women into killing each other. Instead of going himself and sitting between them, he got a large parchment and fixing it to the end of a pole he poked it in between them. The old women heard it rattle and thought it was the boy himself coming to sit between them. Then they turned their backs to the skin and began to hit away at it with their elbows. Every time they stabbed the skin, they cried out, "I am hitting the son of Aioswé! I've hit him! I've hit him!" At last, they got so near each other that they began to hit one another, calling out all the time, "I am hitting the son of Aioswé!" They finally stabbed each other to death and the son of Aioswé escaped this danger also.

When the young man had vanquished the two old women he proceeded on his journey. He had not gone very far when he came to a row of dried human bones hung across the path so that no-one could pass by without making them rattle. Not far away, there was a tent full of people and big dogs. Whenever they heard anyone disturb the bones, they would set upon him and kill him. The old woman who had advised Aioswé's son told him that when he came to this place he could escape by digging a tunnel in the path under the bones.

When he arrived at the spot he began to follow her advice and burrow under. He was careless and when he was very nearly done and completely out of sight, he managed to rattle the bones. At once, the dogs heard and they cried out, "That must be Aioswé's son." All the people ran out at once, but since Aioswé's son was underground in the tunnel they could not see him, so after they had searched for a while they returned. The dogs' said, "We are sure this is the son of Aioswé," and they continued to search.

At length, they found the mouth of the hole Aioswé's son had dug. The dogs came to the edge and began to bark till all the people ran out again with their weapons. Then Aioswé's son took the stuffed ermine skin and poked its head up. All the people saw it and thought it was really ermine. Then they were angry and killed the dogs for lying.

Aioswé's son escaped again and this time he got home. When he drew near his father's wigwam, he could hear his mother crying, and as he approached still closer he saw her. She looked up and saw him coming. She cried out to her husband and co-wife, "My son has come home again."

The old man did not believe it. "It is not possible," he cried. But his wife insisted on it. Then the old man came out and when he saw it was really his son, he was very much frightened for his own safety. He called out to his other wife, "Bring some caribou skins and spread them out for my son to walk on."

But the boy kicked them away. "I have come a long way," said he, "with only my bare feet to walk on."

That night, the boy sang a song about the burning of the world and the old man sang against him but he was not strong enough.

"I am going to set the world on fire," said the boy to his father. "I shall make all the lakes and rivers boil." He took up an arrow and said, "I am going to shoot this arrow into the woods; see if I don't set them on fire." He shot his arrow into the bush and a great blaze sprang up and all the woods

152

began to burn.

"The forest is now on fire," said the old man, "but the water is not yet burning."

"I will show you how I can make the water boil also," said his son. He shot another arrow into the water, and it immediately began to boil. Then the old man who wished to escape said to his son, "How shall we escape?" The old man had been a great bear hunter and had a large quantity of bear's grease preserved in a bark basket.

"Go into your fat basket," said his son, "you will be perfectly safe there."

He then drew a circle on the ground and placed his mother there. The ground enclosed by the circle was not even scorched, but the wicked old man who had believed he would be safe in the grease baskets, was burned to death.

Aioswé's son said to his mother, "Let us become birds. What will you be?

"I'll be a Robin," she said.

"I'll be a Whisky Jack (Canada Jay)," he replied. They flew off together.

Random Thoughts

- Light travels faster than sound. This is why some people appear bright until you hear them speak.

- He who laughs last thinks slowest.

- Change is inevitable, except from a vending machine.

- Those who live by the sword get shot by those who don't.

- Nothing is foolproof to a sufficiently talented fool.

- The 50-50-90 rule: anytime you have a 50:50 chance of getting something right, there is a 90% probability you'll get it wrong.

- The things that come to those who wait will be the things left by those who got there first.

- Give a man a fish and he will eat for a day. Teach a man to fish and he will sit in a boat all day drinking beer.

- Flashlight: a case for holding dead batteries.

- The shin bone is a device for finding furniture in a dark room.

- A fine is a tax for doing wrong. A tax is a fine for doing well.

- When you go into court, you are putting yourself in the hands of 12 people who weren't smart enough to get out of jury duty.

- We all want to live a long time, but none of us wants to grow old.

- To be born a gentleman is an accident – to die one is an achievement.

- Do dustmen have to learn the trade or do they pick it up as they go along? (What rubbish!)

- At a dinner party, it isn't so much what is on the table that matters, as what is on the chairs.

- Marriage is the only Union that can't be organised. Both sides think they are the management.

- Education survives when what we have learnt is forgotten.

- When an agnostic dies, does he go to the 'great perhaps'?

- I wonder why just one letter makes all the difference between here and there.

- I also wonder why we never hear father-in-law jokes.

Anti Nazi Resistance Movement within Germany in World War Two

By Cyril Cook

It is not generally known that during World War Two there was an active resistance movement against the Nazis, operating from the highest level of army hierarchy down to students at a number of universities. General Thiele, for example, passed information to contacts in Switzerland continuously from Army GHQ in Berlin, from the time of the invasion of Russia until he was eventually hanged for complicity in the attempted assassination of the Fuhrer in 1944. Even then, although the Gestapo knew that there was a mole in the headquarters, they never found out who it was. The passing of this information to a superbly organised Russian organisation in Basel

Sophie Scholl

known as the 'Lucy Ring' meant that Russian generals often knew of proposed German movements before even their German opposites had been informed.

One of the leading groups in the opposition to the war was at Munich University. This organisation, led by a brother and sister, Hans and Sophie Scholl, was known as 'The White Rose'. They produced leaflets in opposition to the Nazi movement and the war, until eventually in 1943 they were arrested by the Gestapo and put on trial.

There was no doubt about the outcome of the trial. They had preached sedition which was probably one of the most heinous offences in the Nazi register. They were sentenced to death by the so-called 'Peoples Court'; there was no appeal. They were then executed on the day of their sentencing along with a friend named Christophe Probst. The method of execution? By guillotine.

A total of over thirty thousand German nationals were executed for sedition or similar charges. This figure did not include the tens of thousands of communists, trade union officials, Quakers and so on, incarcerated before the war and who eventually succumbed to the dreadful conditions obtaining in the camps; the forced labour, and eventually if they had survived all that, the forced marches in 1944-5 away from the invading Russians and the British and American armies.

I wonder if there is a memorial to them anywhere?

By Cyril Cook

Although the bill shown here indicates 'Colonel and Mrs Cook,' I have to tell you I was merely a buckshee lieutenant.

I had been granted only four days leave from my parachute unit in which to get married, due to our being on stand-by for an operation. We therefore, living in South London, decided uponTunbridge Wells as a suitably close venue in which to spend our honeymoon. As I said to my wife-to-be, "The last thing we will want to do is to waste time travelling," with which sentiment, I am pleased to say, she heartily agreed.

The hotel was very comfortable, opening on to the famous 'Pantiles' at Tunbridge Wells and was by far the best 'fiver' I ever spent.

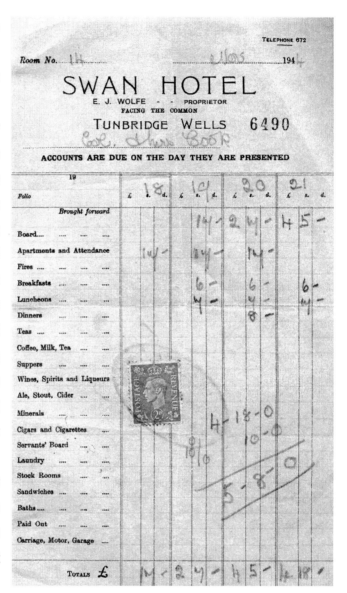

I wonder what it would cost today. But then, as a full lieutenant including my parachuting pay, I received the princely sum of fifteen shillings a day (75p), roughly five pounds a week!!

I Know my Writes

The following are true extracts from letters sent to the City Hall of a large town in Lancashire. The initials which follow each quotation are those of the sender. The excerpts do show however, how, many people write as they think. They know what they mean, there is no reason, therefore, why the recipient should not know what they mean. It is fair to say that these missives did not all arrive in one week; they have been collected over a number of years.

- This is to let you know there is a smell coming from the man next door. - BN

- The toilet seat is cracked – where do I stand? - AH

- I am writing on behalf of my sink, which is running away from the wall. - SH

- I am still having trouble with smoke in my built in drawers. - SS

- I request your permission to remove my drawers in the kitchen. - FT

- Our lavatory seat is broken in half and is now in three pieces. - SR

- Can you please tell me when our repairs are going to be done, as my wife is about to become an expectant mother? - MS

- I want some repairs doing to my cooker, as it has backfired and burnt my knob off. - AT

- The toilet is blocked and we cannot bath the children until it is cleared. - JW

- The person next door has a large erection in his back garden, which is unsightly and dangerous. - JT

- Will you please send me someone to mend our broken path? Yesterday my wife tripped and fell on it and she is now pregnant. - RT

- Our kitchen floor is very damp, we have two children and would like a third so will you please send someone to do something about it. – BG

- Would you please repair our toilet, my son pulled the chain and the box fell on his head. – IK

- Will you please send a man to look at my water, it is a funny colour and not fit to drink. – JP

- Would you please send a man to repair my spout, I am an old age pensioner and need it straight away. – AN

- I awoke this morning and found my water boiling. – RS

- This is to let you know that our lavatory seat is broken and we cannot get BBC2. – JB

Postscript. For clarity's sake we have revised some of the original spelling!

By Bob Adams OBE

A hard sharp sound rang out and disturbed the heavy quietness resting over the rambling group of farm buildings. Over in the upturned sawn off fishing boat the hens stirred lazily and flounced their soft feathers like a sleeper turning under warm, clinging bedclothes. The cockerels stretched themselves preparatory to piercing the peacefulness with the rooster's reveille.

The hard metallic sound repeated itself and gradually became a pattern. The stable door swung open and into the cold dawn air a huge hairy footed horse stumbled out and over the cobbled yard. Bud is thirsty. He made straight for the trough. There he stopped, dipped his shaggy head and slurped the cool water greedily. A few moments later another great horse emerged from the dark, warm, sweet smelling stable into the fresh crisp air. It also turned towards the trough. They stood there, Bud slightly the taller, heads down for a long time, steam rising from their broad flanks.

The ploughman, with his tackety boots making a noise not unlike that of the horses, led the horses, thirst now slaked, down the narrow red granite road to the field. The sky had been as black as the Buchan earth when Alec had risen to harness the horses, but now a grey light spread over the colourless fields; no green has yet come to lighten the early year earth. They turned in to the open gate. The horses were aligned in front of the plough, the harness connected, and with a, "Hup," the day's work began.

In unison the horses gave a mighty pull to overcome the inertia of the lumpen plough. After a few paces of noisy, snorting struggle, the team and the plough settled down to a deep gliding cut. The soil rolled over like the bow wave of a majestic ship as the plough share cut through the tangled roots of last year's crop.

Bud knew the job; the repetitiveness and the variations; knew the sharp commands which guided his response to these variations. Bud knew the man and trusted him; knew too his companion Rose and trusted her to respond also and take her share of the strain. There was a constant sound of rapping as the blades hit the round flint filled stones strewn about the field or when an iron clad hoof kicked one aside.

The little turnip shoots expanded daily and soon the great globes beneath were pushing through the soil and showing pink and orange cheeks. Spring turned to summer and harvest time was soon upon them. Now the hay was cut by a reaper drawn by the horses. In the days that followed, Bud and Rose pulled broad rakes across the field and the farm workers piled the harvest into neat coles. At this time when the food arrived at midday, there were happy shouting children with the women. They all settled down in the sunshine and shared the contents of the baskets. To the children this was a picnic. To the men and horses it was a welcome break from the routine of the field. The children fed hay and grass to the gentle giants. Even three year old Sadie wanted to do her share and was patiently lifted up by young Jake who would much rather have been laying on his back with the others.

At the end of the day the horses plodded homeward with the children on their backs. The two older children rode on Rose. Sadie astride Bud was almost doing the splits on her broad back. Bud strode cautiously his massive feet daintily avoiding the pot holes and cart ruts on the well-worn track.

The harvest was safely in when the man arrived. He was wearing a Service Corps uniform and had official looking papers in his hand. The farmer looked up from the fence he was repairing as he saw the stranger approach.

"Aye aye man. Whit brings you in aboot here? Nae work to dae?"

"Work enough – and maybe harder than mending a puckle fences."

"Weel, it's aye bad news when a stranger comes in aboot to the farm. Whit is it this time?"

"It'll no be good news I'll grant you. I'm from the War Office."

"Well, me and Alec are too auld fur you and the lad's oor young and that's a' we hae – unless you fancy taaking the wife."

"It's no folk I'm looking for. It's horses. How many do you hiv?"

"Only the twae and I couldna dae without them. We man grow food still."

"If you have two I must take one."

"And wha'll pull the plough – Alec and me? Een horse canna dae it."

"You and your neighbour will have to get together for the heavy work. Help each other."

"Wallace help. That po-faced bugger's never done a hands turn for anyone in his life."

"Tell him there's a war on."

"No, you tell him when you tak his horse."

The two men went together to the field where the horses were grazing. Bud and Rose ambled across to the gate on seeing the farmer and nuzzled up to him. The man went into the field and walked around the two animals. He prodded and pinched them and looked carefully at their teeth and hooves. He looked at Bud's broad forehead and twinkling intelligent eyes; his fine straight legs and muscle packed thighs.

"Yon's a braw horse."

"Bud. Aye, you'll be leaving me that one?"

"I man tak the best. From what I hear they'll need to be good out by."

"Bud's the best."

"Well, the truck will be along tomorrow. I'll be on my way. Best of luck Bud." He patted the horse's nose and departed.

The farmer and his wife each at some time during the evening walked over to the field and bade the big horse farewell. The children, with tears in their eyes, spent the morning in the field feeding Bud and walking him about the field on a rope halter. Sadie stroked the soft black skin of his nose and the boys carried a well-filled nosebag of oats to their friend as a special treat. They refused to go in for their own meal and stayed with the horse till the dreaded truck arrived.

Bud now sensed the anxiety around him and was alarmed by the sight of the truck. He galloped off around the field and had to be chased and brought to the vehicle. The horseman who had come with the truck went up the ramp with the rope attached to bud's bridle and pulled but to no avail. Bud decided he was going nowhere with this stranger.

The farmer now let Bud gallop around the field for a time then walked over to him talking softly as he approached. He then took hold of the bridle close to the horse's mouth and still talking softly into his ear, led him up the ramp again and tied him up in a padded corner of the truck.

The farmer remained with Bud and spoke gently for a few minutes and Bud knew he was going to be all right; he trusted the farmer; he had always treated him well. As the truck moved slowly off, three small sobbing faces were pressed against an upstairs window.

The truck passed through nearby Peterhead, where large posters proclaimed, 'Your King and Country Need You,' and lines of eager young men laughed and joked outside the Army Recruiting Office. Fear and bewilderment welled up in Bud as the truck bumped about on the country roads.

Three days of jostling, confusing and frightening travel saw Bud arrive in Salisbury Plains. Here he was amongst hundreds of other horses all equally terrified by the strange surroundings, the bustle and the noise. The horses were well fed but Bud did not eat anything. He did not wish to accept anything from these strange men. He did not trust them.

Bud's training started by him getting acquainted with a new horseman – a man who used different sounds to convey his orders. To begin with Bud did not understand what was required of him. This was not the farmer. Bittle, the horseman, now hit Bud on the broad flank with a whip. Bud felt the sting of the whip and even more the indignity of being so treated. He kicked out savagely. The whip was applied again. After this had happened a few times, Bud remembered his training as a young horse a long time ago at the farm and realised he could not win, so he accepted his fate and settled down. Bittle was a good horseman, so after showing him who was in command they started to work well together. Bud recognised he could work with such a man – a man who took the trouble to use his name, talk quietly as he approached and always work from the same side in the stable. No surprises. No sudden startling movements. The man in turn realised his good fortune in being allocated such a magnificent horse.

Bud was teamed with another horse and taught how to pull a light gun. To Bud it was very similar to pulling a plough but easier; Bud was bigger and stronger than most of the other horses. The hard work and the companionship of his partner, 'Tib', the horseman called him, tired his body and eased his mind respectively. He relaxed and started to eat again.

Bud and a long convoy of horses set off on foot for a channel port. It was a steady march through pleasant countryside – not unlike the Buchan countryside he had so recently come from.

The short sea journey was not comfortable. The air in the ship was pungent and sour and Bud felt sick. When the time came he scrambled up the ramp to the open air more willingly than when he had boarded the ship. Bud was in France.

Bittle led the horses for a few miles to a yard where they were harnessed to a piece of artillery. Anytime they stopped Bud got the same friendly treatment as he had become accustomed to at the farm. The children came out to offer grass and titbits. Even the adults came up and stroked and spoke to these fine looking, big, friendly beasts, and the handsome Bud, looking around with his clear intelligent eyes, as always getting the most attention. Bud was beginning to feel that strangers could be trusted.

As the lines of wheeled guns trundled southwards, the horses could hear the sound of gunfire. The noise became louder with each passing hour. The villages through which they passed smelt of burning. Bud felt himself choking. Men and women walked with bundles on their backs and horses with hanging heads shuffled past pulling a great assortment of carts and carriages. No-one had time to pat Bud's nose now.

The next night, Bud's team made its way quietly with muffled wheels up to the battle line. Yellow flashes cracked across the heavens. Thumping explosions blew pieces of the fields ahead of them high into the air. Shells whined close overhead. The air was filled with the stinging smell of cordite. Throughout this the great stoical beasts plodded steadfastly on. When night came the horsemen slept right beside them.

Next morning they left the road and struck across open countryside. These had been farm fields but little of the fences or hedges remained. To Bud, it was very like walking on ploughed fields, kicking the empty shell cases like the flint filled stones of the Buchan fields.

This became a routine. They were driven up to the frontline once or twice a day to move the gun. When their gun was blown up they went back a long way and brought up another. Sometimes they brought up a new crew. The routine was varied for Bud only by the intensity and proximity of the falling shells.

Then as spring turned to summer, everybody and everything was moving back. The journey became shorter but faster. The gunfire was more intense and the shells were falling nearer. The roads were jammed with hurrying vehicles and people. Smoke hung in great palls over everything, making it difficult to keep to the road and burned the eyes of man and horse. Even Bittle was showing signs of alarm. His calm whispers changed to shouts. The team however, was still working well and overcoming the obstacles better than most.

Then they were confronted by not only a blocked road, but a blocked detour. A team of mules were stuck in deep sludge. An enemy gun team high on a distant hill saw the congestion and after a few sighting shots found the target. A cluster of shells fell on the road and showered everything trapped on the detour with shrapnel. The nearest shell burst not twenty yards from the team. Bud felt the great heaving, shattering impact and reared in fright, the whites of his eyes bulging, as he let out a loud terrified whinny. Tib took the full blast and after one great shuddering jump was silent and heavy, slumped in the harness pulling Bud deep into the mud. Bittle lay still and quiet – blown right over Bud by the blast. Bud felt a sharp pain in his shoulder where a splinter of hot metal had passed over the now dead horse and hit him. When Bud most needed them there were no comforting sounds from the horseman to reassure him.

Bud was trapped – held by the harness to the literally dead weight of his companion and the now very heavy light gun which was slipping deeper into the mire by the minute. All the other animals and men caught in the blast were dead or badly wounded. Bud struggled frantically to free himself, driven to a frenzy by the shells dropping nearby and by the sudden silence of the horseman and of his partner.

His forelegs were clear and he pushed up on them with all his might, but his stronger rear legs were trapped deep in the mud and held there by the combined weight of the gun and the dead horse. He clawed desperately but succeeded only in churning the mud to a broth into which he was sliding and sinking. He turned to Tib for help in the struggle to pull free. The other horse did not respond.

162

The shelling stopped and Bud gave up the struggle and lay still, changing position from time to time to ease the pain. No-one came near them. The wounded men screamed out in pain, but Bud being a horse, that dumbest of animals, suffered in silence.

The sun set and men appeared to rescue the wounded and to clear the path. When that was done a man noticed that Bud's eyes were following him around and realised that the horse was still alive. He unhooked what he could and cut at the harness, then summoned some other soldiers and started coaxing Bud, who, encouraged by the friendly voice, used his great strength to reinforce their efforts to extricate him. With a mammoth heave he pulled his mud-caked bloodstained body free. The freed horse, now ignored, looked around for his horseman; saw nothing he could recognise as Bittle, so bewildered, wandered in the direction which everything was moving.

Bud limped slowly along the road but broke into a trot every time he saw any men. He did not want to get involved further. Several times a soldier tried to catch his trailing harness, but Bud quickened his pace and easily evaded the tired men. So he ambled on listlessly for many miles until he was passing by a wooded lane a voice shouted a clear, "Whoa." Bud stopped instantly and stood stock still. A voice called, "Steady," in a calm tone and a soldier crawled from a ditch and pulled himself up by Bud's bedraggled harness. He patted the horse's nose in a way that made Bud realise this was a friend. With a, "Steady, steady," to ensure the stillness without which he could not hope to mount the tall horse, the wounded man pulled himself painfully up onto Bud's back and collapsed on the great horse's neck. Bud walked slowly on for many miles until he came to a depot he knew, there he turned in and stood patiently until the wounded soldier was noticed and taken carefully from his back.

Then the day came when there were no more shell bursts, no more flares and smoke, no more wounded to be brought back and no more guns to be taken forward. Everything and everyone was moving north towards the coast. Bud made the long journey to the Channel between the shafts of a lorry filled with happy singing soldiers. Every village they passed through was thronged with noisy cheering people. Bud was not disturbed by this modest level of sound and only when some happy child patted the friendly horse too near the hurt shoulder did he quiver. Some children threw a garland of flowers around his neck. Bud sensed that the end of his ordeal was near. His step became more sprightly.

In a seaside town men and animals parted. Bud was marshalled with other horses in a large field. He relaxed and grazed as he had done on the summer evenings in Buchan. No gambolling though and certainly no rolling on the ground – his shoulder was still too sore. Each day some of the horses were taken away and the day came when Bud was led from the field. Each horse was examined by a veterinary officer – some horses were sent one way, some the other. The vet patted, prodded and peered at Bud, nodded, hesitated, looked again at the wounded shoulder, changed his mind and shook his head.

A man took the halter and walked Bud slowly with a sorry line of injured horses. Bud followed trusting the gentle pull of the quiet man. A withered flower from the children's garland hung from his halter like a faded rosette. He could hear an occasional faint shot ahead, but after all he had been through this bothered him not at all. So the tired Bud, looking incongruously large, walked wearily towards the dark building, past a sign on which was printed the word – Abattoir. Happily he could not read it.

⬦⬦⬦⬦⬦⬦⬦⬦⬦⬦⬦⬦⬦⬦⬦⬦⬦⬦⬦⬦⬦⬦⬦⬦⬦⬦⬦⬦⬦⬦⬦⬦⬦⬦

Dictionary for Men

Profundity This is what many authors pretend to. Their works are like the catacombs – deep, dark, and empty.

Projects A game of hazard by which the honest man ruins himself and the knave ruins others.

Rouge A composition which has the property of rendering older women a little more ugly and younger women a little less pretty.

⬦⬦⬦⬦⬦⬦⬦⬦⬦⬦⬦⬦⬦⬦⬦⬦⬦

By Cyril Cook

You may have read elsewhere in this journal of our brigade, 5th Parachute Brigade, being one of the units to take over Singapore when the Japanese surrendered in August 1945. My battalion, 12 Para had made a seaborne landing in Malaya, but were withdrawn, back to our troopship, The Chitral, to sail on to Singapore, where we took over Alexandra Barracks.

When we had been at Alexandra a couple of days, I was told to get my platoon together and to move out along the Pasir Panjang Road to take over certain key installations, still being guarded by the Japanese in many cases. Two interesting things happened. As we rounded a bend in the road we were surprised to see drawn up on the dockside, a complete German U-boat crew, all in best whites and looking very smart indeed.

It is a fact that at what was I suppose a historic moment in my life, the only thing that I clearly remember saying was, "What the hell are you doing here?" Anyway, after much saluting I accepted the surrender of the U-boat, and being at a loss as to know what to do with the crew, told them they'd better stay on board until we got it sorted out. Apparently, the boat had been in the Indian Ocean when the European war ended, and the captain put in at the nearest port which was Singapore. I think it is probable therefore, that I am the only infantryman to take a U-boat prisoner, although I have to say that not only was there not a shot fired, but within a few days my lads were playing football with the German crew!!

Some twenty odd years later I had an order to build some plant for the American tractor people, Alliss Chalmers, in Mold, Flintshire. The Chief Engineer I was working with was named Hoffman, and over a meal one evening I broached the subject of where he came from. He told me he was born in what was then East Germany, was taken prisoner during the war, ended up in Liverpool, applied to stay in the UK as he had no-one close in East Germany, and didn't want to return there. He married a Liverpool girl, and became naturalised British. I said, "Where were you taken." He said he was an engineer officer on a U-boat which eventually surrendered to British Airborne troops in Singapore!! How's that for a small world!

The second interesting thing that happened was that I was to take over a rubber manufacturing plant, about a mile along the road, still being guarded by the Japanese. I took this over, and despatched the Japs under escort back to battalion HQ. The factory was a major supplier of bicycle inner tubes. In those days there were millions of bicycles in SE Asia and this was big business. However, on going around the factory I came to a shop where upon seeing thousands of moulds laying around I was left in no doubt that this was where the Japs made their condoms. On further examination we found hundreds of boxes of the completed articles; but the fascinating thing was that the Jap rubber technology must have been so basic that they had not been able to improve on 'inner-tube' quality – gossamer they were not!!

We stayed on this duty for two to three weeks, being based in an old police station. During this time we were visited by several ex-internees who, on being released from civilian camps, had come back to see what had happened to their factories and houses. They told us harrowing tales of their confinement; many of them had no trace of their wives and children, but lived in the hope of seeing them again. Others had established that in some cases their whole family had died of malnutrition, disease or maltreatment. Some of the stories they told of the inhumanity of their guards – often Korean, who were regarded as second class citizens even by the Japanese – were sickening. It should be remembered that many of the civilian internees were middle-aged and elderly people, and yet they were still made to work, to live under appalling conditions and to exist on very little food. The attitude of the Japanese was, "For years you have trodden on the backs of the coolies, now you are coolies," so they treated them with brutality and a total lack of any humanity. Despite this, they all said that the treatment they received was nothing compared to the mental anguish they endured, as year after year they wondered about the fate of their wives and children living under the same appalling conditions as they were.

The time came when the installations we were securing were taken over by owners or the police, and we returned to Alexandra. I was then given a very interesting job.

On Loan to the Malay Regiment

After my first task of securing certain key installations had been completed, I was told to return to HQ where the Colonel said, "Cookie, I've got a job for you." Throughout my years in the army I was known only by that nickname, my Christian name was never, ever used. Mind you it would be fair to say that I was probably known by many other, not so complimentary names from time to time, but that's a different matter. Some years after the war I met a great friend of mine of those days and he invited me to stay overnight with him in Dudley, which I had to visit. He introduced me to his wife, "This is Cookie," and she said,

"I can't call him that, what's his real name?"

To which Ian replied, "Well, we served together for the best part of four years and I just don't know!!"

However, back to Singapore. I was told that I was to take over a company of the Malay Regiment which was just being reformed. I was to take three of my sergeants and a couple of other NCOs. My first duty was to guard a huge arms and equipment dump built within gigantic caves tunnelled into the hills just north of Bukit Timah, on the road to Jahore. At the same time as carrying out this duty, we were to train the 200 men that I had been allocated, in modern army drill and operational procedures. Apart from a dozen or so Tamils, my men

Sgt Major Abdullah in 'undress' uniform

were all Malays. They had mostly been in the Straits Settlements Volunteer Corps, the Singapore Volunteer Corps or the pre-war Malay Regiment; the remainder were new recruits. Their leader was superb chap called Sgt Major Abdullah, who spoke very good English; ruled the men with a rod of velvet covered iron and made my job an absolute doddle.

We had one or two problems. The men were poorly paid, so to get to see their wives and families on their day off (and a good number of them were married), they had to spend a fair proportion of their pay getting into Singapore town, where most of them lived. Near the barrack block where they were normally housed, there was an empty godown on stilts, very dry and solid. I suggested to the Sgt Major that we could use it as married quarters provided the men were prepared to partition it off in their spare time. This was done, but the Sgt Major said, "Some of the men will require two cubicles."

Like an idiot I said, "What on earth for?" to which he replied,

"Well, some of us have two wives!"

They were of course, entitled to four wives but most of them could only afford one or at the best two. Anyway, it was eventually organised and the families moved in.

It was one of the most delightful times of my army service. The Malay soldier is a cheerful, friendly, and wonderfully loyal comrade as well as being (as they proved in the subsequent twelve year fight against Chinese communists), brave and resourceful. Malay ladies are utterly beautiful, graceful and have this demure presence which is so captivating. The children of course, were an absolute delight. They were forbidden to come near the military installations, but they used to ambush me on my way down the hill from my quarters to the Company HQ, jostling with each other as to which ones would hold my hands, and then disappearing as soon as we got in sight of the sentries. Needless to say, I used to raid the NAAFI for sweets for them, so I shall never know whether it was me or the sweets that was the attraction.

Talking of the NAAFI, it was here a very amusing situation arose. You are all well aware of the Stock Exchange, the Metal Exchange, and the Baltic Exchange etc; well I started a 'Beer Exchange!' I went to the NAAFI to draw my British NCO's beer allowance. Everyone was entitled to a one pint bottle of the famous Singapore 'Tiger Beer' each week. When I arrived I was told, "Oh yes, B Company Malay Regiment, 212 men, that's 212 bottles." I said not a word, but had the stuff loaded into my jeep trailer. If the irony of this has escaped you, it is that of course, Malays are strict teetotallers! As a result the British troops got a bottle a day and with the remainder we 'contracted' the Navy workshops down the road to provide us with a couple of pre-war generators they had found, check all the wiring in our quarters and at Company HQ, start it all up, and there we were, complete with ceiling fans, refrigerator, electric lights, even a pre-war 'mains operated' radio we found. The Colonel turned up without any warning one day (typical!) and said, "By Jove Cookie, you've got things organised here." Needless to say I didn't tell him the source of our organisational ability!

However, good things don't last forever. First the NAAFI cottoned on to what was happening when some goon in another company said he didn't want all his beer, and then I was called back to Battalion HQ where they had another job for me and my NCOs. So with tearful farewells from my Malay soldiers and their families, I very reluctantly left my first posting to the Malay Regiment.

John's Story

However, before I tell you about the 'Jurong affair', I would like to tell you John's story.

When I first took over my Malay soldiers, one of the NCOs – Corporal Osman came to see me and speaking good English asked me if I could take his eleven year old nephew as a bearer. The practice of officers and warrant officers having a servant, known as a bearer, was general throughout the army in the colonies and in India. I of course, had my own batman, Danny Murray (an Irishman about whom, incidentally, I could write a book to rival Jackie Collins any day), who had served with me all through the European campaign and was more a bosom pal than a servant. I asked the Corporal why the lad was not at school and not with his parents. He told me that the boy was nearly twelve years old and had therefore finished school. He then told me about the lad's upbringing. For my sins I cannot remember the boy's Malay name. For some reason I called him John and that is how I remember him.

John and his family lived in a kampong on the fringes of Singapore Town, a vastly different place to the Singapore we know today. Some two or three weeks after the occupation by the Japanese, three drunken Japanese soldiers wandered into the kampong and came to the small house where John, his mother and father and older sister lived. John was about eight at the time and his sister twelve. Before they could escape, the soldiers grabbed his mother and sister and proceeded to violate them. John ran off to fetch his father, working nearby. His father, armed with a machete, came racing back and attacked the soldier raping the young girl, but was shot and wounded by one of the three Japs. They then tied all three of them to the verandah railings and stabbed them to death with the long bayonets the Japs carried. John saw all this from his hiding place in the surrounding undergrowth. The Japs went away, the bodies were buried and John went to live with Corporal Osman and his young family.

I said I would take him on, but it would only be for a short while as soldiers rarely stay in one place for very long and I would not be able to take him with me when I was moved on.

He proved to be a lovely, gentle boy – always smiling. My room in the bungalow where I lived with my NCOs was kept immaculately clean. In that environment you always change your uniform two or three times a day, and he used to take my clothes to the married quarters and wash and iron them. My boots shone so that you could see your face in them, and when I awoke in the morning there was always hot water for me to shave with – a real luxury after years of shaving in cold water except when we were in barracks. The most amusing thing however, was that I had a rope bed put on my verandah for him, along with a blanket and mosquito net. The first night he was there, when I retired for the night, I heard him pull his bed across my door – no intruder was going to get into my room except over his dead body!

One day, I took him in the back of my jeep, Murray driving, to Battalion HQ. By chance when we arrived we met the Colonel coming out. Murray and I jumped to attention and I threw up one of my 18 carat salutes only to see the Colonel looking past me with the wisp of a smile on his face and when I looked round, there was John standing at the salute as good as any guardsman; he had obviously been watching the Malay soldiers being drilled back at camp. That evening I came back to HQ for mess night and the Colonel asked me about him. I told him the story and later he said to me, "Pop into my quarters before you go back, Cookie."

I should tell you that the Colonel was only pint sized. He was about seven and a half stone of leather and whip cord and as tough as old boots. When I went to his quarters, there was a little pile of shorts, PT vests and sundry other things and on the top of the pile a red beret with a Parachute Regiment cap badge. "Give these to the boy," he said, "the women can cut them to fit. Oh! and tell the boy that he only salutes with a cap on!"

I rarely saw John after that without his beret on – in fact I think he probably slept in it! Eventually we moved to Jurong, about ten miles away and he came with me. He became a great favourite of all the NCOs and was sublimely happy, probably for the first time in his life.

Then of course, came the dreadful, inevitable day of parting. War was brewing in Java, and we knew, as special service troops, we would be involved. We were given only days to up sticks and go, so I had to send John back to Corporal Osman. John cried his eyes out. The NCOs all gave him presents or money and when Murray drove him off in the jeep, many of them, battle-hardened toughs that they were, were wiping their eyes.

I never saw John again. I often wonder what happened to him, whether he became the soldier he so dearly wanted to be, and if so whether he was involved in the war against the Chinese communists, and whether he survived.

I do know one thing, my boots were never, ever the same again! And another thing, I shall never, ever, forget John.

The Jurong Story

At the Jurong radio station, I was told that one of the installations being guarded was a very large rice godown, and as a result of the starvation conditions obtaining in Singapore, raids were being made on the collection of warehouses by black market gangs. To quote the Colonel's words, and for that matter, his way of working, "Go and sort it out Cookie!"

I went to Jurong the next day and took over from the officer already there. The company was two thirds Malay, one third Chinese, and the CSM was an ex-jungle fighter named Chang. I walked into the company office which was in fact the gatehouse to the radio station and which doubled as a guard room. A young Eurasian about thirty years of age rose to his feet to greet me and told me his name was Da Silva and he was the company clerk. He was an amazing chap. He spoke fluent English, the Tamil dialect, Mandarin Chinese and Malayan. We immediately struck up a good rapport. I called him Mr Da Silva, and later he told me that I was the first British officer who had ever called him 'Mister'.

I had been told there were three installations to guard. The first was the godown complex, the subject of the raids, the second was the radio station and the third was a small internment camp. It was no ordinary internment camp; in fact it housed some 200 Korean 'comfort' girls brought to Singapore for the pleasure of the Japanese officers.

I allocated two sergeants to the platoons guarding the radio station and the godowns, and then I called in my sergeant, Hankey, from Rudheath, near Northwich in Cheshire, who had been with me all through Europe, and said to him, "I'm putting you in charge of the comfort girls' camp."

At the thought of this his eyes took on a glazed look, like someone who had heard he'd just won the pools.

I said, "That's the good news, the bad news is they've all got the clap or worse."

I then called Mr Da Silva in and asked him where the sergeant major was. He told me it was his day off. I asked him where he was billeted and was told he had taken over the bungalow at the entry to the radio station. I said I had noticed Chinese women there as I passed, to which Da Silva replied, "They were two of his girls."

I was a bit naïve in those days and said, "You mean his daughters?"

"No, sir," he said, "his women."

"If there were two of them, how many has he got?"

He indicated that there was something of a turnover in the personnel of the establishment.

I then went on to ask Da Silva about the raids on the godown. They had taken place at night, the sentries had been overpowered, yet there were two puzzling things that didn't add up. No shots were fired and no weapons were taken. Add to that the fact that to get to and from the godown, which was in a road with a dead end, the lorries had to pass the main guard room. Why wasn't the alarm raised? There were after all, very few trucks about in the middle of the night.

I said to Da Silva that I would see the Sergeant Major and get an ambush organised from inside the godown over the next few nights. Da Silva hesitated for a minute and then said it might be a good idea to keep the Sergeant Major out of my plans.

The penny dropped. So that's where the rice was going. I said, "Thank you for that information. Please leave a note for the Sergeant Major to be in my office at 8 o'clock tomorrow morning and to call a company parade at 10 o'clock.

The Sergeant Major came in promptly at 8 o'clock the next morning. He was of medium height, medium build, early thirties, very wiry and was wearing a beautifully tailored uniform, much better than my issue jungle green! He was wearing a gold wrist watch and a heavy gold ring on each hand. He had fought in Force 136 in the jungle during the Japanese occupation. Force 136 were ruthless fighters who had kept themselves alive for three and a half years by their wits. They were led by British officers, the other ranks being mainly Chinese and communists. He was obviously no fool.

We talked generally. I said I thought it unlikely the rice raiders would come back again and by that means dismissed the subject.

The Raid on the Godown

Leaving the Sergeant Major out of my confidences therefore, I made a plan. I sent Murray, my batman, to battalion HQ to draw three short-wave radio sets. One I had at the radio station where I was billeted, the second with the sergeant at the bungalow near the godown and the last with Sergeant Hankey with the 'comfort girls'. No native troops were told anything as we didn't know which of them CSM Chang had in his pay.

All three posts were manned by British ORs on a rota and at last, about four nights later around 2 o'clock in the morning, a lorry came down the road to the godown, was let in the main gate, and once it was in, the radios went to work. All fourteen of us moved in and caught the Sergeant Major and six civilians red-handed. I sent a runner to the local police station to collect the civilians, which they did, and then I locked the Sergeant Major in the store room at the radio station gatehouse which we used as a guard room. I fixed a padlock on the door and posted an armed Malay guard outside. That was a bad mistake.

At 4 am or thereabouts, Da Silva came and woke me up. He had taken it upon himself to check the guard room and found the padlock broken – the Sergeant Major gone. The guard was still there but said the sergeant major knew where his family lived and would have their throats split if he didn't let him out. I uttered one or two very well chosen words but I had only myself to blame.

Da Silva then said he thought he knew where the CSM would go, for he had a flat in Singapore town, in the red light district of all places. He had taken Da Silva there once. Murray got the jeep out and he, the sergeant, Da Silva and I dashed off. The hood was up and I told Da Silva to bring a blanket so that he could stay reasonably concealed when we got near the flat – I didn't want him to be a marked man.

Dawn was breaking when we reached Chinatown. Da Silva pointed out the flat which was on a first floor landing at the front of the building – the stairway to which started at the back of the building. I jumped out to run up the stairway and as I ran up I met the CSM on his way down at the half landing. I don't know who was more surprised. I had my revolver at the ready, a Colt 45 automatic, which I had 'won' a long time ago in Europe and said something dramatic like, "Put your hands up and walk slowly down." I knew that as he got near me he would kick – we had all been trained to do that, so I was ready for him. Suddenly, he held on to the hand rail and I saw his foot coming up. I moved to one side and caught his foot and gave a terrific lift which took his other leg off the ground and caused him to crash his head on the concrete stairway. Before he could move I struck my revolver in his mouth. Now I know this sounds terribly melodramatic – even a load of bull! But, cub's honour, I promise you it happened and I can assure you that nothing concentrates a man's mind more quickly that the thought that an itchy finger can blow one's brains out if one does anything silly.

We took him straight to the SIB HQ at SEAC where an old mate of mine, Jimmy Absalom, an ex Liverpool copper, was duty officer. He searched him and found he'd got a money belt with thousands of dollars, gold sovereigns and US twenty dollar gold pieces, all of which used to be dropped to Force 136.

Eventually Chang got ten years for black market offences and was put in Outram Road Gaol. As a postscript to this incident, Da Silva got a good job with SIB and subsequently at Mountbatten's HQ. I heard some time later from another old friend of mine, Sammy Isaacs, who stayed on in the police, that Chang escaped after about two years and joined the communists in the jungle. He was apparently killed in action near Port Dickson about 1951.

And so we said goodbye to our cushy billet at Jurong, and to our John, to face a very unpleasant six months in Java. Six months of Victorian style warfare that was really nothing to do with we British - but then, orders is orders!!

From Phyllis and Dennis Palmer (former residents of that beautiful island).

Every year sightings are made of the Tasmanian tiger, usually it is suspected, by people who have experienced something more than a passing relationship with Mr Fosters nectar of the gods. It is, or was, of course as the case may be, not a tiger, nor a cat-like tiger, but a dog-like animal, its proper name being a thylacine.

For thousands of years it lived in Australia, Aboriginal rock paintings being evidence of this, along with fossilised remains having been found throughout the country. However, over the centuries they seem to have become extinct on the mainland, being plentiful in Tasmania when the settlers arrived.

They were extremely wary of humans, living hidden away in the dense forest and undergrowth areas. Nevertheless, they did emerge from time to time to kill smaller live stock of the farming community, as a result of which, in 1830 the government of Tasmania introduced financial incentives to residents to eliminate them. These payments continued into the 20th century, by which time they were more or less wiped out.

In the early 1930s, the last Tasmanian tiger was captured and placed in the zoo at Hobart, where after a short while it died. So, is it extinct? Not if you believe the hundreds of people who would tell you they have seen one. So far, no-one appears to have been able to take a picture of one. Given the superb professionalism of those photographers we never see, but who provide us with all the brilliant wildlife programmes on the television, one would have thought that if there are any around they would by now have been spotted.

So, if you want to make a name for yourself, swap your Baby Brownie for a telescopic, analogic, digitallic instrument, or whatever they call them these days and go and find a Tasmanian tiger!

An Aboriginal Story from Sherry Sawarde, Australia.

At the end of the world, beyond the mountain where Baiame the Great Spirit lived, there was once a land inhabited only by women. These women were famous for their skill in making weapons – spears, boomerangs and nullanullas. They traded them with men for meat and possum skins which they needed for food and warmth, because there were no animals on the other side of Baiame's mountain. Hunters were equally glad to trade with them, for the weapons that the women made were the finest in the world.

It was difficult to reach the land of women. A vast waterless plain had to be traversed. Then the traveller could proceed no further because his way was barred by a deep lake. No-one was allowed to cross it. The traveller would place his load of meat and skins on the bank and retire. When he was out of sight the women would paddle across the lake in their canoes and exchange gifts for weapons. Yet in spite of the high cost and heavy labour, men were ready to go to such lengths for the sake of the beautiful weapons that conferred honour and dignity on those who owned them.

But there are always rebels who will not conform to the pattern set by others. Such a man was Wurrunah.

"It is ridiculous that men should be content to accept what women are prepared to give them," he complained to his brothers. "After all, they are only women, and men should be their masters." If no-one else will do it, I will show them how they ought to be treated."

"How can you possibly do this?" they asked him. "No-one is allowed to cross the lake. We shall not be able to approach them."

175

Wurrunah laughed scornfully.

"Men are always more clever than women," he replied. "Women make them weak by their wiles; but if a man is strong and determined he will always win. I'll tell you what we shall do. First, we must enlist the help of a number of trusty men. We will take no food, no rugs. Instead each man will bring with him a live animal. It doesn't matter what it is so long as it is alive."

"What will we do with the animals?"

"Never mind. You must trust me. I shall tell you what to do when we get there."

With some difficulty a band of men was gathered together and a curious procession set out across the sun-scorched plain. Wurrunah was in the lead, followed by his brothers. After them came a number of men, each carrying a live animal, well-roped and slung across his back.

When at length they reached the edge of the lake, Wurrunah gave his instructions.

"First of all I will turn my two brothers into white swans. They will swim across the lake. The women will notice them and, as they have never seen any birds except Wahn, and Mullian who is Baiame's messenger, they will launch their canoes and try to catch the birds. In the meantime I will go round the lake. When I reach the women's camp I will gather up their complete stock of weapons. This is sure to bring the women back in a hurry. As soon as I see them approaching, I will shout. When I have given the signal I want you to release your animals. The attention of the women will be distracted by them, and while they are going back and chasing the animals, I will make my escape. Then we shall meet and I shall distribute the weapons among you."

Wurrunah conjured up his most powerful magic. His brothers were changed into two beautiful white swans which glided across the calm lake waters. The women, amazed at the sight, launched their canoes and set off in pursuit.

Wurrunah crept up to the deserted camp and tied all the weapons he could find into a bundle, and placed them on his back. As he left the camp, doubled up under his load, the women saw him. They abandoned the chase of the white swans and paddled furiously towards the shore. Wurrunah gave a loud shout, and his men released the animals. Never had the women seen such a sight before. They leaped ashore and ran in all directions trying to capture them. In the confusion Wurrunah made his escape and passed the weapons over to his followers.

They felt no further allegiance towards him. Each man took his newly gained, treasured possession and hurried away to the plain and the long journey back to his home. But Wurrunah was elated with his success. He had conquered the redoubtable women, and felt power flowing through his body. He lifted his eyes up to the summit of the lofty mountain where it was said that the Great Spirit lived, and in a mood of defiance began to climb the sacred slopes. He had not gone far before black thunder clouds rolled across the peak, and vivid shafts of lightening lit the gloom. One spear-

point of light stabbed down the mountain-side and struck his body. Wurrunah fell to earth, bruised and defenceless. The newly won power ebbed away. The magic departed from him, and there was none left to turn his brothers back to their true form. Sobbing for breath, he turned his footsteps towards the plain.

As he plodded across it, Eagle-hawk soared far above him. Mullian had seen the clouds gathering and knew that his master had called him. His attention was caught by two white dots floating on the lake far beneath. He swooped down and was enraged to find that Baiame's preserves had been invaded by the swans. He attacked them fiercely, tearing out their feathers until they drifted across the water in a white cloud.

The swan brothers cried out to their brother for help. Wurrunah heard them from far away, but was powerless. He could only stand and wring his hands. Yet help was close at hand. The mischievous crows, the birds called Wahn, had made their nests in the sacred mountain, under the very beaks of their enemies the Eagle-hawks. They heard the despairing cries of the swans as they sank lower in the water, and took pity on them. They too were rebels against the might of Baiame. They plucked the black feathers from their plumage and scattered them over the swans until they were warm again, and able to swim ashore.

Baiame looked down and was amused at their temerity, and touched by their kindness to the swans; as a reward he allowed the swans to live and decreed that all the swans of Australia would have black feathers instead of white.

Elfie

Reg was digging away at his allotment, glad to be free of the ear-wigging he had received from his better half, Mable, (at least that's what she thought), and his three bolshie kids. As he tidied up around the rhubarb bed he thought he noticed a movement in amongst the greenery, and carefully with his fork, thinking it might be a hedgehog he knew, he pulled a large frond, or whatever it is they call rhubarb leaves, gently to one side, to find to his astonishment a little man. He was dressed in a green suit, had black boots and a black belt, the whole topped by a green bobble hat with a black tassel.

"Who are you?" Reg asked.

"Allo, man, I'm an elf," replied the little fellow, "you can call me Elfie."

Well, to cut a long story short, they met lots of times after that. Elfie led a lonely life being the only elf for miles around, and man Reg was glad to have some pleasant conversation for a change. Then one day, Reg came to the allotment – no Elfie, and this went on day after day, stretching to weeks, by which time he reached the conclusion that a dog or a fox must have made a meal of him.

A couple of years elapsed, with Reg getting greyer every year, when at the same rhubarb patch a voice called out, "Hello, man."

Reg looked round.

"Elfie, where did you spring from? Where have you been? I thought you were dead."

"I've been on my national service."

"National service? There's been no call-up since just after the war," Reg replied.

"Yes there is. Haven't you heard of the national elf service?"

❖❖❖❖❖❖❖❖❖❖❖❖❖❖❖

The Wheelbarrows – A True Story

A wheelbarrow manufacturer in the Midlands exported a container load of heavy builders' barrows to Dublin. They duly arrived; the container was opened, resulting in the manufacturer receiving an irate telephone call from his customer. Apparently, some wag in the despatch department in Walsall had chalked in each barrow:

Lift this end

The Liverpool Supporter – Probably a True Story!

The Liverpool supporter stood in the kitchen of his home at 11.30 on the day of the match, resplendent in his red and white scarf, red and white bobble hat and carrying his rattle with its red and white streamers. The following conversation ensued between him and his wife.

"I'll be off to the match now, luv."

"It's only 11.30, it doesn't start until three."

"Ah, but I want to get down the front of the Kop."

The wife paused for a moment.

"I think you love Liverpool more than you love me."

"The Kop fan paused for a moment.

"I think I love Everton more than I love you."

❖❖❖❖ ❖❖❖❖❖❖❖❖ ❖❖❖❖ ❖❖❖❖❖❖ ❖❖❖❖❖❖❖❖❖❖

Odd Jottings

Being a husband is a full-time job. That is why so many husbands fail; they cannot give their entire attention to it. *Arnold Bennett.*

❖❖❖❖ ❖❖❖❖❖❖❖❖❖ ❖❖❖❖

A woman is as young as her knees. *Mary Quant.*

❖❖❖❖❖ ❖❖❖ ❖❖❖❖❖❖❖ ❖❖

A man soon finds out what is meant by a 'spitting image' when he first tries to feed his infant!

❖❖❖❖❖ ❖❖❖❖❖ ❖❖❖❖❖ ❖❖

Thinking is the hardest work there is, which is probably the reason why so few engage in it. *Henry Ford.*

❖❖❖❖ ❖❖ ❖❖❖❖❖❖ ❖❖❖❖❖ ❖❖

The only sure-fire way to double your money is to fold it in half and put it in your pocket.

❖❖ ❖❖ ❖❖❖❖ ❖❖❖❖❖❖❖ ❖❖ ❖❖❖❖

From Volume 5 – The Chandlers. By Cyril Cook

Sasagawa called it a day, returned to the mine and then drove himself back in his two-seater Kurogane to his base at Frasers Hill, having arranged for the party to meet the next morning to go up to the escarpment. During the half hour drive he pondered as to what he should do next. He had no desire whatsoever to pursue these bastards into the jungle. He was a town man. He would not of course admit it to anyone, but he was petrified at the thought of, even more petrified at the sight of, and even more petrified than that at contact with the smallest spider. Then he told himself being petrified had no scale or degree, you were either petrified or you were not petrified. This internal line of reasoning however, did not mask the fact that he had been told there were spiders in the jungle big enough to snare birds the size of chickens which they would poison and eat. The very thought turned his bowels to vapour. He had in the past fought and conquered miscreants twice his size, but a spider dropping on him engendered total panic. He had been brought up on the Bushido principle that the greatest honour he and his family could achieve would be for him to die for his Emperor. Even when in an impossible situation, fighting against horrendous odds, he should, and would, save his last round for himself. He would never surrender. Somehow that Samurai code did not extend to combating spiders.

As a boy back in provincial Japan he had never liked spiders, even though they were only the common household or garden type which he could easily swat or tread upon. After his training he had been posted to southern Indo-China. He had a comfortable room in a military complex on the outskirts of Saigon, the room looking out over some bushes and miles and miles of paddy fields. One morning he awoke soon after dawn with a feeling he was being watched. Becoming fully conscious he found himself looking into the eyes of a gigantic spider, fully eight or nine inches across from leg-end to leg-end, crouched on the end of his bolster only a foot or so away. It had a yellowy brown speckled body, hugely thick legs covered in black hairs and intense, unblinking eyes. He was terror stricken, totally transfixed for many seconds.

At last he recovered his wits sufficient to enable him to let out a piercing scream, lift up his end of the bolster thus tilting the spider back against the mosquito net which enclosed the bed space, pulled the net up and saw the ghastly creature fall to the floor. As it scuttled to the corner of the room his bearer, a young Vietnamese boy came running in to see this mighty Japanese warrior cowering against the wall pointing toward the spider, now stationery in the corner. The lad walked over to it, swiftly bent down and picked it up, walked to the door and put it on the veranda outside. It disappeared down the steps and into the bushes.

"Why didn't you kill it?" screamed the fearless member from the hand of the Rising Sun.

The bearer understood not a word, but smiled, saying, "It was one of God's creatures!" It was then Warrant Officer Sasagawa became conscious of the fact that since he had been so tucked in beneath his net that a mosquito could not penetrate his sanctuary, the spider must have been in with him, crawling over him, even sucking his blood without him knowing, all night long! This thought so unnerved him he had to run to make the latrine, thereafter each night making a thorough search of the folds of the net and taking a flash-light into bed with him to finally convince himself, when he had tucked the net in, he was alone.

The degree of arachnophobia from which he suffered is not unusual, but he didn't know that. Most people suffer from it to an extent, few to the extreme of the warrant officer. It was something about which he could tell no other soul; he would lose face beyond retrieval.

◇◆◇◆ ◇◆◇◆◇◆◇◆◇◆◇ ◇◆◇◆◇◆◇◆◇◆ ◇◆◇◆◇◆◇◆◇◆◇◆

More Words of Wisdom

The best thing I know between France and England is – the sea. Douglas Jerrold c1830.

◇◆◇◆◇◆◇◆◇◆◇◆◇◆◇◆◇◆

It is impossible to enjoy idling thoroughly unless one has plenty of work to do. Jerome K Jerome 1889.

◇◆◇◆◇◆◇◆◇◆◇◆◇◆◇◆◇◆

Big brother is watching you. George Orwell 1949.

◇◆◇◆◇◆◇◆◇◆◇◆◇◆◇◆

There are few more impressive sights in the world than a Scotsman on the make. J M Barrie.

◇◆◇◆◇◆◇◆◇◆◇◆◇◆◇◆

What's in a Name

By Michael Pine-Coffin

Pine-Coffin is a name that I am very proud to be associated with, but there have been times when I have contemplated changing it to just Pine or Coffin. Most people on hearing the name for the first time will politely ask, "How do you spell that?" while trying to stifle a fit of laughter. Some crack jokes, alas most of these I had heard by the time I left school. Two noticeable exceptions were the nick names I had whilst in the army. The first was rather blunt but did show a degree of imaginative thought, as I was briefly referred to as 'Worm Bait', the second and longer lasting moniker was again far from subtle as I became known as 'Stiff'.

On leaving the army I joined the police and soon universally became known as Pinco. It is as a police officer that I have encountered most difficulties with my name. Some have provided much amusement. Once I arrested a man called Churchyard. This appeared on a court list as Defendant: A Churchyard. Officer in case: PC Pine-Coffin.

My involvement with sudden deaths has proved to have been one of the most sensitive and difficult areas. The following account occurred many years ago while I was serving at Carter Street police station in South East London, where I had to deal with a fatal accident in Camberwell Green.

A local drunk while in an intoxicated state, had failed to notice a large lorry which was descending upon him as he attempted to navigate his way across this major junction. He stepped off the pavement directly in front of the lorry. An eloquent account of the accident was given by the Southwark Coroner, Sir Montague Levine at the inquest. He stated the cause of death was caused by the compression of the cranium between the pneumatic tyres of a pantechnican and the tarmacadam road surface.

The ambulance crew managed to scoop what was left of the casualty off the road and he was driven the short distance to Kings College Hospital, where life was pronounced extinct. It transpired that the victim was an American citizen and his mother had been located in the States by Interpol. A state trooper was despatched to her address, but instead of informing her about the demise of her son, he stated that the metropolitan police wanted to speak to her. Without further ado the trooper phoned the control room and handed the phone over to the victim's mother, who was left to communicate with a slightly flabbergasted officer who had luckily been on duty on the day of the accident, and it was left to him to pass on the sad news.

A few days later the victim's mother flew over to London and I was asked to accompany her to the mortuary to identify her son and then to accompany her to his flat to retrieve his personal belongings. I did not relish this task and had serious doubts as to how she was going to be able to identify her son. The mortuary staff had done a magnificent job. The casualty had been placed behind a glass screen and resembled an Egyptian mummy. The only part of his face not covered was his nose, which protruded from the bandages like an upturned keel of a yacht. This is the one and only time that I have ever seen a body identified by its nose. I was extremely grateful that she had not asked to take a closer look at the body.

The depths to which her son had sunk soon became apparent when we arrived at his flat, a filthy squat located on the North Peckham estate. There was no reply to my repeated knocking, so I put my shoulder to the door which turned out not to be locked, but jammed shut by the amount of rubbish which had accumulated behind the door.

Strewn all around were discarded belongings and empty beer cans, it looked as if the place had been ransacked. Then there was movement amongst the rags. My first thoughts were rats, but then a head suddenly appeared. It was a man called Joe, who could normally be found in the locality in a drunken stupor shouting abuse at all and sundry. He was not very pleased to be woken up and started on one of his tirades. However, his strong Irish accent made it difficult to understand what he was saying, but it was enough to frighten the hell out of the victim's mother. As a probationer I had arrested Joe on many occasions and rather liked to think I could communicate with him. I remember saying, "Joe, just give us five minutes and we will be gone, please wait outside." He dutifully obeyed and the family thought I was wonderful. They were unaware that he was so drunk that he did not know where he was or what he was doing as he staggered out of the door. The family managed to gather a couple of dog-eared photographs off the floor and stated that they were happy that there was nothing else that they wanted from the flat.

We then returned to the car and the victim's mother said to me, "I cannot praise the metropolitan police highly enough, you would not get this service anywhere else in the world. I want to write to the commissioner and tell him how wonderful you all have been. I know the name of the inspector and that your name is Mick, what is your full name so that I can put it in the letter."

I now went into my well practised routine that we mere constables were referred to by our numbers, all she needed to do was state PC 434 M was the officer involved. In the majority of cases this routine worked well but this lady would settle for nothing less than my full name. Reluctantly I told her, knowing that it would not go down well. There was an uneasy silence; I got my warrant card from my pocket as she said, "Is this some sort of sick English joke?"

I assured her that I was deadly serious and showed her my warrant card, then it dawned on me that perhaps 'deadly serious' was not the best words to have used.

Needless to say, a letter never arrived at the police station.

Another Pine-Coffin – From Cyril Cook

When I returned to 7 Para from Octu, I found my new colonel was Lieutenant Colonel Geoffrey Pine-Coffin, Michael's grandfather. The Pine-Coffins were a well known Devonshire family with considerable military service connections. Michael's father was a colonel in the Devons, his uncle, later a colonel in the Paras. The following is an extract from our colonel's personal diary relating to a practise jump carried out prior to Normandy.

My Private Dropping Zone

On an exercise I was put out too soon and came down in the churchyard at Durweston near Blandford (x marks the spot).

Everyone else thought this very funny and said it was the right place for a Pine-Coffin anyway, but I found it very alarming as the tombstones were very solid and some had spiked railings round them too.

I thought I was bound to break a leg at least, but actually got a light landing, my chute remaining draped on the tree.

Padré Ewen MacDonald wrote a fascinating book entitled 'Padré Mac – The Man from Harris'. The following is an account drawn from his story relating to the same Geoffrey Pine-Coffin when he was a major. With my sincere compliments I reproduce it from Padré Mac's excellent and most readable book.

184

Extract from Padré Mac

In early November, the Parachute Brigade, 1st, 2nd and 3rd Battalions, entrained to Liverpool. Once again, from that busy sea port, we set sail into the unknown. This time it turned out to be North Africa.

I found parachuting both frightening and exhilarating. A few years ago I watched Prince Charles being interviewed on American TV by a woman journalist. After many questions, some of them blasphemous or banal, she suddenly asked, "Prince, what is the most frightening experience of your life?" Without hesitation he answered, "My first parachute jump." I agree.

The unremitting tension was now and again relieved by the odd comic incident.

If I remember rightly, Major Pine-Coffin was B Company commander in the 1st Battalion. Well over six feet in height, he sported an enormous walrus moustache. I had struck up a friendship with the Adjutant and at least once a week used to drop into his office for a chat and a cup of tea.

This particular afternoon as my friend and I were exchanging rude remarks, the phone rang. It was Major Pine-Coffin clamouring for a batman. Covering the mouth of the instrument with his hand, Jock, my rude friend said, "Murdo, as you are absolutely idle till next Sunday, look up the battalion list and suggest a suitable batman for Major Pine-Coffin."

This I did and to my astonishment I came across the name of Private Undertaker. "Oh this is terrific," I shouted.

The Adjutant put down the phone and asked, "Pray tell what is terrific."

"Listen Jock," I said. "I've got the perfect batman for Major Pine-Coffin. His name is Private Undertaker."

In all my experience as a preacher, I have never had a more enthusiastic and ecstatic response. Wielding all the clout of his office, the Adjutant despatched a runner to summon Private Undertaker into his presence.

In no time, a compactly built, bandy-legged, private soldier appeared and saluted the Adjutant with impressive panache. "Sir," he asked, "what have I done wrong?"

"Nothing," answered the Adjutant. "On the contrary, I want to make life more comforting and more interesting for you, Undertaker. Would you be prepared to become a batman to the commander of B Company?" Then more persuasively than Dale Carnegie in his best seller, 'How to Win Friends and Influence People', the Adjutant sold him the job – exemption from Sunday chores and parades etc, etc.

185

The following morning before breakfast, Private Undertaker reported to Major Pine-Coffin. The Major was still in bed when his batman brought him a mug of tea. He yawned.

"You're my new batman. What's your name?"

"Undertaker, sir," was the answer. To begin with Pine-Coffin refused to believe it, but later adjusted to reality.

General Browning, who commanded the 1st Airborne Division, imaginatively grasped the propaganda advantages of this amusing relationship between Major Pine-Coffin and Private Undertaker. In the 1st Airborne Division's newsletter there were some arresting headlines. 'Pine-Coffin and Undertaker land in North Africa.' 'Pine-Coffin and Undertaker dropped in Italy.' However absurd, the Pine-Coffin and Undertaker camaraderie, in its own comic way helped morale.

❖❖❖❖❖❖❖❖❖❖❖❖❖❖❖❖❖❖❖❖❖❖❖❖❖❖❖❖❖❖❖❖

A Very BRIEF and Unreliable History of the GREAT GAME

By Frederick Starkey

This is not so much a potted history as a potty history of the Great Game. (A potty history, by the way, is not a history of potties. Rather it is a history which should carry a health warning if it is to be read, imbibed, smoked or otherwise ingested by sane people. Or should that be an ill-health warning?).

(This is a bad start. It is already clear that this writer is parenthetically addicted. Not to worry. I am now wearing a patch which is a substitute, containing, as it does, a smattering of,.-* and". From now on parentheses will be out). (Hopefully).

The Great Game has left its mark. Wander around Flintshire and sooner, or not so sooner, you will come across one of these huge piles of stones. While some of them are higgledy, if not piggledy, others clearly evidence intelligent design, so they are not the geological extrusions you might have first thought them. Indeed for the more romantically minded of us they might be considered noble structures suggesting knightly doings, blah, blah.

They are in fact the decaying archaeological footprints of the Great Game as it was once played in Wales a handful of centuries ago. The Game, by the way, was not played with a leather or plastic ball, neither spherical nor ovoid. It was usually played with pointy things, although many more creative players might use any blunt objects as long as it weighed about half a sheep.

The Great Game was not encumbered with complicated rules and there was no ruling body to speak of. However, there was a fairly well established format. Instead of each side trying to get control of a ball, the basic idea was to claim the pitch. The pitch was of course a piece of real estate, but it could vary in extent from the size of a large back garden to several thousand square miles. The game was played by each side launching arrows at each other, the air rent with dissonant curses. The match didn't end with someone blowing a whistle. It ended more or less when one side had no players left, or at most so few that they had no option but to concede, or perhaps to run away.

One series of matches which was enjoyed – if that is the right expression, for a few hundred years was between Welsh and English teams. This didn't excluded local matches because, you know, it wasn't unusual for your little brother to raise a side and try for half of your pitch, just when you thought you had established your status as champ in those parts. The high points of the season, however, were the English versus

Welsh matches. Now the English teams could be a bit sneaky really because they had a very good tactic; they would build a very large stone wall around their goal area, where severely blunted the Welsh arrows. The Welsh had their moves as well. They would hide behind a tree or a large rock or even behind some wretched hovel. This meant the English had to fire at trees or rocks, which is a bit silly when you think about it, although not as silly as firing at a large wall with a few slits in it.

One of the joys of the Great Game was the latitude it permitted to the players in the matter of tactics. Consequently there were very few fouls but plenty of free kicks, well, kicks anyway, not to mention other grievous bodily harm. For instance, if you were a complete lolly with a bow and arrow, you could throw a spear. Of course, while spear throwing was very good exercise and aesthetically a good deal more impressive than arrowing, it was definitely less accurate. Also, one spear was enough to carry; so once you had thrown it you were a bit stuck.

We talk about the English and Welsh of course, but who were they? The dubiously labelled Celts who dotted themselves around Wales probably originated in the first place from beyond the Alps, and if there is something you might like to call a Welsh physical type you might say Mediterranean, particularly Spanish, rather like Pablo.

As for the English, 'mongrels' doesn't come near it. From the time of the melting of the ice successive visitors had arrived, playing the Game in its more primitive forms – raping, burning, squatting, colonising the pitches. Among early arrivals, possibly the first, were people known as the Beakers. They were potters it is believed, so finding no-one around in Stoke at that time some of them may have made for Buckley or Rhuabon. Who knows? The fact is, over successive centuries the resident teams in England had lost so many matches to the Europeans that most teams could have called themselves the Jutes, the Picts, the Normans, the Danes. They could have given themselves some great team names. The Normans United comes to mind. The Romans of course kept themselves to themselves and called everybody British.

The Welsh may have been largely migrants pushed west by the Romans and others, having lost their pitches in asymmetric matches. The whole picture is very confusing, but gradually over the centuries, things got more organised, games between local teams, who may have had only a poor grasp of who they were, giving way to more regional affairs. The Normans were good organisers and it was they who put the Game on a more quasi-international basis.

You shouldn't think these guys were always playing the Great Game. Sometimes the weather was too bad, or they needed to spend time checking their kit and sharpening the pointed bits. There would be time for some ritual bowing of a different sort. It was a case of, "OK you're too good for us. Just let me be a Prince." This kind of accommodation could well have been resorted to in Flintshire and even in Gwynedd where the players were a feisty lot and much given to feelings of independence.

And now look at the technology, itself a massive field of study. Inevitably it seems, this Game became over the years more and more explosive in character. Arrows gave way to gun powder. Guns became cannons and visa versa. You could overwhelm a very large pitch from a distance, sometimes without even seeing one of the opposing side, as gun platforms and lobbing devices took to the air. Whole cities could be burned away at the whim of some crazy team manager or owner as whole nations, and indeed groups of nations, decided to be world champions.

This Game has become a monster which threatens the very survival of the world. The big teams now have enough mass extermination devices, about six thousand in fact, enough to destroy every trace of civil society in the world several times over.

(God help us).

Old London

About a million years ago Ludgate Hill, on which St Paul's Cathedral stands, was under the sea. When digging the foundations of the Cathedral, Sir Christopher Wren, at that time plain Mr Wren, made many interesting discoveries. Under the bell, or north west tower he found clear evidence of a Roman burial ground and a Roman pottery, in which were lamps, bottles and urns. Far beneath these he found clay, sand, sea shells and a beach, indicating the hill was at one time under the sea.

The two City livery companies traditionally associated with the annual ceremony of 'swan upping' are the Dyers and the Vintners. Each July, half of the young swans along the Thames are 'nicked' on their beaks to show to which of the two companies they belong – the other half are Royal swans.

If you noticed a marble slab which lies face upwards in the grass to the right of the pathway leading to the main door of St Margaret's, Westminster, you would probably assume it to be a gravestone of some description. It is however marked T II, and is a Roman boundary stone.

189

The origins of 'Parliament' go back nearly a thousand years to William the Conqueror. He would discuss affairs of state with his 'Lords Spiritual and Temporal' in the 'parlour' of his home. These talks eventually became known as 'Parliaments'.

In the beautiful Wren church of St James, Garlickhythe, in London's fair city, there resides a most unusual person. Known as 'Jimmy Garlick', he is a well-preserved mummified corpse in an excellent state of preservation. He was discovered in 1880 when the church authorities were clearing out the bones of past parishioners buried there, to be re-interred elsewhere.

Now, if the corpse had been embalmed, he must have been a person of some importance, was the general opinion. Was he once a Lord Mayor or a wealthy city merchant or banker? In any event it was decided it could not be removed with the other remains. There were apparently difficulties regarding re-burial elsewhere, and as a result of the difficulty of finding the money to sort out all the problems, Jimmy Garlick is still there! With one small difference; whereas before 1880 he was in full view of the worshippers, now he is tucked away out of sight – but still there until eventually someone remembers him again and has the cash to find out why he cannot be removed and reburied.

I.   Dianne with 'Barra'

II.   The Teewah Coloured Sands

III. M.V. Rakaia

The Swallow Family – Bickerton, Cheshire

IV. Photo: Ann Lambert

V. The Glass House Mountains

VI. Beerwah – The Mother of the Mountains

VII.   Gwen and Amber

VIII.   John Bury in a Canadian Winter

IX.   Aboriginal Dancers

X.   Playing the Didgeridoo

The Changi Murals

XI. The Nativity

XII. The Last Supper

XIII.   The Crucifixion

XIV.   The Ascension

XV.   St Luke in Prison

XVI.   The Tynwald Ceremony (Photograph Derek Croucher)

XVII.   The Tynwald Chamber

The Lookers

XVIII.

The Looker and his Sheep

Romney Marshes and Lookers Hut

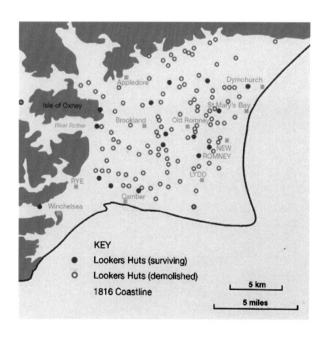

**Lookers Huts Map
Early 20th Century**

The Red Ship

XIX. St Katherine's Dock. 1956 – above. 2006 – below.

The Warrior on the Roundabout

XX.   Thomas Gould's Tomb

XXI.   The Battle of Busaco, where Tomas Gould fought

More Claim Howlers from John Tester

- "I told the police that I was not injured, but on removing my hat found that I had a fractured skull."

- "I was sure the old fellow would never make it to the other side of the road when I struck him."

- "The pedestrian had no idea which way to run as I ran over him."

- "I saw a slow moving sad faced old gentleman as he bounced off the roof of my car."

- "The indirect cause of the accident was a little guy in a small car with a big mouth."

- "The telephone pole was approaching. I was attempting to swerve out of the way when I struck the front end."

- "The gentleman behind me struck me on the backside. He then went to rest in a bush with just his rear end showing."

- "I had been learning to drive with power steering. I turned the wheel to what I thought was enough and found myself in a different direction going the opposite way."

- "I was backing my car out of the driveway in the usual manner, when it was struck by the other car in the same place it had been struck several times before."

From My Australian Representative

My dear friend Phyllis Palmer has sent me the following clangers articulated mainly by well-known Australian politicians. Her husband, Dennis, is a retired legal-eagle in the Canberra megalopolis who used to keep a pet huntsman spider named 'Fred'. Now, if that isn't one-upmanship I don't know what is!

The Clangers

- They are spending money like wounded bulls.

- This is now a city centre that has got too big for its boots.

- It's time to pull the hat trick out of the box.

- One must draw a line in the sand and build a platform under it.

- We can't extend it in perpetuity much longer.

- This is one of the sacred cows coming home to roost.

- They have egg all over their faces from head to toe.

- This is the hot potato coming up over the horizon.

- The Mayor of Adelaide publicising tourism to the city. "If you come to Adelaide, you'll be blown away!"

- *And a couple of newspaper cuttings.*

- "Barry Jones and his elk exploited a constitutional provision ...... "

- "She said this block was an example of what many developers were doing – raising blocks from end to end."

- "The new library has been billed as state-of-the-art, but the collection would also increase in regards to more old fashioned resources such as books.

Thank you Phyllis & Dennis.

More Tommy Cooper Howlers

Our ice-cream man was found lying on the floor of his van covered in hundreds and thousands. Police say he topped himself.

Man goes to the doctor with a strawberry growing out of his head. Doc says, "I'll give you some cream to put on it."

Two elephants walk off a cliff ..... Boom, Boom!

You know, somebody actually complimented me on my driving today. They left a little note on the windscreen. It said, 'Parking fine'. So that was nice.

Ireland's worst ever air disaster occurred early this morning when a small two-seater Cessna plane crashed into a cemetery. Irish search and rescue workers recovered 1826 bodies so far.

By David Jones. Formerly Tutor of Modern Languages.

The life of a missionary in the nineteenth century was, to say the least, a tough one. Inhospitable climates, the necessity of learning a completely alien language and the constant menace of disease were but starting points of the problems surrounding the men who felt the call to go abroad to preach the Gospel in the more distant parts of the planet. For their wives, somewhat less hardened and perhaps lacking some of their husbands' sense of divine mission, the problems and dangers were even greater. When children were born to them their worries could only increase. What kind of education could they receive in those lands?

Thus it was that the London Missionary Society (the missionary arm of the Congregational Church) and the Baptist Missionary Society founded two schools for the children of their far-flung workers – Walthamstow Hall, now established in Sevenoaks for their daughters, and Eltham College for their sons. The latter also started at Walthamstow but later moved to Mornington Crescent, then to Blackheath and finally in 1912 to its present site in Mottingham, South East London.

In those days travel was slow and the missionary outposts could only be reached by sail, followed in many cases by a long trek inland on foot. Consequently the boys of the Home and School for the Sons and Orphans of Missionaries would arrive at the age of between six and ten and not expect to see their parents again until their father's next furlough seven years later. After a further seven years had elapsed they had left the school and were full adults.

There were no holidays. Many of the children were cared for by grandparents, uncles and aunts, or guardians, but some did not enjoy this comfort and spent twelve months of the year in the school. Not for nothing was it called 'Home and School'. (The word 'orphans' in the name was not used lightly either, though it seems that the word could be applied to boys who had lost only one parent). In some years the boys remaining in the school throughout the summer holidays were taken *en masse* for a fortnight to the seaside, and in 1868 a certain Mr Joseph Crossley of Halifax undertook to give the sum of £50 to each of the two mission schools to fund these holidays. Unfortunately he died after the first one had taken place.

Today things have changed. Missionaries are few and far between and travel around the globe is fast and easy. Neither school takes boarders any longer, but the Christian tradition is still preserved and high standards of industry, loyalty and service are still expected.

◇◆◇◆ ◆◇◇◆◇◆◇◇ ◇◆◇◆ ◇◆◇◆

Now read the stories of former pupils:

George Burnett Stalworthy: From the paradise of Samoa in 1855
T Victor Jones: From the deep jungle of Chandraghona, East Bengal in 1926.
Arthur Wyatt: From Shanxi Province, China after the Japanese invasion. 1938.

George Burnett Stalworthy's Story – School for the Sons of Missionaries 1855

This account is drawn from a private publication by George entitled 'Reminiscences', presented to the Old Boys Association of the School for the Sons of Missionaries in 1907, at a London hotel.

George's father was an ordained missionary on the island of Upolu in Samoa in the South Seas. He had been appointed there in 1834 and in 1844 married the daughter of Revd C Wilson of Samoa. George, the younger, was born in 1845 and it is believed his mother died in childbirth.

Two years later his father married Mary Ann Darling, daughter of the Revd David Darling of Tahiti.

George was nearly ten when in 1855 he set sail from the sunny strands and 'coconut' palms of Samoa for the grime and cold of London. The ship which would take him and some twenty odd other youngsters collected from various missions on Polynesian islands was a 300 ton barque named the 'John Williams', commanded by Captain Morgan. This comparatively small craft was to sail the 26,000 miles to Britain, and to round the Cape Horn in the process. It would take six months, another six months to return, therefore the parents waving their sons goodbye would not know they had safely arrived in London for a year, perhaps more. The words, "For Christ's sake and the Gospel's," held a particular meaning when this long period of anxiety was considered. George would never see his father again, who died in Malua in 1859 at the age of fifty. His step-mother returned to England in 1872.

Landing at London docks must have been a pronounced cultural shock to a small boy. He writes, "Our first experience of a railway station alarmed us. It was one of those dock stations where the booking office is built on a bridge over the line, and while we were waiting a fast train came roaring through, enveloping us in white smoke. We quaked from head to foot and crowded round our tutor."

Soon he was introduced to the School for the Sons of Missionaries, then situated in Mornington Crescent, London, where he arrived with his uncle in a 'growler'. I have not as yet been able to identify this type of conveyance!

The matron was a Mrs Flower, the widow of a missionary who had died in India. She used to tell the boys he had 'gone to glory'. She was inevitably nick-named by her young charges as 'Glory'. She had a sure-fire cure for coughs and colds comprising diluted aconite. Aconite is one of the buttercup family having a poisonous root. The drug is obtained from this. The boys would dutifully each take a spoonful of the mixture. It was the same spoon, George reports, "That went in and out of all our mouths, so whatever microbes harboured on our glands got well mixed up!"

Food was basic. Each day breakfast consisted of five lumps of thick bread and thick butter, which apparently he thoroughly enjoyed. On occasion they received porridge in turn, which he found quite inedible, "Crowded with big lumps, as big as nutmegs and covered in sky-blue!"

I have not been able as yet to establish what 'sky-blue' was. On porridge morning you were breadless, unless therefore, you could swap your porridge for a slice of bread out of someone else's five slices, you went hungry.

At breakfast at Mornington Crescent, they had to recite The Commandments – in Latin! He insisted he had hated The Commandments from then on. When the school moved to Blackheath, The Commandments were switched to the Book of Proverbs.

And so the months passed. At holiday times most of the boys would go to relatives. Many had no relatives in Britain, they therefore stayed on at the school – it was not only a school for the sons of missionaries, but also a home for the sons of missionaries.

George left at the age of sixteen, went to New College, was ordained and served as a congregational minister from 1873 to 1910. He died at Billingshurst in Sussex in 1923 aged seventy seven. His abiding memory of being at the School for the Sons of Missionaries was a visit by Doctor Livingstone, who sat him on his lap and spoke kindly to him; otherwise there was little or no kindness there.

✧✧✧✧·✧✧·✧✧✧·✧✧·✧✧·✧✧·✧✧·✧

A Small Boy at Eltham 1926

This is the story of T Victor Jones who was at the School for the Sons of Missionaries from 1926 to 1932, and who sadly passed away only this year as I write – 2007. The school had moved from Mornington Crescent to Blackheath, and when Victor joined it had (since 1912), become Eltham College.

His original home, The Baptist Mission House at Chandraghona in East Bengal was, to say the least of it, in the wilds. From Britain one made a six week journey to Calcutta, an uncomfortable journey by train to Chittagong, followed by several days by river boat up to Chandraghona. The mission comprised a church, a hospital, a school, a leper colony, and of course the pastor's bungalow.

In addition to the help in the bungalow there were, to quote Victor's account, "Other occupants," but these were of an unofficial nature. Chief of those were the snakes that lived in the roof. Every now and then one would fall to the floor, when there would be loud cries for the servants to despatch the creatures with sticks kept by for the purpose. Scorpions were ever present, and white ants which ate away the timber from the inside, the problem being you only discovered their presence when you leaned on an upright on the verandah which promptly gave way!

They lived right on the edge of the jungle and were ever aware of the cries of the animals, particularly the blood-curdling shriek of the jackal. But the main danger was the mosquito. He says, "We had the mosquito net and a goodly supply of quinine to thank for our survival."

His father's first wife died of a tropical germ, and his second wife, Victor's mother, caused his parents early return when she contracted a streptococcal infection, which nearly claimed her life.

In 1926 Victor's father's five year tour of duty was over and they returned to England, Victor to go to Eltham College, whilst his parents would return to India after a year's leave.

So Victor settled into Junior House, and then moved up to Senior House. It was a great deal more comfortable and pleasant than our George Stalworthy had enjoyed, if that is the word, in Mornington Crescent and Blackheath seventy years before. Mind you, seventy years after Victor left the changes were even greater. There were **GIRLS** in the sixth form! In addition, his holidays were spent with relatives in Cambridge or the Isle of Wight, which he loved. To illustrate there is nothing new to sectarian intolerance he tells the story of:

"Grandpa used to spend a great deal of his time sitting in front of the house greeting the passers by. One Sunday evening he observed a group of Roman Catholics on their way to Mass and was heard to shout, 'Quick, quick, mother! Get all the children in.' He was not going to risk his grandchildren being contaminated!"

Victor's mother and father came back to England in 1932. His waiting at the station to meet someone he had not seen for years is described thus:

"I felt strangely passive, bereft of emotion. The train came in. I picked out my father but the blood ties had been diluted by time and distance. The man who was biologically my father had the air of a stranger."

Of his mother he notes:

"When I was re-united with my mother, the bond that had previously existed had weakened. I was never able to love her as I had loved her before. It was not that I did not want to; I had lost the capacity."

This consequence must have been all too common in the days when children of service people, colonials, Empire administrators, and of course missionaries were uprooted at the age of eight to be sent home to be educated, unable to fly back for holidays as they would today.

Victor went on to serve in the Royal Navy through World War Two.

❖❖❖❖❖❖❖❖❖❖❖❖❖❖❖❖❖❖

Arthur Wyatt – School of the Sons of Missionaries 1940

Arthur's father was born in 1895, the son of a Baptist minister in Northamptonshire. During the Great War he served with the Royal Army Medical Corps in Italy as an apprentice to a dentist. On demobilisation, he joined the London Hospital in Dentistry, won a scholarship to practise medicine and qualified as a doctor. He spent one year as a doctor in England, then volunteered to be a medical missionary in China.

In China he married an English teacher - Edith, and in 1928 Ted, the eldest of their four children was born, followed by daughter Ruth, Arthur and George. All three boys came to Eltham in due course, whilst Ruth was sent to Walthamstow Hall in Sevenoaks, the sister school of The School of the Sons of Missionaries.

Ted became a missionary doctor in the Congo, George a doctor in Nigeria, and later Libya, then becoming a consultant epidemiologist in Papua New Guinea.

Arthur was born in Hornsey during his mother's leave in UK and returned to China in 1933. They lived in Taiyuan, the capital of the province of Shanxi, a coal mining area. In 1937 the Japanese invaded China, and by 1938 it was clear they would overrun the province. Although, as British citizens they would be neutrals, Arthur's father decided that Edith, Arthur and Ruth should leave and make for Hong Kong, he travelling with them half the way.

It was not to be an uneventful journey. At one stage the train was attacked by Japanese aircraft, so they decided to change their plan and make their way to Peking. At Scheefoo they boarded a small ice-breaker and made their way to Peking, leaving the father to return to the mission.

That was the last time they saw him.

By this time the province was held in pockets by Chinese irregulars. When Dr Wyatt returned to Taiyuan, he found some missionaries who wished to return to a town some distance away which they had evacuated previously because of the fighting. He volunteered to accompany them. They boarded a small lorry, and in the journey were shot up by one of the irregular groups, thinking presumably they were Japanese. A lady missionary was killed instantly, all jumped out of the lorry to take refuge in the nearby ditch, when Dr Wyatt realised the Chinese driver had been hit. Leaving the comparative safety of the ditch he ran out on to the road to drag the driver out of the vehicle, and was killed instantly.

After a good deal of shouting the remainder of the party were able to establish their identities and the bodies were taken back to Taiyuan and buried in the European cemetery.

In the meantime, Edith and the children secured a passage on the SS Rawalpindi and returned to England. Arthur was then sent as a boarder to Eltham, where he studied until 1950 when he left to do medicine at Barts, qualifying in 1955, and becoming one of London's top surgeons.

We move forward now to 1990. For some years Arthur and his wife Margaret had been trying to get permission from the Chinese authorities to visit the town where Arthur was born and to see his father's grave. During the 'cultural revolution' all churches had been closed, but with the ending of that horrific period of China's history Christianity was growing rapidly. Churches were full, both Catholic and Protestant.

At last an entry permit was granted, the first visits strictly controlled. They took photographs of the house where Arthur had been born and his father's hospital, the officials demanding to know why they wanted to see these places. Eventually they got the go-ahead. The hospital was now three times larger than in Arthur's father's day, but as Arthur reported later it was poorly equipped, the surgical instruments primitive, the whole, fifty years out of date. Upon his return therefore, he raided his own hospital, The Brook at Blackheath, London, and neighbouring hospitals, for all surplus and obsolete equipment and over the next years took suitcases of surgical tools to his father's hospital.

Did they find his father's grave? Well they did and then they didn't. The officials had hedged as only communist officials can over imparting the information as to the whereabouts of the cemetery. Eventually he succeeded in establishing where it was, only to be presented with a great sadness. During the Cultural Revolution all the headstones had been smashed, the site cleared, subsequently an electronics factory had been built on it. How could people do that?

We end on a happy note. When Arthur and Margaret found the house in which he lived as a young child, they were invited upstairs to the sitting room. There, at the top of the stairs was a little wooden gate which Arthur's father had made and fitted so that the toddler did not tumble down the stairs. It was still there and was still being used!

❖❖❖❖❖❖❖❖❖❖❖❖❖❖❖❖❖❖❖❖❖❖❖❖❖❖❖❖❖❖❖

The Talent Contest

By Bob Adams

(George enters a small tatty room with posters of unknown or forgotten entertainers all over the wall. He looks at them. He reads).

"Salome and the Dance of the Seven Snakes." Ugh.

"Gordini and his Goalkeeping Goat." I bet they didn't let any Moroccans in that night.

"Captain Coker and his chorus of Cockatoos.

I think Arthur and the Alarming Alliterating Adman has escaped from the Asylum."

He looks around the room in distaste. He paces about then pulls himself together and takes a piece of paper out of his pocket.

"Right, on in ten minutes. One more run through."

He pulls back his shoulders, and starts talking bright and breezily. He glances at the piece of paper from time to time.

"Hello everyone, and welcome to this evening of fun and glamour. The management has asked me to extend a special welcome to all of you who have had to leave your loved ones behind – and come here with your wives. Not that I see many ladies in the club tonight. But what can you expect with so many women going out to work these days and getting home so tired, they can hardly keep their mouths open. But I do see quite a few senior citizens. There always are when the go-go dancers are on the programme. Reminds me of the secretary of the local branch of the British Legion who invited a stripper to their lest-we-forget dinner.

However, age doesn't matter as long as you keep fit. My wife, wonderful woman, boasts that she can still get into skirts she got into before we got married. I wish I could say the same.

You all right out there. You look a bit crowded. I think we should propose a vote of thanks to the Family Planning Association without whom there might have been a lot more here tonight."

George resumes his normal voice. "The number of times I've been told I should have been a comedian. A bloody sight better comedian than book keeper. I wisnae cut out for anything to do with accountancy. I have to take off all my clothes to count up to twenty one. Well, now's my chance. (Pause) It's a wonderful feeling when you're making people laugh. The best feeling in the world. Timing – that's the secret, and knowing your audience. What will they be like? Not very bright I shouldn't think. Pity I couldn't have come and seen for myself.

It was hard enough to sneak out tonight. The story I told Mabel was as difficult to make up as the script for this show – more difficult. In a mess at the office. Well, that's not a lie. She wouldn't have believed I was after a big prize in a talent contest.

I don't know anyone who does come here. 'The Black Stocking' they call it. I've never been in a night club. Tried once in London with Harry. Down for a trade exhibition. Big boys living it up. Outside the door there was a large sign – 'Topless Waitresses'. They widnae let us in because we hadnae ties on. Imagine. Of course it might be up-market – sophisticated. How would I feel about that? Well, I did all right in Edinburgh that night Sean Connery didn't get his knighthood. Had them in fits.

(Adopts a clipped Bond-like tone) Bond approached the dark building. Unzipping his chinos he slipped effortlessly out of his truss, pulled a pin in the padded pouch and tossed it through the window. Two seconds later the window, half the wall, a framed portrait of Ben Laden and two packets of potato crisps blew out towards him. 'Good old Q,' thought Bond, 'but if that had detonated prematurely it would have been a real cock up.'

Good night that was. But is it still topical? That should be added to timing and audience – topicality.

What would James Bond have done in my position? Not making a fool of himself in a seedy club just to make a few pounds, that's for sure. So what would he have done? Punch someone on the nose – or even shoot someone. That wouldn't help. No-one to shoot? Except myself? A car chase? If I scarpered I don't suppose anyone would come after me. No. Delaying tactics, it has to be.

What a bloody mess to get into. All my own fault too. I can't even ask for sympathy. No-one to blame but myself. Well, maybe old Neilson – a bit. He was bitter of course - being passed over for promotion so often.

'If you can't get your hand on the tiller,' he told me, 'get your hand in the till.'

'Easy,' he said. And he retired with a gold watch – among other things. I covered up for him. No-one to cover up for me. To think I only gave the clerks a new pencil if they brought me back the stub of the old one. I was conscientious. I was good. I was a mug.

Now I am just a liar. A cheap liar. (Pause). But so was our top civil servant – 'Economical with the truth.' No house of correction for him though. No. He goes to the House of bloody Lords. Not right is it?

A breach of trust they'll say. What trust? I didn't trust the people who came to me for a pencil.

We need trust to have a civilised society, they say. But the queen of the greedies said there is no such thing as society – only individuals. But that only applies if you're up there looking down – not down here looking up. Bastards.

I can put it all back ... given time. I don't like that phrase – given time. But now there's word of pay offs. And if I get the heave ho, they'll discover everything. Then I'll even lose my redundancy. If I had waited till now, the redundancy money could have paid for the holiday. But Mabel so wanted that holiday. I couldn't say no. If only I'd waited. But I wasn't to know. Timing.

Only this week we heard of the lay offs. Our great chairman, Jonathan Fotheringham, explained how harsh the economic climate was. His face was flushed as he spoke – but it was the Caribbean climate that had done that.

'We have to face up to the real world. Must get ourselves leaner and fitter,' he said, the folds of his great belly pressing against the desk.

'Business today is like juggling three balls in the air with one hand, and guarding your own with the other.' Well, he was guarding his own all right. Although there were a few feet itching to put that to the test I can tell you.

Those who are kept on, have to take a cut in wages. So, even if I do keep my job, my chance of paying back is nil. If I go – I'm rumbled. For every frying pan there is a fire.

This prize could clear me – or at least buy time, that's all I want – to buy time. So it all depends on the comic material. It's your only talent, chum. Casting my artificial pearls before real swine. Oh God.

Tried the bank. Hadn't been in one for a while. Changed haven't they? Bankers! Always willing to help those better off than themselves. But I went there as broke as The Ten Commandments. That was a joke. I mean my visit to the bank was a joke.

(He mocks himself) I don't have any money but I want to take my wife on a holiday to the sunshine. I could see what the banker was thinking – now here is a man who has his feet firmly planted in mid air. He's the company banker too. Probably knew of the pay offs before we did.

Why don't I go to my friends for help? My friends? Some intelligent character once said – 'Nothing gives a man more pleasure than seeing a friend fall flat on his face.' Or as the Scots put is more succinctly, 'A friend in need is a pain in the arse.'

It was all too easy. The company pays us in sweeties and doesn't give us any feeling that we're trusted. So we help ourselves. Stands to reason doesn't it? No bother. (Voice drops) Don't talk tough. I could never have done this if I hadn't been desperate. I shook every time the auditor came in – and that was before I had nicked anything.

They'll be writing down the stock, so it's going to be impossible to hide the shortage. That's what consultants always do. Write down the stock savagely and blame present management, then make extra profit on it and take the credit. Parasites – canny get a job of their own. Like a man who knows fifty seven different ways to make love, but disnae know any women. That's a good one, should use that – nobody likes consultants.

Nobody likes politicians either. 'Norman Tebbit today appeared in court after having been timed doing one hundred miles an hour on the M25 but when he explained that Mrs Thatcher was in the car with him the charge of joy riding was dropped.' Not topical. And it's too long a sentence. Must keep it snappy. What am I saying? Imagine me saying to the judge, 'That's too long a sentence.'

I've never been in court. Very ritualistic I hear. What will the ritual be for the likes of me? Will he don a red cap before sentencing the debtor?

Mind you, the length of sentence doesn't matter a damn as long as it doesn't come too soon. Mabel will be so ashamed if I went to prison.

Mabel is a good woman. Not always the easiest to live with – but a good woman. She will be mortified. She has faith. She believes in God, ghosts, fairies, the royal family and me. Heaven help her. She was so pleased with the holiday. She had set her heart on going to Greece. Kept talking about it. Of course if she had thought for one moment that I didn't have the money for it she wouldn't have come. We were lucky with the weather. We're always lucky, she kept saying. She lay in the sun to her heart's content – not giving a damn about what the doctors say nowadays.

I remember my dad used to give money to send deprived Glasgow kids to the sunshine for a week. I wonder if he bought any of the wee buggers' skin cancer.

Now the ending. I can't keep changing it. Improvise like Billy Connelly in the middle if I can. But must know the ending."

(Speaking brightly), "It looks as if some of you have had a fair bucket. So be careful when you go home. Remember more than half the people in this country are caused by accidents.

Or, Driving home are you. Think it wisnae so long ago when clunk click every trip was the men doing up the chastity belts on the way out.

Get off really well they say and the punters will forget the rest. And if things are not going great, end early.

End early! 'Before I die,' Mabel said. She's not afraid to say it. I am. 'Three months,' the doctor said. Now that is a sentence. A death sentence. The murderers on death row get longer than that after they're sentenced. A lot longer.

She so wanted that holiday before she died.

I'll give her the best funeral money can buy – with their money. Solid oak coffin, the lot." (He chokes).

"She's holding on well. Very cheerful. But if I get arrested before she goes." (Pause). "She says she's had a good life. A life worth leaving as she puts it.

I wish she wasnae so bloody cheerful. Then I could comfort her. So – all I could do was give her the holiday.

Right, one more time. I've got to go for it." (He stands up. Glances at paper. Then, bright and breezy),

"Hello everyone, and welcome to this evening of fun and glamour. The management has asked me to extend a special welcome to all of you who have had to leave your loved ones," (he chokes), "behind – and come here with your wives." (He breaks down and sobs).

THE END.

❖❖❖❖❖❖❖❖❖❖❖❖❖❖

More from Fernando

Envy finds defects even in perfection.

❖❖❖❖❖❖❖❖❖❖❖❖❖❖

Imagination is the sun of the mind.

❖❖❖❖❖❖❖❖❖❖❖❖❖❖

The ignorant are unhappy because they do not understand anyone; the wise are unhappy because no-one understands them.

❖❖❖❖❖❖❖❖❖❖❖❖❖❖

Life is a mountain we all have to climb.

❖❖❖❖❖❖❖❖❖❖❖❖❖❖

The sea speaks a language only poets understand.

Soldier ● Engineer ● Author
Light removals with horse and cart

I am writing to all gentlemen to acquaint you of a recent experience of mine in the hope that you may gain some benefit from it. I became afflicted with what my self diagnosis decided was lumbago. The reason for the self diagnosis was that had I visited my surgery I might well have had to see our Indian lady doctor. I would like to make it clear that there is no sexism or racism to be inferred from that statement; she is a first class, highly competent, down-to-earth doctor. The problem which might have faced me was that I think she fancies me. If I go to her with a cold, a strained wrist or a bunged up ear she always makes me take my shirt off and sounds my chest and back thoroughly. I think she just likes looking at my body. With that in mind my premonition as to what would happen if I went to her with lumbago I leave to your imagination. She would probably have asked me to cough.

I decided therefore, to seek the advice of my very good friend, the pharmacist at Boots. She is lissom, lovely and Spanish, rejoicing in the name of Maria Gonzales de la Iglesias, and obviously highly intelligent. I explained my problem. She suggested an aerosol spray which has the effect of providing instant heat to the afflicted part and requires no massage. I asked her if she could provide the first treatment so as to give me some temporary relief. She apologised profusely that she was unable to help as she was an unmarried, strict Catholic girl of good hidalgo family, where such things were not permitted. In addition, she pointed to the signs on the shop wall which stated, "No mooning on these premises." She suggested I get one of my neighbours to apply it for me. I explained they had both been in the Navy so I could not take the risk. She seemed a little mystified at that response, so I paid for the spray canister and took my leave.

When I arrived home I removed my garments in order to apply the treatment and secure the relief so urgently required. I then ran up against a problem. Unless you are totally double jointed, with your back to a mirror, you still are unable to see the base of your spine. Secondly, the arm needs to be fitted with universal joints so that, as the instructions on the can indicate, it is held vertically at a distance of six inches from the afflicted part and moved parallel to the surface to be treated.

Well, here goes I thought. So as to have a firm base from which to work, I braced myself by standing legs apart, moved the can out of my line of vision to where I fondly imagined I would spray the lower vertebrae, and pressed hard on the end cap. I speedily realised I had been guilty of what might be termed a directional inexactitude. If you consider the base of the spine to be the bulls-eye, I scored a hit at what rifle shooters would describe as, "An outer at six o'clock." Now, that would have been bad enough, but with legs akimbo (can you have <u>legs</u> akimbo? Anyway you know what I mean), the overspray connected with, and speedily elevated the temperature of certain parts of my anatomy which, under normal circumstances, other outside influences rarely reach. There is, however, usually a silver lining in the most severe of cataclysms, in this case the conflagration engulfing my more sequestered parts made me totally forget my lumbago! Some you win, some you lose.

⟡◇⟡◇⟡◇⟡◇⟡◇⟡◇⟡◇⟡◇⟡◇⟡◇⟡◇⟡◇⟡◇⟡◇⟡◇⟡◇⟡

More Quotations

Courtship to marriage – as a very witty prologue to a very dull play. *Cougreve 1693*

◇⟡◇⟡◇⟡◇⟡◇⟡◇⟡◇⟡◇⟡◇⟡◇⟡◇⟡

Reading is to the mind what exercise is to the body. *Sir Richard Steele C 1700.*

◇⟡◇⟡◇⟡◇⟡◇⟡◇⟡◇⟡◇⟡◇⟡◇⟡◇⟡

There is no such thing as a moral or an immoral book. Books are well written, or badly written. *Oscar Wilde 1891.*

◇⟡◇⟡◇⟡◇⟡◇⟡◇⟡◇⟡◇⟡◇⟡◇⟡

The love of money is the root of all evil. *I Timothy.*

◇⟡◇⟡◇⟡◇⟡◇⟡◇⟡◇⟡◇⟡◇⟡◇⟡

Before the Roman came to Rye or out to Severn strode,
The rolling English drunkard made the rolling English road. *G K Chesterton C 1900.*

◇⟡◇⟡◇⟡◇⟡◇⟡◇⟡◇⟡◇⟡◇⟡◇⟡

When a man is tired of London, he is tired of life; for there is in London all that life can afford. Samuel Johnson 1777.

◇⟡◇⟡◇⟡◇⟡◇⟡◇⟡◇⟡◇⟡◇⟡◇⟡

The US standard railroad gauge (distance between the rails) is 4 feet, 8.5 inches. That's an exceedingly odd number. Why was that gauge used? Because that's the way they built them in England and English expatriates built the US railroads. Why did the English build them like that? Because the first rail lines were built by the same people who built the pre-railroad tramways and that's the gauge they used. Why did 'they' use that gauge then? Because the people who built the tramways used the same jigs and tools that they used for building wagons, which used that wheel spacing. So! Why did the wagons have that particular odd wheel spacing?

Well, if they tried to use any other spacing, the wagon wheels would break on some of the old, long distance roads in England, because that's the spacing of the

wheel ruts. So who built those old rutted roads? Imperial Rome built the first long distance roads in England for their legions. The roads have been used ever since. And the ruts in the roads? Roman war chariots formed the

initial ruts which everyone else had to match for fear of destroying their wagon wheels. Since the chariots were made for Imperial Rome they were all alike in the matter of wheel spacing.

So the United States standard railroad gauge of 4 feet, 8.5 inches is derived from the original specifications for an Imperial Roman war chariot. And bureaucracies' live forever.

So, the next time you are handed a spec and told, "We have always done it that way," and wonder what idiot came up with that, it was because Imperial Roman war chariots were made just wide enough to accommodate the back ends of two war horses.

Now the twist to the story …

When you see a Space Shuttle sitting on its launch pad, there are two big booster rockets attached to the sides of the main fuel tank. These are solid rocket boosters, or SRBs. The SRBs are made in Utah. The engineers who designed the SRBs would have preferred to make them a bit fatter, but the SRBs had to be shipped by train from the factory to the launch site. The railroad line from the factory happens to run through a tunnel in the mountains. The SRBs had to fit through the tunnel. The tunnel is slightly wider than the railroad track and the railroad track, as you now know, is about as wide as two horses' behinds. So a major Space Shuttle design feature of what is arguably the world's most advanced transportation system was determined over two thousand years ago by the width of a horse's backside!

An Inuit (Eskimo) Legend

From John Bury. Loon Lake, Saskatchewan, Canada.

Long ago, in a cold land far away, there lived a brother and sister who loved each other very much. But they quarrelled all the time. They argued about anything and everything. "It's cold," the sister would say.

Her brother would shake his head. "It's not too cold."

"Spring will be here soon," the sister would say happily.

"It's spring already, foolish sister," the brother argued.

Day in and day out they quarrelled. Now we would say they were as different from each other as night from day.

One day the sister awoke and said to her brother, "We must change."

"We must NOT change," he disagreed. But she was determined.

"I think we should transform ourselves into wolves and travel together in harmony as they do.

"Wolves howl," he said. "We must not become wolves."

"We'll become bears," she suggested. "Bears are amiable creatures."

"Bears are blunderers," he said.

"We'll become salmon and swim together down the river."

"The water is cold. We should not become salmon," the brother said firmly.

"Beavers', then," she said. "The Great Spirit praises the beaver who works with his brothers."

"We do not want to have sharp teeth," said the brother. "We must not become beavers."

"Seals then," said the sister. "Their great soft eyes are evidence that they are as kind as we should become."

"Slithery creatures," the brother shuddered. "We should not become seals."

All day they argued. Each time the sister suggested an animal they might become, the brother scowled and said, "No, no, no!" She recommended caribou and musk, oxen, eagles, and deer, but he was not convinced. Each arctic animal the sister suggested brought argument from her brother.

"All right," she said at last. "I will become the sun and rule the skies!" She snatched a flaming torch of moss from the fire and ran outside.

"No, I shall rule the skies," he cried, and he too grabbed a torch and began to chase her. They ran round and round their igloo, their torches flaming brightly.

The sister turned and ran toward the frozen fields, and all the animals watched in wonder as the brother gave chase after her. Deep into the tundra they ran, faster, and until their torches looked like shooting flames. Suddenly the sister began to rise into the sky.

"Oh," she cried as she rose and gazed down at the land to see that her brother too had begun to rise.

"We're moving to the sky," she called, "and I will rule," and with that she reached and put out her brother's torch with the touch of her cold hand. Higher and higher they flew in their chase. "I will put out your light because you need no light. You will not rule the sky," the sister called.

"I will," he argued, but his torch, darkened now, grew silvery in the chilled air. As they rose, the sister held her golden torch and her brother raised his silver flame. Higher and higher they drifted, still arguing until at last they were so high that down below the people and all the village igloos looked like toys dotting the cold, snowy land.

"I will warm the land for our people," the sister said, and her brother looked and felt a pang of longing for the people and the land he loved.

"I have no warmth," he said. "But I will offer light when you are resting."

"That is what we shall do," the sister agreed, for they both loved their people and the land, and they knew they must now share the sky.

And so the brother and the sister became the Sun and the Moon, sharing the task of lighting the world. They still watch over their people, and if you look closely you'll see their faces looking down on the earth. Brother's light is cold and clear and gazed longingly below. Sister's light is the brightest of smiles, for she knows their transformation helped the world to grow. Both of them cherish the power and wisdom of their light and the pleasure it brings to all the people of the Earth.

A True Story of Australia in the 1860s.

It has long been a well known fact that whenever an organisation or gang of Australian bush criminals was able to carry on for any length of time it was mainly because they were practising robbery in districts where a large percentage of the residents were in active or passive sympathy with them. Frank Gardiner and Ben Hall had long careers – for bushrangers, in Western New South Wales, because they were operating in a territory of which the lower classes were on their side as opposed to the forces of law and order. It was the same with the Kellys in northern Victoria. And the Clarke brothers of Monaro were no exception to the rule. It was the old story of 'bush telegraphs' and the sympathetic assistance of those in whom the taint of convictism was still strong enough to smother good citizenship. To them, all government was obnoxious, and the only sort of policeman for whom they had any use was an absent or dead one.

The Clarkes were a bad lot, root and branch. John Clarke, the head of the family, cheated the hangman by dying in Goulburn gaol whilst confined there under a charge of murder. His wife, the mother of the bushrangers with whom we are concerned, had been a Connell, and they were nearly as nice a family as the Clarkes. One of her brothers was charged as an accessory to the brutal murder of a party of policemen, which we will presently consider. Another was doing ten years in Darlinghurst at the time – having already done five for highway robbery, and his wife was locked up in the female division of the same prison for receiving stolen goods. A third died of a policeman's bullet, and a fourth was sentenced to death for robbery under arms and wounding with intent to murder. Two of good old John's sons, Tom and Jack, were hanged for murder, and another got three years for being mixed up with a mail robbery near Queanbeyan. The Clarkes and their cousins must have been a charming clan. However, since there isn't room here for all of them, we will confine ourselves mainly to the criminal careers of the Thomas and John Clarke who were hanged.

On April 9th, Tom Clarke, Pat Connell, Tom Connell, Bill Fletcher and one or two other kindred souls were returning from the Bega races when Clarke bailed up a Chinaman who was journeying from the Gulph gold diggings, and looted all the gold and money he had on him. A little further on they encountered the mail boy, and Tom Clarke forced him to exchange his horse, saddle and bridle for those which had been taken from the Chinaman. They had ridden a few miles further when they encountered Mr John Emmett, and told him to bail up. Emmett refused to do so, wheeled his horse and galloped away. They chased him firing their revolvers at him, and finally wounded him and killed his horse. They took about £100 from him, together with a parcel of gold-dust, and callously left him where he lay. He managed eventually to drag himself to where he could get assistance, but for all the robbers cared he might have bled to death.

The following night they tried to hold up a butcher's shop and met opposition. The argument grew so loud that it disturbed the only policeman in the village, Constable Miles O'Grady, who was sick in bed. He got up, dressed and walked along to the butcher's to see what might be the matter. He at once ordered the gang to leave the shop, whereupon Bill Fletcher fired at him without effect. O'Grady immediately returned the fire, and Fletcher was shot dead. One of the others then shot the plucky constable, who died a few hours later.

O'Grady's murder induced the Government to issue a proclamation against Clark and Connell under the Felon's Apprehension Act.

In the second half of 1866 a small body of secret police, led by a man named Flynn, came into the district to try and break up the gang, but it failed to do much and was eventually withdrawn.

Then a senior warder at Darlinghurst gaol, named Carroll, offered to go after the bushrangers with a party of his own choosing, on condition that he should only be rewarded according to results. If he succeeded in effecting their capture he was to have special promotion in the public service, and his men were to be provided with positions in it also.

They went to the Jindera district in the guise of surveyors, and proceeded to measure out a flat near the residence of old John Clarke, the father of the two 'wanted' men.

Soon after they commenced their 'surveying', the party was murderously attacked in the dark. They had returned to camp for the evening meal, and were afterwards standing round the fire, when suddenly a rifle shot broke the silence of the night, and a bullet struck the tree beneath which they stood. Whilst they were running to the tent for their rifles they were again fired at from several directions. It was a pitch dark night and the special constables couldn't see their attackers, but they returned the fire. No-one was hurt.

After this it was realised that further disguise was useless, and Carroll and his men now openly hunted the outlaws.

After dark on January 8th 1867, Carroll and his party set out on foot from Jinden station, meaning to visit the home of a man named Guiness, about four miles off, to which the Clarkes were said to be in the habit of resorting.

On the following day their bodies were found by some stockmen belonging to Jinden, and it was apparent from the positions in which they were lying that the men had been ambushed and murdered. Those of Phegan and McDonell were riddled with bullets. Carroll and Kennagh lay some distance from the others – it was supposed that, escaping from the first volley, they had run for cover, being pursued and shot down. Carroll had a bullet through the temple, and Phegan one in the throat. On Carroll's chest a £1 note had been pinned as a sort of indication that the special constables hadn't been slain through motives of robbery.

The news of this fourfold murder made a great sensation throughout Australia, and as soon as it came to Sydney the Governor issued a proclamation in a Gazette Extraordinary which offered a reward of £5000 for the murderers or £1000 for any one of them. The government also decided to send a special body of picked men, under a carefully selected officer, to the Braidwood district to hunt the bushrangers relentlessly. A Royal Commission was also sent from Sydney to inquire into conditions in the neighbourhood. So there arrived in due course Sub-Inspector Stephenson, with a contingent of picked men, and Sub-Inspector Brennan brought with him the best blacktrackers in the force.

Before long about 40 mounted troopers were combing the Braidwood countryside.

The end of the hunt was at hand. Senior Constable Wright, a very efficient officer, had been sent to the district to help hunt the outlaws down, and, at last, with four troopers and a smart blacktracker, he accomplished his task.

Wright's party had been camped about twenty miles from Ballalaba, on the road from Jinden and Cooma, and on the afternoon of April 26th, picked up the tracks of the bushrangers, following on foot until darkness and heavy rain baffled them for the time being. Wright's party consisted of Constables Walsh, Egan, Lenehan, James Wright and a blacktracker known as Sir Watkin. They had an idea that the Clarkes were making for the house of a settler a couple of miles away and pushed forward cautiously in that direction.

When they came to the place they were soon satisfied that the men they were after were in the hut, and quietly surrounded it, intending to wait for daylight before attacking. Soon after dawn the two Clarkes came out with bridles on their arms, to catch their horses. They saw the police, and ran back into the hut, firing their revolvers at them as they ran.

When they got inside they opened fire with their rifles through the cracks between the slabs, and for some time a regular fusillade was kept up from both sides. The younger Clarke had been wounded, though not dangerously, in the right breast as the men ran for cover, and Constable Walsh and the tracker were both hit when the bushrangers opened fire from the hut. Before long additional police arrived, and then the brothers, recognising that they were fairly trapped, decided to surrender. They came out of the hut unarmed, and were promptly handcuffed and taken to Ballalaba. Thence they were escorted to Braidwood, where they were eventually committed for trial in Sydney.

No-one had any doubts that the Clarkes were responsible for the murder of the special constables, but it was impossible to procure evidence, so they were charged with having wounded Constable Walsh with intent to murder him – a capital offence. The trial took place at Darlinghurst before the Chief Justice, Sir Alfred Stephen, on May 28th 1867, and though the brothers were most ably defended by Messrs. Dalley and Blake, the jury found them guilty.

In sentencing the Clarkes to death, the Chief Justice made a memorable speech, in which he deplored the misery that had been inflicted on the community by bushranging generally, and enlarged on its futility.

"The balance is all against you." he told the doomed brothers. "I have said I never knew a man, or heard of one, who through a course of bushranging, gained a shilling's worth of property he could call his own, or could gain it if let loose tomorrow morning. Where is there one flourishing in any single respect? I will read you a list of bushrangers, many of whom have come to the gallows within the last four and a half years. I believe they are all caught but one. Many of these were young men, capable of better things, but died violent deaths: Piesley, executed; Davis, sentenced to death; Gardiner, sentenced to thirty two years' hard labour; Gilbert, shot dead; Hall, shot dead; Bow and Fordyce, sentenced to death, but sentence commuted to imprisonment for life; Manns, executed; O'Meally, shot dead; Burke, shot dead; Gordon, sentenced to death; Dunleavy, sentenced to death; Dunn, executed; Lowrie, shot dead; Vane, a long sentence; Foley, a long sentence; Morgan shot dead; yourselves, Thomas and John Clarke, about to be sentenced to death; Fletcher, shot dead; Patrick Connell shot dead; Tom Connell, sentenced to death, but sentence commuted to imprisonment for life; Bill Scott, a companion of your own, believed to have been murdered – by you. There is a list! .... You young men have now to receive the last sentence of the law. You will pass from the country which you might have helped to raise in the estimation of the world. You will pass out of the world, felons, convicts, bushrangers, and I very much fear, murderers."

No more telling indictment of the profession of bushranging has ever been made – of its foolishness and utter futility.

◇◇◇◇ ◇◇◇◇◇ ◇◇◇◇◇◇◇◇ ◇◇◇◇◇◇◇◇◇◇◇ ◇◇◇◇◇◇◇◇◇◇

Words Failed Them

My great friend, **John Tester** was an insurance inspector for one of the largest British companies. Over many years he collected a multitude of statements from drivers trying to summarise the details of their accidents in the least number of possible words, often with hilarious results.

"Coming home I drove into the wrong house and collided with a tree I don't have."

"The other car collided with mine without giving a warning of its intention."

"I collided with a stationary truck coming the other way."

"I thought my window was down, but I found out it was up when I put my head through it."

"A truck backed through my windshield into my wife's face."

"The guy was all over the road. I had to swerve a number of times before I hit him."

"I pulled away from the side of the road, glanced at my mother-in-law and headed over the embankment."

"In an attempt to kill a fly, I drove into a telephone pole."

"I had been driving for 40 years when I fell asleep at the wheel, and had an accident."

"I was on my way to the doctor with rear end trouble when my universal joint gave way causing me to have an accident."

"As I approached the intersection a sign suddenly appeared in a place where no stop sign had ever appeared before. I was unable to stop in time to avoid the accident."

"To avoid hitting the bumper of the car in front I struck the pedestrian."

"My car was legally parked as it backed into the other vehicle."

"An invisible car came out of nowhere, struck my head and vanished."

By Cyril Cook

In the early 1930s air passenger service in the United States was still a novelty, in fact during the depression it all but ceased to exist. Crashes were common. Without sophisticated navigational aids, pilots, mainly World War One ex-service men, flew literally by the seats of their pants in old converted war planes. Flight costs were high; the aircraft were mainly built in wood with a fabric covering. The only thing that kept them financially viable was the fact that the US postal organisation instituted 'air mail' in 1918 between the major cities. It was these contracts which kept them in the air.

In 1932, Jack Frye of TWA asked Douglas to design a, "New transport to incorporate the best of the swiftly emerging aviation technology."

Douglas had built military aircraft up until now on the wood and canvas principle previously mentioned. They set-to, designed, built and flight-tested, an all metal cabin-type aircraft in under one year! This aircraft they designated the DC-1. The wings were of multi-cellular design using lightweight aluminium alloy, the complete aircraft covered in a skin of stressed aluminium sheet. It was designed to last.

The DC-1

After the DC-1 had been tested in July 1933, Douglas carried out a little re-design in that the cabin was stretched thereby adding two more seats. This became the DC-2.

TWA bought twenty five of these aircraft and orders flooded in from home, overseas and the military; of the latter more later. Flight ١ to eighteen hours from New York to Los Angeles rendered other air liners, mainly Curtis Condore and Fokker Triplanes, obsolete, but it in turn became obsolete when Douglas built the DST (Douglas Sleeper Transport) which had bunks for fourteen passengers. It was Pullman comfort.

This aircraft body was twenty six inches wider than the DC-2, had an extra ten feet of wingspan to give more lift, and more powerful engines. However, sleepers were not a large market, thus was born the DC-3 – the subject of the title of this article.

In the DC-3 the wider body of the DST was used and it could carry twenty one passengers. With those numbers in one airplane it was financially viable. The growth was phenomenal. Between 1936 and 1939 four hundred and fifty DC-3s were built, being used by 90% of all US airlines and operated by thirty foreign airlines. An interesting factor in the interior cabin design was a shelf running along beside the seating to accept gentlemen's hats. No self respecting business passenger would dream of not wearing a hat, usually of substantial size – particularly in the southern states.

The C-47 – The Dakota

The American military late in 1938 starting purchasing versions of the DC-3, the first being the C41 – US Army staff transport – a clear case of the generals' looking after their own comfort first!

However, the most famous version of all was the C-47, as known

The C-47 The Dakota

to the American forces, and when delivered to the RAF, who by tradition gave every airplane a name, was called 'The Dakota'. Ten thousand of these planes were built during the war by Douglas and another 9000 by licensees throughout the world.

They were used in every theatre of war, loved by those who flew them, received uncomplimentary nick-names (they were not the most beautiful of aircraft), such as 'Old Fatso' and 'The Goony Bird'. It was universally accepted that you can wreck a Dakota but you can never wear one out.

After the war, during the Berlin airlift, a Dakota was loaded in error with 11500 pounds weight instead of 5500 at Wunsdorf airfield. It <u>just</u> got into the air, and delivered its load!

Back to the DC-3

The last DC-3 was built in 1946, but that was by no means the end. After the war there was big business in converting surplus Dakotas and C-47s, so much so they became the mainstays of new civil fleets. They were primary contributors to the recovery of post-war European airlines, and in the 1950s virtually every airline in the world operated C-47 conversions, putting operators into the business of cargo carriers as well as passenger carriers.

As people carriers it found, except for less travelled routes, it would not compete with the new four-engined planes; but at the end of the 1960s there were still more than sixteen hundred in scheduled service with fifty seven airlines around the world. Even in the 1970s the world's airlines operated more DC-3s than any other single type of aircraft.

Although outclassed in speed, power, technology and size by modern jet aircraft, the DC-3 remains unmatched for its ability to carry relatively large loads for the best pound for pound cost. There are still several hundreds of them around, each in this year of 2006, being at least sixty years old.

You can crash a Dakota – you can't wear it out!

The DC-3 was the plane that changed the world!

◇◇◇◇◇◇◇◇◇◇◇◇◇◇◇◇◇◇◇◇◇◇◇◇◇◇◇◇◇◇◇◇

Beware the fury of a patient man. *John Dryden C 1680.*

◇◇◇◇◇◇◇◇◇◇◇◇◇◇◇◇◇

Power without responsibility – the prerogative of the harlot through the ages. *Rudyard Kipling.*

◇◇◇◇◇◇◇◇◇◇◇◇◇◇◇◇◇

A virtuous woman is a crown to her husband. *Proverbs 12.4*

◇◇◇◇◇◇◇◇◇◇◇◇◇◇◇◇◇

A book that furnishes no quotations is, *me judice*, no book, it is a plaything. *Thomas Love Peacock. 1831.*

◇◇◇◇◇◇◇◇◇◇◇◇◇◇◇◇◇

Il n'y a point de héros pour son valet de chambre.
No man is a hero to his valet. *Mme Cornuel 1728.*

◇◇◇◇◇◇◇◇◇◇◇◇◇◇◇◇◇

The Gordon Riots

By Cyril Cook

It is only a few years ago that a party of Her Majesty's Foot Guards would arrive at the Bank of England to guard it overnight. In these days of maximum security of buildings and a peaceful population, it would seem that an armed force of guardsmen placed in the centre of the City of London was a little over the top. The fact was that it had been going on for two hundred years, and most people had forgotten why. In the army, the most important part of the system, apart from marching in step and saluting officers is – tradition. The Royal Welsh Fusiliers were the last regiment to wear pigtails – so they wore a black flash on the back of their collars. It was tradition. The Gunners wore white lanyards and so on. So why did guardsmen have to waste their time guarding a building which is virtually impregnable anyway? It was all the fault of a Lord George Gordon.

Back in 1780 the government of the day was bringing forward a measure known as, 'The Catholic Relief Act', designed to reduce the existing constraints on Roman Catholics. Lord George Gordon assembled Protestant supporters in Lambeth, leading them to Parliament Square to protest against the measures in the Bill. The column grew and grew on the way, joined by a mass of Huguenots from the City, until it stretched for some four miles. Crying, "No Popery," as it went, the Government quickly ordered the Horse Guards on to the streets to disperse it, fearing a riot.

As a result of the heavy handedness of the troops and the attendant constables, a number of the protesters were injured and some were taken to Newgate. This turned the intended peaceful demonstration into a riot, a section of the crowd breaking away and burning down the chapel of the Catholic Sardinian Ambassador.

The next day was quiet, but the day after that a mob assembled in the City. They burnt houses owned by Catholics in Moorfields, looted a Catholic chapel there, then moved on to Wapping and Spitalfields, in which places they set large areas alight. It was clear that it was now not just an anti-Catholic protest – it was anti-state!

Many were arrested and taken to Newgate. The Lord Mayor turned out troops garrisoned in the Tower, but was unwilling to give them orders to fire on the rioters, not only because of having the casualties on his conscience, but also because he knew that a fair proportion of the soldiers were sympathetic to them.

The rioting then went from bad to worse. The mob, inflamed by what they had already achieved, and the drink they had consumed, marched to Newgate with the intention of freeing those of their comrades who had been arrested. Their first action was to fall upon the Warden's house, at the entrance to the gaol. He piled his furniture against the gaol door to endeavour to prevent their entry, upon which the rioters smeared the door with tar and set light to it. Virtually the whole of the City force of one hundred constables, armed only with their regulation staves, attempted to break up the mob, but were soon overcome and their staves added to the fire.

By now the doors and the furniture behind were well ablaze, the flames rapidly spreading to the prison proper, where the prisoners were in danger of being burnt alive. As a result staff opened the doors and over three hundred of those inside escaped.

Having succeeded in their task at Newgate, the mob moved on to Bloomsbury Square where they burnt down the house of Lord Chief Justice Mansfield. Following this the leaders of the riot declared that unless their demands were met they would fire other prisons, the Bank, the Royal Mint, and the Royal Arsenal. They would throw open the gates of Bedlam and set the lunatics free, but despite this final threat they received no answer to their demands.

On the evening four days after Lord George Gordon's first peaceful march, the anarchy reached new heights. The Fleet prison was burnt down, as also was the King's Bench and the famous Clink prison in Southwark.

But now authority became restored, and with a heavy hand. Further army units were turned out with orders to fire on the mob or mobs. Two hundred were killed, Lord George Gordon, along with hundreds of rioters, was arrested. 'Pour encourager les autres', twenty five were hanged on the spots where they had carried out their felonies. Three young boys had been part of the mob at Lord Mansfield's house. Their youth did not save them; they were hanged on the spot.

And Lord George? Arrested on a charge of high treason he was acquitted on the grounds that he had no treasonable intentions! However, in 1788 he was sentenced to five years in Newgate for, 'Libelling the administration of justice in England.' He lived an extremely sociable life in prison, to the extent of hosting dinners and dances, but because he could find no-one to act as security for his good behaviour when he was due for release he was refused discharge. He died in Newgate in 1793.

◊◊◊◊◊◊◊◊◊◊◊◊◊◊◊◊◊◊◊◊◊◊◊◊◊◊◊◊◊◊◊◊◊◊◊◊◊

From Fernando Beralba

The sea speaks a language that only the poets understand.

◇◇◇◇◇◇◇◇◇◇◇◇◇◇◇◇◇

He wins who loses with dignity.

◇◇◇◇◇◇◇◇◇◇◇◇◇◇◇◇

Die Wahrheit Kommt mit der Zeit.

A Dictionary for Men (Part One)

These extracts are from a tiny book written by John Arondal before the Great War of 1914, which explains one or two references to our German friends in a somewhat unfriendly manner!

A. Abusive   A state of physical and mental exertion which is seldom appreciated by the other person. Produces extraordinary symptoms such as a keen desire on the part of the Germans to ejaculate periodically, "Gott strafe England."

B. Brutality   The effect of ignorance, superstition and militarism. Found in large doses among exponents of 'Kultur'.

C. Coquette   A woman without a heart who dupes a man without a head.

D. Dreams   Illusions that console the poor and terrify the rich.

E. Echo   The only thing that can cheat a woman out of the last word.

F. Fool   An individual whose folly does not accord with that of the majority.

G. Germ   A small insect capable of great mischief. German. A larger insect incapable of small virtues.

H. Hearse   A stage that carries us into the other world, and in which there is always room.

I. Interval   Often the most enjoyable part of the performance.

J. Jury   Twelve men chosen to decide who has the best lawyer.

K. Keep (To)   There are three things which it is very difficult to keep: a citadel, a treasure and a woman.

More to come!

Schooldays at Essemay

By J H Absalom

Sensational headlines in national newspapers drew attention to a brutal attack in Anfield, Liverpool. Television cameras covered the scene and moved around the grounds and buildings. One camera shot stayed for a while on a building which I immediately recognised, although I had lived away from Liverpool for decades and it was over sixty years since I had entered the doors of that building.

It had been the office of our headmaster, Mr Simpson, 'Simon', when he was out of hearing. Regarded with respect, and indeed, almost feared by boys and teaching staff alike, 'Simon' ran a fine school, one of the best in Liverpool, from that small office in the building I suddenly saw on television. Memories flooded back as I watched pictures of the old school grounds. Memories of school friends and fine teachers. School routine and events and camps and growing up. Learning not only maths and art and other subjects, but also learning to make friends, how to relate and how to choose company and how to please caring masters.

'Pip' Lunt was a small, slightly built, teacher of English, who taught his subject in a way that boys enjoyed so that the enjoyment stayed with them. He also had the hardest knuckles! Let him arrive unexpectedly at the side of a boy wasting time and that boy would be 'pipped' by a knuckle rap on the side of his head as if knocked on a closed door. 'Cozzy' Cosnet, the teacher of French, was a crack shot with pieces of chalk … or anything else that came to his hand. Legend had it that when a parent was inattentive during a meeting of parents and teachers Chairman 'Cozzy' dealt with the interrupter as he dealt with noisy lads in class. The parent felt the smack of a piece of chalk above the left ear and paid attention for the rest of that meeting. The former 'Stinks' room, lower 4 had a pipe running around three walls. The pipe had openings in it where Bunsen Burners would have been connected. Rows of two-seater desks accommodated thirty lads who gathered for a maths lesson. The master was a Welshman, whose first name was Eyton. Heartless boys of thirteen and fourteen, unusually, ignored the fact that he had a club foot, put up with his smokers breath and liked him because he would sometimes forget maths and suddenly break into poetry.

Unfortunately, he was also inclined to have fits of temper. When roused, he would suddenly snarl and scream and shout. Just as suddenly his tantrum would cease. We knew he was a member of an amateur dramatic society and wondered if he sometimes put on an act for us. However, boys being boys, we would stir him into a tantrum just to watch the dramatic effects. One particular morning was worse than usual. He ought to have suspected, for there wasn't a sound when he entered the classroom. Heads were bowed over books and pen nibs busily squeaked. Having placed his books on the desk, the tall, thin, black-haired master turned to the blackboard. Thereon he saw, written in chalk in boyish scrawl, "Eyton, Eyton, two dogs fighten, one a black and one a whiten."

There was a deathly hush as he stood reading the words. Boys peered over pens, heads very slightly raised. All could see the master's shoulders quivering, but it wasn't possible to make out whether it was with laughter or rage. Stan Taylor broke the silence. Stan was a big lad, a fine sportsman and into every kind of mischief, but there wasn't an evil thought in him. Sitting near the back of a row of desks and near a hole in the old gas pipe, Stan blew a raspberry into the pipe as a bugler blows a note into a bugle. The raspberry issued forth from other holes around the classroom. The silence was shattered.

Eyton danced around on his toes like a welter weight boxer, faced the class, lunged and grabbed a small inoffensive boy sitting near a hole from which issued one of the deep trumps. Holding the lad at arms length so his feet barely touched the floor, the master screamed, "What you doin' boy? What you makin' that noise for?"

The boy was being shaken like a rabbit. Ever mindful of the need for justice, another half a dozen lads sprang to their feet and shouted as if they were members of a Gilbert and Sullivan chorus, "It wasn't 'im, sir – it was me!"

The rabbit was dropped back into his seat and Eyton danced about in front of the class and then up and down aisles between desks, snarling into the grinning faces of his tormentors until he came face to face with the standing Stan Taylor. "It was you!" he fumed.

"Yes sir, you're right sir," said Stan in a gentle calming voice. Old beyond his years was Stan. "It was me, see – I blew down here," turning to show the hole in the pipe … then, changing the subject with all the wile and innocence at his command … "But I thought the poem was good, didn't you?"

Not even our remarkable Welshman could resist the charms of young Stan when he was at his most charming. Man and boy stood gazing at each other for a full silent minute. Then the master said, in his usual lilting tone of voice, "Well, indeed yes. It is quite clever," and as he turned away from Stanley the Charmer, his shoulders began to shake again, but this time because he was chuckling like one of his own pupil tormentors and saying, almost to himself, "Eyton, Eyton, two dogs fighten, one a black and one a whiten."

Calmly and slowly he took his seat behind the tall teaching desk; looking around the smiling boys he finally looked at Stanley, now seated with folded arms on his desk.

"Taylor, you are a rotten speller, tomorrow morning bring me a paper with the word, 'fighting' on it spelt properly, one hundred times and another paper explaining the meaning, as you see it, of the word 'whiten', do you understand?"

"Oh, yes sir, I do sir," the Charmer replied. It wasn't long before Stan was in more trouble and I was to join him, receiving punishment. But that's another story.

❖❖❖❖❖❖❖❖❖❖❖❖❖❖❖❖❖

The Paomnnehal Pweor of the Hmuan Mnid

Aoccdrnig to rcneet rscheearch at Cmabrigde Uinervtisy it deosn't mttaer in waht oredr the ltteers in a wrod are, the olny iprmoatnt tihng is taht the frist and lsat ltteer are in the rghit pclae. The rset can be a taotl mses and you can sitil raed it wouthit problem. Tihs is bcuseae the huamn mnid deos not raed ervey lteter by istlef, but the wrod as a wlohe.

❖❖❖❖❖❖❖❖❖❖❖❖❖❖❖

Monsieur Wagner a de beaux moments, mais de mauvais quart d'heures.
Wagner has lovely moments but awful quarters of an hour. *Rossini 1867.*

❖❖❖❖❖❖❖❖❖❖❖❖❖❖❖

Any man who hates dogs and babies can't be all bad. *WC Fields 1939.*

❖❖❖❖❖❖❖❖❖❖❖❖❖❖❖

Quotations

If once you have paid him the Dane – gold
You never get rid of the Dane. *Kipling.*

Oh Love! Thou bane of the most generous souls!
Thou doubtful pleasure, and thou certain pain. *Granville 1698*

The Old Soldier

A True Story by Cyril Cook

1966
I lay in my hospital bed
In the bemused half awake, half asleep
That follows after surgery.

White fronted angels floated by
Serene, competent, smelling of security
"Drink this Mr Cook, it will do you good."

Even the dragon sister came and held my hand
I was conscious enough to think
She is afraid she may be losing me.

It was late evening and getting dark
Across the ward the old soldier was singing
Very quietly on the end of his bed.

"There's a long long trail awinding
Into the land of my dreams
Where the nightingale is singing
And the bright moon beams.
There's a long long trail awinding
Until my dreams all come true
To the day when I'll be going
Down that long long trail with you."

Softly he sang, his eighty years
Giving poignancy to the words
And finishing the words, re-hummed the tune.

Sleep overtook me, pain put in storage
Occasionally awakening, mouth dry, angel attending
And back to oblivion until the morning light.

On awakening, across the ward the empty bed
Expertly made, hospital corners as regimental
As the old soldier himself had been.

When he was singing, did he know?
Was he ready for his passing out parade?
Would the Heavenly Sergeant Major welcome him?

2006
I am an old soldier now
Though there were many times in many places
When I didn't think I would ever be.

Will serenity overtake me so that I too
When the day comes, as it surely will,
Can sit on the end of my bed and softly sing.

"There's a long long trail awinding
Into the land of my dreams ....

A Fairy Tale

One day, long, long ago there lived a woman who never, ever, nagged, hated shoes, and loved her husband to go to football matches. She never was heard to say she had 'nothing to wear', and would never think of even trying to keep up with the Jones's!

But this **was** a long time ago.

And it **was** only for one day.

And it is a **fairy tale**.

The End.

It is tough to climb the ladder of success especially if you are trying to keep your nose to the grindstone, your shoulder to the wheel, your eye on the ball, and your ear to the ground.

Of all things you wear, your expression is the most important.

Why does a slight tax increase cost you £100 and a substantial tax cut save you 20p?

Old London

In 1822 a certain Charles Dickens, aged 20 and at that time a newspaper reporter, went on strike with others of his profession demanding more pay.

The tower of London is not in the City of London.

FA Cup winners 1881? Old Curthusians beat Old Etonians. No kissing or diving in that match I'll wager.

Achaanwaapush

A Cree Legend from John Bury, Saskatchewan, Canada.

I don't know what the other communities call it, but here in Whapmagoostui, we call this legend Achaanwaapush (Cannibal Rabbit). He was a cannibalistic creature. He was a person with the features of a rabbit and he habitually slaughtered people.

There was a family of Lynx people camped out on the land. One day, the Lynx adults were getting ready to set off for a beaver hunt. As they left, they said to their young Lynx children, "Achaanwaapush will reach our camp today." The young Lynx were forewarned what would happen. The adult Lynx said, "When Achaanwaapush enters our tepee, he'll want the place warm and he'll want to be scratched and soothed. But make sure that you don't use your claws so Achaanwaapush will become frustrated and will want to be scratched more vigorously. After he tells you to scratch him more forcefully, rip him open along his ribs."

The Lynx men left with their wives to hunt for Beaver. Only the children were left at the camp.

During the day, the old Cannibal Rabbit reached the camp of the Lynx and entered the tepee. As he opened the door flap and saw the young Lynx children sitting around inside the tepee he said, "Grandchildren, put some wood in the fire and I'll warm up and you'll scratch my back." The Lynx children agreed. They fed the fire and the place was nice and toasty. Achaanwaapush got undressed and told the Lynx children to scratch his back. The children began rubbing Achaanwaapush's back using only their paws.

The old Cannibal Rabbit stopped them and asked,

"What's going on? How come you're not scratching me? Let me check your claws. I told you to scratch my back. Do it with more force." The Lynx children agreed.

The old Cannibal Rabbit laid down again. The young Lynx children put their paws along his spine and stuck out their claws and pulled down along his ribs. They ripped the Cannibal Rabbit's skin and teared him open. The Lynx children killed Achaanwaapush. As they joyfully butchered him, they said, "Our parents will eat the abdomen meat."

After hunting Beaver, the Lynx adults said, "Let's go home. Achaanwaapush must have reached our children." On their way back, they saw the Cannibal Rabbit's trail leading to their camp. Just seeing this trail frightened them. The Lynx men told their wives to walk far behind. The Lynx men snuck up to their tepee as they got near. One Lynx man jumped in the entrance and the other pounced for the smoke hole of their tepee to attack Achaanwaapush. They believed the Cannibal Rabbit had slaughtered their children but the startled Lynx children said,

"What are you doing? We've killed Achaanwaapush." The Lynx men were glad and said,

"It's a good thing you did that." When the wives of the Lynx arrived, the rest of the camp was already rejoicing and happily cooking a feast of the Cannibal Rabbit. This is the legend that I heard.

◈◇◈◇◈◇◈◇◈◈◇◈◇◇◈◇◈◈◇◈◇◇◈◈◇◈◇◈◇◈◇◇◈◈◇◈◇◇◈◈

Tail Piece

When you are in deep trouble –

say nothing and just try to look inconspicuous!

On the north eastern point of Singapore island lies the Changi promontory. It housed in 1941, Changi village, seven large guns designed to fire on ships approaching from the Johore Straits, three large barrack blocks, and the notorious Changi Gaol.

Bombardier Stanley Warren arrived early in 1942. (A bombardier is a corporal in the Royal Artillery). The island was quickly overrun and Stanley became one of the thousands of prisoners, being marched into captivity to Roberts Barracks, one of the Changi blocks, and one of the other barracks – Changi Gaol being packed out with civilians, of which more later.

A fellow captive was a Padré, Reverend F H Stafford. He approached the Japanese commander to ask permission to use one of the rooms in the block as a chapel, this permission being surprisingly granted. He came to hear that Stanley Warren was a commercial artist, and a devout Christian. Stanley had in civilian life been a cinema billboard artist for Granada and readily agreed to use his talents to paint murals on the new chapel walls, despite the fact he was very ill with dysentery.

The chapel was to be dedicated to Saint Luke the Physician, an apt choice since it was adjacent to the hospital block, and in mid August 1942 the work began. Prisoners scrounged wood and made benches to sit on, fashioned a lectern and even found an old harmonium which was restored. The walls had an 'old gold' distempered finish, the next problem being where to scrounge the paint to use for the murals.

The Nativity

Meanwhile, although very ill, Stanley sketched his proposals on all manner of pieces of paper he and others for him, could lay their hands on. The paint for mural one 'The Nativity', which was to be approximately three metres long by one and a half high, was gradually accumulated, comprising ex WD turf brown camouflage paint, a small tin of violent crimson, a larger tin of white oil paint, and six cubes of billiard chalk, which crunched up and added to some of the white provided blue paint.

Stanley set to work, but could only paint for fifteen minutes at a time before having to rest. It took him nearly four months, being finished at Christmas 1942.

His health was now improving; he started on mural two the Ascension.

The Ascension

He decided to paint this one so that if he died he felt it was important he had shown Christ's time on earth. More paint had to be found. A large drum of grey paint had been discovered. Prisoners scraped different colours off abandoned cars, lorries and from a large variety of scrapped metal objects to colour the grey. As a result he was able to produce mural two.

His next depiction was the Crucifixion. He painted Jesus' eyes closed. He said he felt he had not the impertinence to look into the eyes of Christ!

This mural was also to show forgiveness for the atrocities their captors were inflicting upon them. "Father, forgive them, they know not what they do." It is to be hoped that the few Japanese who could read English would find significance in that heading.

His next offering was 'The Last Supper'. By now he was out of blue paint.

The final mural was that of Saint Luke in prison which shows the saint writing his gospel.

The Crucifixion

The murals were completed in May 1943 but had a comparatively short initial life. In May 1944 the Japanese moved the prisoners out, housed their own troops in Roberts Barracks, and distempered the walls, covering up the murals.

The Last Supper

And there they remained, under the distemper, until 1958 when a member of the RAF was billeted in that room and discovered them beneath successive layers of distemper. Gradually the distemper was very carefully removed, and on three occasions Stanley returned at the invitation of the Singapore authorities to restore them.

Stanley died in February 1992, his murals live on.

The above excerpts were taken with permission from Peter W Stubbs excellent book,
'The Changi Murals', published by Handmark Books in Singapore.

Ambition

(By S Tarrant)

Let the school-boy have a care,
Ambition plays a lion's share,
When all the truth is out.

Napoleon was lost at school,
But rose to fight a world-wide duel,
When all the truth is out.

And why bemoan the fate he saw,
Success can even be a bore,
When all the truth is out.

So let ambition have its fling,
It achieves most anything,
When all the truth is out.

244

I knew a headmaster; in fact he was a very close relative of mine, who ran a large high school in the West Midlands. In addition to his management and organisational skills, which were required for such a successful establishment, he was also very keen to seize every possible opportunity to engage individual pupils in private conversation. Both parties benefitted; one feeling 'special' talking to the boss, the other discovering what made his charges 'tick'.

An example of this was to be provided by the Domestic Science department. Senior girls in turn were given the opportunity to prepare and serve the Head with coffee each morning break, in his room. During one particular week a biscuit was provided in addition to the customary beverage. This disturbed the Head, so on the third morning he challenged the girl in question.

"It is very kind of you to provide me with a biscuit with my coffee but I am concerned that you are spending your own money on me in this way!"

"Oh that's alright sir," was the reply. "My sister works at the biscuit factory and she brings them out in her knickers."

In the 1960s in a newly built senior school on Merseyside, we operated a prefectorial system. Not for the purpose of helping to maintain discipline, but to take on small jobs of responsibility to add to their development. These prefects changed on a regular basis but their tasks remained the same. One of the tasks that most of the children who were involved enjoyed, was clearing away and washing up the tea cups left by colleagues in the staffroom at the end of the morning and afternoon breaks. I think the attraction for what one would describe as a menial task was to have the opportunity to enter what they believed to be the 'inner sanctuary'.

The children were allowed only a certain length of time to complete the operation before returning to class. On the occasion a much longer time than normal elapsed, so the teacher, anxious as to know why, rushed to the staffroom. There she found three very worried pupils in the staff toilet. The cups and saucers had been duly washed, dried and set out on the tray but the teapot stood there minus its rubber spout extension.

"What's the problem children? Why are you taking so long?"

"Well miss, when we emptied the tea pot dregs into the toilet, the rubber spout dropped into the lavatory water. We don't know why, but we've always managed to get it back before!"

Practical teaching practice in schools was a significant component in the training of student teachers to enable them to qualify to become a member of the profession.

However competent intellectually, it was one's efforts and capabilities in the classroom that determined success or failure.

I remember clearly an incident in the sixties when the importance of a particular student's strengths and weaknesses was put to the test.

It took place in a junior school in a class of ten and eleven year old children. It was the student's final teaching practice, this being the most important one of all. The student's academic achievement was not in question, but previous teaching practices had been somewhat borderline. So it was decided that on this occasion a lesson, chosen by the student would be viewed by his college tutor, head and class teacher. Forewarned, the student realised the importance of this exercise. Being interested in thespian activities he decided to tell the story of David and Goliath, hoping that he would hold the attention of a 'not so easy' class, and impress the judges.

The morning arrived, the stage was set and the story introduced. With the right change of pace in the telling and apt dramatic pauses, the children responded beautifully.

Little David selected the most suitable pebble from the stream and placed it carefully in his sling. With appropriate dramatic movement the imaginary sling was circled round David's head gathering speed and then when the time was right, released towards its target.

PAUSE. Silence pervaded the classroom.

The pebble plummeted into Goliath's forehead.

STOP. All was still.

The panel exchanged glances of approval as the children hung on the edge of their seats waiting for the next word.

The student who had by this time been transported into another world – he could not believe how receptive his charges had been – was about to proceed with the telling when the silence was broken.

Little Johnny on the front row could contain himself no longer and blurted out,

"Did it 'urt 'im sir?"

Emotionally drained and somewhat frustrated and annoyed, the student replied,

"Urt 'im, it effing well killed the bastard, didn't it?"

The question is – did he pass or fail?

In July 1979 the parliament of Ellan Vannin was graced by the presence of Her Majesty Queen Elizabeth II to celebrate its millennium, though many scholars claim it pre-dates that. And where is Ellan Vannin? It is known to us as the Isle of Man, famous for its three legs, the TT races, and its kippers long before the wealthy settled there to take advantage of its tax incentives.

The parliament, known as 'Tynwald', Norse for 'assembly place', meets every year on Tynwald Hill, and has done so ever since the Viking freemen of the ninth century, who occupied the island at that time, used to meet to hear complaints.

The Parliament today consists of a lower chamber, elected by the people known as 'The House of Keys'. There is an upper house which in addition to having eight elected members from the House of Keys, has the President of Tynwald, the Bishop of Sodor and Man, and the Manx Attorney General.

In July each year both Houses meet on a mound called Tynwald Hill, where laws passed during the year are read in English and Manx, the Manx language being derived from the ancient Celtic peoples who sailed from France in the Dark Ages. The Norsemen endeavoured to introduce their tongue, but little of it remains. When the laws have been read they are put on the Statute Book, provided no Manx person airs any grievance he may have toward them. This rarely happens; Manx people seem to be able to sort out their differences without a lot of aggravation.

The Tynwald Chamber
(Eve of Man Photography)

View of Tynwald ceremony with the hill Slien Whallian in the background
(Photograph Derek Croucher)

Some interesting facts about the Isle of Man

‣ Emmeline Pankhurst was the daughter of a Manx woman.

‣ In 1881 the Manx Parliament was the first in the world to give votes to women.

‣ Women's votes were restricted to owners of real estate valued at £4 or above.

‣ In 1919 all women were included in the suffrage.

‣ The Hill, Slien Whallion, has a fearsome reputation. In days gone by if a woman was suspected of being a witch she was put in a barrel and rolled down the hill.

‣ By some strange logic those who survived were without doubt deemed to be witches, otherwise they would not have lived through the ordeal. As a consequence they were killed!

‣ The first ever 'Derby' was raced on the Isle of Man. The 7th Earl, who sponsored it, would only allow Manx bred horses to run in it.

'On Trek'

By Philip Burkinshaw

From 1949 Philip Burkinshaw was posted to Sierra Leone, having joined the Colonial Administrative Service, where he served, mainly up-country, for over six years. In those days that part of the world was known as 'the white man's grave'.

The following is an excerpt from his excellent book 'Alarms and Excursions'. This fascinating book covers a lifetime of soldiering, colonial service in many insalubrious countries, followed by a million miles of travel all over the world as one of that illustrious Corps of Queen's Messengers, of which more will be read later.

We take up his story with him being posted to an outpost of Empire known as the Tonkolili District in Northern Sierra Leone.

I often made the long hard slog through the hills of northern Sierra Leone to Bendugu in the course of the next few years whilst stationed in Tonkolili District. The first stage of the journey was to Bumbuna where one spent the night in the rest house on the hill looking down on the village and its centre piece, a massive (near one hundred foot) cotton tree. The rest house was not one of the most comfortable and I recall on one occasion during the rains spending a sleepless night on a camp bed wearing a mackintosh and with an umbrella suspended on top of my mosquito net. Such was the sieve like nature of the grass roof!

From Bumbuna the walking began. Although something of a trial in the rains, in the dry season it was an interesting experience, and if one was lucky, one might see or at least hear a variety of wild life – elephant, leopard and bush cow (the West African buffalo). Chimpanzees, baboons and many varieties of monkeys were fairly common in the area; crocs abounded in the larger rivers which one had to cross in dug out canoes. Unfordable smaller rivers had to be traversed over locally constructed bamboo suspension bridges or merely tree trunks, over which one had to do a balancing act. After heavy rain, one would come across a mixed bag of snakes, green mambas, cobras or pythons basking astride the sunlit path which had been cut through the dense bush. One hazard in the remoter parts might be a trail of black ants (or driver ants) over which one had to sprint if, as often occurred, they entirely covered the track. Part of the route passed through tropical rain forest which blotted out the sky with its dense canopy of foliage.

The first night's stop would be at a remote spot called Sakasakala where one would be greeted on arrival by the section chief who would have prepared the rest house. He would usually come with a 'shake hand', a small present, as a token of welcome. Sometimes this would be in the form of eggs which he had been saving up for several weeks! No-one seemed to catch salmonella in those days! A suitable gift, perhaps a packet of shot gun cartridges, would be given to the chief in return. The rest house was a mud hut. The Sakasakala model had no doors or windows and an uneven floor upon which one's canvas camp bed with mosquito net would be precariously erected. The Union Jack was hung proudly from a bamboo pole alongside the mud walls outside to show that the District Commissioner was in residence and available, for what would today be called 'a surgery' for those who had any problems or grievances for which they might obtain redress from an independent arbiter. A queue would inevitably form before the District Commissioner had had time to change his shirt and the session might go on until the evening!

The hut would have been dutifully swept out before one's arrival and water from a nearby stream provided for cooking and bathing. The accommodation was, as the reader may have guessed, fairly basic, but Sakasakala was merely a resting point after a long day's slog. After a soak in the canvas bath, a meal of tinned soup, tinned meat or tinned something else, with perhaps a few sweet potatoes, I would usually lose myself in a book or read over my address to the Chief and Native Authority at Bendugu, whence I was heading, before turning in.

Serenaded by the morning chorus of a thousand birds, one raised oneself from one's camp bed at about 5.00 am so as to get off to an early start and cover a fair distance before the intense heat of the day made limbs ache, feet blister and every step a tedium.

Bendugu was the headquarters of a somewhat formidable old paramount chief with strong feudal tendencies who was feared by his people. In his early days he and his 'war boys' had been involved in some violent skirmishes with his neighbours over land and these disputes had led to clashes with authority. In this respect however, he was a reformed character, age having mellowed him. His drive in another direction however, was as unrestrained as ever, as he maintained a veritable regiment of wives, his household dominating the town from one of four hills from which he could survey the activities of his subjects.

One of the chief's entourage would be blowing a deafening greeting to the stranger on a hollow horn, and another, in the style of the troubadours, would be intoning in an ear piercing voice the praises and achievements of the chief and his illustrious visitor! It was all a rather daunting experience for any young administrative officer on a first visit, particularly as the chief, after gripping you by the hand, would not release it until you had gone through the sequence of the customary greetings in the language of this tribe, Koranko, which was not only little used but difficult!

On the evening of my arrival a queue of complainants at the rest house would bring a wide variety of problems for me to consider, from perhaps a call for assistance to deal with a marauding leopard which had been killing stock to a request for the sinking of a village borehole, or the building of a new bridge. Following the 'surgery' there would be a meeting with the chief to discuss the next three days' programme.

Depending on the time of year, the first full day would be spent in the court at a public meeting, either collecting the poll tax from village headmen and section chiefs or considering with the chief and elders the Native Authority estimates for the next financial year, a draft of which I would have already prepared for discussion, and approval or otherwise.

Almost inevitably there would be appeals to be heard against the judgement of the chief's court. If there were a decision in a land or bush dispute to be reviewed the site would have to be visited. This might be anything up to ten miles away and would involve another hike through the bush. If one couldn't get back before dark, one would have to take some iron rations and camp bed so as to be able to spend the night in a village hut. Bush disputes could become very heated and it was never advisable to give one's decision on the spot or else one might have a minor battle on one's hands and, on occasion, bloodshed. There might be contracts for the construction of Native Authority buildings to be signed and any work already done inspected, or a trace for a new road to be surveyed.

On one such sortie in connection with a road survey when I was spending the night in an African hut in a remote village in Tonkolili, I was roused in the early hours by shouting and people running about outside. Switching on my torch, which I kept under the pillow on my camp bed, I soon discovered the reason for the disturbance. The mud floor of the hut was covered with thousands of black ants, some of which were already on my bed and others dropping on to me through the mesh of my mosquito net. I have never moved out of bed or a dwelling so quickly and, joined by my faithful court messenger orderly, Komra Sise, who was never far away if I was in need of help, we followed the village people into the adjoining bush away from the black invaders, which have, incidentally, been known to kill and eat tethered horses and cattle. This was indeed 'the stuff which (bad) dreams are made of!'

As general factotum, the District Commissioner never found any shortage of work during the days he spent on trek at a chief's headquarters. In fact, it was sometimes with a feeling of relief that he set off on the relaxing march through the bush back to base.

Taken with permission from:
Alarms and Excursions. Philip Burkinshaw OBE. ISBN 09517742 0 4

Paramount Chief Kullio Yallu.
Terror of the north when young. Now had seventy two wives!

On Trek thirty miles in the bush,
with police and carriers.

To My Readers (both of them)

By Cyril Cook

It occurred to me that you might be interested in the photocopy of a new club tie my daughter and son-in-law bought me for Christmas – replacing one which had, by dint of long service, been somewhat disfigured by sundry drippings from my soldiers, gravy stains, and assorted similar hazards. The club referred to above is: **The South Cheshire Pheasant Pluckers Club.**

The club is affiliated to the Guild of Pheasant Pluckers which dates back to the Crusades. In fact a Pheasant Plucker was one of the first to enter Jerusalem after it was seized from the Sarazens. To become a member of the Pheasant Pluckers Club you have to be either a Pheasant Plucker or come from a Pheasant Plucking family. Part of the initiation ceremony involves proving the ability to show pheasant plucking to be a fine art. The candidate must not go at a bird like a bull at a barn door, but must make his approach gently, removing the outer coverings with finesse so as to have the satisfaction of having firm undamaged, enticing flesh beneath. A Pheasant Plucker is expected to follow this genteel practice in other aspects of his life.

Pheasant Pluckers originated the

253

expression, "A feather in his cap," as when a candidate is admitted to the Guild of Pheasant Pluckers he is given a tail feather to wear in his headgear. On seeing another member thus attired he is obliged to call out firmly, "You're a Pheasant Plucker," to which the reply has to be made equally loudly, "You're a Pheasant Plucker too." Should this challenge and reply not be properly made, no matter what or where the circumstances, be it in church, council meetings, public toilets, or wherever, the Pheasant Plucking members are fined heavily.

A Pheasant Plucker must display his feather at all times, even if he is not wearing a headdress. This applies even in the shower, where it is considered that with a little dexterity on the part of the Pheasant Plucker the feather can be housed temporarily in a secure position.

Should you be interested in this ancient and noble guild I could introduce you. The entry fee, payable to me in used twenty pound notes, is £500.00 plus an annual subscription to be advised. Should there be another crusade you would be called upon to take part and provide your own horse. By being a member of this ancient guild you would have the satisfaction of knowing that all the world will be aware that you are a Pheasant Plucker – there can be no higher accolade.

❖❖❖❖❖❖❖❖❖❖❖❖❖❖❖❖❖❖❖❖❖❖❖❖❖❖❖❖❖❖❖❖❖❖❖❖

Pissed as a Newt

This very rude expression is known to suggest an advanced state of inebriation observed in another, or experienced in oneself. However, why a newt? Since newts live in water one assumes they are most unlikely to come into contact with alcoholic beverages and thus render themselves intoxicated. The answer lies in the East End of London a century or more ago.

In those days you had three sets of circumstances. One: families were big, two: houses were small and overcrowded, three: family funerals were a common occurrence, and were as lavish as the circumstances enjoyed by the organising relatives could afford.

After the funeral, mourners would repair to the family home, with the consequent gathering resembling the shoulder to shoulder of a pre-war football crowd. It was part of the undertaker's duty in those days to provide alcoholic beverages to those present, plus the necessary glassware. The drink almost always provided was port wine. The problem was getting the drink to the would-be consumers, which in many cases was the only reason they came to the funeral in the first place. It was necessary therefore to employ small youths for this task since they could weave their way through the throngs in the tiny rooms more adroitly than the heftier pallbearers, and because of this they were called newts.

The remainder of the explanation tells itself. One newt carrying trays of port wine naturally samples the goods at any given opportunity, particularly since it was free! I wager there was no shortage of applicants for the job, constant hangover or no!

❖❖❖❖❖❖❖❖❖❖❖❖❖❖❖❖❖❖❖❖❖❖❖❖❖❖❖❖❖❖❖❖❖❖❖❖

By Cyril Cook

It was October 1958. My wife and I along with our daughter and my father-in-law were returning from holiday in Grasse, in the south of France in our very comfortable Armstrong Siddeley Sapphire. (Show off). It should be remembered that this was 1958, there were no motorways in those days, petrol in France was severely rationed due to the country's economic difficulties, therefore traffic as you know it today was non-existent.

The Armstrong. (Show off).

We stopped in the country for lunch, which we had carried with us from our holiday home in Grasse, and which was contained along with our luggage, travel documents, passports etc, in the capacious boot of this beautiful motor. (Show off).

I asked my father-in-law if he would get the food out whilst I disappeared into the bushes. I should not have done that. My father-in-law was what is generally described as 'heavy-handed'. The handle opening the boot turned 90° to the right. As I returned from my very necessary visit to the bushes I saw my father-in-law trying to pull it directly towards him, and not having any joy in this endeavour, putting his foot up on the bumper to give him extra leverage. Before I could stop him, the handle, an aluminium alloy die-casting, came away in his hand leaving us incapable of opening up the boot. NO LUNCH.

We climbed back into the car with the intention of finding a garage with a 'Reparation' sign on it. Now, what I have not told you is that it was a SUNDAY, and because of the aforementioned economic situation the few petrol stations we had encountered had no mechanics on the premises.

We began to get a trifle concerned. Food we could buy, but the boot contained our passports, and to get a bed in a hotel in those days you had to show your passport. In addition, our car ferry documents were all securely locked away. Eventually we came, late afternoon, to the outskirts of Lyon. Needing to fill up with petrol I pulled onto the forecourt of a largish garage with the 'Reparation' sign on it, and asked the attendant in my fluent French (show off), whether they could help. He said their workshop was closed on Sundays, but we might find a mechanic working in a small row of lock-ups some 300- 400 metres along the road. He did private work at weekends, although he might have gone home now.

We crossed everything - fingers, legs, even the windscreen wipers, and dashed to the man, hopefully in the lock-ups. We were lucky. He was literally closing the double doors as we arrived.

He was a man in his middle to late thirties, of few words, but immediately sized up the situation and set to work. He drilled out the remainder of the handle, cut out the locking mechanism which left a hefty hole in the lid of the boot. He then started to probe inside the boot lid. What I didn't know, and which obviously he did, the lock on the outside of the boot did not in fact unlock the boot itself, but by means of an extension piece operated a mechanism some fifteen inches under the boot cover which in turn actuated the securing devices on each side.

He had been working now for a good half hour, and my mind switched to finance. Now it is well known that garage men of all nationalities and particularly the French are of the most avaricious, grasping, greedy rapacious breed known to man. Even worse if they have you over a barrel and worse still if they know a stupid Englishman is on the end of their line and will probably pay anything not to miss his ferry booking. I began to mentally count how much cash I had. The boot opened. Well, at least we shall be able to catch the ferry, even if we have no money left for a hotel or food – there were no such things as credit cards in those days, only travellers' cheques, for which a back street mechanic would find no use.

Our mechanic then set-to to make up a tool which would connect up through the hole in the boot cover to the actuating device. This was a lengthy piece of steel rod, fitted with a handle at one end and bent to a delicate shape at the other, which when engaged in a comparatively small slot in the afore-mentioned actuating device, hey presto, opened the boot.

There were smiles and hand claps all round, except for the nagging feeling in my water as to 'how much?!' He had been working for well over an hour on a very finicky

257

job; I had a feeling I was in for a belting. With a casualness I far from felt I asked (as I thanked him profusely),

"Now, how much do we owe you?"

"Nothing."

"Nothing? But you have been working on a Sunday for over an hour."

"Nothing."

"But why nothing?"

"Because in the war I was a soldier in the French army. I escaped to Dunkirk where I was saved by British sailors. When I was in England I was taken into English homes and made welcome. This is the first opportunity I have had to repay any of those kindnesses. You owe me nothing."

How lucky can you get??

◇◇◇◇◇◇◇◇ ◇◇◇◇◇◇◇◇ ◇◇◇◇◇ ◇◇◇◇◇◇◇ ◇◇◇◇◇◇◇ ◇◇◇◇◇◇◇◇

An Oldie

As I, Cyril Cook, am a fully paid up, registered oldie, I am allowed to make jokes about such illustrious members of the human race. In addition, since I am also a 'deafy', I am allowed to similarly do the same in respect of those unfortunates. So hear(?) goes.

An elderly gentleman had serious hearing problems for a number of years. He went to the doctor and the doctor was able to have him fitted for a set of hearing aids that allowed the gentleman to hear 100%.

The elderly gentleman went back in a month to the doctor and the doctor said, "Your hearing is perfect. Your family must be really pleased that you can hear again."

The gentleman replied, "Oh, I haven't told my family yet. I just sit around and listen to the conversations. I've changed my will three times!"

◇◇◇◇◇◇◇◇ ◇◇◇◇◇◇◇ ◇◇◇◇◇◇

Two elderly gentlemen from a retirement centre were sitting on a bench under a tree when one turns to the other and says, "Jim, I'm 83 years old now and I'm just full of aches and pains; "I know you're about my age. How do you feel?"

Slim says, "I feel just like a newborn baby."

"Really?! Like a newborn baby?!"

"Yep. No hair, no teeth, and I think I just wet my pants."

◇◇◇◇◇◇◇◇◇◇◇◇◇◇◇◇◇

From Cherry Cheshire

Many people have expressed to me their complete lack of understanding of the Neanderthal grunts and indecipherable syntax used by London youth but spreading rapidly and inexorably throughout the land. I have made a close study of this phenomenon and offer a translation of a number of the more common expressions as follows.

ASSA COMMONS – Our Parliament building.

ART ATTACK – Extremely perturbed, as in, "Don't tell Sharon, she'll have an art attack."

BANNSA – A person employed to deny access or eject troublemakers at a club. "Dave's got izself a job as a bannsa."

BOAF – The two. "Oi Dave, ooja fancy most, Sharon or Tracy?" Boaf is the reply.

CANCEL – Administrative body of a town. "Darren, wive ad annuvva letter from the cancel."

CANTAFIT – Fake, as in money.

CHOONA – An edible fish purchased in a tin and usually prepared with mayonnaise.

CORT A PANDA – A big hamburger (smaller than an arf panda).

DANSTEZ – On the ground floor, where the biggest telly is.

FINGY – A person or object whose name doesn't come to mind. "I ad it off wiv fingy last night."

HAITCH – Letter of the alphabet between G and I.

IFFY – Dubious. "Ere, Trace, I fink this bread pudding you made last munf's a bit iffy."

KAF – Eating house open during the day.

KAFFY – A girl's name.

LEVVA – Material made from the skin of an animal.

NARTAMEAN – Do you know what I mean? (Sometimes used as janartamean).

PANS AN ANNSIS – Imperial weight system.

RANDEER – Locally. "There ain't much call for it randeer."

SAWTED – Done, arranged, resolved.

TOP EVVY – A woman of plentiful bosom. "Ere look at that, Darren, she's well top evvy."

YAFTA – You must. "Even if yer guilty, yafta av mitigating circumstances."
(Second issue – see page 288)

(Second issue – see page 288)

❖❖❖❖❖❖❖❖❖❖❖❖❖❖❖❖❖❖❖❖❖❖❖❖❖❖❖❖❖❖

Profundity

He who hesitates is sometimes saved.

❖❖❖❖❖❖❖❖❖❖❖❖❖❖❖❖❖

Young people are changed by natural impetuosity and the aged by habit.

❖❖❖❖❖❖❖❖❖❖❖❖❖❖❖❖

Life is what happened between your plans. *John Lennon*

❖❖❖❖❖❖❖❖❖❖❖❖❖❖❖.

Genius is knowing where to stop. *Goethe.*

❖❖❖❖❖❖❖❖❖❖❖❖❖❖❖

I am an optimist – but an optimist who carries a raincoat. *Harold Wilson.*

❖❖❖❖❖❖❖❖❖❖❖❖❖❖❖

By Roger Geeson

Well, I wasn't quite a 'war baby', but a slightly pre-war baby. How very brave it was of my parents to even contemplate starting a family in the summer of 1937, with the diplomatic rumblings of future European conflict looming on the horizon, as must by then have been worryingly obvious, even to relatively unsophisticated political observers such as they.

Not only were the diplomatic signs not good, but with my father earning the grand sum of just over two pounds a week as a journeyman carpenter and joiner, and my mother probably only a little more than half that as a trained milliner, with a weekly mortgage repayment of eight shillings and ninepence to find on their new three bed roomed end-of-terrace 'ideal home' in suburban Sidcup, it was scarcely a propitious time to be embarking on any venture requiring cash and security, let alone a house and family. It should be said, in order to emphasise the extent of their problems and the enormity of their undertaking, that they deliberated long and hard over whether to go for the more 'up-market' end-of-terrace or for what they could more nearly afford – namely the mid-terrace plot which would have set them back just seven shillings and sixpence per week! Eventually, the Jones or Bouquet syndrome kicked in and they cast caution (and one shilling and threepence per week) to the wind and went for the end-of-terrace!

Yes, I owe my very existence to the pluck and courage displayed by my parents in taking a long-term chance on their own spirit, love and propensity for hard work, at a time when the world seemed about ready to cave in on them. I came into that world in March 1938, just six months before Neville Chamberlain returned from Munich bearing the Fuhrer's infamous 'note' guaranteeing peace, twelve months before the break up of Czechoslovakia and the secession to Germany of the Czech Sudetenland and about eighteen months before Hitler, reneging on his promise not to invade Poland, plunged Europe into the hell of major international warfare. The world would never be the same again and I know that I am a different and possibly better individual for having experienced, and for having been fortunate enough to survive, the rigours and privations that the process of global war imposed on all of us.

My mother and I were, and of course he was too, extremely fortunate in that as a skilled construction craftsman my father was classified as being in a 'reserved occupation' and as such was not called up for military service. I think he possibly felt a slight pang of guilt that he was not really seen to be 'doing his bit', particularly as his younger brother was an aircraft fitter in the RAF, but from what I can gather he certainly ran his fair share of risks during his frequent call-outs to shore up and also help evacuate the injured from badly bomb damaged buildings. In addition to working long hours in an arduous occupation, he was engaged most nights as an ARP warden and firewatcher and so certainly made every bit of his fair share of contribution to the war effort.

Blissfully unaware of the fears and uncertainties that beset my parents as I lay gurgling in my cot or crawling around the floor molesting poor Judy, our long-suffering mongrel dog, or bitch to be strictly accurate, we passed through the period of the 'phoney war', as it was called when not very much appeared to happen.

Once war was properly engaged, and with the import convoys bringing in food stuffs and vital war supplies being savaged by the U-boat packs, rationing was soon imposed. My poor mother, along with thousands of others contrived, aided and abetted by countless food gurus broadcasting helpful advice on the BBC, to feed her family on 2 oz of this and 4 oz of that per person per week. With great skill and ingenuity, she nevertheless managed to concoct quite tasty and nutritious meals from what today would have seemed like the best part of nothing at all. Although far too young at that stage to appreciate her efforts, I am led to believe that she did extraordinarily well, and that although we were lean, we were quite fit with it. Far fitter, dare I say, than today's youngsters who have plenty, if not more than enough, but of all the wrong things!

Destined as I was, always to be something of a trial and a constant worry to my long-suffering mother, I started as I meant to go on by arriving as a large, bouncy lump of some nine and a half pounds birth weight. This factor coupled with a seeming reluctance, possibly due to a vision of what lay ahead for us all, to join the rest of humanity in such a troubled world, caused me to keep her in labour for some thirty six distressing and very uncomfortable hours.

This inevitably gave rise to some obstetric complications, prompting the medical staff to advise my mother that there was a fair chance that she might not conceive again. Of course, thereafter, as what was possibly to be their only son, I was spoiled quite noticeably by my parents until a dreadful day some six and a half years later when I was quietly taken to one side to be informed that by some miracle of medical science or more probably of patriarchal skill and persistence, I was shortly to be gifted with a brother or sister! Sometime later I was indeed presented with a baby sister who, whilst our early years could be said to have sometimes been somewhat abrasive, has since proved to be a sister in a million and one of whom I think the world. However, for much of the first seven years of my unworthy existence, I continued to be spoiled out of all proportion to my importance and contribution to the family and have since learned to my everlasting shame that I happily consumed all of the powdered egg ration, most of the butter and almost certainly all the meagre allowance of sugar that came into the house. The latter indulgence, I profess to this day, is believed to be entirely responsible for my incredibly sweet tooth and a pathetic reliance on sugar that remains with me still. Nevertheless, although over-indulged in that respect, I was very fortunate to have been over indulged with very little in terms of actual substance, which prevented my becoming the obese couch potato which otherwise could so easily have been the case.

A particular consequence of rationing, and a rather fond memory which has remained with me throughout my life, was the almost rigid pattern of food preparation which stemmed from the need to avoid waste at all costs and to stretch the available food sources to the very limit. As a result I vividly recall that, from the time when Mother was able to obtain one and I was able to remember it, a miniscule joint of meat such as pork, lamb or occasionally beef would appear on the Sunday table as a roast, from which paper thin slices would be carefully carved and served. This would be accompanied by quantities of potatoes, carrots and swede or cabbage and a huge baking tin of Yorkshire pudding steeped in the meat juices and gravy. The Sunday roast was a feast and something of a ritual.

Needless to say, we all sat around the family table to partake of all our meals with me strapped securely into a folding high chair which cunningly split and hinged to become a crawler on little wheels. There was never a suggestion, even many years later when we finally acquired a small television set, that anyone should eat from their laps, or otherwise fail to join the family meal table without an exceptionally good excuse.

Monday, for an obscure reason that I have never really fathomed, then being the traditional day to tackle the weekly wash, Mother was busy all day, and really had no time to prepare and cook the family dinner. Lo and behold the scraggy remains of Sunday's joint would be produced with a flourish, again thinly sliced, garnished with onions and pickle and served up with vegetables reserved from the weekend feast. These were often mashed up together, moulded into round patties, fried until dark and crispy on the outside and presented as that most wonderful of British culinary delight – bubble and squeak.

Thereafter, on Tuesday, Mother acquired the skills of both a vulture and a magician, stripping the joint to the bone of every last morsel of edible meat. This she carefully minced with a fearsome nickel plated mincing machine which clamped to the leaf of the kitchen table. The mincer retained, throughout its long and useful life, an alarming propensity to detach itself when you were in mid-wind with the handle and unless you were very quick witted, the contents of its capacious hopper would distribute themselves all over the table or worse still – the floor, earning the careless mincer operator a clip on the ear! From this you will have gathered that, from the time when I was old enough to be relied upon not to add my fingers to the remains of the joint in the hopper, when I was around, I became Mother's chief 'mincer', fortunately not a characteristic which I carried with me into adulthood! The minced meat, all the better and more tender for having already been cooked once, was bulked up with minced carrot, a few peas if there were some, heated through and served with mashed potato. Delicious!

Detailed recollections of the remainder of the week's fare elude me but vague memories of such things as spaghetti, cauliflower and macaroni cheese and corned beef hash are surely some of the basic but substantial meals with which my mother sustained her family. We scarcely lived like lords but we certainly never went short. By dint of careful and efficient household management, she saw to that.

At some stage in the very early years of the war, our household, along with thousands of others in areas at risk of enemy bombing and who were fortunate enough to have a small garden, was provided with an Anderson shelter. This ingenious protective measure comprised of six large, curved sheets of heavy gauge corrugated iron which, bolted together and with the long legs of the sheets sunk some three feet into the ground, formed a shelter about six feet six inches by four feet six inches on plan.

With the curved roof covered with the soil from the three feet deep excavation and the ends protected with steel 'blast' plates, these cheap and cheerful contrivances provided adequate shelter from the then daytime bombing and the liberal scattering of shell burst shrapnel. This felt like hot steel rain when the anti-aircraft 'Ack Ack' gunners, in conjunction with the cannon and machine guns of the RAF fighters, were doing their best to blast marauding Heinkel and Dornier bombers from the skies over London as well as provincial cities and dockyards, railway termini and industrial targets everywhere.

Designed principally for daytime use, the 'Andersons' were cold and damp, not at all popular when night-time bombing became the norm and in which people were expected to sleep during raids.

Of course, my father being something of a perfectionist and being 'in the trade' as it were, our Anderson was a work of art, the excavation being provided with a concrete floor and half height wall and a miniature flight of concreted steps down from garden level. The shelter was fitted with two timber framed and steel mesh in-filled bunks and I had a third bunk set slightly higher and across my parents feet. Since even as a small child I slept like a log, even when the air raid sirens sounded their mournful wailing, I was frequently carried down to the end of the garden wrapped in a blanket and, still fast asleep, placed gently in my bunk. If the bombing had been persistent and extended, I frequently awoke the following morning a little surprised to find myself no longer tucked up in my cheerful, pastel yellow painted nursery, complete with cartoon characters, a large teddy and a gyrating mobile. Instead, I was reposing just a few inches below a cold, rust streaked, white distempered, corrugated steel ceiling which dripped droplets of condensation onto my blankets and with the never to be forgotten smell of the faithful Valor paraffin heater, the acrid but not altogether unpleasant aroma of candles and, even in Dad's 'Ritz' of an Anderson, that all pervading smell of dampness in my nostrils. That musty odour which you could taste in your mouth, which permeated your clothing and characterised the semi-troglodyte lifestyle which, for that mercifully short period of the war, one almost became used to.

I mentioned the Valor stove and what a wonderful piece of kit that was. Standing about two feet high or so and about nine inches in diameter, it had a hinged top section which gave access to the brass paraffin container surmounted by the tubular wick holder with its knurled adjustment knob and which was topped off by a narrow metal flue. The flue and the outer casing had little oval mica windows conveniently located so that you could check the state of the flame. The top of the hinged outer section was decoratively perforated, which when the stove was alight, would cast a kaleidoscopic pattern on the ceiling. The secret to getting the vest from a Valor stove was keeping the wick properly trimmed and adjusted. Get it wrong and the beast would produce a smoky yellow flame which burned cold and produced lots of carbon 'lamp black' and fumes which choked you. Get it right and the flame burned blue, with no offensive by-products and hot enough to toast bread on the top plate, which we often did.

I suppose in fairness that I can only possibly have hazy residual memories of the tail-end of the bombing 'Blitz' as it was called, from the German term 'Blitzkrieg', as it ended in May 1941 when I would have been a little over three years old. However, sub-conscious memories are hard to shift and can apparently invoke unusual behavioural patterns, of which I would later experience at least one example. I had evidently become used to sleeping in a steel box, the Anderson in my early formative years, and then subsequently, the 'Morrison' as well and I would later on display a peculiar tendency to sleepwalk in the early hours. During such nocturnal perambulations I would head not for the larder or the ice-box (we did not have refrigerators in those austere days) as might be expected, but for the enamelled cast iron bath in the bathroom. Therein, I would curl up and sleep the sleep of the innocent, sometimes with the benefit of a blanket or quilt dragged from my bed, but most times without. How I failed to succumb to the rigours of pneumonia I shall never know, bearing in mind that central heating was a future luxury, and that in our house one scraped the ice off the *inside* of the windows in order to check what the weather was like outside! Anyway, I never did and since I also appear to have resisted the temptation to turn on the taps, thereby running the risk of drowning myself, I seemed to suffer no ill-effects other than lowering my body temperature by several degrees. Fortunately this strange habit appears to have terminated with the onset of puberty, only to be replaced by other, equally strange, habits over which one should perhaps draw a discretionary veil!

I am sure that, had this odd activity persisted into adulthood, any psychoanalyst armed with a Freudian text book, and a set of suggestive ink blots would have conjured up from my curious behaviour a diagnosis of some heinous, sectionable deviancy. So, fortunately, I was saved from the shrinks in white coats and, so far as I am aware, have never suffered from somnambulism since.

I referred earlier to the ice-box and to the household's lack of a refrigerator. Prior to the arrival of the ice-box, the bottled milk delivered by the milkman (remember them?) together with our meagre margarine ration and other perishables, were preserved in the summer months for a day or two by being stored in a hole about a cubic foot in size which my father had dug in the small lawn just outside the kitchen door. The hole was lined to keep out the bugs and father had provided it with a close fitting timber lid. Not ideal, as it was a step or two to fetch the milk in when required, but it served its purpose and worked very well, even in the hottest of summers. Several years later Dad came by this old wooden ice-box which to us was a luxury. Lined with zinc sheet and very heavily insulated with compressed straw and cork crumb, its internal capacity was a fraction of its external size which was about that of a small chest of drawers. Large hinged doors on the front, secured with proper spring loaded cold store latches, gave access to the main storage section whilst a small door allowed crushed ice to be poured into a separate compartment at the end. This had its own integral drainage and collection tray for when the ice eventually melted. Crude, but very effective, I think would sum up its performance but, since there was no room for it in our ludicrously small kitchen, it ended up in the garden shed, to where it was of course an even longer hike to fetch the milk than the hole in the ground!

I also made reference to the saga of wash day Monday. In those austere days of the 40s, washing day for the majority was sheer drudgery. Washing machines were a far off dream except for the very well off and my poor mother kept all of us spotless with the crudest of equipment, more in tune with a ship's engine room than a domestic kitchen.

We had a gas heated copper which first had to be physically dragged out from under the teak draining board, filled with cold water via a hose from the sink tap and then fired up with a long lighted spill through the little ignition port in front of the enamelled casing. After what seemed like an eternity the copper would at last be boiling and Mother would add the Rinso or Oxydol flakes or something similar, perhaps some soda crystals depending on the wash and pile in the soiled laundry which she would agitate and pummel with a wooden batten, bleached and grainily eroded through long exposure to boiling, soapy water. Especially heavily soiled articles, which I assume were usually mine, were scrubbed on a ribbed washboard with yellow cake soap and a stiff bristle brush until seen to pass the exceptionally high standards of the launderer. When deemed to be 'done', the laundry would be hauled out of the copper with a pair of similarly bleached and eroded spring hinged wooden tongs and transferred to the deep white earthenware belfast sink for rinsing by hand. After thorough rinsing, roughly ringing out by hand and placing in a large bowl, the heavy wet washing would be carried outside, regardless of weather conditions and 'mangled'.

In our house, to my eternal regret, we never aspired to a Victorian model cast iron framed mangle. These awesome but strangely beautiful machines, which I feel sure must have been designed by Stephenson or Trevithick, were fitted with a pair of five inch diameter, heavy spring tensioned, lathe turned wooden rollers operated by a twelve or fifteen inch diameter geared hand wheel. This dreadnought I am certain could have coped with hot rolled iron girders if pressed, since the rollers were possessed of a potentially lethal crushing capability. No, we had a much more modest modern light steel angle framed 'wringer' with a pair of two inch diameter rubber faced rollers and a flimsy cranked winding handle which, I was later to discover to my considerable chagrin, possessed a lethal crushing capacity almost the equal of its gargantuan Victorian forbears . Having wrung the majority of the water from the washing, after perhaps several passes through the wringer and the possible loss of several buttons to the unforgiving rollers, Mother would then peg the laundry onto the braided rope clothes line, which ran the length of the garden. This was done regardless of weather conditions, excepting of course rain, and with luck they would be dry enough to iron on Tuesday or Wednesday. Having committed the laundry to the rigours of the washing line, and sometimes, in the winter, I have seen my parents 'cracking' frozen bed sheets in order to fold them up small enough to bring into the house, it was then back to draining the copper. This was done by means of a brass tap at the bottom, into a bowl or bucket and thence to the sink for disposal. By this time, as may be imagined the kitchen floor was generally awash and had to be mopped over and dried thoroughly. Little wonder then, after the foregoing saga, that my mother had neither the energy nor inclination to cook a family meal and that the above described 'cold meat and pickles' was therefore generally the Monday standby.

Even less wonder then when years later, as we took delivery of our first Hotpoint top loader with integral powered wringer, Mother breathed a sigh of relief which could be heard, so they say, all the was to Chiesmans in Lewisham, from which august emporium the aforesaid labour, and possibly life, saving machine had been purchased! Said acquisition would possibly have necessitated the provision of another little compartment labelled 'HP' in the cash box of which more will later be revealed.

I touched earlier upon the lethal crushing capacity of our pathetic little wringer and therein lies the clue to my subsequent misfortune, as I 'touched upon' a part which bit back! I was then, as a small boy of I suppose some five or six years of age, and still am, inherently curious, particularly of things mechanical. Regrettably, this innate and well honed curiosity and desire to 'take things apart to see how they work' was not always matched by a guaranteed ability to reconstruct the dismantled item. At least it was not matched by an ability to reconstruct so that the unfortunate object still worked after my inept and amateurish scrutiny. On many an occasion in my formative years I found it necessary either to seek the assistance of a 'grown up' to satisfactorily rebuild one of my demolition jobs or, even more shamefacedly, to casually replace the assorted cogs, spindles and washers haphazardly and then to strenuously deny having every been anywhere near it when the stricken item was eventually discovered to be malfunctioning! However, enough of my true confessions for now, back to the saga of my contretemps with our wringer.

At the end of each roller was attached a steel cog wheel and from one roller cog wheel protruded a cranked handle. The two cogs intermeshed and, little Einstein as I then was, I had worked out that by turning one roller with the handle the meshing cogs would make the other roller turn as well, albeit in the opposite direction. Excitedly anxious to impart this gem of mechanical wisdom to my mother who I felt sure, in a particularly early display of chauvinism, would not be privy to such male orientated knowledge, I tugged at her sleeve, attempted to explain this marvellous technical phenomenon, and pointed to the meshing gears which, unfortunately for me, she was winding at the time. I remember that it was cold outside where the wringing out was being done and that in consequence I was wearing woollen gloves. Not *just* gloves you understand but as an accompaniment to my normal winter attire! As I pointed, the cogs caught my gloves and with it the tip of my index finger. My agonised screams produced a lightening reaction in my mother who, with credible presence of mind, immediately ceased her exertions on the handle. Ever sensible, or maybe she just couldn't bear the sight of blood or the thought of what she might find, she did not remove my glove but instead, straightaway rushed me the quarter mile down the road to our local doctor's surgery, one Dr Jackson I recall. Now this was pre-NHS days you will realise when, on the debit side you paid the doctor to come out and indeed for whatever treatment he doled out if you went to him. On the credit side, doctors then were doctors and thus dispensed 'doctoring', by which I mean the broader spectrum of medical attention as distinct from the medicinal administrative treatment which passes for 'doctoring' in our enlightened society.

In those days you went to the doctor and, except in those suffering the most serious of conditions, the doctor treated you, cleaned, sterilised and patched you up, or set a broken bone in plaster rather than, as now, confining their treatment to a rapid diagnosis, prescribing of drugs you probably don't need and which are beset with possibly unpleasant side effects and, in the event of the merest hint of blood or minor injury, shipping you off to the A & E Department of some far distant general hospital! There you may possibly die of boredom, expire from malnutrition after several days of waiting, or attract a dose of lethal staphylococcus or MRSA from idly fingering a trolley in the corridor.

On the contrary, this proper doctor calmly but carefully removed the by now blood soaked and soggy glove from my injured paw, observed that the tip of my index finger remained attached to the rest of said digit by the merest thread and, calmly sitting me on his couch proceeded to sew the fingertip back on with commensurate skill and some nifty needle work. I bear the scar to this day but, to the credit of an excellent local GP, I suffered no loss of sensation or any other long-term ill effects. How I wish that, painfully recalling the many hours that I have frittered away during what have been mercifully few subsequent visits to A & E in later life, we could regress a little and revert to using some of the good old systems. They worked!

Back to the war, where an added complication to our lives had arisen as a result of my maternal grandparents having been bombed out of their property in Whitechapel during one of the raids on London's docks.

In consequence, having nowhere else to stay and we having a little spare space, it was arranged that they should come and live with us until alternative and more permanent arrangements could be made. They were both then middle-aged and Granddad was still working at his fishmonger's shop in Whitechapel; not that in those deprived times he had very much fish to 'monger'.

Quite apart from the fact that the Anderson was already a bit cramped with the three of us using it, my grandparents had reached the stage in their lives when getting up from their relatively warm back bedroom in the middle of the night, getting partially dressed and traipsing down to the far end of the garden every time the siren sounded, was a considerable problem.

In fact it was for them, on balance, quite likely to become a more dangerous impairment to their future wellbeing than anything the Luftwaffe was likely to deliver in our direction. In addition, actually getting down into the shelter via the narrow and sometimes slippery concrete steps presented something of a physical challenge to their slightly arthritic old joints and it soon became very clear that alternative arrangements needed to be made now that they were billeted with us permanently.

Fortunately, albeit very rarely as I have subsequently come to realise, the Government put into effect at around that time an idea which was to solve our problem. Although the Anderson was very effective, and certainly ours was above average quality and comfort as air raid shelters went, and would have been rated at about two start on the Michelin scale, the persistent night bombing and the general dislike of this shelter prompted the all caring Government to come up with a slightly better alternative.

The shelter Mk II, proletariat for the use of, was at least designed for use *indoors* thereby avoiding the additional problems of British weather conditions adding to the unpleasantness of the Fuehrer's efforts. Whilst I rather doubt that he personally had anything to do with its design, Herbert Morrison took credit for and gave his name to the new breed of 'Morrison' shelter. This was basically a six feet six inch, by four feet six inch sheet of one quarter inch steel plate, steel framed and supported on angle iron legs, and was designed to be installed inside a ground floor room. It was less than three feet high, apparently to allow it to double as a dining table, and was the cause of many a sore head if you sat up in bed suddenly for any reason.

As usual, whether by Government recommendation or not, Father had gone more than the extra mile in converting our front room into a mini fortress. As well as the steel Morrison shelter, he had shored up the entire room with heavy timbers so that, even if the whole house collapsed from blast upon it, the cell would have survived intact. He had also sealed the room against gas attack. The floor boards were plugged with folded newspapers punched into the gaps, window casements sealed with adhesive tape, the fireplace sealed, gaps around the door frame filled with foam strips and all air bricks temporarily papered over. Father took the view that chlorine was for swimming pools and the only way he was prepared to take mustard was on the side of his plate. There was certainly no way that Adolf was going to get his fiendish concoctions into *our* front room if my father had anything to do with it! Mind you, how long the air in the room would have lasted with sometimes five people taking advantage of the security it afforded, poses a question which I do not believe was ever the subject of scientific examination or review.

Had we experienced a near hit, causing us to be trapped within this modern sarcophagus for any length of time, we might well have presented the authorities with the unusual phenomena of uncovering possibly five bodies from the debris, quite unmarked, but who had all expired from shortness of breath! Not a pleasant thought but maybe I exaggerate the risk, and perhaps Father's 'room sealing' capabilities were not as hermetically perfect as he may have imagined.

So for the duration of hostilities at home, Granny and Granddad slept each night in the Morrison shelter. In the event of an alarm, dependant I suppose upon the actual time of the raid and the general clemency of conditions outside, I would be whipped out of bed and we would all either pile into the Morrison together, head to toe like sardines in a can, or just the three of us would decamp to the Anderson if conditions were not too cold or wet.

Whilst I have mentioned Sunday, Monday and Tuesday in respect of their meals ritual, and Monday as a traditional washing day, I cannot remember anything special about Wednesday. Nothing that is except the old adage that, "Wednesday's child if full of woe," so maybe that's a good enough reason for glossing over Wednesdays.

Thursday of course was 'pay day' for Dad and, as such, very important. Not so much because of the actual receipt of the paltry pay packet, but because Thursday evening was when my mother sat down at the kitchen table with her lined foolscap book and the little black enamelled lockable tin cash box, which my father had carefully divided with thin plywood strips into small compartments, each of which Mother had carefully labelled either as – mortgage, rates, electric, gas, Prudential, birthdays, milkman, housekeeping etc. Should there have been a copper or two left over after Mother had carefully apportioned the income amongst the essential divisions, then this would go into another little compartment labelled 'surplus', to be set against emergencies, the occasional luxury or as a hedge against an unforeseen shortfall in any other department. Needless to say, there was rarely as much as a copper or two for the 'surplus' compartment and this accumulated exceedingly slowly!

Each week a page of the foolscap account book would be dated and record entries made as each contribution was paid into its designated compartment of the cashbox. With luck, as each monthly or quarterly payment became due there would be a little extra in its section within the box, which would be transferred, with just a wee trace of smug triumphalism, into the 'surplus' section.

My mother was as much a financial genius with the family's sparse resources as my father was hopeless. With Dad, if he had a penny he'd lend or even give it to you, but if he hadn't – then it was bad luck. There was no question of cash flow planning or saving for a rainy day, and, had it not been for Mother, we would have acquired very little in material terms.

In years to come, thanks to her careful custodianship of the family finances, a further tier would be added and additional little compartments constructed within the cash box, labelled 'car, telephone, TV licence, and holidays' among others. Yes, Dad's hard work and her prudent money management brought us a reasonably comfortable standard of living well above that which we might have otherwise expected.

Her prudence extended to avenues beyond stringent cash management, for she knitted and darned constantly to keep everyone smartly turned out. I well recall a particular pair of swimming trunks which she knitted for me shortly after the war in readiness for a day trip to the seaside. Well perhaps seaside was stretching credulity just a little as the trip was to Allhallows, about halfway down the Thames estuary, but it was a start and I loved it. The swimming trunks were fine until I had the temerity to actually venture into the water, whereupon they stretched from waist to ankle and looked positively ridiculous. This may account for why one sees so few sheep swimming I reckon. Come to think of it, I do believe that Wednesday would probably have been 'ironing, darning and mending day' – no wonder Wednesday's child was full of woe!

However, very few of my mother's attempts at couture, haute or otherwise met with failure or were as disastrous as the knitted trunks. I well remember that shortly after the war ended, when all clothing was rationed and coupons were like gold dust, I was dressed in the smartest of khaki drill shorts and tan silk shirts. I was the envy of my school friends and I'm sure their parents were utterly convinced that my mother was in league with a 'spiv' or involved in something highly dubious to be able to obtain such superb clothes for me. Little did they know that, in Woolwich market via a long walk to Bexleyheath and a 696 trolleybus ride to Beresford Square, my mother was buying war surplus WD kit bags and huge triangular panels of parachute silk, apparently available to anyone without coupons. From these work-a-day, lack lustre materials she was, very skilfully and laboriously making my shorts and shirts. I have no idea how many hours my mother spent at the dining room table, bent over her faithful old hand-operated Singer sewing machine, but I do know that it wasn't that easy, as I sometimes got to wind the cotton bobbins for her. I'm also told that it took a bit of soaking and scrubbing to get the stencilled, 'name, rank & number' off the kit bags, for which process I was duly grateful since it rendered the rather tough and resilient material soft enough for comfort. If you know how tough an army kit bag is, you'll have some idea of how indestructible my shorts were. Good news in a boisterous and adventurous eight year old!

Friday of course was 'bath night' or, as advertisements for the popular shampoo, current at the time, ran, 'Friday night's Amami night!' Now, although I must emphasise that our smart 'ideal homes' three bed end-of-terrace did boast a separate bathroom, unlike many houses at that time, it must be remembered that the questionable joys of central heating were years into the future, and that our house only had solid fuel fireplaces, one in the living room, one in the front room and in each of the two big bedrooms. Before the war the front room would, in all probability, have been called the parlour but things moved on. Due to quite severe fuel rationing it was not normal to light a fire in the front room unless it was to be used for entertaining, and not much of that went on during those war years. In addition, you may remember that my father had 'gas proofed' the front room and that involved sealing the flue.

Fires were never to the best of my recollection laid in the bedrooms, sheet ice on the window panes and freezing cold linoleum between the occasional rug providing our own domestic 'Gordonstoun' toughening up process. However, the living room and the fireplace in there concealed a secret. Behind the grate there lurked a cunning contrivance known as a 'back boiler'. This was a very small water tank with large, twin galvanised barrel pipes running up the side of the chimney breast, connecting it to a large, square, galvanised hot water cistern in the back bedroom airing cupboard. When a decently banked up fire was lit in the grate, this tiny tank heated a cistern of hot water very efficiently by way of convection in the flow and return pipes. So hot water was available but, in winter the bathroom was like an igloo – as was the remainder of the house. Only an Inuit would have felt comfortable in there. So, as a youngster, I was bathed in an oval zinc bath laboriously filled from the kitchen tap and placed on the hearth rug in front of the living room fire. This was of course an effective way of saving precious hot water as the amount needed to give a comfortable depth in the zinc bath would have had me sitting in about an inch of water in the proper bath.

Whilst this was great fun and very pleasant for me, as the overall dimensions of the zinc bath were somewhat restrictive, I suspect that my unfortunate parents had to endure the freezing conditions in the bathroom, come what may. Later on my multi-talented father, at a time when the word CORGI referred only to a breed of small Welsh dog much favoured by our Royal family, acquired and installed a gas heater in the bathroom. Having cut and tapped into the supply to the gas point by the back bedroom fireplace and extended it to the bathroom, Dad fitted this imposing, almost art deco style, gas radiator. It comprised twin, cast iron, tapering box columns with, at the base of each column, a framed orange glazed lift up flap through which to light the fishtail burners. This appliance made winter use of the bathroom much more bearable, facilitated the rapid drying of wet towels and the warm orange light from the glass windows imparted a psychological warming effect, even if the gas jets, as they generally would be, were set at their lowest economy level.

Some years later, when my father and I installed central heating throughout the house, the back boiler and pipe work were removed and replaced by a gas boiler in the kitchen, serving panel radiators in every room. Out of curiosity, we took off the access plate of the back boiler and found to our astonishment a cavity within the accumulated lime scale barely larger than an orange. Similarly the one and a quarter inch bore of the flow and return pipes had been reduced to about half an inch diameter adjacent to the boiler. These discoveries were testament not only to the extreme hardness of Thames Valley water, but to the incredible efficiency of the principle of convection. No accelerator pump was fitted to that type of system and it is remarkable that it ever delivered hot water at all – but it did!

It was whilst I was using Dad's trusty Primus paraffin fuelled blow lamp (easy, clean, convenient bottled gas blow lamps which didn't seem to get half as hot, had not yet become available) to sweat the yorkshire soldiered joints of the copper tubing in the central heating system, that my memory was stirred and I was reminded of something that I had witnessed years before.

In order the produce the required level of heat to melt and run the solder, the blow lamp had first to be primed and pre-heated with a little fuel on a scrap of paper burning in a small brass cup just below the nozzle. When sufficient heat and pressure had built up the vaporised paraffin in the tank would rise, under pressure, to exit at the nozzle and burn with a fierce tongue of bright blue flame and a fearsome, deep throated menacing roar. Now where had I seen and heard that particular combination of sight and sound before? Then I remembered what it reminded me of.

It would have been in the summer of 1944, sometime between June and September maybe, when I would have been just over six years old. I say between June and September although I really cannot recall exactly. I just know that it was a Sunday lunchtime, because Dad was at home with us and that it was a warm and beautiful summer day. Quite obviously, the air raid siren had warned of imminent attack but because it was such a marvellous day, my mother and father had opted to decamp to the old Anderson shelter which they kept in good order and perfectly habitable in the garden.

In the circumstances they figured that this would be infinitely preferable to joining my grandparents, who would have been occupying the Morrison shelter, in the stuffy, airless confines of the front room. I remember it so vividly and, to this day, can almost smell the flowers in the garden mingled with the familiar musty smell of the shelter. It was around lunchtime when the air raid warning had sounded. Plates and cutlery were gathered up, and the pudding, to which point in our repast we had progressed at the juncture of Goering's untimely interruption, was transferred with us to the far end of the garden.

I was standing on the steps which went down from the garden path to the floor level of the shelter, earnestly gazing up into the sky and obviously hoping to see the RAF Spitfires or Hurricanes up from Biggin Hill and adjacent airfields. I had often been lucky enough to watch those beautiful aircraft wheeling and banking as their young pilots bravely engaged either the enemy bombers direct or, which was much more exciting, did battle in dogfights with the Messerschmitt ME109 fighters which usually accompanied the bombers and provided protective cover on their raids over London and the Home Counties.

I had in my hand a small bowl of stewed plums and custard, or what passed for custard in those austere days – very little powdered milk and almost no sugar! Now I come to think of it, since the plums would undoubtedly have been Victoria plums from our own tree, which overhung the shelter, it was probably September time rather than earlier in the summer. Having said that, Mother was a dab hand with the Kilner preserving jars and they could possibly have been plums harvested in previous years. But I digress...

So there I was, gazing skywards, clutching this bowl of plums and custard in one hand and a spoon in another, for even in those dark and belligerent days we maintained the highest standards of etiquette and decorum in table manners, searching the skies for any signs of aerial combat or other activity. I searched in vain for the familiar fighters on this occasion. Not for a the first time during that awful summer of 1944, since the very first one had landed, explosively but harmlessly in farmland at Swanscombe in Kent at around dawn on June 13th; this was not a bombing raid in the accepted sense. I continued to scan the skies, but sight was not my initial intimation of foreign visitors, as that dreadful sound first came to my ears. That was the droning, spluttering, throaty roar of the crude pulse jet, 'blow lamp' engine mounted on the fuselage of a dreaded V-1, flying bomb or 'Doodle Bug' as they were soon universally christened.

Then in a virtually clear blue sky I saw it and, fascinated, I continued to watch the Doodle Bug's unerring progress. My parents meanwhile, sat unconcerned on their bunks, probably listening to Tommy Handley and ITMA on the battery powered radio they habitually took with them to the shelter. Never mind that there's a war on, one simply couldn't miss Tommy Handley and the ITMA on a Sunday afternoon. It was an institution and remained such for years after the war ended.

Suddenly, simply by way of a helpful running commentary on the progress of the war that afternoon, I called out, "Dad, the flame's gone out!"

Never before can five, small, unremarkable and relatively innocent little words have initiated such a profound reaction from a body. Whilst I was still gazing skywards, my right arm was seized in a vice like grip and I was instantly propelled, sideways and downwards, into the bowels of the Anderson. My bowl of plums and precious, if sugarless, custard went one way, the spoon another and I ended up in an untidy heap on the shelter floor, conscious of the fact that my father's not inconsiderable bulk was draped over me in what I later and gratefully realised was a protective mantle.

Although it seemed like a lifetime, I suppose not more than a few seconds elapsed whilst we sorted ourselves out and my parents established that my untimely dumping on the shelter floor had caused no lasting damage, when the ground shook and there was a muffled 'crump' immediately followed by a louder, more cracking explosion as its warhead of some 850 Kg of TNT erupted. The V-1 landed on a shallow glide path, took out part of Holy Trinity Church and, not content with its afternoon's work, skipped across the road, completely demolishing the Odeon cinema; both not a mile from our vantage point.

Whilst we suffered no harm, I of course never quite forgave my parents for their totally 'over the top' precautionary action in depriving me of the one chance I'd had that summer of plotting an actual landing of one of those fiendish devices. I could of course have wound up in heaven, with my golden pencil and mother-of-pearl notepad, reporting the scene from and altogether more ethereal perspective, so I suppose they had a point.

It was indeed surprising to learn, much later, that of just over 9200 V-1 missiles, plotted as crossing the English coastline, no less than 4150 or almost fifty percent were destroyed before reaching their targets. Of these 'kills', almost 3900 were brought down by either gunfire or fighter planes in almost equal numbers, whilst barrage balloon tethering cables accounted for nearly 300 more.

Perhaps the most bizarre defensive procedure brought to bear against the V-1 that emerged, was the practice undertaken by some 'devil may care' fighter pilots. This involved flying alongside a missile, matching their airspeed precisely at about 330 mph and, having waited until they were over open country or an otherwise safe area, and then very bravely nudging the flying bomb off course and into a terminal dive with their wing tip. This first example of this perhaps foolhardy, but nonetheless effective, method of despatch was reported by a young Australian fighter ace flying a new MK XIV Spitfire for 91 Squadron based at West Malling. Having expended all his ammunition in attempting to shoot down the V-1, he resorted to this cunning manoeuvre and was delighted when it worked. He reported the incident and the outcome to his intelligence officer, but his claim of success was at first treated with some scepticism by both ground staff and his fellow pilots. Only when his plane was examined and his wing tip found to be marked with traces of fresh black paint was his story given credence.

Needless to say, the technique was soon widely copied throughout the squadrons of Fighter Command which had to deal with this particular menace.

Regrettably, no such similar defences to those used so relatively successfully against the V-1 could be employed to counter the ravages of its successor.

Whilst the V-1 did possess the positive advantage of being both seen and heard to be coming, thus giving a gambling man half a chance of betting on whether or not his 'name was on it', the truly evil spawn of the Doodle Bug, the V-2 rocket, displayed no such sporting pretensions.

Being a true rocket, fired on a parabolic trajectory into the stratosphere before falling back to earth, the V-2 arrived out of the blue, suddenly, silently and at nearly four times the speed of sound with absolutely no warning. On impact, its one ton warhead blew its landing site to pieces without the unfortunate recipients even realising that they were under attack. A true vengeance weapon – Vergeltungswaffe zwei, as Hitler had personally designated his fiendish means of retribution.

The very first V-2 rocket, fired at England from Walcheren Island off the Dutch coast, plunged into Chiswick on September 8th 1944, killing three, seriously injuring seventeen and leaving a thirty foot wide crater in the ground. Phase two of Hitler's final offensive against English soil had begun and would continue on its course of murderous destruction until the final rocket, fired as a last desperate hurrah, fell in Court Road Orpington on 27th March 1945. This rocket, whilst injuring many, was responsible for the sole fatality – one unfortunate lady who had previously survived a very near miss in January 1945 by virtually the last V-1 flying bomb, which had, by some cruel twist of fate, also landed in Court Road.

Of a total of 1115 V-2 rocket hits reported, 517 reached London with the balance of 598 spread randomly throughout the Home Counties and East Anglia.

At the time when the last V-2 fell and by now just seven years old, I continued to attend the infants school in Dorchester Avenue, where I had started at age four and a half. For a long time after the war finally ended, I continued to locate and collect, to my mother's evident discomfort, odd pieces of shrapnel which could be found in ditches and hedgerows everywhere. My father once acquired the de-fused magnesium body of an incendiary bomb which, for me, came in extremely useful when I later developed a keen interest in chemistry, and hack-sawed and filed this block to produce magnesium powder for various experiments.

One infamous relic of offensive weaponry, about which I have been warned in the direst terms and for which I searched diligently and most carefully, but without success, throughout the war proper, was the 'butterfly bomb'.

It was said that the cunning Bosch had designed a small anti-personnel bomb to look like a colourful butterfly which, when dropped during raids, would drift down, on a small parachute I believe and hang suspended in tress or shrubs, daring inquisitive youngsters to pick it up or pluck it from the branches. Those who found one and ignored official warnings 'not to touch' would pay dearly for their curiosity with the loss of limbs or even of life itself. However, whilst I assume that they existed, perhaps fortunately, I never actually saw one.

VE or Victory in Europe Day in May 1945 (VJ Day denoting victory in Japan did not follow until August of that year) saw the most lavish of street parties. Everyone it seemed, though they may have suffered actual loss of loved ones, homes or possessions, was ready to celebrate that great day and parties went on for a very long time in many places. Quite where the 'goodies' came from to celebrate in such style and with such flamboyance is unlikely ever to be known; but the British are masters of improvisation, and there did seem to be more than enough to celebrate with.

I suppose that, all in all, I was extremely lucky and I didn't have a bad war. Certainly, one subsequently heard horror stories of the misery, rejection, privations and even cruelty suffered by some children who were lifted from their families, and familiar environments, and evacuated from those areas likely to have suffered bombing.

Shipped off to total strangers in unfamiliar parts of the countryside, usually with just a small cardboard suitcase of essential items, a label tied to their sleeve and the brown cardboard box containing the obligatory gas mask slung around their necks, many were desperately unhappy. Although, of course not all were treated badly and there were many who thoroughly enjoyed their evacuee experiences, boarded with caring and loving second families in countryside or seaside environments, of which not a few had been previously totally unaware. I remain so glad that I was allowed to stay with my own parents throughout the duration of hostilities. Sure enough there were severe difficulties. Nights of lost sleep for some; although I'm not aware that I suffered in that direction. The dank and murky shelters. For thousands, nights spent sleeping on tube station platforms. The constant fear of enemy attack, either by conventional or incendiary bombing, and of course the flying bombs, rockets and land mines.

In addition, those who stayed behind coped with the problems caused by blast damaged homes, fractured gas and water mains interrupting vital services, bomb damage, debris strewn streets and the ubiquitous little shored up excavations which cropped up everywhere as the incredibly brave Royal Engineers Bomb Disposal Squads dealt with increasing numbers of unexploded ordnance. All this, plus the ever-present 'blackout' with stern warnings to 'mind that light' and the knock on the door by the ARP wardens should any chink of illumination be seen from anywhere outside!

Finally, there was always the distinct possibility that one could have been unlucky enough to have taken a near or even direct hit, resulting in death or injury, but all things considered, and with of course that indispensable ingredient known as hindsight

I'm glad I stayed!

◇◇◇◇◇◇◇◇◇◇◇◇◇◇◇◇◇◇◇◇◇◇◇◇◇◇◇◇◇◇◇◇◇◇

Strokes – A Serious Matter

Sometimes the symptoms of a stroke are difficult to identify. Unfortunately, this lack of awareness can spell disaster. The stroke victim may suffer severe brain damage when people nearby fail to recognise the symptoms.

Now doctors say that a bystander can recognise a possible stroke by asking three simple questions, perhaps remembered by the initials S.T.R.

S   Ask the individual to SMILE.

T   Ask the person to TALK and SPEAK a simple sentence coherently (eg It is a sunny   day today).

R   Ask the victim to RAISE BOTH ARMS.

If they have any trouble with ANY ONE of these tasks, call 999 immediately and describe the symptoms to the operator.

<u>A new sign of a stroke</u> - Stick out your tongue!
If the tongue is crooked or if it goes to one side or the other, that is also an indication of a stroke.
Remember these simple tests – you never know, you could
SAVE A LIFE!

By Bob Adams

Lawrence is sitting in a comfortable seat in the first class buffet car having a drink. He is smiling contentedly. He spies a friend – Graham and hails him.

Lawrence:	Graham old boy. Long time. Sit yourself down and join me. What'll you have?
Graham:	Lawrence. How nice. Yes, please. Whisky.
Lawrence:	(Beckons steward) Two whiskies please.
Graham:	Thanks. What brings you north in mid week? Not another takeover?
Lawrence:	Not business at all. Pleasure, pure pleasure.
Graham:	I thought last time...
Lawrence:	This is different.
Graham:	Go on! You're in love. Don't give me that.

The steward (or stewardess) puts the whiskies down before them.

Lawrence:	Cheers Graham. No. Of course not. No, but it's beautiful.
Graham:	Cheers. I'm sure it is. Well I hope you're not raising expectations in some poor lass's breast.
Lawrence:	Not at all. Her only expectation is of my next visit. No she's a married woman. A happily married woman.
Graham:	Married! How could you?
Lawrence:	Very well I can tell you. Of course she's married. I'm married aren't I? All carefully thought out. Nobody gets hurt.
Graham:	Not even Judith?
Lawrence:	Especially not Judith. I'm happier because of my little interludes. I'm a better husband. Doing Judith a favour.
Graham:	And your mistress's husband? Doing him a favour as well?
Lawrence:	Not mistress, please. I'm sure I am. When I first met her she was bored to distraction – and grumpy. My, she was grumpy. I wouldn't like to have lived with her then. No, she'll be much better now.
Graham:	But you'll be rumbled. Always are.

Lawrence:	No chance. He goes fishing. She drives him to the station. Sees him off before driving back to the house and waiting for me. A signal and in I go.
Graham:	And if he comes back by surprise?
Lawrence:	Not possible. She has to go to the station to pick him up by which time I'm well n my way – and there's no early train. So, perfect. In fact his train will be passing *(looks at his watch)* in two minutes. Have another?
Graham:	Hardly time have we? OK one more.
Lawrence:	Steward. Same again please.
Steward:	Sorry sir. Buffet closing.
Lawrence:	Right, how much do I owe you?
Steward:	Five pounds forty please.

Lawrence reaches into his jacket pocket and pulls out some papers and looks surprised.

Lawrence:	My wallet. Where's my wallet?

He pats his other pockets without success. He looks at the papers. He looks at the jacket.

Graham:	OK, OK. I'll get it.

Graham hands some money to the steward. Lawrence looks closely at the garment in his hand.

Lawrence:	This isn't my jacket.

Pause.

Graham:	Then, where is your jacket?

Lawrence's head sinks into his hands.

Lawrence:	Oh my God.

A train rushes past going the other way.

The End.

❖❖❖❖❖❖❖❖❖❖❖❖❖❖❖❖❖❖❖❖❖❖❖❖❖❖❖❖

An excerpt from volume three of 'The Chandlers'
By Cyril Cook

The evening went with a swing, the happy couple leaving at eight o'clock for Birmingham where they would stay at The Midland overnight, going on to North Wales for their honeymoon on Sunday in a small rented cottage on the coast of Bangor. The party, under the considerable persuasion and example of Mr Maguire, developed into almost a repeat of the stag night to the extent of providing the most riotously funny incident any of the people there had ever seen in their whole lives. The priest who had conducted the service – a friend of the Maguires as well as their father confessor – was a bulky person and known to like a drink or two. On this occasion, being as it were almost one of the family, he was naturally invited to the festivities, at which he let his hair down well and truly, aided and abetted by Eamonn Maguire to the extent that his glass was not only never empty, but not even left half empty! By eleven o'clock when the party had to end, Father Kelly was slumped back on a chair against the wall totally incapable of standing up, singing 'Mother Macree' at the top of his voice. Mr Maguire and several of his Catholic friends stood looking down at this mountainous heap of clerical inebriation. Attempting to lift him to his feet was Herculean in itself, until they found that there was to be no assistance whatsoever forthcoming from the functioning of the priest's legs. Whatever message to indicate locomotion was coming from Father Kelly's brain was being waylaid somewhere, since it certainly was not reaching his lower extremities. They let him slump back onto his chair whilst Eamonn myopically sized up the situation. "It'll take six of us to carry the bugger," was Eamonn's judgement.

"I'll get a barrow and some four by two," one of Eamonn's friends – a builder with a yard not fifty yards from the hall – announced to his companions in the newly constituted ecclesiastical relocation committee. He hurried off, accompanied by another of the guests, neither moving in what could be described even loosely as a straight line. They returned in about ten minutes with a huge wooden wheelbarrow, the accomplice carrying two lengths of four by two on his shoulder. Six of them, David being one, picked the padre up and lowered him not too reverently into the wheelbarrow, one of the ladies slipping the cushion off the piano seat under his head a second before it would have made contact with the front edge. David volunteered to wheel the barrow but as soon as he lifted the sixteen stone cleric along with the wheelbarrow which itself felt as though it weighed a ton, he urgently regretted his foolhardiness. Nevertheless there was no going back – there was no way he could announce the task was beyond him, particularly with his sister and fiancée watching him through their uncontrolled tears of laughter.

He wheeled the barrow through the door from the hall to find himself confronted by four broad steps down on to the pathway. He then saw the purpose for the pieces of four by two. The builder guest had met this problem before. How do you get a barrowful of wet cement, or in this case, a thoroughly soaked man of the cloth, down a flight of steps without spilling anything?

"Turn the barrow round captain, so he goes down feet first," bade the builder in charge of this delicate operation. David complied.

"Now put the four by two under." This was accomplished.

"Now, two on each end of the wood. When I say lift, lift slowly. No, not yet Michael you blithering idiot." Michael was a big strong fellow, and in lifting his end had dislodged the grips of the two on the other end of the timber, which fell to the floor, in the process turning the baulk of wood into a lever, thereby almost turning the barrow over and dumping Father Kelly on to the top step of his own parish hall. They reorganised.

"Now lift slowly." This was now accomplished without further mishap.

"Now slowly down the steps – and KEEP IT LEVEL." This was easier said than done. It must be remembered that each and every one suffered a height differential from his companion on the timber. Secondly each and every one had had copious quantities to drink. Thirdly half of them were so close to hysteria at the whole bloody shebang they were almost useless anyway.

Somehow or other Father Kelly arrived safely on the pathway, by this time snoring loud enough to wake half the neighbourhood. It was about a hundred yards along the main road to his lodgings at The Priory, once he got going David finding his task to be not utterly beyond him. It was a bright moonlit night when two policemen on bicycles coming from the opposite direction spotted a most unusual cavalcade of men, talking loudly, some carrying baulks of timber followed by a cortege of well-dressed ladies, most in hats, the whole preceded by a somewhat bulky army officer in full service dress wheeling a large wheelbarrow containing a body. It was not a sight they normally met, even on a Saturday night, in the fair borough of Aylesbury. They decided to make a 'U' turn on their velocipedes, which they really should not have done. As they completed their turn they both took their eyes off the road, and off each other, to look at the body in the barrow, to their astonishment recognising the extremely well known, if at present recumbent figure of Father Kelly no less. Their surprise compounding their previous inattention caused their front wheels to become interlocked as a result of which from the elevated seats of their sit up and beg machines they were deposited on the pavement right in front of David's barrow. David stopped, let the barrow down with a bit of a bump, which in turn disturbed his cargo, who promptly started to sing 'Mother Macree' all over again.

Things went from bad to worse. Two of the guests ran, or rather staggered, round to help the policemen up. However, Buckinghamshire policemen are not recruited unless they have the build of heavyweight boxers. As a result the aforementioned guests found the task beyond them. In bending down to perform the enterprise, their equilibrium being somewhat disturbed by the adverse ratio of alcohol to blood within their systems, they found their good intentions did not compensate for the marked lack of physical strength they had previously considered they possessed. To put it plainly, they were too pissed to be of any use to anybody, as a result they both found themselves prostrated on the unwelcoming bodies of two members of the constabulary; a race which normally considers it is at the top of the pile, not the underdogs. Willing hands pulled the would-be helping hands up, thus allowing the pride of the Buckingham Constabulary to re-establish the vertical thus bringing some pretence of law and order to the streets of Aylesbury.

By now Father Kelly had gone back to sleep. The senior policeman announced in suitably officious tones they had better get 'him' home before they were all in trouble. One wag from within the party proclaimed, "When the super sees your bikes I reckon you will be the ones in trouble." All eyes turned to the specimens of police mobility lying in the gutter. Each front wheel instead of presenting a perfect circle now curved in altogether different directions. Buckled, bulged, contorted, warped, however one might describe them, there was no way they could be wheeled, let alone ridden. The party had the highly satisfying sight of two burly policemen each carrying a bicycle back to what would undoubtedly be a committee of enquiry constituted from on high after which they would be court martialled, or whatever it is they do in the police force to people who marmalise property belonging to the 'Old Bill'.

The evening was not over.

David's arms felt they were being slowly but painfully removed from their sockets, he was therefore mightily relieved to hear Eamonn announce, "We're here. Well done David my boy." They were at the bottom of a flight of some half a dozen steep steps leading up to the front door of The Priory.

One of the crowd asked, Who's going to ring the bell?" David thought this question was surely unnecessary; anyone could ring a blasted doorbell! However, as he soon was informed it was not the actual ringing of the bell, which presented a problem; it was the facing of Sarah McGonicle, Father Kelly's housekeeper, who would be the one to answer it. The fierce and utterly devoted Sarah had looked after the Father ever since he came to the parish in 1919. It was firmly believed that she was descended from a long line of inquisitors, since no-one could disturb the peace of Father Kelly without undergoing a third degree grilling to establish whether their business was a matter of life or death before they were allowed beyond the front door.

David heard himself saying, "I'll ring it," and then discovered himself thinking, "you silly sod, you've volunteered again!" Having made the statement, to the unbounded relief of the parishioners, he climbed the stairs to carry out the enterprise. He had not long to wait after tugging the jangling bell-pull.

He could hear footsteps slap-slapping across the bare boards inside, the door opened, and a thin faced, grey haired lady, wearing a housecoat and a mauve coloured hair net, faced him, with a mouth half open to declare, "What do you want?" in no uncertain terms, until she saw a handsome army officer in full service dress, Sam Browne, medal ribbons and all standing there in the moonlight. Instead of the expected tongue-lashing, the guests on the steps heard her say, "Good evening to you sir, can I help you at all?"

"I have been a guest at Mary Maguire's wedding. Father Kelly was also there, as you will doubtless know. It was very warm in the hall, in fact it has been a very warm day altogether, has it not?" Not waiting for a reply he continued, "As a result of the hot room and the fact that Father Kelly was very tired after a long day, he fell soundly asleep, so we've brought him home."

Her attitude changed. "What you are saying captain – you are a captain are you not? – is that you and the Maguire clan have got him drunk. You all ought to be ashamed of yourselves so you should," she yelled at the crowd assembled around the wheelbarrow, which she discerned for the first time. "And wheeling him through the town in a wheelbarrow – oh the shame of it, oh the shame of it."

"He really was quite comfortable," David assured her, and then could not help adding for sheer devilment, "Even the two policemen who stopped us agreed he was quite comfortable and being well looked after."

At this, Sarah was speechless, at last spluttering, "Bring him in."

The four by two wheelbarrow raising party fell in. They found it was much more difficult carrying their load up the steep steps than it had been carrying it down the shallow steps at the hall. Eventually, after what would have seemed an extremely hazardous flight, had the passenger been capable of experiencing it, they reached the top level by the front door.

"You are not bringing that blasted thing in on my polished floor." harangued Sarah McGonicle.

Adding fire to the flames Eamonn called out, "Sarah, you've just said a naughty word, I shall have to have a word with the Father tomorrow." She looked at him, unable to find words with which to chastise him.

"Wait here," she commanded and scurried off, returning a minute later with a long narrow Persian hearth rug. "Lay him on the end of that," she ordered. Half a dozen of them picked the Father up out of the barrow and laid him as gently as they could on the rug. Sarah picked up the loose end and started to tug the recumbent incumbent on his rug across the highly polished floor. David, seeing that she was making very heavy weather of it, jumped to her aid and they dragged him down the hallway into the sitting room and across to the fireplace where the remains of a wood fire were at their last gasp. Quickly Sarah put a cushion from the sofa under his head, got two travelling rugs out of a sandalwood box against the wall and put them over him. It occurred to David that this was not the first time she had performed this service for her beloved padre. She looked at David. "He'll be alright there. He has slept in far worse places. He was three years in the trenches and won the military cross you know". Her voice was that of someone having a deep love for another. It lasted only a minute. She went back to the door. "Away with you all, you should be ashamed of yourselves," and with that slammed the door on them.

They made their various ways to their beds, sides still aching, and with a story that would be told from Lands End to John O' Groats and even further for years to come.

More Quotes

One more such victory and we are lost. *Pyrrhus. 279 BC*

You can always tell an old soldier by the inside of his holsters and cartridge boxes.
The young ones carry pistols; the old ones, grub. *GBS 1898.*

The optimist proclaims that we live in the best of all possible worlds.
The pessimist fears this is true. *James Cabell. C 1920.*

By Cyril Cook

William Bingham Baring Esquire, a member of the wealthy Baring Brothers banking family was being served his breakfast at 'The Grange', his mansion near the village of Northington, some eight miles from the beautiful city of Winchester. It was Monday the nineteenth of November 1830 and as he surveyed his misty Hampshire acres he undoubtedly would be sensing clouds on his immediate family horizon for the first time in his carefully cushioned life. A century ago his great grandfather, John Baring, son of a Lutheran pastor, had left the family home in Bremen and had settled down in Devonshire making cloth. John's son Francis, although profoundly handicapped by deafness, founded the House which was to become Baring Brothers, built it into a major city institution, and was acknowledged a financial genius. His son Alexander married Anne Bingham from one of America's wealthiest families, and their son William was he who now sombrely faced his day from amidst his splendid rolling estates where he played the part of a JP and country gentleman of considerable means.

The cause of the air of despondency lodging over Mr Baring's head and many of the other landowners and clergy in the counties of Kent, Sussex and Hampshire, was what has since become known as the 1830 riots - agricultural unrest which began in Kent and swept across Sussex and Hampshire and other southern counties like a forest fire. There were two main causes for the discontent. The first was the abysmal starvation rates of pay of farm workers. Married men received eight shillings a week and single men five shillings. The men were demanding twelve shillings a week for married men and eight shillings for a single man, which would still only lift them from grinding poverty to just over subsistence level.

The second cause was the introduction of threshing machines and other types of horse drawn mechanical equipment on to the land. A threshing machine for example, could do the work of six men; as a result the labourers feared that soon many of them would be thrown out of work, and if they lived in tied cottages, which many of them did, not only would they lose their living but in addition could find themselves without a roof over their heads into the bargain.

Agricultural workers in general were a passive, quiescent section of the community. They knew their place in a society which was dominated by 'The Big House' from whence control was delegated to the agent, the tenant farmers, their bailiffs and foremen, with the ever vigilant power of the Church, firmly subject to the landowners often for their very living watching over them.

At the end of 1829 and during 1830 a new breed of outsider began to arrive in the country districts – the agitator. The most well-known was William Cobbett who had written a best seller of its time some ten years before, entitled 'Rural Rides'. He was a most complex character, a mixture of idealism, radicalism, and love of the countryside. He violently opposed the harsh legal system weighted in favour of the landowners, he felt the low wages paid to agricultural workers to be iniquitous and he actively exposed corruption and extravagance on the part of government. He didn't like clergymen very much to boot!

Cobbett and a man named Hunt made fiery speeches at the Rotunda in Winchester and elsewhere urging the labourers to go to their employers together and to demand a higher wage. If the employers bought machines the men were urged to smash them so as to secure their jobs. (In this of course they would be following in the footsteps of Ned Ludd of Leicester who in 1779 destroyed stocking making frames for the same reason and in the process caused a new word to be entered into the English vocabulary).

As a result of the activities of people like Cobbett, risings of land workers took place firstly in Kent. The landowners and their supporters in Parliament immediately enacted laws which made the demanding of more pay or the smashing of machines **capital offences**. In other words you could be hanged for asking your employer, who if not himself a magistrate would certainly have immediate access to one, for another four shillings a week.

These draconian laws added fuel to the fire of unrest. In 1760 there had been around sixty offences which carried the death penalty – by 1830 there were around two hundred and fifty! In this situation it was no wonder Mr Baring was not quite as complacent as he had been hitherto.

Our story now moves to the pretty little village of Micheldever situated just on the western side of the old Roman road from Winchester to London and not five miles away from where Mr Baring was eating his breakfast. Here a small group of men from the village had assembled, among whom was a nineteen year old farm labourer named Henry Cook. He lived with his parents John and Ruth in their cottage in the village, had received no schooling whatsoever, and the furthest he had ever travelled was the eight miles or so to Winchester. According to all accounts he had little idea of what he was getting himself involved in and 'ran headlong with the rest'.

The men having come together moved off to the neighbouring village of East Stratton where they met others, and as a party of over thirty, led by Robert Silcock and George Pace (both committed machine breakers), they proceeded to Northingdon

Down Farm, part of the Baring estate tenanted by Mr Thomas Dowden. He was the owner of the machine they were on the way to smash.

Meanwhile word had been got to Mr Baring as to what was happening; as a result he rode towards East Stratton and confronted the marchers. Silcock told him they were going to Northingdon Down Farm to 'break a machine'. Mr Baring turned and rode back to the Grange, enlisted twenty five men on his staff to come with him and then made for the farm. When he arrived the damage had been done and Silcock faced him saying two or three times, "We have broken this machine and intend to break others." In his capacity as a JP Mr Baring attempted to arrest Silcock but the mob snatched him back and it is at this point the chain of events overtake Henry Cook, lift him up and eventually carry him on to the gallows at Winchester prison.

There are three different accounts as to Cook's participation in what happened next. The first is that he took no part other than just being there, although that of course in itself would be a capital offence, as indeed it was for all the others. Secondly, some said he went forward angrily and knocked Mr Baring's hat off. However thirdly, Mr Baring said in evidence at the eventual trial, and this was corroborated by one of his men George Harding, that Cook struck him between the shoulder blades with a sledge hammer; as a result of which he was, "Incapable of bearing up against it and sunk instantly, losing his senses for the moment." This testimony, even though it was backed by George Harding, who was after all his servant, would appear to be suspect to say the least. Firstly, if a nineteen year old labourer, strong in the arm from working for a number of years in the fields and being knowledgeable in the way of swinging a sledgehammer, was of a mind to strike someone, one would have thought he would cause a considerable amount of damage to the recipient of such a blow. This was obviously not the case. Secondly, Mr Baring said he was struck in the back. Mr Baring was facing the mob with twenty five of his men at least at his back; how then could Cook separate himself from his fellow breakers, go into Mr Baring's party and strike him in the back without Baring's followers attempting to prevent him from so doing?

Whatever the truth of the matter he was eventually charged, among other counts, with, "Striking Mr Baring with a sledge-hammer with intent to murder." Another charge made against each and all the breakers was that of robbery – again a capital offence. When the mobs throughout the southern counties roamed the countryside to find and smash machines they invariably demanded money from farmers, clergy and others they considered to be monied people so that they could buy food. In this case, after smashing the machine and before the arrival of Mr Baring, the ringleaders had demanded and received two guineas from Mr Dowden. As a result Henry Cook, with the others, was eventually charged with robbery.

So far this day, therefore, the nineteenth of November 1830, he had committed offences which could result in his being hanged on **three counts,** but it would become obvious that his greatest crime was the assault on the person of Mr Baring, compared to which all else paled into insignificance.

The scene now moves to the Winchester Assize Court where over three hundred and twenty alleged breakers and rioters from various parts of the county of Hampshire, rounded up by special constables sworn in by JPs like Mr Baring, were to be tried under the Special Commission for the County. It is a matter of interest that five persons refused to be sworn in for this service and themselves were arrested to appear at the next Winchester Assizes.

To prosecute these mainly illiterate men, none of whom were being legally represented, the Crown provided the services of none other than the Attorney General himself – Baron Vaughan. The trial was by jury which to their credit found some seventy of the accused not guilty and in others recommended leniency on account of the previous good conduct of the accused. In the case of a man named Robert Mason, who was convicted of robbing the Curate of Barton Stacey of five shillings, this leniency was evidenced by (although he was sentenced to death – **yes**, sentenced to **death!**), his sentence being subsequently commuted to transportation for life.

When Henry Cook was charged it is reported that Baron Vaughan made a, "Perspicuous recapitulation of the evidence," given in person by Mr Baring and George Harding. As a result Henry Cook, along with twenty others, was placed at the bar and after, "An impressive address by the Attorney General," they were summarily sentenced to death en bloc. The proceedings lasted a fortnight. At the end of the trial the number sentenced to death was one hundred and one, of which six, including Henry Cook had their execution fixed for the 15th January 1831 – a little under two weeks time. 'Justice' had certainly been swift. In addition to those condemned, ninety four were sentenced to transportation or imprisonment at home and fifty four bound over to keep the peace. One curious fact was that Silcock and Pace, although the known ringleaders of the Northingdon Down Farm mob, and participants in other breakings, escaped the death penalty receiving the lesser sentence of seven years transportation.

The trial finished and those convicted were removed to Winchester jail. The Hampshire Chronicle reported that, "The wives and relatives of the prisoners have resorted to the jail in great numbers and their interviews have been of the most heartrending description." Heartrending or not it did not deter the paper from reporting in the next issue, "It will be gratifying to observe that the first amateur concert and ball of the season will shortly take place."

Over 700 of the local gentry and tradesmen signed a petition which was sent to His Majesty praying that the awful sentences may be commuted for a less severe punishment. Similar petitions were sent from Southampton, Basingstoke, Portsmouth and other places; as a result all but two of those condemned to death had their sentences reduced to transportation, mostly for life. The two unfortunates left to face the hangman were James Cooper and Henry Cook.

There is no question that this Commission, powered as it was by the Attorney General himself, had to make an example, "Pour encourager les autres." Cooper was an obvious choice as he had a history of acting as the leader of machine breaking mobs at farms in the vicinity of Fordingbridge on the borders of Hampshire and Dorset. Worse than that he had attacked the premises of two manufacturers of equipment and caused considerable damage to their property. The law would not tolerate damage to property at that level. Finally an indictment was also pending against him at the Special Assizes at Dorchester for outrages committed in that county. He therefore would never have stood a chance of reprieve.

But Henry Cook – why Henry Cook? He was only nineteen, one of the youngest if not the youngest of all the accused. Until that fateful day he had been in no trouble, he was no agitator; he lived at home with this parents who were very respectable people, but like many others before him and many since, he was at the wrong place at the wrong time and above all, struck the **wrong person**. The fact that he was convicted of attempting to murder Mr William Bingham Baring JP immediately singled him out for special treatment and it was special treatment he unquestionably received. His cause was not helped by William Cobbett. As soon as Henry Cook was sentenced and whilst a reprieve was at least in theory being considered, Cobbett published papers saying that it was Mr Baring who was the cause of Henry Cook being condemned. Whether he genuinely thought this action on his part would help the granting of Cook's reprieve is most unlikely; he must have known that by attempting to blacken Mr Baring's name he would only stir further animosity against Cook in an establishment which was determined to prevent in England a repetition of the dreadful events which had taken place in France only a relatively short time before; happenings still very fresh in the minds of the aristocracy and gentry against whom the 1830 riots were targeted. Perhaps he was actively fabricating a martyr for the cause; a teenage illiterate could readily fit the bill. We shall never know.

On the morning of January 17th 1831 therefore James Cooper and Henry Cook were brought forward, "To expiate their offences by the sacrifice of their lives." Those prisoners against whom sentence of death had been recorded, along with those who were standing for trial for similar offences of a capital nature at the next Assizes, were brought

291

into the yard to watch the grim proceedings. It is recorded that great distress was suffered by many prisoners, both Cook and Cooper being known to a number of them. Extra constables were brought into the city to counter the possible unrest from members of the local public reinforced by an expected influx of strangers from various parts of the country. In the event they were not needed, the persons who assembled to witness the executions were less in number than was anticipated, "Much less than have been noticed at previous melancholy occasions of this nature," as one reporter put it.

At eight o'clock therefore, after joining the Chaplain in prayer they were conducted to the scaffold. With final cries of, "Lord have mercy on me," the bolt was withdrawn and as the Hampshire Chronicle graphically described the event, "They quickly passed from time to eternity."

Later that morning Henry Cook was taken down and borne by his grieving parents to Micheldever where he was buried in the village churchyard. Legend surrounds his final resting place which has it that snow never remains on his grave, though it may lie deep elsewhere. It is not known whether the same legend obtains in respect of the other seventy odd unfortunates who were executed at various places in the southern counties for the same types of offences during that year. What is indisputable is that the full majesty of the law became in fact the full terror of the law, determined to maintain the ruling class as the ruling class and to ensure the labouring classes would think twice in the future before challenging the establishment.

Justice is the means by which established injustices are sanctioned. Anatole France.

The quotation above is illustrated by the following postscript.

A short time after Henry Cook was laid to rest, the same Justice of the Peace, William Bingham Baring was himself brought before his fellow magistrates. He was charged with brutally assaulting a prisoner with a heavy stick. The labourer concerned was being held in custody and at the time of the beating had been made to wear handcuffs. For this cold-blooded abuse of a prisoner, who was in fact subsequently proved to be innocent of any charge, Baring was ordered to pay damages of £50.

This amount of course would be possibly the equivalent of more than two years pay to a labourer, but would have been pocket money to Mr Baring. Bearing in mind the punishment handed out to the breakers and would-be breakers for their offences, was there ever a clearer example of one law for the rich and a totally different one for the poor?

They have had some pretty eccentric people in the House of Commons in days gone by. Dennis Healey was in the habit of singing in the lift. Electioneering in Bishops Stortford he is reputed to have stopped a lady in the shopping centre saying, "Be alert! Britain needs more lerts." At another election meeting he was being severely heckled by a National Front supporter until he jumped from the platform to thump the person in question. It is the only time a Special Branch officer has had to intervene to protect the public from a politician!

A well recorded incident is of Winston Churchill, after the 1945 election when labour had sent him from power, going to the gents in the House, to find labour Prime Minister Attlee the only other occupant. Winnie walked way down the other end away from Attlee, causing the PM afterwards to say that though they were strong opponents in the House they had no reason to be distant outside it. "Yes," replied Winnie, "but the trouble with you lot is if you see anything worth having, you nationalise it!"

Eric Heffer was renowned for 'walking out' of meetings when he could not get his way. At one NEC meeting at the House, not at Labour headquarters, he staged one of his tantrums. The first door by which he endeavoured to leave opened on to a loo, the second turned out to be a cupboard and the third was locked. "Oh, bugger it," he said, and sat down again!

Dennis Skinner, even today, won't even have a cup of tea with a journalist unless he compromises his socialism.

It takes all sorts.

The Law

▸ If you 'usurp' the ROYAL ARMS the penalty is still 'beheading'.

▸ It is still against the law, under an act of 1313, for an MP to appear in the Houses of Parliament in a suit of armour.

General Summary of the Sentences at Winchester

DEATH: to be executed Jan. 15, 1831.

James Thomas Cooper.] Attainted of riotously as-
Henry Eldridge. } sembling and feloniously
with force demolishing machinery.
John Gilmore. Attainted of riotously assembling
and feloniously with force beginning to demo-
lish machinery.
Robert Holdaway. Attainted of riotously assem-
bling and with force demolishing a house.
James Annalls. ? Attainted of robbery.
Henry Cooke. }

DEATH RECORDED.

*Attainted of riotously assembling and feloniously
with force demolishing machinery employed in
manufactures.*

Amey, Joseph	Deadman, Aaron	Philpott, Geo.
Clarke, George	Hayter, Chas.	Quinton, Sam.
Fulford, John	Newman, Wm.	Read, Charles

*Attainted of riotously assembling and feloniously
with force beginning to demolish machinery employed in manufactures.*

Blatch, Joseph	Green, Thomas	Myland, George
Ellis, John	Manns, James	Shepherd, Wm.
Fay, Charles	Manns, Isaac	Stanmore, Wm.

*Attainted of riotously assembling and with force
demolishing a house.*

Harding, Aaron	Heath, John	Painter, James
Harding, T.	James, Henry	Triggs, Matt.

[Robbins and Wheeler, Printers and Stationers to the County of Southampton.]

DEATH RECORDED.

Attainted of robbery.

Adams, Wm.	Farmer, Wm.	Pain, Charles
Annetts, John	Farmer, J.	Painter, John
Annetts, James	Freemantle, N.	Payne, Daniel
Baker, John	Glasspole, Jas.	Pearce, James
Baker, James	Goodall, T.	Primer, Wm.
Batten, John	Gregory, T.	Pumphrey, Jas.
Berriman, T. sen.	Harding B.	Rampton, Rd.
Bishop, Thos.	Hill, Isaac, sen.	Rolte, George
Bulter, W. sen.	Hill, Isaac	Sims, Daniel
Brummell, C.	Hopgood, Geo.	Sims, John
Bulpitt, John	Isles, Isaac	Sims, William
Bulpitt, Charles	Kent, John	Smith, Wm.
Bunce, Henry	Keens, Richard	Steele, George
Burgess, Wm.	Keens, John	Stroud, Wm.
Carter, George	Kimber, John	Summerbee, W.
Carter, Jos.	Kingshott, J.	Sutton, Wm.
Childs, A.	Lawrence, Laz.	Tollard, John
Clark, George	Martin, James	Trew, James
Clarke, George	Marshall, Thos.	Turner, Jacob
Cook, James	Mason, Robt.	Wareham, Wm.
Cook, Robert	Mason, Joseph	Warwick, Thos.
Coleman, G.	Nash, John	Wiltshire, Jacob
Conduit, Wm.	Neale, Thomas	Winkworth, W.
Cropp, James	Nutbean, E. C.	

Attainted of felony.

TRANSPORTED for the TERM of their NATURAL LIVES.

Chas. Shepherd—Geo. Webb—John Weeks, John
Slade—John Newman.

SEVEN YEARS' TRANSPORTATION.

Attainted of felony.

Allen, John	Ford, James	Paice, George
Arney, Wm.	Fussell, James	Palmer, George
Berkingham, R.	Heighes, Thos.	Silcock, John
Bayes, John	Hill, Wm.	Sydenham, Ed.
Brackstone, W.	Hopgood, John	Toogs, John
Champ, David	Houghton, P.	Watts, Wm.
Collins, John	Hudson, John	Webb, Wm.
Collins, George	Jemman, Wm.	White, John
Cooper, J. T.	Jemmay, Geo.	Witcher, Wm.
Duke, John	Lush, John	
Fielder, A.	Morey, S. jun.	

18 months' imp. to hard lab.

Bown, Benj.	Prior, T. jun.	Varnell, James
Camis, James	Stagg, Thomas	

12 months' imp. to hard lab.

Chalk, John	Kinchin, Wm.	Stonenge, John
Etherington, R.	Reeves, John	Todd, George
Hooper, Thos.	Rogers, Henry	
Kelsey, Wm.	Smith, John	

3 months' imp.

Jon. Woodlard—C. Bryant.

Misdemeanor.

2 years' imp.

Cobb, John	Hoar, Wm.	Hoare, Thos.
S. Bundy.) Convicted of two misdemeanors—		
Rich. Lane.) 18 months' imp. to hard labour.		

1 year's imp.

Bone, Henry	Reeves, Wm.	Trimming, J.
	White, James	

C. Bratcher.) Convicted of two misdemeanors—
John Webb.) 12 cal. months' imp.
Robert Cull.) Convicted of two misdemeanors—
Wm. Lane.) 9 cal. months' imp.

Misdemeanor.

6 months' imp.

Butcher, Izaac	Hamblin, Thos.	Skelton, Wm.
Cull, J.	Harding, John	Smith, Ben.
Dickson, Jas.	Newland, John	Webb, Richard
Doling, Edw.	Sanders, Saml.	

3 months' imp.

Bundy, Henry	Cavell, Henry	Southwell, Wm.

1 month's imp.

Abraham, Wm.	Grantham, W.	Mullens, H.
Blackman, J.	Hampton, Geo.	Oliver, Barnard
Carter, George	Holt, George	Oxer, George
Cook, Thomas	Hopkins, C.	Pike, George
Cooper, John	Ilsley, David	Thorp, Henry

6 weeks' imp.

Wm. Varndell.

*Convicted of misdemeanor, but discharged on their
recognizance to keep the peace and be of good
behaviour.*

Adams, James	Gold, John	Page, Thomas
Astridge, Wm.	Grant, James	Payne, John
Baker, M.	Hoar, Richard	Piper, John
Bartholomew, B.	Holloway, R.	Pragnell, A.
Bennett, T.	Judd, James	Robinson, Dan.
Brown, Henry	Kerby, Charles	Rogers, William
Burlinge, Wm.	Kneller, James	Rose, William
Cole, James	Knight, Geo.	Scammell, T.
Cooke, Henry	Lawrence, Jos.	Scoates, Thos.
Day, Wm.	Martin, Thos.	Stacey, Thomas
Delacourt, John	Martin, Charles	Steel, Isaac
Dennett, Jos.	Mouly, Thos.	Sturgess, G.
Etheridge, A.	Mouly, James	Tubb, John
Fabian, Henry	Mouly, John	Turton, John
Ford, James	Noble, W. jun.	Wells, Henry
Forder, Chas.	Nottley, Chas.	West, Henry
Gale, Henry	Offer, Isaac	Windybank, D.
Giles, James	Oliver, Ben.	Wren, Joshua

A Report from the Hampshire Chronicle of that Date

H.C Monday, January 3rd, 1831.

Winchester.—At a late hour on Thursday evening, the proceedings under the special Commission for the County were brought to a conclusion, and the judges released from their arduous duties, which will be resumed at Salisbury on Saturday morning. On Thursday evening some of the petty jurors applied to Mr. Justice Alderson for a remuneration for the time they had been detained, and the consequent heavy expense to which they had been subjected. His lordship expressed regret that he had no power to make any order for the expenses of the jury. The only thing he could do was to take care that they should not be again called upon for some time to serve. Many prisoners pleaded guilty on Thursday, among whom were 11 young men, apparently all farmers' servants, who after an admonition, were released on their own recognisances. The trial of John Boyes and James Fussell, charged with having obtained money by threats from Mrs. Long of Marwell Hall, excited considerable interest. The Attorney-General stated that Boyes went about with the mob with a paper which was to this effect : " We the undersigned agree to give 2s. per day to our married labourers and 9s. per week to single men, in consideration of having our rent and tithes abated." This was signed by several farmers and landholders, some of whom had been compelled to put their names to it, and the ostensible object of the mob going about was to get signatures to this paper, though in several instances they made demands of money, and by threats and menaces obtained it. The prisoner Fussell was actually engaged in this mob at the time of the robbery. Mrs. Long's servant proved that a mob came to the house and demanded £12 or £14, and, after remonstrating with them, went to his mistress, who, on his advice, gave him £5 to give to the mob, which was done under an apprehension that they would do mischief. It was also proved by Grace Locke, a servant, living at the Earl of Northesk's, at Rose Hill, that both prisoners came there on the same day; they inquired for threshing machines and said they came to destroy them. They demanded money and insisted on getting £5, which at length they obtained. They then gave three cheers and said, " Now for the machine," and proceeded to where the winnowing machine was kept, and broke it. Prisoners were found guilty and sentenced to seven years' transportation. Several other prisoners received sentence of transportation for life, and others to seven years' transportation, 18 months' imprisonment, and 12 months' imprisonment. The Rev. J. H. Hutton declined to prosecute the men of the Leckford mob and others who rioted and robbed at his house in Stockbridge on the 22nd November, although there were several of them who might particularly have been sworn to, Mr. Justice Alderson expressed a hope that the humane interposition of the rev. gentleman would make the persons who were thus passed over, and who so narrowly escaped the severity of the law, sensible of the lenity shown them, attached for the future in duty to their pastor, and in zeal for his protection and interest.

Among the prisoners were John Silcock and George Pace, who were charged with breaking machinery, the property of Thomas Dowden, of Northington. It was proved by John Hayward, bailiff to Mr. Dowden, that about 30 came with hammers, bars of iron, and sticks, went to the barn and destroyed the machine. Mr. Baring arrived, on which Silcock went out from among the mob, and Mr. Baring seized him by the collar and said, " You're my prisoner." The mob then pressed forward and rescued him. The mob went through the house and came to the front. Mr. Baring said : " What do you mean by this wanton destruction of property ?" Then Mr. Silcock replied, " We break machines wherever we find them." Both prisoners were found guilty.

Robert Mason stood indicted for robbing the Rev. James Jolliffe, Curate of Barton Stacey, of 5s. Mr. Jolliffe proved that about 60 persons, armed with sticks, came to his house demanding victuals and drink. The prisoner said, " You have more than we have, and must give us something." On inquiring how much, they said 5s., which witness gave them to prevent their breaking the windows and taking what they could find in the house. The prisoner, in his defence, said he was forced to join the mob, and was sure that if the learned Counsel by whom he was prosecuted (the Attorney-General) had been there in a smock frock instead of his gown, and a straw hat instead of his wig, he would have been obliged to do as he did and have been tried at that bar. The jury found prisoner guilty, but strongly recommended him to mercy on account of his previous good character.

Henry Cooke was indicted for breaking a thrashing machine at Northington Down Farm and for assaulting Bingham Baring, Esq., by knocking him down with a sledge hammer. The Attorney-General briefly stated the case to the jury, and called William Bingham Baring, Esq., whose testimony was to the effect that on the 19th November he met from 30 to 40 persons proceeding from Stratton towards Northington Down Farm, some bearing hammers and others sticks. They told him they were going to Northington Down Farm to break the machines. On learning this he went back to obtain assistance from the Grange, and returned with 25 persons to the farm. When he arrived there he was told the machine was broken, and he saw the mob standing near Mr. Dowden's house. He went forward and expostulated with the mob, and while so doing one said, " I did not know Mr. Baring was good to the poor." Shortly after, that gentleman called for their spokesman, when Silcock came forward and said, " We have broken this machine and intend to break others." He repeated this twice or thrice, and, before Mr. Baring could turn round, he was knocked down by a blow between the shoulders. It was given by some heavy instrument, as witness was incapable of bearing up against it, and sunk instantly. He lost his senses for the moment, and found himself on recovering with his own men. . . . George Harding accompanied

295

Mr. Baring back to Northington, and corroborated the preceding testimony. The person with a sledge hammer said to the bystanders, "God damn you, get out of the way," and struck Mr. Baring down, using both hands to the sledge hammer. Witness saw him lifting it again as if he was about to repeat the blow. Witness said to him, "You blackguard rascal, would you hit him again," and then struck him down and seized the hammer. Mr. Wright, the magistrate before whom Cook was brought, proved the confession of the culprit, and produced a large quantity of sledge hammers which he had taken from the rioters on the Monday following at Itchen, and who were with the mob when Mr. Baring was assaulted. Being asked what he had to urge in his defence, the prisoner said he begged Mr. Baring's pardon. After a perspicuous recapitulation of the evidence by Mr. Baron Vaughan, the jury found the prisoner guilty.

Twenty prisoners (including Henry Cook) were placed at the bar, upon whom, after an impressive address from Baron Vaughan, sentence of death was recorded.

Mr. Baron Vaughan, observing Mr. Ricketts in Court, took occasion to express the gratification which he himself and his learned brothers experienced in noticing the efficient state of the Constabulary Force under his direction. It was a truly constitutional force. He was happy to see persons associated for the preservation of their own property, and for the purpose of endeavouring to preserve the peace, which they had done in a most excellent manner. Mr. Justice Parke wished it to be publicly known that every magistrate on the application of five householders had the power of swearing in special constables. He was sorry to say there was an indictment against five persons which had been traversed to the next Assizes, for refusing to be sworn in as special constables during the time of these tumultuous and riotous mobs.

The total number of prisoners in the county gaol against whom sentence of death has been recorded is 95, in addition to the six left for execution. The wives and relations of the prisoners since the conclusion of the Assizes, have resorted to the gaol in great numbers every day, and their interviews have been of the most heart-rending description.

A petition from the inhabitants of this city to his Majesty is now in course of signature, supplicating the Royal clemency in favour of the six unhappy men condemned at the Special Commission for the county to suffer the extreme penalty of the law. The unwearied patience, humanity and discrimination bestowed by the Commission in investigating the numerous charges is admitted to have been almost without precedent in our political annals; but entertaining an opinion that the rights of the peaceable and well-disposed may be sufficiently vindicated without having recourse to the punishment of death, the petitioners earnestly implore his Majesty to direct a commutation of that heavy penalty.

Monday, January 10, 1831.

Winchester.—The convicts who were left for execution at the close of the special Commission for Hampshire, still continue under sentence of death, to suffer on Saturday next, excepting Robert Holdaway, for destroying the poor house at Headley and joining in the riots at Selborne, who has been respited till the 5th of February on special grounds, to allow time for inquiring into certain affidavits which have been tendered to the judge on his behalf. The petition to his Majesty from this city praying that the awful sentence may be commuted for a less severe punishment was signed by about 700 of the gentry and tradesmen, and on Thursday was forwarded to London for presentation. A similar petition has been forwarded from Southampton, and by a reference to our intelligence from that place it may be seen that an opinion prevails there that the prayer will not be totally disregarded, although it appears certain that the terror of the law must take its course with some of the unfortunate condemned men. Petitions for commutation of punishment have also been transmitted from Basingstoke, Romsey, Portsmouth, Gosport, Whitchurch, and other places.

The disturbances which lately agitated various parts of the county caused a suspension of all amusements at this festive season of the year. Now that tranquility is happily restored, it will be gratifying to observe that the first Winchester amateur concert and ball for the season will shortly take place.

On Wednesday a deputation waited upon the Lord Mayor at the Mansion House for the purpose of requesting his signature to a petition to his Majesty to spare the lives of the unfortunate men sentenced at the late special Assizes for this county to die for machine-breaking. His lordship was about to sign the petition from the impulse of the moment, but afterwards begged that it should be left for him to reflect upon.

The General Quarter Sessions for the county commenced on Tuesday. The calendar contained a list of 40 prisoners who were disposed of as follows :—14 years transportation—George Thorne, for stealing a quantity of barley at Brockenhurst, the property of Henry Cole; and William Harding, for stealing several articles of furniture the property of J. Hollis, at Bishop's Stoke. Seven years transportation—James Cullan, for stealing at Bishops Stoke a lock, the property of Charles Smyth Esq; Richard Coombs, for stealing four bushels of wheat from a barn at Headley, belonging to Robert Parker; and Edward Pinkess, for having at Boldre stolen a quantity of barley, the property of John Apsey. Others were sentenced to various periods of imprisonment and the remainder were either acquitted or discharged for want of prosecution. Mr. Josiah Rose Anderson, the celebrated vocalist, was convicted for an assault on a gamekeeper in the service of Lord Palmerston, and was fined £10, which he paid with much sang froid and departed.

At present the number of prisoners in the county goal for trial at the ensuing Lent Assizes is 35. They are charged with the crimes of murder, arson, highway robbery, burglary, horse and sheep stealing &c.

Winchester. — This morning James Thomas Cooper and Henry Cooke, two of the six unfortunate men doomed at the late special Assizes for this county to expiate their offences by the sacrifice of their lives, were executed at the County Gaol. It is already known that a respite until the 5th of next month was last week received for Robert Holdaway in order that the judges on their return to town might have an opportunity of examining certain affidavits in his behalf which had been forwarded to them. On Thursday morning a respite during his Majesty's pleasure was received by the Governor of the Gaol for James Annalls, Henry Eldridge, and John Gilmore.

From the time of their sentence these unhappy men conducted themselves with great propriety, paying the strictest and apparently most devout attention to their religious duties. All of them admitted their participation in the different outrages of which they were convicted, at the same time asserting in the strongest manner that they were not the original instigators of them, and that they were pressed into the mobs by others. Cooper and Gilmore could read and write, and had received a tolerable education; the other three could neither read or write, and were most deplorably ignorant of even the first principles of the Christian religion. Gilmore never entertained a hope of mercy, and from the first moment evinced such calmness of mind and humble resignation to the Divine Will as are rarely witnessed. He received the intelligence of his respite with becoming gratitude and firmness. Eldridge and Annalls were deply affected, falling on their knees to thank the Almighty for the mercy they had experienced, immediately after which Eldridge requested that a letter might be written to his former friends and associates in his native village entreating them to take warning by his example, and particularly requesting them to observe the Sabbath and to abstain from cricket and other games on that day, to the neglect of which he attributed his own miserable fate.

That Cooper and Cooke were in expectation of a reprieve was proved by the excess of their feelings when it was announced to them that the lives of their companions were spared, and that in their cases the law would certainly take its course. On recovering from the shock, which was quite overpowering, they expressed the greatest anxiety for the welfare of their souls, manifesting the deepest contrition for their past sins, and seeking for mercy through the merits of the Redeemer.

Cooper persisted in the statement he made, and supported by respectable testimony at his trial, that he left his mother's house in the morning for the purpose of removing some sheep, and on his return was met by the mob and forced to accompany them. With respect to the report that he was connected with Cobbett and Hunt, and had been a frequent attendant at the Rotunda, he declared that he had never seen either of these persons in the whole of his life, and he had not been in London more than once for many years past, and that was in July last, shortly after his wife eloped from him, and then only for a single day, having left East Grinstead on the Sunday evening and returned to the same place on the follow-

ing Tuesday. With this exception and a week spent in Southampton, he had not been absent from home more than a single day until he went into the service of Mr. Mussell at Whaddon, with whom he resided at the time he joined the mob.

On the Chaplain visiting the prison early this morning he found both prisoners very composed. They had slept the early part of the night. After joining in prayer and other acts of devotion with the reverend gentleman with the greatest fervency till eight o'clock, they were then conducted from the condemned cell through the ante-room to the platform at the back of the gaol. Cooke was dreadfully affected, crying and groaning bitterly, and his hapless associate, although he exhibited less external demonstration of terror, was evidently labouring under extreme mental agony.

The awful preparations being complete, the Rev. Chaplain concluded his solemn and very distressing duties in a most impressive manner, the prisoners joining in and fervently ejaculating " Lord have mercy upon me." The bolt was then withdrawn and they quickly passed from time to eternity. The numerous prisoners against whom sentence of death was recorded for participation in the late acts of riot and robbery, and those for trial at the next Assizes witnessed the awful spectacle from the yards in which they were severally confined.

297

NATIONAL MEMORIAL TO PRISONERS OF WAR

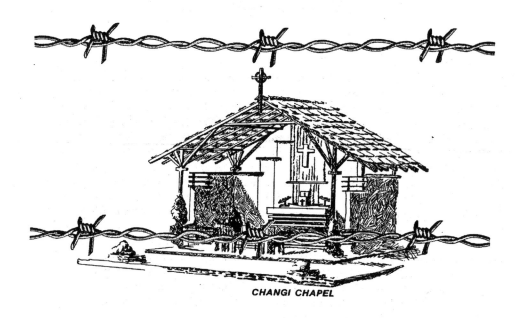

CHANGI CHAPEL

ROYAL MILITARY COLLEGE, DUNTROON, A.C.T.

THE ORIGINAL CHAPEL—RE-ERECTED
IN THE GROUNDS OF THE
ROYAL MILITARY COLLEGE, DUNTROON IN 1988

Following the entry of Japan into World War 2, its military forces conducted a series of campaigns to gain control over Asia and the Pacific. A key target was Singapore which was the focus of the British presence in the region, including its military forces. Singapore Island was captured by Japanese forces on 15 February 1942 (Wigmore 1957). The fall of Singapore and a series of other campaigns by the Japanese forces resulted in a large number of Allied service personnel, including Australians, being taken prisoner. The surrender of Allied forces on Singapore included about 15,000 Australians. This was by far the largest number of Australians captured in the region during the war. In order to accommodate these and other prisoners, the Changi Gaol was established on 17 February 1942 as the Prisoner-of-War Headquarters for Singapore. Changi was up to that time a British army barracks. Changi remained a prisoner-of-war camp until the end of the war. However, the number of Australians housed there varied because the Japanese used the prisoners as a work force for projects away from Singapore. Notwithstanding this fluctuation in numbers, Changi remained the largest Australian prisoner-of-war camp in the region. Prisoners of war from the 8th Division AIF were interned in the Changi Gaol Camp from 1943 onwards, and within weeks of their arrival had determined to build a Catholic Chapel. Originally a simple post and beam structure with a frond floor was erected under the guidance of Lieutenants Hamish Cameron-Smith and Hugh Simon-Thwaites. A more elaborate Chapel was designed by Cameron-Smith who was an architect in civilian life. The Chapel evolved over an extended period in 1944 and utilised found materials.

It was used as a place of worship until the end of the war. In October 1945 the War Graves Unit, including Corporal Max Lee, spent a few days by chance in the Changi Camp, en route to Sumatra. Corporal Lee made a request to the British to save the Chapel, which was one of the few structures that had not been destroyed by fire. Permission was granted and after extensive photographs were taken and dimensioned drawings and sketches were made by Lee, the Chapel was dismantled by a working party of surrendered Japanese personnel. It was crated to Australia in 1947, with the intention that the Chapel be reconstructed as afitting memorial for 'prisoners of war who had little recognition for the extreme adversity under which many had lived and died' (attributed to Lee). The crates were stored in the Australian War Memorial where they remained for 40 years. The Chapel was finally offered to the Australian Defence Force Academy and in 1987 reconstruction work commenced.

The work was undertaken by the Royal Australian Engineer Corps. Following an unsuccessful application for Bicentennial funding the Army launched a nation-wide public appeal for funds. In consultation with the Australian Heritage Commission a site at Duntroon was chosen in the centre of a small parkland close to the Duntroon Chapel. The items inside the crates were marked with alphabetic and numerical codes enabling accurate reconstruction. Included were: the cross from the roof and roof tiles, panels from above the altar and the altar, most of the floor tiles, two roof beams and struts, timber framing from the side walls, a few pieces of timber trim, corrugated iron skirting, electrical switchboard, and electrical light fittings. Missing were two front posts and the remainder of the roof frame. Replacement timbers were provided. Some of the roof tiles were broken. Originally the tiles were from the Malabar tile works and Feroke in India, and identical replacement tiles were obtained from Saint Mary's Church at Rose Hill, Sydney.

There was no attempt to replace missing floor tiles. Although photographs and sketches from 1945-46 indicate the Chapel was not wired, an electrical switchboard and wiring were found in a crate and this was installed. Paint samples were matched at the then Canberra College of Advanced Education, and the Chapel painted in its original colours. The Chapel was dedicated as a National Memorial to all Australian prisoners of war on 15 August 1988, the anniversary of the end of the war, and was attended by Max Lee and many of the Changi survivors and their relatives. Both Simon-Thwaites, a Catholic priest in England, and Cameron-Smith, an architect in Zambia, were traced though too late to enable them to attend the dedication ceremony. They were subsequently brought to Australia in May 1990 when Father Simon-Thwaites celebrated mass in the Chapel. Physical Description,The reconstructed Chapel is an open structure, 12 by 16 feet, made mainly from timber, masonite and galvanised iron. Its pitchedroof of reddish terra cotta tiles is raised several feet above the walls. The roof is supported by four large wooden posts, one at each corner of the structure. The altar wall at the back of the Chapel is a stepped wall of masonite, painted white with a green trim. The wooden altar is centrally placed, and directly above it is a rectangle of green galvanised iron with a white cross superimposed on it. The sides of the structure are comprised partially of a wall and partially a green altar rail, while the front of the Chapel is a green altar rail only with a small gate at the centre. There is a large light fixed to the centre of the roof which lights the altar. The Chapel has been reconstructed on a concrete slab 20 by 26 feet, with concrete tubs, each with rosemary growing in it, at each corner of the front. In front on the left hand side is a plaque which reads, 'National Prisoner of War Memorial dedicated to the 35,000 Australian servicemen and women taken prisoner in the following wars: War in South Africa, Boer War 1899-1902 World War I 1914-1918 World War II 1939-1945 Korean War 1950-1953'

WATERCOLOUR PAINTED BY
PRISONER OF WAR DICK COCHRAN
IN CHANGI IN 1945

Unveiled by a former prisoner of war on 15 August 1988 in front of the right hand side is a plaque which reads, 'This Chapel was originally constructed by prisoners of war in Changi Camp, Singapore Island in 1944. Its construction was an act of enduring faith in the midst of extreme adversity. After the war the Chapel was returned to Australia for preservation. It was erected on this site as a National Memorial to all Australian prisoners of war on 15 August 1988. Funds for erection and maintenance of this memorial were provided by public subscription.' The landscape of the site is intended to symbolise the original Changi site. It is built in a grassy parkland, with the axis of the Chapel centred on existing gum trees. Several seats are located in the grassed area in front of the Chapel. Discussion of Significance The Chapel is a relocated structure and this raises a question about its significance as a place. Certainly the removal of theChapel from its original location at Changi has reduced at least one aspect of its heritage value. However, the values of the Chapel have changed. In its original setting its values related to it being a place of Catholic worship for prisoners in the hostile wartime environment of Changi. In its new setting it has become a memorial to all Australian prisoners in four wars although it appears to retain a very particular significance for the former prisoners of Changi. The intrinsic values of the structure have only been marginally affected by the relocation.

Condition

The Chapel is in good condition and is largely intact. The Chapel was originally located at Changi prisoner-of-war camp in Singapore but was dismantled and brought to Australia in 1947. It was reconstructed at Duntroon in 1987-88. As part of the reconstruction process some new materials, such as timber posts and roof members, and roof tiles, were used to replace missing materials. (August 1994)

Bibliographic references

NATIONAL MEMORIAL TO PRISONERS OF WAR, NO DATE, (PAMPHLET).
PETER FREEMAN AND ASSOCIATES, CONSERVATION PLAN, RE-CONSTRUCTION OF CHANGI CHAPEL AS A NATIONAL POW MEMORIAL, RMC DUNTROON, CANBERRA.
WIGMORE, LIONEL, AUSTRALIA IN THE WAR OF 1939-45, SERIES ONE, VOLUME IV, THE JAPANESE THRUST, AUSTRALIAN WAR MEMORIAL, CANBERRA 1957.

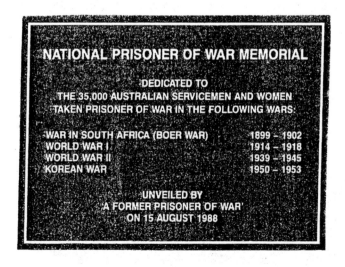

By Cyril Cook

The following is a précis of an article written in 1882 which appeared in The Encyclopaedia Britannica that year.

I am old enough to have had a father who served in the army in India and South Africa in the 1890s. The paper that follows indicating as it does the extent of medical knowledge of tropical diseases at the time, makes one wonder how any of our soldiers and empire builders lived to tell the tale. This particularly since an army posting to say India, Africa, Malaya and so on would have been almost certainly for five years.

One can catch a lot of complaints in five years!

Malaria

The name malaria is derived from the Italian 'mala' – bad 'aria' – air, and is known as marsh fever, ague, jungle fever and by several other names.

Malaria has been estimated to produce one half of the mortality of the human race and inasmuch as it is the most frequent cause of sickness and death in those parts of the globe which are most densely populated, the estimate may be taken as rhetorically correct.

In the British Isles sporadic cases of ague may occur anywhere but it is not endemic except in a few localities such as the Essex marshes. In France there are several districts which are notoriously malarious for example the Loire Valley, parts of the Rhone Valley and the marshes in the Mediterranean area. The disease is endemic in Schleswig Holstein, Hanover and Westphalia and most of Holland and the lower parts of Belgium. The Danube from Vienna to the sea has areas which are so malarious as to be uninhabitable.

The most malarious localities are the estuaries and deltas of rivers (Ganges, Euphrates, Po, Mississippi, Orinoco etc), and in areas of mangrove swamps. In contrast malaria is found in rocky terrain and sandy plains (Hong Kong, the Deccan, Andes etc).

It is concluded therefore that malaria is a specific poison generated in the wet ground. Attempts have been made to separate a malarious poison from the gases generated by swamps, or from the air of malarious localities, without success. It acts for the most part only within a few feet of the ground. In the East Indies the raising of dwellings on poles serves to keep off, or at least lessen, the liability to fever, and the Indians in South America escape it by sleeping in the branches of trees. Although it is not known to act beyond a few feet from the earth's surface it may produce fever in localities situated at a height of 7,000 – 9,000 feet above sea level. It sometimes acts at a distance from its supposed place of origin. Thus it is said to have caused fever on board ships lying 2 – 3 miles off a malarious shore. In West Indian experience it has been known to render the high limestone ridge more unhealthy than the swamp at its foot, and a similar experience has occurred on the Kentish shore of the Thames Estuary, and at other parts of the English Channel coast. Although a still night is most favourable for its production there is a popular opinion that it is carried by the wind and that a belt of trees or even a wall will 'keep it off'. Situations to the windward of a malarious swamp are usually reckoned safe.

The treatment for malaria universally applied is the taking of quinine. Arsenic has proved to be one of the most efficient substitutes for quinine, and dwellers in malarious localities have found in opium a palliative of the misery induced by malaria.

❖❖❖❖ ❖❖❖❖❖❖ ❖❖❖❖❖❖ ❖❖❖❖❖❖ ❖❖❖❖❖❖❖❖❖

More Oldies from Cyril, OAP and Bar

Hospital regulations require a wheel chair for patients being discharged. However, while working as a student nurse, I found one elderly gentleman already dressed and sitting on the bed with a suitcase at his feet, who insisted he didn't need my help to leave the hospital.

After a chat about rules being rules, he reluctantly let me wheel him to the elevator. On the way down I asked him if his wife was meeting him.

"I don't know," he said. "She's still upstairs in the bathroom changing out of her hospital gown."

❖❖❖❖ ❖❖ ❖❖❖❖❖❖ ❖❖❖❖❖❖ ❖❖

A couple in their nineties are both having problems remembering things. During a check-up, the doctor tells them that they're physically okay, but they might want to start writing things down to help them remember.

Later that night, while watching TV, the old man gets up from his chair. "Want anything while I'm in the kitchen?" he asks.

"Certainly! Don't you think you should write it down so you can remember it?" she asks.

"No, I can remember it."

"Well, I'd like some strawberries on top, too. Maybe you should write it down, so's not to forget it?"

He says, "I can remember that. You want a bowl of ice-cream with the strawberries?"

"I'd also like whipped cream. I'm certain you'll forget that, write it down?" she asks.

Irritated, he says, "I don't need to write it down, I can remember it! Ice-cream with strawberries and whipped cream – I got it, for goodness sake."

Then he toddles into the kitchen. After about twenty minutes, the old man returns from the kitchen and hands his wife a plate of bacon and eggs.

She stares at the plate for a moment.

"Where's my toast?"

◈◈◇◇◇◇◈◈◇◈◇◇◈◈◇◈◇◇◈◈

A senior citizen said to his eighty year old friend, "So I hear you're getting married?"

"I certainly am."

"Do I know her?"

"No."

"This woman, is she good looking?"

"Not really."

"Is she a good cook?"

"No, she can't cook at all."

"Does she have lots of money?"

"No! Poor as a church mouse."

Well then, is she good in bed?"

"I don't know."

"Why in the world do you want to marry her then?"

"Because she can still drive!"

◈◈◇◇◇◈◈◈◇◈◇◇◈◈◇◈◇◇◈◈

Three old guys out walking.

First one says, "Windy isn't it?"

Second one says, "No, it's Thursday"

Third one says, "So am I. Let's go and get a beer."

◇◇◈◈ ◈◈◇◈◇◇◈◈◇◈◇◇◈ ◈◈◇◈

An elderly couple had dinner at another couple's house, and after eating, the wives left the table and went into the kitchen. The two gentlemen were talking, and one said, "Last night we went to a new restaurant and it was really great. I would recommend it highly.

The other man said, "What is the name of the restaurant?"

The first man thought and thought and finally said, "What is the name of that flower you give to someone you love? You know … the one that's red and has thorns."

304

"Do you mean a rose?"

"Yes, that's the one," replied the man. He then turned towards the kitchen and yelled, "Rose, what's the name of that restaurant we went to last night?"

❖❖❖❖❖❖❖❖❖❖❖❖❖❖❖❖❖❖❖❖❖❖❖❖❖❖❖❖❖❖❖❖❖

A Banbury senior citizen drove his brand new BMW Z3 convertible out of the car salesroom. Taking off down the motorway, he floored it to 90 mph, enjoying the wind blowing through what little hair he had left. "Amazing!" he thought as he flew down the M40, enjoying pushing the pedal to the metal even more. Looking in his rear view mirror, he saw a police car behind him, blue lights flashing and siren blaring.

"I can get away from him – no problem!" thought the elderly nutcase as he floored it to 110 mph, then 120, then 130. Suddenly, he thought, "What on earth am I doing? I'm too old for this nonsense!" So he pulled over to the side of the road and waited for the police car to catch up with him.

Pulling in behind him, the police officer walked up to the driver's side of the BMW, looked at his watch and said, "Sir, my shift ends in ten minutes. Today is Friday and I'm off for the weekend. If you can give me a reason why you were speeding that I've never heard before, I'll let you go."

The man looked very seriously at the policeman and replied, "Years ago, my wife ran off with a policeman. I thought you were bringing her back."

"Have a good day, sir," said the policeman.

◈◇◈◇◈◇◈◇◈◇◈◇◈◇◈◇◈◇◈◇◈◇◈

Hades

Charlie dies and finds himself in hell. As he is wallowing in despair he has his first meeting with the devil …

Satan: Why so glum?

Charlie: What do you think? I'm in hell!

Satan: Hell's not so bad. We actually have a lot of fun down here. You a drinking man?

Charlie: Sure, I love to drink.

Satan: Well you're going to love Mondays then. On Mondays that's all we do is drink. Whisky, tequila, Guinness, wine coolers, vodka and colas. We drink till we throw up and then we drink some more! And we don't worry about getting a hangover because you're dead anyway.

Charlie: That sounds great!

Satan: You a smoker?

Charlie: Oh, definitely.

Satan: All right! You're going to love Tuesdays. We get the finest cigars from all over the world and smoke our lungs out. If you get cancer – no problem, you're already dead remember?

Charlie: That sounds great.

Satan: I bet you like to gamble.

Charlie: Why yes, as a matter of fact I do.

Satan: Wednesdays you can gamble all you want. Craps, Blackjack, Roulette, Poker, Slots. If you go bankrupt … you're dead anyhow. What about drugs?

Charlie: Are you kidding? I love drugs! You don't mean …

Satan: That's right! Thursday is drugs day. Help yourself to a great big bowl of crack, or smack. Smoke a doobie the size of a submarine. You can do all the drugs you want, you're dead. Who cares?

Charlie: Wow! I never realised Hell was such a cool place!

Satan: You gay?

Charlie: No! DEFINITELY NOT.

Satan: Ooooh, you're going to hate Fridays!!

◇◈◇◈ ◇◇◈◇ ◈◇ ◇◇◇◇◇ ◈◇ ◇◈◇◇

Grandma's 100th

It was Grandma's 100th birthday. She had received her telegram that morning; her second treat of the day was to have a picnic on the lawn, an occasion she enjoyed greatly.

Grandma had had a stroke, was wobbly on her pins, and was therefore wheeled out in her invalid chair. In addition, the stroke had left her voiceless, as a result she was provided with a writing pad and biro with which to make her requirements known, and to answer questions made to her.

As she sat in her chair watching the family lay out the tea things on the tablecloth-covered rug on the lawn, the family noticed she was falling over to the right. They immediately ran to her, one with a pillow which was placed so as to keep her upright. A few minutes later she was noticed leaning over to the left. A second pillow was found and placed again to set her upright. A few minutes later she was seen to be falling forward. A scarf was found and put round her and the back of the chair to prevent this happening.

When this had been accomplished she was joined by her favourite grandson who had just arrived. "Hello Grandma, are you having a great time?" he asked. She pointed to her writing pad, which he gave her, and upon which she wrote:

"THEY WON'T LET ME FART."

❖❖❖❖❖❖❖❖❖❖❖❖❖❖❖❖❖❖❖

Liverpool Girls

Three men were sitting together bragging about how they had given their new wives duties to perform.

Terry had married a woman from America and bragged that he had told his new wife to do the dishes and all the cleaning in the house.

He said it took a couple of days but on the third day he came home to a clean house and all the dishes were washed and put away.

James had married a woman from Australia and he bragged that he had given his new wife orders to do all the cleaning, the dishes and the cooking.

He told them the first day he didn't see any results, but the next day it was better and by the third day his house was clean, the dishes done and there was a huge meal on the table.

The third man said he had married a girl from Liverpool. He boasted that the duties he had ordered her to do were to keep the house cleaned, the dishes washed, lawn mowed, laundry washed and hot meals on the table every day.

He said the first day he didn't see anything, the second day he didn't see anything, but by the third day most of the swelling had gone down and he could see a little bit out of his left eye.

Enough to make himself a bite to eat, load the dishwasher and call a gardener.

❖❖❖❖❖❖❖❖❖❖❖❖❖❖❖❖❖❖❖❖❖❖❖❖❖❖❖

By the Seaside

In the 1920s and early 30s the most that working families could expect for a family holiday would be an occasional day trip to the seaside, usually on a Sunday. What is of particular interest to us today is the clothes they wore for this much anticipated outing. The photo, indicating an obviously comfortably off family who would not dream of dressing for comfort! The ladies are not only wearing their hats, but they are of a quality one would see these days only at a wedding or at Ascot.

And the men? Collars and ties. The gent on the right wearing lace up boots and showing a substantial amount of long-john, whilst the other gent has at least discarded his homburg hat for the benefit of the photographer.

There is an old country saying that 'a change is as good as a rest!' Perhaps the coach journey combined with sitting on the sand and looking out at the sea, perhaps even having a paddle would provide as much pleasure as present day jet-setters obtain from flying off to Ibiza. There would certainly have been far less hassle involved, to say nothing of the pleasure of the charabanc stopping at the half-way house for a drink on the way home to end the day on the right note.

The only sad part? Work tomorrow.

The Knight of Everest and the Bowler Hatted Pigeon

By Jim Absalom – retired Prison Governor

During the nineteen-sixties when every aspect of life in England was changing, those who trod the corridors of power decided that penal practices and policies also had to change. Realising that many of those who trod, seldom did so in the straight and steady lines we of HM Prison Service were then used to treading, many of us looked forward with considerable trepidation to threatened changes.

However, there was one change, one innovation, many of us thought was excellent. Used properly it could be of great benefit to the Prison Service, to prisoners, and to staff. It was parole.

The following story is not about the system as such, but about a few of the people involved in setting up parole, and about a few who might benefit. It is also about a prison pigeon that wore a bowler hat.

Because HM Prison Wandsworth, West London, held many prisoners serving long terms of imprisonment, some of whom had been transferred to Wandsworth as 'unsuitable' for the long term prisons to which they had been allocated, and because the gaol was easily accessible to those who visited, it seemed clear that Wandsworth would be one of the first, if not the first, establishment to have to deal with parole matters. These would include writing and producing reports, carrying out interviews and assessments, setting up panels and boards and so on and so forth. However, before all those activities commenced, a parole supremo had to be appointed and a parole board of wise people had to be established.

It may well have been that the Government, then Labour, and Home Secretary, James Callaghan in particular, began to see that the setting up of parole was a formidable mountain to be mastered. Maybe it was decided that a master mountaineer was required. Whatever process led to the decision to choose a supremo, a famous mountaineer *was* recruited. His appointment was a stroke of genius.

The leader of the team that conquered Mount Everest, Sir John Hunt, later to be a member of the House of Lords, visited Wandsworth Prison as soon as he was appointed to head the new Parole Board. I met him at the gate and as we walked from the gate to the governor's office, the strongly built, upright ex-army colonel acknowledged with a smile and a 'thank you' the prison officers who obviously admired him, giving him the smartest open-handed military salutes I had ever seen them present to anyone! Sir John clearly had the gift of immediately being able to establish an easy rapport with staff and inmates alike.

The Governor was a tough character highly respected throughout the service. Beneath the somewhat cold and unsmiling appearance was an artistic, cultured and caring man with a great sense of humour. Jack Beisty OBE had been a soldier before the Second World War and, like me, had risen from the basic ranks of the prison service. He and I went back a long way but that is a story for another time.

The Governor had just returned to his office from 'rounds' as Sir John and I entered his room. As Deputy Governor I stayed a little in the background and took great pleasure in observing the two fine characters as they chatted easily together, until Governor Jack said to me, in his quiet, controlled voice, "Well Dep, I think you had better take Sir John on a guided tour. You know the prison better than anyone and I am sure he will enjoy going with you."

I was proud to be guide to one of the nicest men I ever met and when, in answer to my question, "Is there anything in particular you would like to see Sir John?" he replied,

"Everything, Mr Absalom!" I decided to deliver the works!

Since the arrival of Jack Beisty as Governor, and myself as his deputy a few months previously, many security changes had been made. For example, the perimeter security of the Victorian prison had been greatly improved. As we approached one corner of the perimeter I said to the famous mountaineer, "What do you think of that for a wall, sir?"

"Not bad, not bad at all," he replied quietly, pausing and looking up and down the twenty feet of smooth flat bricks that towered above us and seemed to me to be un-climbable without aids. "But," he continued, "it can be climbed." When I expressed doubt he said, eyes twinkling,

Would you like me to show you?"

It really would have been thrilling to see him conquer that climb but I had no doubt that there were many pairs of eyes watching us and, once some of the owners of some of those eyes saw the wall overcome, there was every likelihood that efforts would be made to demonstrate that there were unfulfilled mountaineers behind bars who were just waiting for an opportunity to show that they too might sometime conquer their own Everest. Subsequent to our discussions, and now convinced that the wall could be defeated, further modifications were carried out. To my knowledge, the only time that the 'Great Wall of Wandsworth' has been surmounted since that time was when a party of sadly misguided students taking part in a Rag Week attacked it from the outside, using ropes. At the approach of prison staff most of that party got down in a terrible rush and fled leaving just a few in fancy dress atop and astride the rough summit of a very steep vertical structure. There they had to remain for several long hours nervously peering down both sides of the wall at snarling, breathless slobbering and smoking members of the prison dog team … and their dogs, until the local constabulary arrived. They were then encouraged to dismount in dismay, proceed to dungeons disparate, there to be dispassionately directed to forgo future disorderly conduct, then dismissed, no doubt after being given mugs of hot sweet tea and doorstep cheese sandwiches, as is the custom of the custodians and upholders of law and order in this country when dealing with such demonstrators.

Walking at a steady pace I guided Sir John Hunt on a tour of all parts of that prison where I had served in uniform a decade and a half earlier. A town within a town, we visited cells and landings, the bath-house and hospital, the brush maker's shop and the cobbler's shop, where boots with two inch soles belonging to the Brigade of Guards were repaired. Then to the kitchen where, in the caterer's small office, a sample of a midday meal was being laid out for tasting on a shining airline-type tray on a table with a spotless white cloth.

I knew that the Principal Officer Caterer Geoff Matthews would welcome me as was his wont. "All correct sir," he reported, touching his forelock with two 'v' shaped fingers, in far from correct Royal Navy fashion. Then, as he shook hands with Sir John, the ex-Royal Navy petty officer made his usual request in an aside to me, "Kindly do not slam the door, sir," and as I very gently shut the door, I joined him and a nearby kitchen prisoner in the chorus, "or you'll blow the duff off the table!"

Vastly amused, our guest left the kitchen with me after chatting amicably to groups of smiling kitchen prisoners who clustered around him, hanging on every word that was spoken and looking as if they longed to touch his sleeve or the hem of his jacket in frank admiration.

Out in the yards again I unlocked another blue door that opened into a long workshop where busy prisoners were chalking and cutting navy blue cloth for uniforms. We strolled around the tailor's cutting shop chatting to instructors and workers. As we were about to reach the door to leave the shop, one small prisoner stopped marking cloth on a long bench and, turning to me, said through the side of his mouth, "Have you seen the bird, Gov'nor?"

"Not yet, not today, George," I replied conspiratorially, "I'll pass the word when I do."

"Okay, Guv," he said, and we left the workshop.

I paused outside to lock the door and the gate behind us. Sir John asked, "What was that about Mr Absalom? The bird?"

As we strolled on, crossing the exercise paths encircling the flower beds full of roses, and aiming for the administration block and a welcome cup of tea, I explained as follows.

"I walk around this prison at various times during the day when I can chat to prisoners and staff and keep in touch with whatever is going on. I walk around in the evenings several times a week. The rules demand that the Governor shall pay night visits. Here I often relieve my Governor, who recently had heart trouble. All governor grades at the prison are required to carry out night visits as a matter of course. During evening visits I sometimes see a pigeon fly off a cell window sill then suddenly stop in mid-air. Wings beating madly it moves backwards to the sill. Mailbag twine has been tied to its leg and it is the 'pet' of a prisoner in the cell. Every effort has been made to stop this sad custom without much success. Pigeons are menaces in institutions like this, for a number of reasons.

Among the flocks of birds that fly around the prison (their home), is a shiny black one which has a white mark over its beak and – it is wearing on its head, probably stuck on with glue from the brush shop, a small perfectly shaped black bowler hat. On the front of the bowler hat are the initials 'HMP' in red ink or red paint! Prisoners place bets on where that bowler-hatted pigeon will be seen at a certain time during the day. If a report is received that it has been seen, then a prisoner who reports the sighting will receive 'roll ups' as his winnings.

The majority of inmates here believe I know everything that is going on in the slammer. It would be silly to disillusion them! So, at some stage, one of the prisoners asking me about the pigeon sighting will be a bookmaker checking that the report he received from a potential winning backer is correct.

Now, I have to try to do two things. One is to recognise the bookie and keep an eye on him in case he corners all the business; the other is to ensure that I know a backer – a prisoner who is short of tobacco. He is the only one to whom I deliver news of the sighting! I have to hope that the bookie doesn't realise that I am on the side of the losers! Sir, justice comes in all colours and shapes."

As we sat down to drink our mugs of hot sweet tea Sir John was still chuckling and expressing a kind of wonder, at the introduction he had received to the different world in which the inmate, (staff and prisoners) lived at Wandsworth.

About twenty years later, after I had retired, I was national vice-president of an organisation helping young people. We held a reception in the Cholmondeley Room at the House of Lords. My Lord John was acting as host. He and I had a happy reunion, prefaced by his words, "Jim, I wonder what happened to your bowler-hatted pigeon?" I often wonder.

I know that not long before I left Wandsworth, to take charge of Gloucester gaol, I walked one evening near the kitchen and came almost face to face with the bowler-hatted pigeon that was perched on a low wall. I am sure he gave me a knowing wink before flying to the loft of the C of E Chapel. Maybe he was wearing a halo on that occasion.

◇◇◇

- In 1832 a certain Charles Dickens, aged 20 and at that time a newspaper reporter, went on strike with others of his profession demanding more pay.

- The Tower of London is not in the City of London

- FA Cup winners 1881? Old Carthusians beat Old Etonians. No kissing or diving in that match I'll wager

- *C'est un métier que de faire un livre, comme de faire une pendule.il faut plus que de l'esprit pour être auteur*

  .Making a book is a craft, as is making a clock. It takes more than wit to become an author. *Jean de la Bruyère 1688.*

- Many a man owes his success to his first wife and his second wife to his success.

- The man who can smile when things go wrong has thought of someone else that he can blame it on.

- By the time you have money to burn, the fire has gone out.

◇◇◇◇◇◇◇◇◇◇◇◇◇◇◇◇◇◇◇◇◇◇◇◇

From Margaret Dickenson

The First Lookers

Stand anywhere on Romney Marsh, where Romans once panned salt as payment for their troops, and you are surrounded by history. Some as hidden archaeology or ruins, such as St Martins Oratory, dating from 670 when Romney was a hidden Saxon Borough. Others like the Norman Church of St Nicholas. Still standing proud and resonating to the voices of its congregation, choir and bells; over 900 years since its construction by Bishop Odo, half brother to Duke William.

Stroll the banks of the Military Canal, or around Martello Towers, and echoes of Napoleonic War are roused.

Then walk the fields and meadows with their flocks of Romney sheep, in the footsteps of "wool smugglers", inspect a restored "Lookers Hut," where once Lookers sheltered out of the weather, slept on the small bed and ate the mutton and vegetable Lookers Pie, while tending to the flocks owned by the absentee landlords.

Romney Sheep

Picture courtesy of www.norwoodfarmnewchurch.co.uk

The pastures of Romney Marsh provide ideal grazing for sheep, indeed history records, "A long woolled, strong and highly valuable sheep has been kept on Romney Marsh since time immemorial."

The unique environment of the marsh has developed a breed of large framed, hardy animals that are docile, good foragers, and resistant to foot rot. The Romney sheep provided the foundation for the English woollen industry. Their long but dense fleece was highly prized, leading to widespread wool smuggling. Romney's are also well known for their meat, with its delicate taste even in older lambs. The sheep were so important to the marsh that during the Second World War, they were evacuated ahead of the women and children!

Why Lookers

The marsh has always been a difficult environment to survive in. By the 16th Century disease and poverty had struck, and many farms, houses, and churches were abandoned as the population dwindled.

The land was bought up by absentee landlords, who lived some distance away, to form larger holdings. These were laid down to pasture for sheep, which was less labour intensive than the growing of crops. This led to a huge increase in sheep numbers on the marsh. It is estimated that by 1890 there were about 225,000 sheep. There were also many types of pasture and flocks needed to be moved many times during a year. There was a huge demand for those who could shepherd the flocks and instead of employing several shepherds to tend their large flocks many of the landowners used the service of a 'Looker'.

The Lookers were independent, self-employed shepherds who would travel with the flocks and stay with them out at pasture. They would often be responsible for a number of flocks, for several landowners, spread over large areas of land.

The Looker would have been a hardy breed. He would have covered many miles in a day, criss-crossing the marsh on foot or by horse. His knowledge of the marsh would have been invaluable; allowing him to speedily move from flock to flock.

How they Lived

The life of a Looker was a lonely one. To be close to the flocks the Looker was forced to live away from his family, and therefore needed shelter out on the marsh, this led to the construction of Lookers huts. The Looker's hut was a simple building, generally about 10ft by 10ft, built mostly of brick with a tiled roof, and chimney. Inside would have been; a small storage area, a sleeping

Picture courtesy of Romney Marsh Countryside Project

would use this hut to store tools, to tend sickly sheep, as well as a shelter. Their only comfort would have been the fireplace; there the Looker could keep warm, heat milk for lambs, and food for themselves. Surrounding the hut would have been numerous pens where sick sheep could be kept close at hand. The huts were mainly used during lambing, but also for shearing or attending to disease in the summer months. The Looker could spend six weeks at a time in the hut, relying on his family to bring his provisions.

There are still people living on the Marsh who remember sleeping in these buildings. Many a farmer's son, when the family got too big, was relegated to sleeping in the Looker's hut.

Looker's huts are still dotted across the Marsh today, although most have fallen into disrepair through lack of use, as changing farming methods have reduced the need for Lookers.

◈◈◈◈◈◈◈◈◈◈◈◈◈◈◈◈◈

Lookers Pie

Ingredients
1½lbs Lean Lamb
8oz Potatoes
1 tbsp chopped mint
½ glass of red wine
1 beaten egg to glaze

8oz Onions
½ pt lamb stock
Salt & Pepper to season
10oz short crust pastry

Dice the lamb and brown in a little oil. Chop and brown the onions in a little butter.
Place Lamb and onions in a casserole dish with the wine, stock and mint.
Season with salt and pepper.

Cook for 1½ hours in oven at 160°C.
In meantime peel and part boil the potatoes for about 5 mins. Chop potatoes into chunks and stir into the casserole once cooked.

Roll out half the pastry and line the bottom of a pie dish. Spoon the casserole contents into the dish. Use remaining pastry to make a crust to cover the dish. Glaze top of pie with a little beaten egg. Cook pie for 25mins at 170°C

Lookers Hut Map - Distribution of huts in the early 20th century

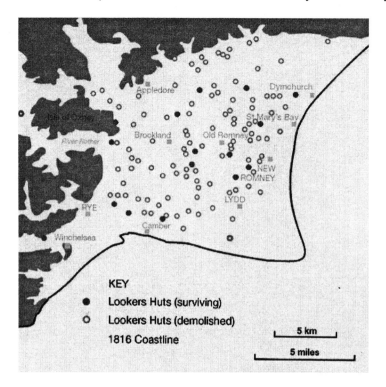

More Quotes

'Tis better to have loved and lost
Than never to have loved at all. *Alfred Lord Tennyson 1847.*

For when the wine is in, the wit is out. *Thomas Bacon c1542.*

Like all the very young we took it for granted that making love is child's play. *Nancy Mitford.*

Il faut manger pour vivre et non pas vivre pour manger.
One should eat to live, and not live to eat. *Molière 1668.*

Music, the greatest good that mortals know,
And all of heaven we have below. *Joseph Addison. c1700.*

The boss of a big company needed to call one of his employees about an urgent problem with one of the main computers, dialled the employee's home phone number and was greeted with a child's whisper.

"Hello."

"Is your daddy home?" he asked.

"Yes," whispered the small voice.

"May I talk to him?"

The child whispered, "No."

Surprised and wanting to talk with an adult, the boss asked, "Is your Mummy there?"

"Yes."

"May I talk to her?"

Again the small voice whispered, "No."

Hoping there was somebody with whom he could leave a message, the boss asked, "Is anybody else there?"

"Yes," whispered the child, "a policeman."

Wondering what a policeman would be doing at his employee's home, the boss asked, "May I speak with the policeman?"

"No, he's busy," whispered the child.

"Busy doing what?"

"Talking to Daddy and Mummy and the fireman," came the whispered answer. Growing concerned and even worried as he heard what sounded like a helicopter through the earpiece on the phone the boss asked, "What is that noise?"

"A hello-copper," answered the whispering voice.

"What is going on there?" asked the boss, now truly alarmed.

In an awed whispering voice the child answered, "The search team just landed the hello-copper."

Alarmed, concerned, and even more than just a little frustrated the boss asked, "What are they searching for?"

Still whispering, the young voice replied along with a muffled giggle, "ME."

◈◇◈◇◈◇◈◇◈◇◈◇◈◇◈◇◈◇◈◇◈◇◈

More from Allison

A man wanted to get married. He was having trouble choosing among three likely candidates. He gives each woman a present of £5000 and watches to see what they do with the money. The first does a total makeover. She goes to a fancy beauty salon, gets her hair done, new make up and buys several new outfits and dresses up very nicely for the man. She tells him that she has done this to be more attractive for him because she loves him so much.

The man was impressed.

The second goes shopping to buy the man gifts. She gets him a new set of golf clubs, some new gizmos for his computer, and some expensive clothes. As she presents these gifts, she tells him that she has spent all the money on him because she loves him so much.

Again the man is impressed.

The third invests the money in the stock market. She earns several times the £5000. She gives him back the £5000 and reinvests the remainder in a joint account. She tells him that she wants to save for their future because she loves him so much.

Obviously the man was impressed.

The man thought for a long time about what each woman had done with the money he'd given her.

Then he married the one with the biggest boobs.

Men are like that.

❖◇❖◇❖◇❖◇❖◇❖◇❖◇❖◇◇❖◇◇❖◇◇◇❖◇◇❖◇❖◇❖◇◇◇❖◇❖◇◇◇❖◇❖◇◇◇❖◇❖

From Baralba

"The weak may appear strong, but the ignorant have no way to appear wise."

"Orators only influence those who listen, but that do not hear, and those that hear but do not understand."

"No dog is silent if another dog barks."

"Inferior is he whose superiority depends upon the inferiority of others."

"As a man gains power, so he loses his reason."

The Torment of Gabrielle Schlicter

From The Chandlers – Volume Four

By Cyril Cook

It was New Year's Eve 1941. Gabrielle was a second year medical student at Munich University. As the bells rang out announcing the New Year, she threw a handful of leaflets from a balcony in a large beer hall on to the crowds below, condemning the war and calling on the people to put an end to it. Whilst trying to make her getaway she was arrested and handed over to the Gestapo.

Now read on …

When arrested, she was not roughly handled, which surprised her, knowing the reputation of the police in general and assuming the Gestapo would be even heavier handed. She was taken down into the basement of the police headquarters and put into a room, not a cell exactly, but a room with just a solitary chair in it. They had allowed her to keep her watch, although they had taken her purse, and some letters she had in an inside pocket of her topcoat. It was 1.15 am. It was very cold in the unheated room. One comparatively small bulb which stayed on all the time was the only lighting. She sat on the chair and waited, getting colder and colder despite still wearing her coat. From time to time she got up and ran up and down the small room in order to get warm. She carried out simple callisthenics for the same purpose, then she tired, sat back on the chair, got cold again, the whole cycle then being repeated.

At 6 am a small hatchway opened in the door and a tray with a mug of water and thick slice of black bread appeared. Removing these items from the tray, the tray was removed and the hatch fastened outside. Not a word had been spoken; neither could she see who it was who had brought her this sumptuous meal.

On New Year's Day she was left alone all day, getting sleepier and sleepier, but only being able to have catnaps sitting on the chair. At 6 pm the hatch opened again and a repetition of the feast presented in the morning was offered her. During the day she had badly needed to go to the lavatory, but although she shouted no-one answered her, and at long last she had to find a place in the corner of the room to relieve her bowels and bladder. She felt dirty and ashamed.

Another night was spent as she had the previous one. A succession of trying to get warm, looking at her watch, catnapping on the chair and finally and disgustingly having to relieve herself again in the corner. At 6 am she was brought bread and water again.

321

She was waiting for the hatch to open, immediately shouting to whoever was out there she must go to the lavatory. There was no reply as the hatch was slammed down and latched.

At nine o'clock she heard heavy footsteps outside. The door opened and a heavily built woman, thirty five-ish appeared, followed by a huge man in dungarees. He had a vacant, mongoloid appearance, obviously a Russian prisoner now working for the Germans. On entering, the woman immediately put a handkerchief to her nose, pointing to the mess in the corner she told the Kapo, "Clear that up," then turning to the prisoner said in a kindly voice, "I'm sorry about that, they should have left a lidded bucket for you, being New Year it must have been overlooked." As she spoke, two more men arrived carrying a table with another chair lodged on it, placing it in the middle of the room. "Bring your chair up and sit down," she asked, still using a friendly conversational tone of voice. The mess having been cleared up, the Russian stood in one corner whilst the two women sat down facing each other at the table.

"Now, what is your name and how old are you?"

"I am Gabrielle Schlicter, a student at the university, I am twenty years old."

"Now, I have a written deposition from a reliable witness who saw you throw a number of these leaflets onto people in the central bierkeller on New Year's Eve. Similar outrages occurred at other festive occasions which shows there is an organised group of you. This is an offence against the state, which, as you must know, could carry the death penalty." She was speaking in a soft, friendly voice. "Now, I have investigated your family background; your parents are prosperous people who own a cinema in the city centre; your father is a party member; your younger brother is in the Hitler Youth. With that background I am sure you have been led astray by others. Now, all I want to know is the names of those others and you will be free to go and resume your studies in the new session."

She opened a notebook.

"Well?"

"I'm sorry, I don't know any others. A woman gave me the leaflets and asked me to throw them at midnight."

"Did you not read the leaflet?"

"No, I just threw them."

"Look Gabrielle, I am a very friendly person. Sooner or later you will tell us who these other people are. I quite understand young university students' latch on to crazy campaigns like this," she looked at the leaflet, "Wanting to kill the Fuhrer indeed!"

"It doesn't say anything about wanting to kill the Fuhrer."

They looked at each other. Gabrielle knew she was caught. She was tired and she had been led into an elementary trap. There was no going back.

There was an edge to the woman's voice as she continued, "Now Gabrielle, we both know where we stand. My first offer is still there, you tell us of the others and you can go, if you don't, there will be other methods used – do you understand? I don't want that, I have a young sister of your age; I would not want her to be dealt with in that way. Now, write down here the names of the rest of your group." She pushed the notebook over to Gabrielle.

"I can't do it." She was thinking furiously, even if she gave the names there was no certainty this woman would keep her word. In fact it was probably just a wicked ploy; she probably did not have the authority to offer such terms. They will probably try and beat the information out of me – God, how I wish I didn't know who the others were, they could kill me then and I would not tell.

Her inquisitor sat back looking at her steadily. "I am sorry you said that. I will give you one last chance. You will die in this building if you do not tell me what I need to know. That is not all. Before you die terrible things will be done to you, why don't you see sense!" The last words spoken very loudly, making Gabrielle jump and causing the jailer to move from his torpor in anticipation of pleasures to come.

"I'm sorry, I can't do it."

"Very well, I did not want to have to use Ivan, but you leave me no choice." Thus cleansing whatever little conscience she had she looked at Ivan and nodded towards the door. Ivan went to the door reappearing with a vicious looking cane.

"Bend over the table."

Gabrielle hesitated. Ivan moved with astonishing speed for such a big man, pulled her up by her hair, kicked the chair away and bent her double over the table. The inquisitor pushed down on her shoulders whilst Ivan beat her on the buttocks with terrible ferocity a dozen times. She screamed with the sudden agony, when he stopped she lay sobbing across the table.

"Now will you tell me?"

"I can't."

Ivan repeated the punishment, Gabrielle by now lapsing into a state of semi-consciousness as a result of the searing pain spreading through her body. Again she refused to tell. The inquisitor nodded again to Ivan, who went to the door returning with another similar cane, this one having one end split down in several places. He rolled Gabrielle over on the table onto her back, undid the buckle on her skirt and pulled it down, pulled her knickers down, rolled her back onto her stomach and bared her backside. Standing away he brought the split ends down onto her buttocks again, some seven or eight times with such force that the skin was broken in numerous places, as a consequence at the last two strokes the inquisitor herself was splattered with Gabrielle's blood. After a second session of this she was almost unconscious with the pain. The inquisitor called a halt. Again, lifting Gabrielle by the hair Ivan sat her back on the chair, her pain being so great she hardly noticed the extra agony of being seated.

That will be all – today. Gabrielle, listen to me." Gabrielle looked up through the tears of pain and outrage.

"Are you a virgin?" She nodded in the affirmative.

"Well tomorrow I shall have Ivan re-arrange all that for you. Ivan loves to de-flower German girls." Ivan standing beside her was making obscene gestures with his right forearm and wiping the saliva from his mouth with his other hand.

"So I shall ask you for the names in the morning. Remember, we have only just begun."

With that the evil pair left, leaving Gabrielle crumpled on the chair, sobbing with terror and desperation, shivering with the cold on her half naked body. Slowly she gathered her faculties together, levering herself off the chair, in the course of so doing inflicting further agonising pain on herself, she stood leaning on the table until she found the strength to dress herself again and to recover her coat which her tormentors had thrown in the corner of the room. With the marginal recovery in her bodily comfort she began to reason what she could do. She could give half a dozen false names and addresses, but that would mean only a stay in her ordeal whilst they were checked out, and who knows what sort of distress would be inflicted on the people living in the addresses she gave. She could, and no-one could blame her, give the names of the people with whom she had been associated. She ruled that out straight away; she could not live with herself afterwards if she did and anyway they were probably going to execute her – they would never release her to tell others of her experiences. She steadily gained control of her thinking. There was only one way out. Before those two depraved cretins returned in the morning she would have to do away with herself. But how? Hanging was out of the question. Even if she could tear her clothing into strips to make a rope, there was absolutely no projection anywhere from which to suspend it. Even the window, small as it was at the top of the end wall, was in the form of solid glass blocks; it had no frame and was not covered by bars. Sobbing quietly to herself she wondered if she could use the electric light socket to electrocute herself, but even though she could reach it by standing on the table left behind from the morning's inquisition, the bulb was concealed in a heavy glass cover screwed into a metal ring flush with the ceiling, and anyhow she reasoned it would only be 110 volts, not enough to kill anyone unless they could hold on for a time, and since she would have to push her fingers into the socket that would not be practicable.

Exhausted by her constant hurt she sank back onto the chair only to cry out with the further agony of being seated on the hard wood. She laid her arms on the table and her head on her arms and quietly sobbed herself into a sleep, disturbed by the arrival of the inevitable slice of black bread and mug of water. She slowly made her painful way to the door, trying to get a glimpse of whoever it was out there.

"Who are you?" she asked in a broken tearful voice. There was no reply. She took the bread and water. Washing the water around her mouth, dry with fear and with the constant breathing through it while her nose was blocked, she saw immediately what she could do. It was a tin mug, once upon a time enamelled probably, but with now most of its colour chipped off. The walls of the cellar were rough untreated sandstone. If she rubbed one part of the rim of the mug against the sandstone wall it would gradually become sharp, bit by bit, she would be able to turn the mug to obtain a two inch section honed like a razor. She would then cut her wrists.

The horror that struck her at the solution at which she had arrived sent her again into sobs of fear and total despair. Gradually she recovered, examined the wall for a fairly smooth piece of stone, reckoning this would give her a smoother, finer blade, and proceeded to move the mug rim laterally backwards and forwards until she had sharpened a small section. Repeating this, after nearly an hour she had achieved her goal, at the same time her mental demeanour had calmed to a steely determination to go through with this great sacrifice.

Gabrielle Schlicter was a deeply religious Catholic girl. Up until now the thought of the great sin she was to commit in taking her own life had not presented itself to her. But now, as the moment approached when she was to go to meet her maker she had fears of the purgatory she would surely endure. In great pain, she sank to her knees against the chair and prayed.

"Dear God, forgive me this great sin I have to commit. If I live until tomorrow I am sure the abominable torture I shall receive will result in my giving the names of my friends who have worked with me in opposing this dreadful war. They too will then perhaps name others I do not know when they too are tortured."

She paused for a few moments, crying silently.

"Dear God, take care of my dear mother, father, brother and sister upon whom I have now placed such anguish and distress. Comfort them in their torment, soothe their heartache, and bring them peace."

She was silent again for a short while, and then raising her face to Heaven, concluded her prayers.

"Dear God, I entreat you to absolve me from this wrongdoing and accept my soul into heaven."

Lifting herself from her knees, she gradually lowered her suffering body onto the chair, placing her arms uppermost in front of her on the table. Sobbing quietly, and very afraid, she cut first one wrist and then the other. Softly she began to sing a song she used to sing in her school choir and which she had always loved so much. It was about a young man telling how his loved one had pledged her devotion to him with the gift of a ring, but then had gone away from him, the ring then breaking in two.

IIn einem kuhlen grunde, da geht ein Muhlenrad
Mein liebste ist verschwunden, die dort gewohnet hat
Mein liebste ist verschwunden, die dort gewohnet hat.

Sie hat mir treu versprochen, gab mir ein ring dabei
Sie hat die treu gebrochen, mein ringlein sprang entzwei
Sie hat die treu gebrochen, mein ringlein sprang entzwei.

Ich mocht als Spielman reisen, weit in die Welt hinaus,
Und singen …

Beginning the third verse, the sweet, sad haunting Schubert melody faded away as she lapsed slowly into unconsciousness. Fifteen minutes later her soul left her.

There is a horrific sequel to this evil event. When the inquisitor arrived with Ivan the following morning they found the girl dead. Ivan displayed such rage at being denied the prospect of ravishing this beautiful young woman that he stormed around, his face seething with hatred of she who commanded him. As a result, since she now feared she could no longer control him, she had him returned to the Russian Asiatic prisoners' compound at Mauthausen. Ivan was well nourished after his months at Munich. The night he arrived they set on him. He was a match for any one of them, but not for all of them. They killed him and ate him. They were starving. Cannibalism was not uncommon among Asiatic prisoners.

By Cyril Cook

Joseph Stalin, 'Uncle Joe', had a dream. For ships to leave the White Sea in the far north of Russia to carry their valuable cargoes of timber and ore to European ports, they had the hazardous journey out through the Barents Sea and down the four hundred mile coast of Norway. Stalin decided he could build a canal, The White Sea Canal, from Belomorsk in the North, to Leningrad on the Baltic, utilising existing lakes and waterways on route. The means of construction? Slave labour. Method of construction? Entirely by hand. Tools? Shovels, picks, wheelbarrows, scaffolding, all made by hand from wood from the forests. Accommodation? Built by prisoners with timber from the forests.

The canal was to be dug to a depth of four metres. There would be approximately one hundred and fifty miles of actual canal, plus the existing waterways, and it would require the building of five dams and some twenty or more locks – and Stalin decreed it should start in September 1931, - only seven months after he first broached the idea – and be completed in twenty one months! This meant the workers would have to toil through two winters in sub zero temperatures, shift every rock and every bucket of frozen earth by hand, work night shifts aided by generator powered electric lights, all on starvation rations.

But is <u>was</u> completed on time. Stalin made a much publicised trip down it on a small steam vessel, books were written about it, plays were performed about it. As Uncle Joe made his triumphant journey he would have passed the point where a tablet denotes, "To the innocents who died building the White Sea Canal 1931-1933." It does not give a number. It is calculated nearly fifty thousand died building this waterway, but then fifty thousand deaths represents only a drop in the ocean of millions of deaths which can be directly placed on the conscience of Joseph Stalin.

And this engineering masterpiece today? A muddy waterway bearing the occasional barge. The railway is vastly quicker.

By Cyril Cook

When I was a boy I lived on a farm at Mottingham, Kent. I was very popular with the boys of the village, but I have to confess this was not entirely due to my undoubted charm, my sporting ability or any superfluity of worldly goods. It was due to the fact that we had a **field**. When the lads therefore wanted to play cricket or have a kick-about at football, or even a place for a jumbo sized bonfire on November 5th, I was the one they came to.

The field in question was the only one near the village which was reasonably level. There were a number of other fields of course on the farm, but these were either on a slope or cultivated for hay, root crops and kale to winter-feed the sixty odd head of cattle kept on the farm. It was known as 'The Paddock' and was used, along with a couple of others, for the cattle to graze between morning and afternoon milking.

And there came the rub. As cows are no respecters of cricket pitches, football pitches, or prospective bonfire sites, inevitably our greatest hazard was 'pancakes', by which genteel name the hazards in question were generally known. In addition to bats, ball and stumps, a main piece of our playing equipment was a shovel, but although it was comparatively easy to clear the pancakes on the pitch between the wickets, it was a vastly different kettle of fish to clear the out field.

If you let your mind run on this fascinating situation, you can readily imagine the kinds of incidents that can occur. Cows will obviously eat the sweetest grass and crop it short. When they come to a patch of dock or thistle, they will eat round it. This leaves an oasis of rough, in the middle of which for good measure one of them will have left a pancake. You are playing at square leg – Loftie Johnson hits one up in the air towards you – you run backwards to catch him out, get caught up in the rough and go arse over tip backwards into the pancake. I've seen it happen many times.

Again, you are playing at third man – Porky Murray makes a good drive and you race round to field it hoping to make a name for yourself and the second before you field it – it hits a pancake and it is definitely not egg you get on your face.

We had a local rule for this particular situation. As soon as the ball hit a pancake the batsmen completed the run they were on and stopped. This then gave the fielder time to clean the ball in the grass and throw it back in, hopefully not hitting another pancake on the way.

Football was a different matter altogether. We would put the coats down for goal posts on clear patches, but there was no way you could avoid the pancakes when you were playing. Furthermore, you can imagine that volunteers to play goalkeeper were few and far between, in view of the fact that every time they made a save they further distanced themselves from the rest of humanity. Here again we had a local rule. If the ball landed 'plop in' then the game stopped, the ball was cleaned and the game restarted with a dropped ball one yard from the pancake. They never had to do that at Wembley!

If you consider the foregoing to be at the least a little adventurous, Bonfire Night was even more so. At least in daylight you can see the pancakes, in the dim light of bonfire night they were more or less camouflaged. Furthermore **girls** used to come to the Bonfire Night, and they, for some unknown reason, couldn't accept that if you put your foot in a pancake you just rubbed your shoe on the grass and carried on. We could never discern whether the girls were squealing because of the noise of the fireworks, encountering a pancake, or the normal reason for squealing when they are with the lads of the village in the half dark.

In the light of all this, you will probably think that we must have been a pretty smelly lot, but I honestly can't remember that we were. It was a fact of life that there were pancakes, and that at some time or other you would tread in one. Of course, we had to take our boots off before we went into the house, but that was standard practice for life on the farm. My mother would have crowned my dad if he had walked into the kitchen in his working boots. However, I think the bank manager's son from Avondale Road and perhaps one or two others from the village were looked at askance when they arrived home from playing with those rough boys on the farm – Eau de Cologne they did not smell of at all!

Those were the days.

✧❖✧❖❖✧❖✧✧❖✧❖✧✧❖❖✧✧❖✧❖✧❖✧✧✧❖✧❖✧✧✧❖❖✧❖✧✧❖❖✧❖✧✧❖✧✧❖✧

Mark Twain's Reflections

When angry, count a hundred; when very angry swear.

✧❖✧✧❖✧❖❖✧✧❖✧✧❖✧✧❖✧✧

Man is the only animal that blushes. Or needs to!

✧❖✧✧❖✧❖✧❖✧❖✧✧❖✧❖✧❖✧✧

There ain't no way to dind out why a snorer can's hear himself snore.

✧❖✧❖✧❖✧❖✧❖✧✧❖❖✧✧❖✧❖✧✧

The report of my death was an exaggeration!

✧❖✧❖❖✧❖✧❖✧❖❖✧❖✧❖✧✧❖❖✧✧

A classic: something that everyone wants to have read and nobody wants to read.

329

Uncle Joe on a Day Out

By Cyril Cook

Uncle Joe's dream of Heaven was 'Sarfend', (Southend in Essex to you!), in the sun, with a stop on the way down for a pint, a plentiful supply of bottles on the sands (carefully guarded), and a further stop at the 'halfway house' on the way back to Peckham.

While he was there he naturally got undressed, in that he took off his shoes and socks, ate several basins of cockles, followed by an ice-cream cornet.

Uncle Joe at the seaside

If he was feeling very daring he might well have had a paddle, taking care not to make his trousers and long-johns wet, above all, ensuring his beer was having a trustworthy eye kept on it, preferably by a non-drinker, although to be fair, there wouldn't have been many of those around.

He may not have been a millionaire, lushing it up on the beach at Cannes, but you have to agree he was most definitely a happy little seasider!

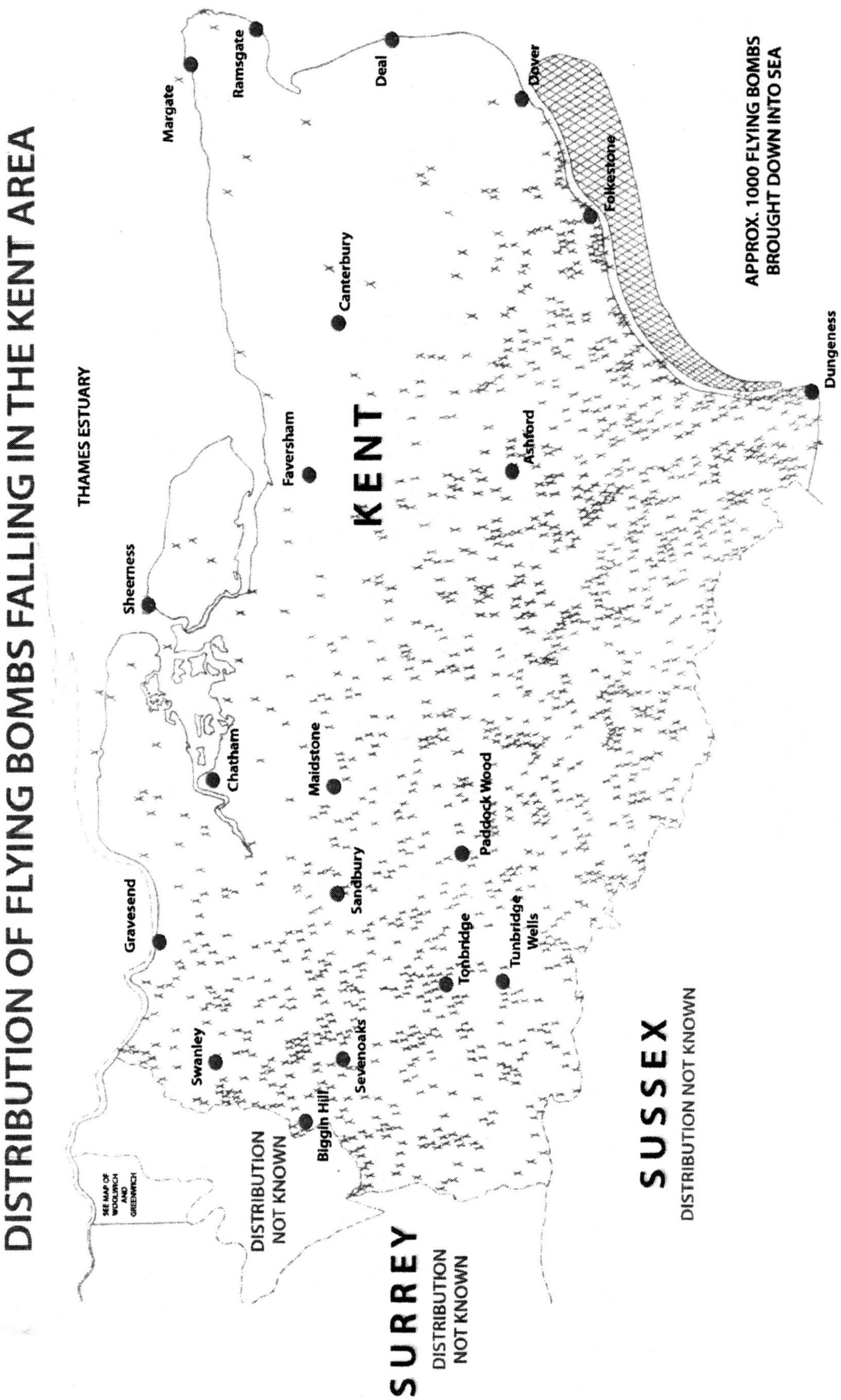

DISTRIBUTION OF FLYING BOMBS FALLING IN THE KENT AREA

THAMES ESTUARY

Margate

Ramsgate

Deal

Dover

Folkestone

APPROX. 1000 FLYING BOMBS
BROUGHT DOWN INTO SEA

Canterbury

Dungeness

KENT

Faversham

Ashford

Sheerness

Chatham

Maidstone

Paddock Wood

Gravesend

Sandbury

Tonbridge

Tunbridge
Wells

Swanley

Sevenoaks

Biggin Hill

DISTRIBUTION
NOT KNOWN

SEE MAP OF
WOOLWICH
AND
GREENWICH

SURREY

DISTRIBUTION
NOT KNOWN

SUSSEX

DISTRIBUTION NOT KNOWN

Flying Bombs in Kent

The Woman and Her Bear

An Inuit (Eskimo) Legend from John Bury, Loon Lake, Canada.

Long ago in the far north, there lived a village of people known as the Inuit. They lived on the shores of the icy Arctic, and they depended upon the bounty of the salmon and seal and the creatures of the snow to feed themselves. All the young men of the village were hunters and fishermen. One old woman lived alone. She had no husband and no sons to hunt or fish for her, and though her neighbours shared their food with her, as was their custom, she was lonely. She longed for a family of her own. She often walked along the shore, looking far out to sea, praying that the gods might send her a son.

One cold winter day, the woman was walking by the sea when she spotted a tiny white polar bear sitting all alone on the thick ice. At once she felt a kinship toward him, for he looked as lonely as she. His mother was nowhere in sight. "Someone must have killed her," she said softly, and she walked onto the ice, picked up the cub and looked into his eyes. "You will be my son," she said. She called him Kunik.

The old woman took her cub back to her home. From that day on, she shared all of her food with Kunik, and a strong bond grew between the two.

The village children loved Kunik too. Now the woman was never lonely, for her son, the bear, and all the village children kept her company all day. She would stand by her igloo and smile as Kunik and the children rolled in the snow and slid on the ice. Kunik was gentle with the children as if they were his brothers and sisters.

Kunik grew taller and smarter. The children taught him to fish. By springtime he was fishing on his own, and every afternoon he came home carrying fresh salmon for his mother. The old woman was now the happiest of all the villagers. She had plenty of food and a son she loved with all her heart. She was so proud of her little bear that whenever he returned home, she would say proudly to anyone nearby, "He's the finest fisherman in all the village!"

Before long the men began to whisper among themselves. They knew the bear was the most skilful fisherman of the village. They began to feel envious.

"What will we do?" they asked each other. "That bear brings home the fattest seals and the biggest salmon."

"He must be stopped," one of the men said. "He puts us to shame." They all turned and looked at him. They nodded slowly for although they were envious, they knew how much the old woman loved the bear.

"We will have to kill him. He has grown far too big," one man said. One by one the others agreed, for their envy made them stupid and mean.

332

"Yes," the others said. "He is a danger to our families."

A little boy overheard the men talking. He ran to the old woman's home to tell her of the terrible plan. When the old woman heard the news, she threw her arms around her bear and wept. "No," she said, "they must not kill my child." At once she set off to visit every house in the village. She begged each man not to kill her beautiful bear. "Kill me instead," she wept. "He is my child. I love him dearly."

"He is fat," some of the village men said. "He will make a great feast for the whole village."

"He is a danger to our children," the others said. "We cannot let him live."

The old woman saw that the men were determined to kill her son. She rushed home and sat down beside him. "Your life is in danger, Kunik. You must run away. Run away and do not return, my child." She wept as she spoke and held him close. "Run away but do not go so far that I cannot find you," she whispered. And though her heart was breaking, she sent Kunik away. He had tears in his eyes, but he obeyed his mother's wishes.

For many days the old woman and the children grieved their loss. Then one day the old woman rose at dawn and was determined to find Kunik. She walked and walked, calling out his name. After many hours, just as the old woman feared she would never find him, she saw her bear running toward her. He was fat and strong, and his coat was shimmering white. They embraced, and the old woman whispered, "I love you."

But Kunik could see that his mother was hungry, and so he ran to get her fresh meat and fish. With tears in her eyes, the old woman cut up the seal and gave her son the choicest slices of blubber. Promising to return the next day, she set off for home, carrying her meat, her heart filled with joy.

The next day, as she had promised, she went to visit her son. And every day after that, the old woman and her son met, and the bear brought his mother fresh meat and fish.

After a while the villagers grew to understand the love between the woman and the bear was strong and true. And from that point on, they told with pride and respect the tale of the unbroken love between the old woman and her son.

❖❖❖ ❖❖❖ ❖ ❖❖ ❖❖ ❖ ❖❖ ❖❖ ❖❖❖ ❖❖ ❖ ❖❖ ❖❖❖ ❖❖❖ ❖❖ ❖ ❖❖❖

Miles Kington, the well known columnist of the Daily Telegraph wrote the following article, a plea from one of his readers in Dorset. Miles, not being what you might call an 'agony uncle', reprinted the letter, trusting that among the erudite subscribers to his illustrious paper there would be a knight in shining armour who could save the day. To broaden the field only a fraction it must be said, I am reprinting his final words. Over to you readers.

Dear Mr Kington

I am secretary of a large golf club in Dorset, and one of my tasks is to organise the 5 November bonfire and fireworks, which the golf club has traditionally organised every year for members' families.

Last year we very nearly did not have a firework display at all, as the cost of insurance against damage and personal injury was almost more than the cost of the event itself.

This year the insurance premiums have gone up so much that we decided we would either be forced to cancel the show or stage it in a very different form.

By a stroke of good fortune, we found that one of our members, a talented cameraman called Trevor Wilkins, had made an impressive 15 minute film of last year's display, and we decided to show that on a big screen outside the golf club, complete with special effects and recorded noises and even a bit of the '1812 Overture'.

The film was a great success, especially as Trevor Wilkins had cleverly edited it and intercut it with funny moments from the club year and bits of interviews with the most popular characters in the club. So although fireworks on a screen are never quite as good as the real thing, we thought the evening went very well and had been a big hit. And because we had charged a small entry fee, and sold refreshments, we did not even make a loss. We felt very pleased with ourselves.

That was before we received a visit next day from the local council officer who looks after health and safety, and similar regulations.

"I hear you had a bonfire night at the club last night which contravenes public safety regulations," he said.

We explained that the fireworks had been on film and could therefore not be a hazard.

"That is my precise point," he said. "You were, in effect, presenting a film show. You were running an outdoor cinema, to which you charged entry. There are many conditions attached to putting on a cinematographical exhibition. You are required to provide decent toilet facilities, to have disabled access, to have emergency exits in case of fire, to have fixed seating, to have fire-proofed projection equipment..."

I won't go on; suffice to say that in our attempt not to burn anything or anyone to death, we appear to have broken more than forty safety regulations, even down to selling unlicensed and untested home-made popcorn.

And that was not all.

"I take it," said this odious official before leaving, "that the firework film was licensed for public display? I mean, it had been submitted to the British Board of Film Classification to be awarded the correct certificate?"

Well, of course it hadn't. Who submits their home-made movies to the censors? But it turned out that by charging for entry, we had automatically become cinema exhibitors and therefore subject to censorship. It may be hard to imagine a film of fireworks which could deprave and corrupt, but the man said he had no choice but to prosecute us for unlawful cinema exhibition.

"I shall also have to investigate the question of money passing hands in the making of the film," he said.

"There wasn't any!" I said. "The people in it appeared for free! The filming was done for free."

"Use of unpaid film extras," said the bureaucrat, writing all this down. "Uncopyrighted use of a public firework display..."

"Oh, for heavens sake!" I said, losing my temper. "This is political correctness gone mad!"

"We don't use the word 'mad' anymore, sir," said the official, making more notes, his eyes glinting strangely. "I think you will regret having said that."

And that is how the matter stands. These prosecutions may well ruin the club. Do you have any suggestions as to how we should proceed?

Over to you readers.

The Red Ship

By Cyril Cook

In the summer of 1956 my friend Dennis Carter, who lives in Bournemouth and is an artist of repute, found himself at St Katherine's Dock in East London, still much battered from World War Two bombing – the dock that is, not Dennis.

Across the dock he saw a red ship leaving. As this was far from being an everyday event he took out the sketch pad he always carried and speedily transferred the scene on to paper.

The sheets of paper upon which he made his first impressions were put into a box with countless others, and there they remained year after year until he retired and rediscovered them, resulting in the picture illustrated above, completed in 2001.

This raises the question, why was a ship painted red? I approached my great friend Captain John Bury, who in addition to being a seafarer was also one of the Elder Brethren of Trinity House. He told me it would almost certainly have been an Antarctic survey vessel, painted in that colour so that it showed up against the ice.

There arose then another twist to the story …

I bought an H Salmon Ltd calendar from W H Smith, and upon turning it to August discovered a photograph of St Katherine's Dock as it is today – the picture having been taken from almost the exact position from which Dennis had made his sketches nearly fifty years before. That was coincidence number one.

And the Red Ship?

Captain John told me of a friend of his, Captain Woodfield OBE who sailed in these vessels at that time, which led me to coincidence number two. Captain Woodfield told me he could well have been on that ship at that time, since he made a tour in the summer of 1956, sailing from St Katherine's.

And what did The Red Ship do? Or at least the intrepid people who sailed in her? We shall tell you more in due course!

A Dictionary for Men (Part Two)

L. **Lace**   Lace, like charity, covers a multitude of sinners.

     Lover   That one of her admirers whom a woman acknowledges in public.

M. **Man**   Man is made of dust and his wife shakes it out of him.

     Ministry   A post attacked by all desirous of occupying it.

     Money   A liniment capable of softening the harshest temper.

N. **Neutral Person**   One who never says yes.

O. **Optimism**   The system of those who, wanting nothing, contend that everything is for the best in the best of all possible worlds.

P. **Pianist**   Anyone who plays the piano and comes to England from a foreign country.

     Poor Devil   An individual who has to resolve, every morning, whether he shall eat in the course of the day.

     Profundity   What many authors pretend to. Their works are like catacombs – deep, dark and empty.

R. **Relations**   A tedious pack of people without the smallest instinct about when to die.

S. **Sinner**   A person who gets found out.

T. **Tragedian**   A man who gets into a passion for so much a night.

V. **Visiting Card**   A memorial left by someone who is delighted at not having seen you.

W. **Wedding**   A trade in which the bride is given away and the groom often sold.

     Women   God made many women smart, a few clever, and some good.

Y. **Youth**   The age of a man till he is twenty, and of a woman till she is fifty.

Manx Folklore

In the days when Charles II was King of England, and Charles, Earl of Derby King in Mann, Peel Castle was always garrisoned by soldiers. The guard room was just inside the great entrance of the castle and a passage used to lead through one of the old churches, to the Captain of the Guard's Room. At the end of the day one of the soldiers would lock the castle gates and carry the keys back down the dark passage to the Captain. The soldiers used to take turns to do this duty.

About this time a big black dog with rough curly hair was seen, sometimes in this room, next time in a different room. He did not belong to anyone there; apparently no-one knew anything about him. But every night, when the lamps were lighted in the guard room and the fire was burning bright, he would walk down the dark passage and lay himself down by the hearth. He made no movement but lay there until the break of day, when he would then get up and go back along the passage.

The soldiers were at first terrified of him but after some time they were used to the sight of him and lost some of their fear, though they still looked upon him as something more than mortal. Whilst he was in the room the men were always sober, and no bad words were spoken. When the hour came to carry the keys to the Captain, two of them would always go together – no man would dare walk down that passage alone.

One night however, one foolish fellow had drunk more than was good for him. He began to brag and boast that he was not afraid of the dog. It was his turn to take the keys, but to show how brave he was, he said that he would go alone. He dared the dog to follow him.

"Let him come," he shouted, laughing; "I'll see whether he be dog or devil." His friends were terrified and tried to hold him back, but he snatched up the keys and went out into the passage. The black dog slowly got up from before the fire and followed him.

There was a deathly silence in the guard room; no sound was heard except the dashing of the waves on the steep rocks of the Castle Islet.

After a few minutes, there came from the dark passage the most unearthly screams and howls, but not a soldier dared to move to see what was happening. They looked at each other in horror.

Presently they heard steps and the rash fellow came back into the room. His face was ghastly pale and twisted with fear. He spoke not a word, then or later. In three days he was dead and nobody even knew what had happened to him on that fearful night. The black dog has never been seen again.

The Night of the Hurricane – October 16th 1987

By Cyril Cook

On Thursday October 16th 1987, my wife and I drove to Eastbourne from our home in Eltham, South London, to attend a conference of District 113 of Rotary International, which would end on Sunday 18th. The weather was horrendous, torrential rain and gusting winds making driving quite unpleasant. At Polegate, just north of Eastbourne, the road was flooded, but we managed, with great care, to drive through. We were the lucky ones, the police closed the road a short while after we had passed.

We spent the evening with old friends, and making new, then made for bed at a reasonable hour, knowing that if previous Rotary conferences were anything to go by, the next two nights would be early morning occasions!

At around two o'clock my wife awakened me, saying there was a terrible wind blowing and that she was afraid the window would be blown in, it was rattling so badly. I replied that the wind often reached gale force on the coast, and that there was nothing to worry about, turned over and promptly went back to sleep!

Our friends, Roy and Audrey Grant, being higher up in the Rotary scheme of things than we were, were staying with the nobs in The Clarendon, a posh hotel right on the front. They got very little sleep. Our Rotary padré occupied a room overlooking the sea. In the next room there was an elderly lady from the east end of London, and in the next room to her was her daughter, who had brought her to the seaside for a relaxing weekend.

The roar of the wind became more and more terrifying. The waves washed up tons of sand and gravel onto the gardens and road all along the front. This was no ordinary storm.

At around three o'clock our padre heard a tremendous crash from the adjacent elderly lady's room. He rushed into the corridor to be met by the daughter who had her mother's door key. The scene inside the room was apocalyptic. The curtains were blowing horizontally from their fixings, furniture had been blown over, and draped over the end of the bed was the window frame which had been previously some three or four paces away, and one would have thought been firmly fixed for all time. There was glass everywhere, and in the middle of it all, the elderly lady was sitting up in bed, quite unperturbed it would appear, as she announced, "Bugger this for a lark, I want a cup of tea." Well, she had, it transpired, been all through the Blitz in the East End, so this was really a bit of a sideshow.

At the height of the storm the National Grid gave up the ghost, blacking out London and most of Southern England. In some places it would be days before the supply was renewed, despite the heroic efforts of the public utility workers, private contractors, and the army who were called in to help clear the thousands of trees which had brought the power lines down.

Back to our friends Roy and Audrey. They live in an imposing property near the small town of Old Bexley. Adjoining their beautiful Georgian mansion they had built a granny flat to house Audrey's mother. At six o'clock in the morning, as the worst of the hurricane had passed Eastbourne, they received a telephone call to say a tree had been blown down across the front door of the granny flat, and that much other damage had been inflicted on the rest of the property. They decided to leave immediately. Their car was in the car park behind the hotel, which presented them with their first shock as they approached it to load their suitcases into the boot. Tiles and slates, blown off the roof of The Clarendon had targeted the nobs Jaguars, BMWs etc indiscriminately. Roy had a brand new, top of the range model which had received a slate through the rear window, shattering glass all over the place and not doing the interior upholstery any good to say the least. They had a 'tidy up' and started off to Bexley, but this was easier said than done. With trees down everywhere, often bringing roadside power cables and supporting posts with them, they suffered a nightmare of diversions, not made any easier by signposts having been bodily lifted out of the ground so that they found themselves frequently in the middle of nowhere.

This nightmare was nothing compared to what they found when they reached home. The River Cray runs through their property. On the far bank they had a thick belt of very tall trees, beyond which in the near distance was the town of Old Bexley, a view they had never experienced from their house before. Now some fifty odd trees, many of them eighty to one hundred feet high were either flattened or had assumed grotesque angles, and they saw Old Bexley clearly for the first time. It took years to clear and in many cases, replant, but I am pleased to tell you that nature has now recovered and that beautiful wood has grown back.

We returned to London on the Sunday, by which time the main road had been partially cleared, but many of our fellow Rotarians failed to make it, Sir Bernard Weatherill, Speaker of the House of Commons, who was to open the conference on the Saturday being in that number.

We shall not forget Eastbourne in a hurry!

This photograph of Seal Chart near Sevenoaks was taken some years ago. In the meantime the trees had grown over from each side of the road to provide a covered avenue.

This is how it looked after the hurricane once the debris had been cleared.

My sincere thanks to Bob Ogley, who published a magnificent book, "In the Wake of the Hurricane," from which these pictures were taken, for allowing me to reproduce them.

In days gone by when you turned off the A11 at Bromley Bow to join the inevitable queue to go south through the single Blackwall Tunnel, you were confronted by this sign.

I remember that I used to say, as a matter of routine, "And you!" I am convinced I was not the only one!

❖❖❖❖ ❖ ❖❖❖ ❖❖❖ ❖❖❖ ❖❖ ❖❖❖❖

What God Looks Like

An infant school teacher was walking around her class of children who were having a drawing lesson. Studying the various efforts she came to one little girl working very hard with evident concentration. She asked the little girl what she was drawing.

The little girl replied, "I'm drawing God."

The teacher thought for a moment or two and suggested, "But no-one knows what God looks like."

As quick as a flash the little girl countered, "Well, if you hang about for a few minutes you'll find out won't you?"

❖❖❖❖ ❖❖❖ ❖❖❖❖ ❖❖❖ ❖ ❖❖

Church Notice board

Come work for the Lord. The work is hard, the hours are long and the pay is low. But the retirement benefits are out of this world!

◈◈◈◈◈◈ ◈◈◈◈◈◈ ◈◈◈◈◈◈◈

First Fight

Three weeks after her wedding day, Barbara called her minister.

"Reverend," she wailed, "Nat and I have had a terrible fight."

"Calm down my child," said the minister, "it's not half as bad as you think. Every marriage has to have its first fight."

"I know, I know," Barbara replied, "but what am I going to do with the body?"

◈◈◈◈ ◈◈◈◈◈◈◈◈◈◈ ◈◈◈◈

Sailor clings to buoy for 17 hours. *Brighton Evening Argus.*

◈◈◈◈◈◈◈◈◈ ◈◈◈◈◈◈◈◈◈◈

Wisdom of Daniel Defoe (c1700)

The best of men cannot suspend their fate
The good die early, and the bad die late.

◈◈◈◈ ◈◈◈◈◈◈◈◈◈◈◈ ◈◈◈

From this amphibious ill-born mob began
That vain ill-natured thing, an Englishman.

◈◈◈◈ ◈◈◈◈◈◈◈◈◈◈ ◈◈◈

Necessity makes an honest man a knave.

◈◈◈◈◈◈◈◈ ◈◈◈◈◈◈◈◈◈◈

And of all plagues with which mankind are cursed
Ecclesiastic tyranny's the worst.

◈◈◈◈ ◈◈◈◈◈◈◈◈◈◈◈ ◈◈◈

In trouble to be troubled
Is to have your trouble doubled.

344

The Lazy Wife

A Manx Fairy Tale by Sophia Morrison

Well, there was a woman once, and she was scandalous lazy. She was that lazy she would do nothing but sit in the corner of the *choillagh* warming herself, or going on the houses for newses the day long. And one day her man gives her some wool, to spin for him; he was terrible badly off for clothes to wear, for she was letting them get all ragged on him. He had told her to mend them until he was tired, but all he could get out of her was, *"Traa dy liooar."* Time enough!

One day he comes to her and says,

"Thou liggey my hraa, here is some wool for thee to spin, and if it is not done a month from this day, I'll throw thee out on the side of the road. Thou and thy *Traa dy liooar* have left me nearly bare."

Well, she was too lazy to spin, but she would be pretending to be working hard when the husband was in the house. She used to put the wheel out on the floor every night before the husband came in from work, to let on to him that she had been spinning.

The husband was asking her was the thread getting near spun, for he said he was seeing the wheel so often on the floor that he wanted to know if she had enough to take to the weaver. When it came to the last week but one, she had only one ball spun, and that one was knotted and as coarse as gorse. When her husband says to her, "I'm seeing the wheel middling often on the floor when I come home at night; maybe there's enough thread spun at thee now for me to take to the weaver next week?"

"I don't know, at all" says the wife. "Maybe there is let us count the balls."

Then the play began! Up she went on the *lout*, and flung the ball through the hole, down to him. "Keep count thyself, and fling the balls back again to me," says she to the man. And as fast as he flung the ball up to her, so fast she flung it down to him again. When he had counted the ball, maybe, two score times, she says to him, "That's all that's in."

"Aw, 'deed, you've spun well, woman, for all," says he; "there's plenty done at thee for the weaver."

Aw, then she was in a great fix, and didn't know in her senses what to do to save herself. She knew she would sup sorrow if she was found out, but she could think of nothing.

At last she bethought herself of the giant that lived in a lonesome place up the mountain, for she had heard tell he was good to work, and the woman, she says to herself, "I've a mind to go my ways to him." She took the road early next morning, she and her rolls of wool, and she walked up hills, down gills, till at last she came to the giant's house.

"What are thou wanting here?" says the giant.

"I'm wanting thee to help me," says she; and she up and told him about the ball of thread and everything.

"I'll spin the wool for thee," says the giant, "if thou'll tell me my name when thou come for the balls a week from this day. Are thou satisfied?"

"Why shouldn't I be satisfied?" says the woman; for she thought to herself it would be a middling queer thing if she couldn't find out his name within a week. Well, the woman she tried every way to find out the giant's name, but, go where she might, no-one had ever heard tell of it. The time was getting over fast, and she was no nearer to the giant's name. At last it came to the last day but one.

Now as it happened, the husband was coming home from the mountain that day in the little evening, and as he neared the giant's house, he saw it all in a blaze of light, and there was a great whirling and whistling coming to his ears, and along with it came singing, and laughing and shouting. So he drew near the window, and then he sees the big giant inside sitting at a wheel, spinning like the wind, and his hands flying with the thread to and fro, to and fro, like the lightning, and he shouting to the whistling wheel, "Spin, wheel, spin faster; and sing, wheel, sing louder!"

And as he sings, as the wheel whirls faster and faster

"Snieu queeyl, snieu; 'rane, queeyl, 'rane;
Dy aooilley clea er y thie, snieu er my skyn.
Lheeish yn ollan, lhiams y snaie,
S'beg fys t'ec yn ven litcheragh
Dy re Mollyndroat my ennym!"

Spin, wheel, spin; sing, wheel sing;
Every beam on the house, spin overhead
Herself's is the wool, mine is the thread
How little she knows, the lazy wife,
That my name is Mollyndroat!

When the husband got home that evening he was late, and his wife said to him, "Where have you been so late? Did thou hear anything new?"

Then he said, "Thou are middling good to spin thyself, *ven thie;* but I'm thinking there's one in that's better than thee, for all. Never in all my born days did I see such spinning, a thread as fine as a cobweb, and hear such singing as there was going on in the giant's house tonight."

"What was he singing?" said the wife. And he sang the song to her,

"Snieu queeyl, snieu; 'rane, queeyl, 'rane;

Dy chooilley clea er y thie, snieu er my skyn.
Lheeish yn ollan, lhiams y snaie,
S'beg fys t'ec yn ven litcheragh
Dy re Mollyndroat my ennym!"

Well, well, the joy the woman took when she heard the song!

"Aw, what sweet music! Sing it again, my good man," says she.

And he sang it to her again, till she knew it by heart.

Early next morning she went as fast as her feet could carry her to the Giant's house. The road was long and a bit lonesome under the trees, and to keep up her heart she sang to herself,

"Snieu, queeyl, snieu; snien, queeyl, snieu
Dy chooilley vangan er y vffiey, snieu er my skyn.
S'lesh hene yn ofian, as lesh my hene y snaie,
Son shenn Mollyndroat cha vow eh dy braa."

Spin, wheel, spin; spin, wheel, spin;
Every branch on the tree, spin overhead.
The wool is Himself's, the thread is my own,
For old Mollyndroat will never get it.

When she got to the house, she found the door open before her, and in she went.

"I've come again for the thread," says she.

"Aisy, aisy, good woman," says the giant. "If thou don't tell me my name thou won't get the thread – that was the bargain." Andsayshe, "Now, what's my name?"

"Is it Mollyrea?" says she, to let on that she didn't know it.

"No, it is not," says he.

"Are you one of the Mollyruiy ones?" says she.

"I'm not one of that clan," says he.

"Are they calling you Mollyvridey?" says she.

"They are not," says he.

"I'll warrant your name is Mollychreest?" says she.

"You are wrong, though," says he.

"Are you going by the name of Mollyvoirrey?" says she.

"Deed I am not," says he.

"Maybe your name is Mollyvartin?" says she.

"And, maybe, it's not at all," says he.

"They're saying," says she, "that there was only seven families living on the islan' at one time, and their names all began with 'Molly'; and so," says she, "if you are not a Mollycharaine, you are none of the rael, oul' Manx ones at all."

347

"I am not a Mollycharaine," says he. "Now, be careful, woman; next guess is your last."

At that she pretended to be frightened, and says she, slowly, pointing her finger at him,

"s'lesh hene yn ollan, as lesh my hene y snaie,
Son shenn-Moll-YN-DROAT cha vow eh dy braa."

The wool is Himself's, and the thread is my own,
For old-Moll-YN-DROAT will never get it.

Well the giant he was done, and he was in a red rage, and he cries, "Bad luck to you. You never would have found out my name unless you're *mummig yn aishnee.*"

"Bad luck to yourself, my boy," say she, "for trying to steal a dacent woman' wool."

"Go to the devil, yourself and you fortune-telling," shouts he, jumping up and flinging the balls at her. And away home with her, and her balls of thread. And if she didn't spin her own wool for ever after, that's nothing to do with you and me.

Lingua Franca (Part Two)

From Cherry Cheshire

(Part One – Page 205)

ARST – Past tense of ask. "Jordan, I must've arst ya free fazzund times to clear up yer room."

DREKKUN – Do you consider? As in, "Which dog drekkun'll win the next race?"

EFTY – Considerable. "Ere, Trace, this credit card bill's a bit efty."

EYEBROW – Cultured, intellectual.

FATCHA – Margaret, British Prime Minister 1979 on.

GRAND – A football stadium. "It all wennoff atside the pub near the grand."

IPS – An unknown area of a woman's body to which chocolate travels. "That Mars Bar will go straight to me ips."

JA – Do you, did you. "Ja like me new airdo, Sharon."

JAFTA – Is it really necessary? "Oi mate, jafta keep doing that?"

NARRA – Lacking breadth, with little margin. "Mum wannid to come rand but changed er mind. That was a narra escape."

PACIFIC – Specific

REBAND – Period of recovery after rejection by a lover. "I couldn't 'elp it. I was on the reband from Craig."

ROOFLESS – Without compassion.

From AJ Duffy, Chester.

If ever you find yourself travelling through the city of Chester and in particular close to the area by the Magistrate's and County Courts you will undoubtedly travel around the busy Grosvenor Roundabout. This roundabout is unusual in that it is also the final resting place of among others, one Thomas Gould. His solitary tombstone can be clearly seen close the side exiting onto Nicholas Street.

Grosvenor Roundabout and Thomas Gould's tomb

When the roundabout was originally built it cut through the graveyard of the former St Bridget's Church. The remains of many of the graves were reinterred, but there are still some graves remaining on the traffic island – only one of which has a stone, that one belonging to Thomas Gould.

From the inscription on his tombstone we learn that Thomas Gould died on 1st November 1865 aged seventy two years. Forty six of those years had been spent in the service of his country. During this extraordinarily long service he was a soldier in the 52nd Regiment of the Foot Light Infantry and had fought in many campaigns including fighting under the Duke of Wellington against Napoleon and his armies at the Battle of Waterloo.

The 43rd and 52nd Light Infantry at the Battle of Busaco

The inscription records his presence in the following military engagements: Vimera, Coruna, Crossing the Goe near Almeida, Bsaco, Pumbal, Redinha, Condeixa, Foz D'Avoca, Sabugal, Fuentes Donole, storming of Cuidad Rodigo and Radasos Salmanca, San Munos (injured and taken prisoner), St Milan, Vittoria, Pyrenees, storming of the French establishment of Vera (where he was wounded), Nivelle, passage of the Neve Orthes, Tarbes, Toulouse and of course Waterloo.

In his long army career he received the Peninsular Medal with 13 clasp and also received the Waterloo Medal. We know too from the inscription that he spent time as a prisoner and was also seriously wounded during at least one campaign.

One can only begin to imagine the horrors he saw and personally endured during his forty six long years of service, fighting in what were undoubtedly, savage, hand to hand military combat campaigns. It seems the brave warrior has swapped a life spent amid the brutal battles, noise and chaos of a nineteenth century soldier's life for a resting place alongside the cars, buses, traffic and general hustle bustle of a busy city roundabout.

Let us hope he still manages to 'Rest in Peace'.

Thomas Gould's final resting place.

MOVING UP:

12 Para North West Germany 1945

Right to left: Sergeant Vaisey, Pte Williams, L/Cpl Reilly

By Roger Geeson

They do say that if you lift the engine room hatch on any merchant ship operating under virtually any national flag in the world and shout, "Jock!" then someone will come up. Well I believe that if you scratch the surface of practically any British male, who does still have red blood running in his veins, you will find a love of the sea and ships in almost all of them, in varying degrees.

This probably has a great deal to do with us Brits being an island nation, and the fact that countless generations, as far back as Neanderthal Man with his dug out canoe, have relied upon boats of some description in their everyday lives. As a result, something of the sea has become irrevocably lodged in the British psyche and traces of those ancient maritime skills have been embedded within the DNA of our genes.

As a young lad I was no different from that established pattern, and from a very early age I learned to swim, and developed an affinity with water in general and boats in particular. This love of things marine, maritime or aquatic was to stay with me for life, albeit as a love which for a number of reasons latterly remained unrequited. It should be said for the record, lest someone should think to correct it, that my affinity with water was of course confined to paddling or swimming in it, dabbling in it, mucking about in boats on it, (and frequently in it) fishing from it and using it for assistance with making mud pies and such other childish delights. The finer and more civilised uses for this universally available, globally prolific resource, such as washing, general personal ablutions and mixing in small measure with decent Scotch, were only visited upon me at a very much later stage of my development. It is, naturally, only the experiences of playing and exercising so many leisure hours in it, on it and with it, which I have any desire to share.

As a family of four on an extremely tight budget, annual holidays always presented a severe financial problem for my parents, as of course they did for most other families struggling to rebuild their lives in late forties post war Britain. In addition to monetary considerations we were restrained to a large extent by the parochialism and insularity of my dear father who, even had cash been unlimited, would have stuck pins in his eyes rather than have ventured abroad or taken the family to a hotel for a holiday. It simply wasn't for him and, much as my mother would have loved to have been pampered by a hotel break occasionally, she knew as we all did that Dad would have been thoroughly miserable for the entire holiday and would desperately have missed his home comforts and familiar surroundings.

So it was self-catering holidays for us and although not much of a break from normal routine for our poor mother it was a least a change of scene and it kept everyone happy.

I suppose it would have been around 1949, when I was eleven and my sister about four years old, that the family rented for a fortnight, a holiday chalet on an embryonic camp site at Swalecliffe, a small village midway between Whitstable and Herne Bay on the north Kent coast. The site at that time formed part of Kite Farm, comprising sheep grazing and arable farm land about eight to ten feet above sea level. It was bounded on the seaward side by low friable clay marl cliffs dropping to a steeply shelving shingle beach and leading onto hundreds of yards of estuarial sandy mud flats and cockle beds when the tide receded. For children, it was heaven on earth and, all things considered, for caring parents it was a relatively safe haven in which to allow their precious offspring to play, explore, and investigate the delights of nature, with reasonable peace of mind.

Many, many happy hours were spent trawling up and down the shallows with a home-made shrimping net, digging in the mud for cockles which were so numerous they practically jumped into one's bucket by themselves, and collecting shells and seaweed. The shrimps were delicious although a little on the small side and possibly required the expenditure of almost as much calorific energy from shelling them as was subsequently derived from their eventual consumption. The cockles had a good flavour but, regardless of one's diligence in soaking them and changing the water several times, they always contrived to retain just a few grains of sand making for a crunchiness in the mouth which decently prepared cockles simply should not have. Nevertheless, during the course of our many years of weekend and annual holidays as a family at Swalecliffe, we must have consumed countless gallons of the unfortunate crustaceans along, I dare say, with several pounds of salty estuary grit!

The site was divided between static chalets on one field and caravans, mainly static but with some visiting tourers, on another field. The site was backed up by fields of yellow corn in summer and with views across the open estuary towards Clacton and Brightlingsea. It was not only idyllic but fairly easily accessible and within the price range of my parents. Added interest was provided by the view, on a clear day, of the wartime gunnery forts on Shivering Sands, which stood as silent sentinels and reminders of recent hostilities. In fact they always brought to my mind the impression of Wellsian Martian war machines on stilt like legs, advancing over the horizon against a sleeping London innocently unaware of its impending doom, but then I did always have quite a vivid imagination! These same forts were years later to achieve a totally different notoriety when some of them became the temporary home of pirate radio stations, in company with the roguish, swashbuckling and much loved Radio Caroline ship which moored in the estuary and more or less took over from where the original Radio Luxembourg station left off when I was a youth.

Indeed, so idyllic and secure was this spot on the Kentish coast that, after only one holiday there in a rented chalet, my parents were determined that we should have our own holiday 'villa' on the site. I believe the arrangement was that a nominal sum was paid for a site and the lessee then erected their own chalet, to a pre-determined maximum size and style, paying annual ground rent to the site owners. Alternatively, one could purchase an existing chalet from its owner for an agreed sum. However, my parents had particular ideas about what they wanted and decided to wait for a site to become available upon which they could erect their own chalet, having carefully saved up what would for them have been a great deal of money.

After a pleasantly short period of anxious waiting, a site from which an existing chalet had been removed became available and my father set to work. Utilising his prodigious skills as both a designer and a woodworker, Father first drew up plans for a timber framed sectional building of some sixteen feet long by ten wide and with a pitched roof of about twelve feet high to the ridge. The front ten feet or so by the full width constituted the living/dining area with a small kitchen to the right rear and a double bedroom to the left. The really clever part of Dad's design was a centrally located narrow companion way – OK, steep stairs to you landlubbers – at the side of the kitchen partition which lead up to two bunks for my sister and I, one over the kitchen and one over the double bedroom area. Alright, granted they weren't full size bunks and the headroom was a wee bit restricted, but they were absolutely perfect for two young children and what could be better than being by the seaside and sleeping in bunks, akin to a real ship?

The landing was provided with a small fanlight window in the rear gable which enabled me, because between my sister and me, I was definitely the senior officer, to lie in bed and look out over the estuary, thus keeping an imperious eye on any marine activity. I fear that I suffered with delusions of grandeur even then! The arrangement had the added advantage that, once we had been 'put down' for the night, a heavy curtain closed off the stairs leaving the living area free for our parents to read, play cards or otherwise entertain friends for the rest of the evening without disturbing, or being disturbed by two inquisitive children. The truth was that after a day at, on, by or generally in, the sea, during which we expended enough energy to power a small town for a week, we were ready for bed and usually went out like lights after a few moments of mischief and the usual childish banter.

To construct our new chalet, Father set up a level timber platform on our back lawn at home and pre-fabricated the entire frame, complete with windows, double entrance doors, floor, wall and roof sections, stairs, partitions and the internal structure. The whole thing was sectional and designed to be bolted together on site. Came the great day, Dad hired a lorry and with the help of a few friends the skeleton sections were laboriously manhandled through our garden and onto the flatbed. Securely stabilised and roped down and with all the secondary joinery, insulation and cladding materials loaded on as well, we all set off in various cars and proceeded to follow the truck to Swalecliffe at what was probably a fairly slow, very careful and, for my father, possibly a worrying pace. Happily, nothing fell off or was damaged during the journey and we all arrived safely and in anticipation of a very hard days work ahead.

The base foundation blocks had been levelled in and secured on a previous visit and it seemed like no time at all before the floor and wall frames were erected, plumbed up and bolted together and the roof rafters cut and fitted. Once the framework was in position and secured and deemed to be to Father's complete satisfaction, the whole of the structure was cocooned in 'sisalkraft' bituminised building paper as an initial protection against the elements until the external cladding could be fitted on a subsequent weekend. Such clever innovations as 'tanalised' or similarly pressure impregnated preserved timber was not available in those days and great care had to be taken to ensure that the frame was perfectly dry before being finally enclosed for fear that the dreaded 'dry rot' might set in, with calamitous results for the future.

The exterior cladding, I am now somewhat loath to admit, was ¼ inch thick flat asbestos cement sheets, each of which were carefully drilled and countersunk at about 16 inch centres around the edges and at points coinciding with the wall frame studding for screwing to timber. Of course neither my father, or indeed anybody else then, had absolutely any idea of the incredible dangers to health posed by all asbestos products when they were drilled or sawn, releasing the minute fibres into the atmosphere. The construction and other diverse industries, knowingly or unknowingly, continued to use asbestos in its myriad forms quite happily until the risks became known and finally began to be publicised, when it was eventually phased out in the 70s or thereabouts.

Of course by then the damage had been done and, in a whole raft of industrial processes which utilised asbestos, many thousands of workers who had been innocently exposed to the effects of its deadly airborne fibres suffered irreparable lung damage and died prematurely. The withdrawal of this material from use gave designers considerable scope for finding suitable alternative materials and of course its demise was also an opportunity to develop the extremely lucrative industry of asbestos removal which continues to flourish and expand to this day, such was the enormously widespread use of the stuff!

However, for the long term protection of a timber structure set not more than fifty yards from the beach, asbestos cement sheet was probably the best thing which could have been used. Although painted for decorative effect, it would easily have withstood the onslaught of salt laden winds in its raw state for many years.

The exterior having been fully clad and the joints mastic sealed and masked with timber cover fillets, it was now possible to insulate the voids between the timbers with glass fibre quilt and to cover the inside walls with plasterboard sheets nailed on.

With the nail heads and board joints filled and taped ready for painting, it made for a quick economic and dry internal finish. Once the doors and windows were fitted, the kitchen units installed, bed bases fixed and sundry joinery all completed, it only remained for Dad to run the Calor gas supply to the cooker and light fittings from the bottle store outside and our 'country house' was almost complete. At this stage it was my mother's happy task to make and fit curtains, valances and to generally equip the place with the household paraphernalia and ornaments etc, to turn it from a glorified, if very large garden shed, into a very comfortable 'home from home'. Emergency lighting was provided by paraffin 'Alladin' lamps which had silk mantles and tall glass chimneys atop chromed ornate base tanks. These were very reliable and, if properly trimmed and adjusted, gave an excellent level of light, although care had to be exercised when moving them due to the extreme fragility of the mantles once they were initially burnt in.

I have not mentioned sanitation since the chalets were not connected to either mains water or drainage. Fresh water was collected in a large enamel jug from communal taps dotted around the site and one's ablutions were carried out in one of several large communal toilet blocks with waste water from washing up etc being carried to the disposal point in buckets.

Collection and disposal of water was of course designated as my job and a 'pocket money earner', just as shoe cleaning, occasional washing up and car cleaning were too. These sanitation arrangements gave rise to some fairly horrendous sights of a morning as some ladies threw caution and decorum to the wind and wandered off to the toilet blocks clad in carpet slippers and some pretty terrifying dressing gowns. With their hair screwed into tight rollers and wrapped in scarves, many of them would certainly have frightened the horses had there been any in the vicinity!

To complete the picture of rustic and bucolic under-development and reminiscent of a pre-war simplicity of life, when we first arrived on site, fresh milk would be delivered daily. No surprise there one might think except that the milk was conveyed in a couple of shiny steel churns secured on the back of a small pony and trap. In retrospect, perhaps the pony may have been frightened by the 'dressing gowns and curlers brigade' in the mornings, but he was a docile 'Thelwellian' little chap who had no doubt seen it all before and took it all in his diminutive stride. The milkman, who I assume to have been a local farmer or one of his hands and who had also no doubt seen it all before, would proceed up each line of chalets and caravans ringing a hand bell. Stopping every so often, he would wait while folk wanting milk gathered round with their jugs or containers and would then dispense their requirements with one of two calibrated measures, either pint or half pint. These were narrow steel tubes with long hooked handles and when brim full they each held a precise measure, periodically checked by Weights and Measures and with official verification stamped on their brass rims. When sales to a particular section were complete, he would slap the churn lid back on and go on his way, cheerfully ringing his bell. What fun today's clip board toting Health and Safety 'Obergruppenfuehrers' would have had with that little scenario can only be guessed at! It would surely have necessitated the poor little pony defecating only once, within six feel of the open milk churns to have had the milkman incarcerated in Canterbury jail and the whole site fumigated and declared out of bounds for a fortnight!

As no-one had electricity and therefore had no refrigerators – what am I saying, we didn't even have a 'frig at home - the milkman called each day and so one only bought enough to last for 24 hours. It was so fresh however that even in really hot weather it very rarely went sour. Now we buy our milk from supermarkets at possibly less per litre than we paid ten years ago, and almost certainly only a copper or two more than it costs farmers to produce, and the doorstep deliveries are fast vanishing from our streets. The product comes in plastic flasks, had been treated in some way to make it last for days and when its time clock mysteriously expires it suddenly turn to sour yoghurt without warning. Progress?

Eventually, once the building works were complete and the paint dry, we spent most summer weekends and all of our holidays at the chalet. Poor Dad had to learn to look after himself at home during the week and commuted to the chalet at weekends when we were there during the long school holidays with Mother.

The foregoing is of course only relevant to describing how I came to be fortunate enough as a youngster to spend sufficient time by the sea to acquire more than a passing interest in boats.

As a family we soon made friends with the Daws who had a chalet a little further up Row K from our No 5. Their son, another Roger rather confusingly, was a year or two older than I but we hit it off very well, especially when our mutual interest in boats became apparent. Shortly after we met, Roger acquired his own boat, a sturdy clinker built rowing dinghy of some ten feet in length. She had evidently been laid up for some considerable period before Roger took ownership and as a result her planking had shrunk a wee bit, and so she took a little water when she was re-launched. Undeterred, we acquired a small saucepan which served as an excellent bailer and thereafter, took turns in vigorously despatching the sea water in the bilges from whence it came, until such time as the planking swelled and she was again 'tight'. She was of course a simple rowing skiff and we expended vast quantities of energy ploughing up and down the coastline, about fifty yards from the shore, perfecting our rowing skills in all weathers.

It was a useful coalition really, because the boat, being stoutly constructed from solid timber, was quite weighty and altogether too heavy for either one of us to manhandle up and down the beach alone. Together however, we were a great team, or crew as we preferred to be called, and spent many happy hours recreating, in our own minds, the adventures of Arthur Ransome's Swallows and Amazons, all of whom were our heroes. There was of course a significant snag, given our respective names, in that when she eventually became a 'sailing dinghy', it did occasionally become rather confusing when passing orders from the bridge, as the stern steering thwart was referred to. "OK, ready about-'lee hoh' Roger!" would be the command, and, "Roger, Roger!" the inevitable response!

As I have indicated, confining our nautical prowess to rowing Roger's small dinghy up and down a relatively restricted expanse of sea shore soon became rather passé. Given that we were only about twelve or fourteen years old, we were hardly robust enough to row enormous distances, and soon the talk between the pair of us turned to the possibility of converting this trusty little craft into a fully fledged sailing dinghy, so that we could embark upon proper 'voyages'!

Allowing for the naturally straitened financial circumstances of two small boys, all of the equipment necessary for this marine conversion had either to be scrounged, borrowed on a more or less permanent basis, or, as an absolute last resort, purchased.

With the paucity of marine construction skills between us, the conversion to sail power had to be not only cheap but relatively simple as well, whilst at the same time leaving the craft safe and seaworthy.

The pros of the boat's mooted conversion were argued with great skill and tenacity considering our tender years, whereas the cons were dismissed as mere incidentals. The cons of the debate were, needless to say, exclusively raised by anxious and doubting parents who, whilst obviously were very concerned for our wellbeing and safety, could undoubtedly foresee the venture as inevitably impinging upon their pockets at some stage of the proceedings. We were going to create this beautiful sailing 'swan' from the bare bones of the 'ugly duckling' that we already had, and that was it and all about it! With the degree of enthusiasm we had between us we were unstoppable, and in the end both sets of parents, putting their concerns and prejudices on one side, gave us their tacit although not at that stage, their financial support.

Having apparently won the moral argument, and fired with renewed enthusiasm for the now practical rather than theoretical venture we were embarking upon, it was time to prove ourselves and buckle down to the task of becoming proper dinghy sailors.

We both studied books on sailing, re-read Swallows and Amazons for the rekindling of amateur ideas and hand to mouth solutions and, after due deliberation, agreed jointly that a conversion to a gaff rigged skiff should be within both our financial and craft skill parameters.

Visits to acquaintances with boats, boatyards at Seasalter and Whitstable harbour and general scrounging around, yielded the three lengths of round spruce that were more or less essential for a the mast, gaff and boom. The mast, which was stepped in existing holes in the forward thwart and keel board, indicating that she had perhaps once been a sailing dinghy, was properly stayed with galvanised wire shrouds secured with shackles to screw eyes in the mast head and with straining links to eyebolts in the port and starboard gunwhales and the stem. Whilst I had learned to back-splice and eye-splice hemp and manilla ropes in the Boy Scouts, these skills had never extended to splicing wire shrouds which were totally beyond me. In consequence, the shrouds were returned around the eyes and secured with waxed twine whippings of at least three inches in length on both ends. Needless to say, whilst this method of securing the shroud tails was acceptable for anything up to a light breeze on the Beaufort scale, it singularly failed to cope with our first encounter with something approaching 'moderate to fresh'! There we were, creaming along with a bow wave like a destroyer, and with both of us sitting on the weather gunwhale in order to balance the heel of the boat, when … 'twang' went the weather shroud and over the side went the whole kit and caboodle of mast, gaff, boom and sail on the lee side whilst Roger and Roger were dumped unceremoniously, and backsides first into the sea on the weather side!

Nowadays of course, it is totally unnecessary to bother learning the ancient art of wire splicing, with its attendant loss of blood and fingernails, as one simply trots along to one's friendly yacht chandler requesting stainless steel shroud wires of a precise length. He of course cannot wire splice any more than you can but he has the advantage of a small hydraulic press which can squeeze an alloy ferrule onto the wires under untold pressure. For a consideration of several pounds sterling, he can guarantee you a pull out strain of sufficient tonnes to ensure that your rigging does not go overboard because of shroud failure, even in a force nine! Talurit splices they used to be called but I've no doubt there are now many variations on the original theme.

Returning to the boat conversion, we now had a mast, stayed by the appropriate rigging, and a boom, which was secured to the mast with a simple arrangement of three screw eyes – one on the boom end and two close together on the mast – with a galvanised drop bolt which passed through all three. Crude but very effective and we never had to modify or strengthen this rudimentary arrangement. The gaff was loose footed, as we hadn't the 'nouse' to dream up a method of loosely attaching the foot so that it slid up the mast. It was therefore attached to the head of the sail and was hauled up the mast by a halyard, attached to the gaff at about two thirds distance from the peak of the sail, run through a sheave at the masthead and secured to a cleat at the bottom.

At this juncture we had a stroke of luck which was desperately needed as we had reached the crisis point of needing a sail! Now you can scarcely beg, borrow or steal a sail, especially one that has to be a particular shape and size and we had collectively been much engaged by the problem of how this crucially important component was to be obtained.

Roger's parents, having seen that we were really keen to effect the conversion and had made a fair job of the work up to that point, undertook to get us a sail for the boat. Mast and spars were laid out on the grass and accurate measurements taken and relayed to Daws senior. In due course a large off-white sheet was presented to us, precisely cut and double hem stitched to the dimensions we had provided. One or two faintly coloured marks and smudges on the 'sail' gave a possible hint to its antecedents and we strongly suspected that it had begun life as a decorator's unbleached rough linen dust sheet! Nevertheless, it was perfect so far as we were concerned and whilst obviously not sailcloth, we felt that with care it would put up with anything we were likely to ask of it. After all, Nancy Blackett and her Amazon pirates had confined their adventures to a Cumbrian lake and had not felt compelled to round the Horn or tackle the North West Passage and we felt similarly restrained in our own ambitions.

We set about punching brass eyelets (which disastrously we had actually had to purchase since by no means devious or otherwise had we been able to scrounge them), into the head and foot of the sail and to making up short rope strops with which to attach it to the gaff and boom. We were forced to resort to these fairly crude methods of attachment since we could not afford the proper tracks and it would not have been possible to sew the necessary bolt ropes to the sail edges. In any event, once attached, the sail remained firmly fixed to the spars and so the relatively inconvenient fastenings were not a problem.

The flailing boom end was controlled with a main sheet (rope) shackled to an eye on one side of the transom, run through a block on the boom end and back through another block on the other side of the transom. Whilst not an ideal arrangement, it coped adequately and never came near to decapitating either of us in a gybe.

We were almost ready to sail but we still lacked two essentials. The first was a means of steering the beast and the second, a method of preventing our shallow draught vessel from skidding sideways across the water when working under anything other than a stern wind, in other words, carrying leeway. We found that our collective, rudimentary carpentry skills, with just a little kindly supervisory encouragement from my father, were sufficient to fashion a workable plywood rudder attached to a mahogany rudder post. This in turn was fixed to the transome board with another cheap but very effective 'pintle and gudgeon' arrangement, consisting of screw eyes and drop bolts. This type of fixing was necessary because when beaching the boat, the rudder, which hung deeper than the boat's skeg, had to be smartly lifted off as it touched bottom. The fixings could not therefore be permanent and had to allow for rapid detachment. A broom handle tiller was fixed to the top of the rudder post and we had steering! We later got really clever and devised a hinged tiller extension so that we could both sit forr'ard to better balance the boat.

Leeway, being that sideways movement of the boat across the water now remained the only, but perhaps the most difficult problem which we needed to resolve. A centreboard was the ideal solution but that was out of the question, not only because we lacked the skills to fabricate such a modification, but because it is doubtful that the boat's construction and condition would have tolerated such a radical intrusion.

Now it happens that in those far off, wonderful days, Thames barges regularly and sometimes on rare occasions even the odd Norfolk wherry, used to ply the river estuary and beyond to Brightlingsea, Colchester and various ports of East Anglia. They ran into Whitstable harbour to discharge sand and ballast, grain, malt and other bulk cargoes. I have even seen a barge unloading sheaves of Norfolk reed, which I assume to have been bound for some exotic property in the Weald of Kent or elsewhere which required its roof to be re-thatched. Since Roger and I spent many hours wandering around the harbour foraging for useful bits of timber, lengths of discarded rope and suchlike, it wasn't too long before we spotted the answer to our leeway problem. The barges too were fairly shallow draught, as they needed to be in order to navigate the shallow estuaries and clear the bars and sandbanks that bedevil that area, and of course a drop centreboard with its large casing above the keelson would have seriously impeded their cargo hold space.

The centuries old solution to the problem of leeway designed by the shipwrights of so long ago was 'leeboards'.

In the case of the Thames barges, these were enormous boards, constructed of several planks, strapped together with barnacle encrusted wrought iron banding and fixed to both port and starboard sides of the boats at roughly the point of broadest beam. The boards were of sufficient length to project below the keel depth when lowered vertically and were pivoted on huge iron pins through the topsides. They would have been extremely heavy and were raised and lowered by hoist ropes directed through pulley blocks on small gaff spars down to steam or hand operated capstan winches. The board would be lowered on the lee side, hence the name, depending upon which tack the barge was sailing on. Should you be sailing with the wind blowing onto the left, or port side of the boat, you would be on the port tack and the starboard side leeboard would be lowered to present a large resistance area to the sideways drift of the boat and vice versa.

In our case we did not need two boards as it would be possible to swing a single board from one side to the other as the boat went about onto the opposite tack. We duly fashioned a stout plywood board which was simply attached to the boat my means of a single length of rope knotted through a hole at the top of the board and run to the centre point on the 'midships thwart. The length of rope was such that it was taut when the board hung down vertically in the water on either side of the boat and, once positioned by the crew man, the water pressure tended to maintain the board in position. As with either centreboards or leeboards, they only minimise rather than eliminate leeway drift, but our contraption worked creditably well considering the minimal financial outlay. Since the boat was not initially fitted with a jib sail, the crew man had nothing to do when going about or gybing, other than to smartly change sides and duck low when the sail and boom swung over and to remember to swap the leeboard to the opposite beam!

The good old leeboard has another useful function, which one always hoped not to have to call upon but frequently had to, and that is to act as a lever when endeavouring to right a capsized dinghy. It is of course no match for the help afforded by the true centreboard upon which one can clamber when the boat lies on her beam ends and the centreboard extends horizontally just below the surface. One endeavours to stand on, or at least kneel upon the board, dependant upon conditions and, grasping the gunwhale and leaning right back, it is usually possible to return the craft to the vertical plane. Not so easy with a loose and floppy leeboard but it does provide some leverage and is certainly better than nothing.

Indeed for the first few days when we were actually learning to sail the hard way, namely by trial and error whilst metaphorically clutching a soggy copy of the sailing manual, we actually seemed to spend more time with the mast horizontal than in the near vertical plane. However, no real harm, apart from bruised egos and baskets full of soaking wet clothing, was occasioned by these embryonic sailing lessons and the way we did it at least guaranteed that one learned fast.

The leeboard certainly earned its corn during those early days and we would surely have been lost without it. We weren't of course always able to right the boat ourselves and, even when we could, it was still not always possible to bail the boat out and restore positive buoyancy. When fully flooded, and without the benefit at that stage of designed buoyancy tanks or bags, a dinghy sits very low in the water and certain short choppy seas would persistently refill the hull faster than even an energetic and, dare one say, desperate crew could bail out. In those cases we had two options. One was to drop the little kedge anchor that we always carried, swim ashore and go and collect the boat when the tide went out, or alternatively, wave and holler until some kind soul ashore spotted our plight and got one or other of the pleasure boatmen to come out and tow us in. This was always the better option as one could never fully guarantee that the kedge anchor would hold, with the risk that the boat might drift either beyond low tide range or just too far away to permit easy recovery later. She was very precious to us and we would not willingly have abandoned her. A little later, now aware of some of the more basic problems and rapidly ascending the learning curve, we incorporated a measure of positive buoyancy which at least guaranteed that we should be able to bail out the vessel in anything less than very choppy sea. Once again, ingenuity and a shortage of both cash and expertise brought out the inventive streak in us and the positive buoyancy was achieved with the use of large plastic drums firmly secured under the bow, 'midships and stern thwarts. These drums restricted stowage space a little but ensured that in the event of a 'knock down' by a squall, we could right her and get her home.

Thus it was in those halcyon days of the very early fifties that we wiled away our summer weekends and school holidays, sometimes helping with the grain harvesting on the farm, perhaps assisting the man with the tractor and trailer who delivered replacement gas cylinders throughout the site and even giving a hand with litter picking to keep the camp spick and span. Nevertheless, the love of our young lives remained the sea and the best times were those happy hours spend messing about in the boat.

Even when the weather was bad there was still pleasure to be gained. When the winds howled across the North Sea and funnelled into the estuary, driving white horses and spray before it, we could be found on the cliff tops in our weatherproofs watching in awe as huge waves broke on the pebble beach, roaring as they drove up the slope doing battle with the battered and weather beaten timber groynes and then hissing and sighing as the water receded, dragging the smaller stones and fine shingle with it. Afterwards, when the winds abated or the tide ebbed, we would walk the high tide line searching for interesting flotsam or attractive driftwood. Occasionally, when conditions were particularly stormy, we would walk along the cliff top or beach towards Hampton, where the land rose and the cliffs were sixty or seventy feet high, when it was sometimes possible to watch enormous chunks of the muddy clay cliffs falling onto the beach. The cliff top road at this point was closed and huge tracts of road slab had already succumbed to the ravages of coastal erosion. Only later did we discover that, long before we acquired our chalet, there had been bungalows on the seaward side of the road which was now slowly falling onto the beach and that those bungalows had long since disappeared into the sea.

This of course accounted for the number of rounded and worn red orange pebbles which littered the beach along the whole sea front as these were remnants of brick and roofing tiles, broken up and weathered by constant pounding in the breakers.

These first hand experiences of the power of the sea and of nature's constant reminders of her supremacy over man's feeble attempts to manage her, would be brought very firmly home to roost in the great East Coast flood of 1953.

On the night of 31st January 1953, a north easterly gale in conjunction with low pressure and an abnormally high tide, drove a tidal surge down the North Sea coast which impacted upon the pitiful sea defences of East Anglia, Essex and north Kent. Canvey Island being virtually at or even below sea level was especially hard hit and was extensively flooded, with many people unfortunately losing their lives.

On the opposite side of the estuary, the low lying areas of north Kent from Herne Bay up to the Isle of Sheppey, fell victim to the surge tides which inundated thousands of acres of the natural flood plain. Seasalter, Swalecliffe and Kite Farm camp were no exception, and with no sea defences whatsoever, were totally at the mercy of the tidal onslaught. My parents obviously heard about the crisis on the radio news reports and enquiries of the campsite management confirmed their worse fears in that damage was widespread.

At the first opportunity we went down to the coast to see the problem for ourselves and so that my father could assess the damage and plan future action. When we arrived, we could scarcely believe the sight which confronted us. Approach to the camp was via a lane alongside the principal caravan field and the carnage was widespread. Caravans had been tossed around like corks and had caused most damage by crashing into their neighbouring vans. When we got to our part of the site, it had been almost swept clear. The incoming tidal surge had simply lifted the timber chalets clear of their foundation blocks and swept them inland for hundreds of feet until they piled up against one another at the rear of the field as the wave ran out of steam and allowed them to settle back on the ground.

Unfortunately, some chalets which were either old and decrepit, or just poorly constructed, had been unable to stand the strain of such violent upheaval and had more or less collapsed or were so badly damaged as to make repair unviable. Our own chalet, which you will recall was no more than fifty yards from the beach, fetched up well over one hundred yards inland. As the onshore rush of water had been so sudden and of such volume, the chalets had floated off their foundation blocks and been blown inland by the gale force winds before natural leakage through door and floor panels etc permitted them to ground. Unfortunately, when our chalet was finally deposited by the receding waters, it landed awkwardly on the large foundation blocks of another, forcibly vacated chalet site, severely damaging the floor joists and boards. However, the whole unit had been so well and soundly constructed by my father that, apart from the floor and the filthy tide mark several feet up the walls, it was virtually unscathed. Naturally, rugs and some furniture were affected by the flood waters, but all in all we had been incredibly lucky and it could have been so much worse. We thanked God for our good fortune and spared many a thought for the thousands of poor souls whose principal dwellings had been badly damaged or even destroyed.

In the case of our holiday home, the primary problem was of course, just how to get the beast back on its foundation blocks after the general site clean up had been completed. Apart from ensuring that the foundation was accurately replaced, I do not believe that we were involved in reinstating the chalet which was carried out with an enormous crane and probably organised by the insurers in conjunction with the site management team. Although it was the closed season, we were allowed to come down at weekends to dry out the property and to sort out the damage, and surprisingly, all was ready for the holiday season when the camp opened again in April. Not unnaturally, the site bore the scars of Mother Nature's tantrum for a considerable time, but quite soon the grass grew through the layer of silt, roads and paths were restored and everything quite rapidly returned to normal.

Possibly as a result of the flood damage, I'm not sure, but shortly afterwards the Daws gave up their chalet and, of course, with their departure went my opportunities for boating. I was devastated and desperately missed both Roger and the good times we had enjoyed on the water. When Ratty of Wind in the Willows fame opined to Mole that, "There's nothing – absolutely nothing – half so much worth doing as simply messing about in boats," he certainly wasn't wrong and I confess that I pined for it very badly. My father, seeing exactly how much of a loss I was at without a boat to mess about in, talked vaguely of buying one, but with everything else that the family needed at that time, the cost of a boat of almost any description would have been both extravagant and of very low priority. This I perfectly well understood and accepted without question.

If I had dismissed the immediate prospect of a boat then my dad certainly hadn't. This was to say the least surprising, since he had never taken any real interest in Roger's dinghy other than to row her about occasionally. This he enjoyed, more as a form of exercise than anything more specific, although he had rowed in a coxed eight as a teenager.

One day to my total surprise and quite out of the blue, he said, "Why don't I help you to build a boat?" I was nonplussed but he explained that he had been admiring a plywood sailing dinghy somewhere or other and the owner had said that he'd built it from a kit of parts. From his description I deduced that it had probably been an Enterprise or GP14 dinghy, one of a fairly new breed of dinghy which were being designed specifically to reduce the enormous cost of boat building in the traditional style. For example, the type of boats sailed by the majority of serious dinghy racers from the Whitstable Yacht Club were the Firefly, which had a hot moulded laminated wooden hull; the Merlin Rocket which was a beautiful, traditionally clinker built mahogany boat and the fabulous Flying Dutchman, which was an out and out racing machine and one of the classes then competed for in the Olympics. All fantastic boats in their different styles but all coming in at an enormous cost. The new breed of cheaper to build, plywood single or double chined hulled boats included the 13' 0 " Enterprise, the 14' 0" GP 14, and the around 11' 0" Heron and Mirror class dinghies.

We looked around, toured the harbours and the yacht clubs, talked to anyone with a boat who was prepared to listen and we of course went to The Boat Show. There, on the Jack Holt stand we, or rather I, fell in love with the Heron dinghy. This was a gaff rigged sloop, cleverly designed so that all the spars fitted inside the hull for easy trailing and storage and was specifically designed to be home built from either a kit of parts or from scratch from a set of plans. Naturally, with Dad's trade connections, his undoubted skills and a garden workshop crammed with timber off-cuts, we bought the plans.

When Dad had suggested that he could help me build a boat, what he of course really meant was 'would I like to help *him* build one', since it was quite beyond my skills at that stage. I could do it myself now, but only because in my many long years since then I have not only picked up so many tips and hints from my talented father but I have since inherited his magnificent kit of joinery tools.

So it was that I helped him build the boat and what a beauty she turned out to be. It was constructed on a set of frames, each a different size and angle to give the hull its sweep and graceful shape. Having made the individual frames, they were erected upside down on extended side legs and were then fitted with the keelson and skeg, the chines and the gunwhales. These formed the skeleton upon which the 6mm marine plywood hull planking was screwed.

Of course my father being Father and never known to build anything to last less than a millennium, went over the top on the specification. For the frames, the plans suggested mahogany which we used; whilst for the chines and gunwhales the suggested material was either spruce or oak. With possible future racing in mind, I was all for using the lighter spruce. Father however, on the pretext that spruce was difficult to obtain, went for the oak which, whilst perhaps making for a stronger frame, added several pounds to the overall weight. I was carrying a handicap already and we hadn't even put to sea!

The work progressed well and I lost count of the hundreds of ¾" No.6 countersunk brass screws that I carefully drilled for, countersunk and screwed home when laying the deck and planking. The screws to the hull planking were more deeply recessed for filling as this area was to be gloss painted whilst those to the foredeck and side coamings were kept perfectly flush for a varnished finish.

Eventually we sent off to Jack Holt for the suit of sails and registration and in due course they arrived, all pristine white and emblazoned on both sides of the mainsail with the Heron profile and the number – 996!

The Heron dinghy was officially designated as the 'Heron car top dinghy', having been specifically designed for transportation, upside down, on a car roof rack. However, I do not believe that this was ever really a practical proposition for anybody other than perhaps twin weightlifters, without serious risk of damage to either the boat, the car or the crew – or even all three! So we opted for a boat trailer which again was largely home built and saved us a lot of money. I particularly remember carefully cutting a blue plastic washing up bowl in half to make a pair of mudguards for the trailer wheels. The bowl even matched the sky blue of the hull – how's that for design co-ordination?

With the boat safely transported to Swalecliffe, we carefully carried her down the beach to avoid scratching her spotless paint finish on the pebbles, a procedure which failed to last for long as the first flush of pride wore off, and officially launched her with a bottle of beer poured over the prow as we couldn't risk broken glass on the beach.

With the launching, we named her 'Finisterre' which was proudly displayed on her transome in gold letters.

The weather was fine, if a little too blustery for my liking on the maiden launching but as there was no reason, other than my nerves, to delay the inevitable I pushed off from the shore and nimbly leapt over the side decking and into the boat, hoping against hope that I could remember everything I had learned in the little single-sailed gaffer which was the only other boat I had ever sailed. This time I was not only sailing solo but I had a jib sail to worry about as well and that was something I wasn't used to. Too late to worry now – we were off!

The wind caught the main sail and I hauled in the sheet, causing the boat to heel over as it pointed up into the wind and headed rapidly out to sea. I was vaguely aware of a nervous squeal from my mother and a shouted enquiry from Dad as to whether I was sure of what I was doing, but their words were flung away in the wind and in any case I was far too busy and adrenalin charged to attend to anything other than staying upright and steering a reasonable course.

I became aware that the jib was flapping and realised that this useful addition would not look after itself and needed trimming occasionally as the wind fluked and eddied around its leading edge. So many things to do at the same time – balance the boat, steer a course, check the burgee for wind direction, trim the main, trim the jib, remember to drop the centreboard (so that's why we were sliding inexorably sideways in relation to a moored boat ahead!), remember to pull down the lifting blade of the rudder to gain full effect and, finally, remember to breathe! I realised that I had been holding my breath since leaving the beach, but with so much multi-tasking I suppose something had to go. After a few moments of excited action, and, if I'm honest, not a little trepidation, things settled down and I began to enjoy myself. I looked back towards the shore which did seem to be an awfully long way away and immediately had visions of my distraught mother calling out the Coastguard and rescue services. I was really enjoying this and idly began planning voyages and expeditions to all points of the compass – well perhaps the Isle of Sheppey, Harty Ferry or Upnor for starters, when my reverie was rudely disturbed. A sharp gust of wind, for which I should have been better prepared knowing the area as I did, caught me napping and very nearly laid the boat flat. Nanoseconds later, with feet hooked under the toe straps and leaning back off the side decking to the limit of the extension tiller, I counterbalanced the heel and brought her up into the wind a little to relieve the pressure. That was a close call I thought, but I resolved to be a little more alert to the fluky wind conditions prevailing as I really didn't want to practise righting a capsize on my first day out. Besides, I was by now well off shore and I knew that my parents would be glued to the eyepieces of their binoculars and that if the boat was laid down the Coastguard *would* be alerted – no question!

I continued to stooge around for some time, thoroughly enjoying both the sensation of sailing and of some pride in my newly acquired skills at managing a boat single handed until I became aware that the tide was ebbing. It was time to return home as the tide recedes very rapidly in those shallow estuary waters and I did not wish to fetch up on the sands (mud) hundreds of yards from the beach and have a nightmare getting the boat back to where it belonged. Believe me, trudging through the ooze was bad enough alone, but hauling quite a heavy boat across it single handed would not have been at all easy, if not completely impossible. So I headed back, this time running before the onshore breeze, 'goose-winged' with the mainsail and jib on opposite sides of the boat. She was really creaming along with 'a bone in her teeth', as the exaggerated bow wave is colloquially referred to, and with that wonderful sound of the water gurgling and slapping under the forefoot that confirms how rapid one's progress is. I was elated and believe I actually burst into song for some time, until I thought a little about the process of bringing her in without, hopefully, making too much of a fool of myself. I knew that friends and neighbours would be watching and that only made it worse.

Once again, so many things to do at once and each of them more or less critical to the success of the manoeuvre but, nothing ventured, nothing for it but to have a go. By this time, on the ebb tide, the wind had slackened slightly as it is often prone to do, which made things a little less hectic and it was blowing diagonally onto the beach. I headed for the point at which I wished to make a landfall and a few yards off the beach, released the rudder shock cord, allowing the blade to float up. Just as I judged that the boat was about to ground, I raised the centreboard, released the jib sheet, put the helm hard down to turn her up into the wind and stopped almost magically with the boat's stern skeg just brushing the shingle and with the sails slatting idly in the breeze. A perfect landing and I stepped out of the boat and into the water feeling like a cross between Thor Heyerdahl and Nancy Blackett. I had done it and, more importantly, I had done it without making a complete fool of myself. There would however, be plenty of other opportunities for making a fool of myself, which I would later grasp with both hands and put on a real exhibition, but of course I didn't know that then.

That outing was just the first of many, many days of my youth spent 'messing about in boats'. An occupation which I can heartily concur with Ratty's opinion, that there is simply nothing so much worth doing!

Of course the majority of my sailing was coastal from Swalecliffe but we trailed the boat to various public slipways at Upnor and Harty Ferry and enjoyed innumerable adventures, mainly cruising around and exploring rather than competitive racing. I was based a little too far distant and my visits were rather too erratic to have made joining either Whitstable or Herne Bay yacht clubs a viable proposition, always supposing that they would have done me the honour of allowing me to sully their exalted ranks. To be known locally as the Commodore of either club was a little akin to carrying the post-war rank of Wing Commander or Brigadier and tales of the rather snooty procedures at yacht clubs were legion. Besides which, in those early days, the Heron class dinghy was not as universally popular as it later became and there were very few about. Racing in either of the two local clubs would therefore have been confined to handicap racing, rather than class racing with pretty well identical boats, and frankly that did not really appeal to me. Apart from that, the entrance fees and subscriptions to both clubs, assuming that I had not been 'black balled' upon application, were fairly steep and one needed to be around all the time to partake of the social as well as the sailing aspects in order to justify the costs.

So my sailing at that stage was largely restricted to pottering about from my home 'port' of Swalecliffe, a rapidly ageing Swallow searching relentlessly for a like-minded Amazon! I did in fact find my Amazon, although whether she was entirely 'like-minded' remains a matter of conjecture, in the shape, and a very pleasant shape it was too, of the site owner's daughter Susan.

I was by this time about nineteen I suppose and Sue would gamely accompany me on my sailing excursions, getting soaked to the skin and ruining her hair, hands and fingernails in the process, whilst stoutly professing to be enjoying herself. I strongly suspect that she only did it out of duty and a totally misguided sense of loyalty to me and always felt that she would surely certainly have preferred to have spent her leisure hours indulging in a little light retail therapy in Canterbury's finest emporiums or in an hour or two of horse grooming in the comfort of a warm and dry stable. However, for whatever reason, she sailed with me and a stronger demonstration of true love would be hard to find I suggest, but, sadly the liaison did not last. At the age of twenty, having sorely tried the patience of the War Office by repeatedly extending my deferment whilst attempting to gain professional qualifications, I was peremptorily drafted into National Service, trained as a Royal Artilleryman and whisked off to Cyprus for eighteen months. Regrettably, whilst absence is alleged to make the heart grow fonder, it almost invariably makes the feet grow itchier and in due course I received what was, amongst military personnel, universally referred to as a 'Dear John' letter. When I returned home, she was engaged to an Italian who drove a smart car, cooked like an angel it was alleged and had not the slightest interest in sailing dinghies! No contest really.

Eventually, when my sister was about sixteen and, understandably, no longer as keen to spend so many weekends away from all her friends, it was decided that campsite holidays had run their course and that our beloved chalet would be sold.

The boat was taken home and for some years I sailed, somewhat sporadically, from Gravesend Yacht Club and sometimes Harty Ferry. On one occasion I have been sailing off Sheppey when I was caught in a rainstorm. After some time beating back to the landing slip in torrential rain, the sails were thoroughly soaked and, necessarily, had to be packed away whilst still wet. Something untoward happened when I got home and I forgot to get the sails out of their bag and dry them properly. The next day it was too late the inevitable had happened and my pristine white sailed were flecked with mildew. Washing and scrubbing had no effect whatever. Say what you like about mildew, it's unsightly, it smells, but it's a tenacious little devil and you just cannot shift it. Ever the resourceful one, my mother said, in an effort to cheer me up, "Why not dye them?" Why not indeed, if you can't beat 'em and all that. So we dyed the sails a beautiful shade of royal blue, deep enough to mask the mildew but not so deep as to conceal the black registration number and Heron insignia. Set off against the Cambridge blue hull it was a very fetching combination and solved the problem quite economically.

Around this period, the parents of my sister's new boyfriend and soon to be husband sailed a Silhouette cruiser from Upnor and, once we got to know them, they quite often invited me to crew with them. This of course was even more fun than dinghy sailing as the trips were of longer duration and one could even sleep aboard.

On one memorable trip from Upnor to Brightlingsea which we had started in absolutely ideal conditions, we found ourselves suddenly enveloped in dense fog in mid-estuary. Believe me, in what are some pretty busy shipping lanes, that was a frightening experience. The boat was equipped with all the necessary charts and an echo sounder which was extremely useful, particularly when all other visual directional senses are denied to you, but there is nothing worse and more totally disorientating that being fog bound on water. Having heard the mournful tolling of one of the channel buoys, we navigated towards it and by sheer luck, did eventually find the thing. Even then, and this remained a standing joke within the family for years, we had to sail right up to the buoy and practically turn it round to read its name and establish our position. The reassuring fact that we had found a buoy, a red, port hand can buoy, at least indicated that we were not actually in the principal shipping lane and this realisation came as a considerable relief to us. We stooged around for an hour or two, carefully remaining within earshot of the buoy, until at last the fog lifted sufficiently for us to feel confident in venturing across the estuary in search of Brightlingsea. The Essex coast eventually hove welcomingly into sight and we soon found the harbour where, after a good meal and a considerable quantity of beer, we spent a restful night. All in all, a lesson well learned in that one must never take the sea for granted. What starts out as an enchanting idyll can so soon and so easily turn into a dangerous nightmare for the untrained and the unwary.

Inevitably, now thirty two and with a new wife who hated boats and water and young babies to worry about, poor old Finisterre fell into both disuse and disrepair and was eventually disposed of. However, once the love of the sea is in one's blood, it never leaves you. It lurks beneath the surface and makes it hard to pass a harbour without a wistful, yearning examination of the yachts bobbing on their moorings. The plaintive cry of the gulls, the slap, slap of halliards on masts and the moan of the wind, not in the Willows but in the shrouds, are all reminders of so many happy times spent afloat. One day …. One day …

※◇◆◇ ◇◇◇ ◇◇◇ ◇ ◇◇◇ ◇◇◇◇◇◇ ◇◇ ◇◇◇ ◇◇◇ ◇◇ ◇◇ ◇◇◇

One Liners

- "Why do people seem to take an instant dislike to me?"
  "It saves so much time."

- "I spent most of my money on booze and women. The rest I wasted." *George Best.*

- Senility prayer: Grant me the senility to forget the people I never liked anyway, the good fortune to run into the ones I do, and the eyesight to tell the difference.

- Notice outside a church: Want a new look? Have your faith lifted here!

- She: "You used to be happy if you could see me for just a few minutes each day."
  He: "That's still true."

- GBS was asked after a party, "Have you enjoyed yourself?"
  He replied, "Yes, and that's all I have enjoyed."

- "Punctuality is something that, if you have it, there is often no-one around to share it." *Hilda Baker*

- William Mann picks the early Shostakovich opera 'The Nose' as a virtuoso performance. Robert Layton was also tempted to pick 'The Nose'. *Soviet Weekly.*

- An inspector paying a visit to a school went into a class where the children were studying 'Hamlet'. His first question to them was, "Who wrote Hamlet?" and pointing to one rather nervous little chap, he received the answer,
  "P… P … Please, sir, it wasn't me."
  This answer highly amused the inspector, and so later, when discussing his visit with the Chairman of Governors he related the incident just as it had happened. The Chairman laughed heartily for some time, then in a rather convincing tone said, "And I reckon it was the little bugger all the time!"

- A child writing about Milton said, "He was a poet. He got married. He wrote 'Paradise Lost'. His wife died. He wrote Paradise Regained!"

- A gentleman is a man who gives up his seat to a lady in a public convenience.

- Florence Nightingale never got any sleep for three years because she was continually being needed by the soldiers.

- Contralto is a low form of music that women sing.

- A Christian is allowed only one wife; this is called monotony.

- A bachelor is a man who has done without marriage.

- Henry VIII had six wives and a man called Cardinal Wolsey to help him.

- Drake circumcised the world in a small ship.

- An upright man is a man who never sits down on his laurels.

- Paradise is what happens when part of your body goes stiff.

- Abraham had two wives. He kept one at home and turned the other into the desert where she became a pillar of salt by day and a pillar of fire by night.

- After Raleigh put down his cloak, Her Majesty remarked, "I'm afraid I've spoilt your cloak." To that the gallant knight replied, "Dieu et mon droit!" which means, "By God, you're right."

- A class had been asked to write an essay on, "The funniest thing I ever saw." The lazy boy of the class sat dreaming away while the children were busy writing. Soon his teacher went up to him to see his efforts. "Well have you finished?"
  "Yes, miss."
  It ran as follows, "The funniest thing I ever saw was too funny for words."

◇◇◇ ◇◇◇◇ ◇◇◇◇◇◇◇◇ ◇◇◇◇◇◇◇◇◇◇ ◇◇◇◇◇◇ ◇◇◇◇◇

And a Contrast

This is a picture taken by the Tass News Agency in Russia during World War Two. How many times such an event was multiplied throughout Europe and the Soviet Union in those dreadful years, in China, Japan, the Philippines and elsewhere, we shall never know.
Cyril.

Get up Mummy!

Farewell to a Para

From The Chandlers – Volume Five
By Cyril Cook

Whilst on an exercise training for D-Day Private Elliott's parachute had failed to open. Now read on.

The funeral of Elliott 73 had been arranged for Friday 7th April. It had come to the ears of 'R' Battalion second in command, Major Hamish Gillespie, that Private Elliott had arrived in the Parachute Regiment from the Cameronians, a famous Scottish regiment, the home for nearly twenty years of the major himself. He buttonholed the RSM after their meeting with the CO.

"Mr Forster."

"Sir."

"Elliott was a Cameronian. I wonder if we can provide the sort of funeral normally provided for a member of that illustrious regiment!"

"What would that entail sir?"

"Well, first of all, all church parades of any description are held with armed sentries at the church door. Secondly, at the internment, sentries are posted north, south, east and west of the grave at a reasonable distance facing outwards."

"Is there a special reason for this, sir?"

"It dates back to the Jacobite days. The Cameronians were a Protestant regiment so they mounted sentries in order that their church services should not be interrupted by Catholics. Most regiments have some little way of being different."

"Well, sir, in the City Rifles we are of course different to all others by common consent."

"Common just about describes it."

They both laughed. The major was right. Every regiment had its little quirks and fancies, something to make it different from others. It assisted in making a soldier proud of the individuality of his unit, whether it was wearing a replica of the front cap badge on the back of the headdress, like the Gloucesters, or NCOs stripes on only one arm like the City Rifles, or a peaked cap so covering the eyes, like the Guards, that they could hardly see, it was all part of family pride.

"Right, sir, I'll have a word with Mr O'Riordan and we will work out a drill." He saluted punctiliously and made his way to 'B' Company's spider.

Paddy had organised the battalion pioneer platoon to fabricate a piece of multi-plywood in the shape of a base of a coffin. This they had fixed to a nine inch diameter log about six feet long. The log was normally used in PT exercises, where one group of men threw it to another group and for other uses in negotiating assault courses – the bane of every infantryman. Using this they had simulated the removal of the coffin from the hearse, the carrying of it, and putting it down. The bearer party would comprise six men of equal height, a sergeant in command, and an orderly to do the odd jobs, carrying the bearer party's berets, arranging the trestle to support the coffin in church and so on.

Then there would be the firing party who would fire over the grave, commanded by a corporal or another sergeant.

These were all being rehearsed as RSM Forster approached them.

"Mr O'Riorden."

Paddy turned.

"Good morning sir." He did not salute of course. The RSM might, next to the CO and adjutant, be among the archangels of military life, but he still did not merit a salute, despite the fact that chinless wonders of second lieutenants, just out of diapers, did require that acknowledgement.

"We've got to conform to a suggestion by the second in command that we conduct the funeral as carried out by the Cameronians."

"The Cameronians sir? Are they a sort of colonial regiment?

"Don't let our Hamish hear you say that or you'll be back in the cookhouse washing dishes before you know where you are."

"Well, what do they do different to us sir?"

"The procedure is the same, but we have to mount two sentries at the church door, and four at the cardinal points around the grave."

"What's that for?"

"So that you Catholics don't charge in and bust up the Protestant service."

"Holy Mary, sir you're kidding?"

"No. That apparently is how it all started, and Elliott was a Cameronian. All it means is that we have two of the smartest men, a lance corporal and a private soldier, to be positioned at the door, and when we get there for you to place the grave-watch party, facing outwards of course. They will be the last to march off, after the bearer party and the firing party, when the committal is over."

"Right, sir, I'll work out a simple drill for them."

On the day of the funeral the men paraded for the company commander's – David's inspection. Six men, a sergeant and the orderly in the bearer's party, six men and a sergeant in the firing party, and six men as sentries. With David, Jimmy James, Elliott's platoon commander, and Paddy there would be a presence of twenty four of the paratrooper's peers on his last parade, plus a bugler from battalion HQ.

Command had sent a coach in which to transport the men, the one hundred and fifty miles or so to the little village outside Peterborough where he was to be laid to rest. David, Jimmy and Paddy would travel in the CO's Humber staff car.

Arriving at church in good time, Paddy's first job was to establish where his lookout sentries would be positioned. There were no problems, no wall in the way or any other stumbling block. It was a fine day; graveyards are notoriously slippery if it is, or had been, raining hard.

The hearse arrived, the bearer party took posts facing the back of the vehicle; the orderly collected their headdresses, in this case six red berets. A minor detail – each beret had the name of its owner in white paint inside so that the orderly could return the correct beret to its owner. Such minor details ensure the proper carrying out of any parade.

The sergeant, in a muted voice, (there would be no parade ground commands at this parade), gave the first command.

"Inward turn." The three men on either side turned to face each other, as the coffin, covered by the Union Flag, on the top of which was placed a red beret, was gradually moved out into the strong hands of the bearer party.

"Lift." They lifted it shoulder high.

"Right and left, turn."

"Step." At this command the left hand file stepped off with the left foot, the right hand with the right foot. This is, in fact, the only time a soldier steps off with the right foot, thus ensuring their burden is carried smoothly.

In slow time the procession made its way down the aisle, the family leaving it to be seated in the pews, the coffin carried forward to be positioned on trestles positioned by the orderly.

"Halt."

"Inward turn."

"Lower." The coffin was lowered onto the trestles.

"Left and right, turn."

"Slow march." The bearer party moved to the rear of the church.

David, Jimmy and Paddy had, in the meantime, been conducted to their seats with the family. As one does, David remembered other occasions in which he had been a sad participant in this service. His first wife Pat killed in a German air attack. His mother, dying in the prime of her life and there was his dear friend and brother in law, Jeremy, who he buried at the battle of Calais with the accompaniment of only a hasty prayer from the padré to see him on his way.

The parson took his text from St John – "He was a burning and a shining light," – a text he said was so apt. He had known John Elliott since he was a boy at Sunday school. He knew him as a choirboy and then as a young man, proud of his uniform, and then so proud of his red beret. His valediction was sincerely expressed and could only, in David's estimation, bring comfort to the mother, father and two siblings who now had to face the world without him.

The service over, the bearer party took up their positions again, lifted the coffin, turned and slow marched to the open grave. 'As the bearer party emerged from the porch, the NCO in charge of the sentries gave the order.

"Sentries, take posts," at which the four men marched to their previously appointed positions, halted and faced outwards. The bearer party lowered their burden onto the struts positioned across the grave, and took up the tapes with which they would be required to lower Private Elliott to his final resting place. The committal then took place, after which, "Bearer party, right and left turn. Quick march."

The bearer party marched off to a nearby path, where they were ordered to, "Replace headdress." There is a drill even for that operation.

Meanwhile, the firing party, waiting nearby was ordered.

"Bugler and firing party, take posts."

"They slow marched to the graveside, three men on either side, the bugler at the head.

"Inward turn. Present. Fire." The shots rang out over the grave, startling an enormous flock of rooks, gathered in the tall elms nearby.

"Order arms."

Without further command the bugler took a pace forward. It is every bugler's nightmare that, not having had the opportunity to have a few practice blows, he will 'drop a clanger' on the first note. On such an occasion as this that would be a disaster, the thought of which increases the horror. The first call however rang out loud and clear.

Firstly.	Regimental call. Each regiment has its distinctive command.
Secondly.	No more parades today. Given at the end of each working day.
Thirdly.	The Last Post.
Fourthly.	Silence for one minute.
Fifthly.	Long Reveille.

The NCO in charge of the firing party waited a few seconds.

"Firing party. Right and left turn."

"Bugler and firing party, to your duties, quick march."

The party marched off to join the bearer party, the whole then marching off to the vehicle park.

David, Jimmy and Paddy stepped forward, saluted the grave together, and then turned to join the family group.

Only when the mourners had left the graveside were the sentries commanded to fall in, they then being marched off to join their comrades. Everything had been carried out in a solemn, martial manner, as befits the laying to rest of one's comrade, be he a private soldier or a general. During the conversation outside the porch Mr and Mrs Elliott approached David and shook hands with him and with Jimmy and Paddy, thanking them so very, very, much for coming all this way.

"He was our comrade, Mrs Elliott; he was part of our family as well."

Those words remained in the minds of John Elliott's parents all their days, as indeed they did in the minds of others who had overheard them.

The sad thing was that nearly half of those providing the various parties so impeccably, would themselves be placed in the soft earth of Normandy in only a few weeks' time.

Jimmy James would be among their number.

***

Bible Truths

Leviticus 19:18   Thou shalt love thy neighbour as thyself.

Numbers 23   What hath God wrought! (This was the first electric telegraph message sent by Samuel Morse in Washington May 1844).

I Samuel 16:7   For the Lord seeth not as a man seeth: for man looketh on the outward appearance, but the Lord looketh on the heart.

I Kings 18:21   How long halt ye between two opinions?

Job 5:7   Man is born unto trouble, as the sparks fly upwards.

Proverbs 4:7   Wisdom is the principal thing: therefore get wisdom: and with all thy getting get understanding.

Proverbs 18   There be three things which are too wonderful for me, yea, four which I know not. The way of an eagle in the air; the way of a serpent upon a rock; the way of a ship in the midst of the sea; and the way of a man with a maid.

Ecclesiastics 15   A man hath no better thing under the sun, than to eat, and to drink, and to be merry.

Isaiah 2:4   They shall beat their swords into plowshares, and their spears into pruning hooks: nation shall not lift up sword against nation, neither shall they learn war any more.

Isaiah 22   There is no peace, saith the Lord, unto the wicked.

St Luke 22   Judge not and ye shall not be judged.

St Luke 7   For the labourer is worthy of his hire.

Horns of the Unicorns

By Annette De Laughter

Trumpeting vibrations sounding throughout the heavens!
Salutations and sorrowful proclamations!
Shouting for the avenging of a unicorn long time standing,
Against the mighty Eloheim!

A unicorn so forlorn from his original state
Whose only course remains to spread his hate
To go as far as imagining such treachery
As to try and still God's masterpiece.

God's centrepiece in the heavens, his bossom of joy
His well beloved, His treasured Adonoi.
His Covenant of Promise, yes his treasure to sacrifice
For what?

The horns of the Unicorns reveal the secret
Of that dark and mournful day
As they layed the master away.

It hadn't been but what seemed a short time before
That the Horns of the Unicorn paraded in escort
Proclaiming the heavenly Father's pride and joy
Which provoked the forlorn unicorn.

Even other innocents died with this prize
This promise to paradise, this heavenly seed with
'written decrees'
What price could be paid that dark & mournful day
As the horns of the Unicorn trumpet and play.

<u>For you,</u> are the mystery and the prize
It was for you, the innocents died
For of a truth and reality,
Death could not hold, this precious heavenly seed!

For your cleansing, yes in his death, he did bleed
In His Blood bears heavens deed.
Declarations of a higher court
Avenged this forlorn unicorn
This unicorn imagined himself to be heavens Majesty!
Such deception caused him to flee!

All for what?

Don't be like the forlorn unicorn
To give your place, when Adonai bore your thorns,

Do not harken to the trumpet of another horn.

If you listen quietly to the horns of the Unicorns
That trumpeted that day, in escount, when Adonai was born
For they wait excitedly for you to sign heavens deed
For your words of heart to join to Adonai's creed:

To covenant with Him and become one with the Father!
For you will become a reigning Son or Daughter!

To listen my friend, to the horns of the unicorns
For, soon, it may be you they trumpet to be born!

[Psalms 22:21
Save me from the lion's mouth:
for thou hast heard me from
the horns of the unicorns.]

**(Annette DeLaughter
Mineola, Texas.)**

❖❖❖❖❖ ❖❖ ❖❖❖❖ ❖❖❖❖❖ ❖❖❖❖❖ ❖❖ ❖❖❖❖ ❖❖ ❖❖❖❖ ❖❖ ❖❖

Answers Section

Armchair Referee 147

1. *Play continues. Going outside the field of play may be considered as part of a playing movement, but players are expected, as a general rule, to remain within the playing area.*

2. *The referee stops play, sends off the player guilty of violent conduct, cautions the substitute for unsporting behaviour and instructs him to leave the field of play. The match is re-started with an indirect free kick to the opposing team where the ball was when play was stopped.*

3. *No. Only the referee can send off a player from the field of play.*

4. *The defending player is sent off for violent conduct and shown the red card. The referee re-starts the match with a throw-in, since the ball was out of play when the offence occurred.*

5. *The referee allows play to continue and cautions the defender for deliberately leaving the field of play without the referee's permission, when the ball is next out of play.*

6. *The referee cautions them or sends them off and re-starts play with an indirect free kick to the opposing team from the place where the offence occurred.*

7. *An indirect free kick is awarded to the opposing team.*

8. *The kick is re-taken since the ball is not in play until it has passed outside the penalty area.*

9. He allows play to continue.

10. Yes, provided the correct penalty kick procedures have been followed.

Picture Puzzle 105

The New Denver International Airport, Colarado, USA.

Acknowledgements and Thanks from Cyril

In a volume of this nature with such a variety of highly gifted contributors, where does one start? I sent a synopsis to an extremely erudite friend of mine knowing I would receive a scrupulously honest criticism, no matter how much I paid him. He wrote back to the effect that he much enjoyed reading such an individual and eclectic book. I had to go to my Oxford English Dictionary to find out what 'eclectic' meant, which as you will all undoubtedly know is 'selecting ideas or beliefs from various sources'. A person who carried out such an exercise is named an 'eclectic'.

I have been called many things in my long and not uneventful life, so it was with a certain amount of gratification I found I was being called something nice for a change. Then it came to me that I was basking in the reflected glory of – **yourselves**.

It is mind-boggling to think of the hours of work you – the contributors – have put into producing your individual presentations. In many cases even more so with regard to the circumstances which prompted the story in the first place. Where in the world would you find another volume with the breadth of experience, knowledge, sensibility, and fun which you have demonstrated in these pages? As a lawyer might say – I rest my case!

So **thank you** to you all, from one-liners to multi-pagers. I will end this tribute by quoting Ben Johnson who somewhere around the year 1600 wrote,

"I confess thy writings to be such
As neither man, nor muse, can praise too much."

I could not have put it better.

And now my thanks to two ladies who have made the presentation of this volume possible.

Lian Beckett
Prior to my moving from London to my new home in Cheshire, Lian was instrumental in producing the layout of the front cover and subsequent thirty specimen pages for the synopsis to present to the publisher. It was no easy task.

From this I was able to plan the full contents of the prepared volume thus making for a professional presentation. I already had good reason to thank her for her hard work in putting five of my six volumes of 'The Chandlers' into her magic machine to very good effect – she is now slaving over my new trilogy (if I live that long), 'The Manninghams'.

So thank you Lian for the good start.

Amanda Duffy
It was obvious when I moved here to Cheshire that, although I had the bulk of OWIL in bits and pieces, putting it together in a readable format was going to require considerable expertise and close co-operation with another genius with another magic machine. I fell on my feet a second time when I became introduced to Amanda.

Articles of varying lengths, some containing photographs to be strategically placed, ending at all sorts of dimensions down the page, thus leaving a blank space to be filled, were a sort of literary jigsaw puzzle. Amanda sailed through these difficulties with the aplomb of a captain of a battleship, the result you can readily agree providing an outstandingly professional result.

Again then, thank you Amanda for your skill and expertise, to say nothing of your total lack of flappability, required at frequent intervals!